Goodbye Forever

Volume I

Ngakpa Chögyam

Ngak'chang Rinpoche

Aro Books WORLDWIDE

2020

Aro Books WORLDWIDE
PO Box 111, Aro Khalding Tsang,
5 Court Close, Cardiff,
CF14 1JR, Wales, UK

© 2020 by Ngakpa Chögyam

First edition 2020

ISBN: 978-1-898185-51-2 (Paperback)

*Dedicated to Kyabjé Düd'jom Rinpoche Jig'drèl Yeshé Dorje—
who asked me to establish the gö kar chang lo'i dé in the West
—and to his twin incarnations Kyabjé Düd'jom Rinpoche
Sang-gyé Pema and Kyabjé Düd'jom Rinpoche Ten'dzin Yeshé
Dorje who have shown me great kindness in remembering me as
the student of their previous incarnation.*

'Kyabjé Düd'jom Rinpoche Jig'drèl Yeshé Dorje told me that he had dwelt upon the nature of the White Lady and that she also had the name Khyungchen Aro Lingma: Garuda who Tastes the Primordial A. *She was a gTértön. She had taken rainbow body earlier in the century. I had been her son in my previous life. My name had been Aro Yeshé. That was what he knew at the present time – but when he knew more, he would tell me. He said that Aro Lingma was known to him—and had been known by Düd'jom Lingpa—but no Lama to whom he had spoken had heard of her apart from Kyabjé Dilgo Khyentsé Rinpoche, who had said that he had heard the name many years before as a yogini who had realised Ja'lü in Southern Tibet.'*

from page 3, Chapter 19, *demon destroyer.*

Acknowledgments

Firstly it gives me great pleasure to acknowledge my Sangyum, wife, and teaching partner: Khandro Déchen Tsédrüp Rolpa'i Yeshé. Her influence, encouragement, support, and unflagging enthusiasm for the lineage are incomparable. Kyabjé Düd'jom Rinpoche Jig'drèl Yeshé Dorje, Kyabjé Künzang Dorje Rinpoche and Jomo Sam'phel Déchen Rinpoche all stressed that it was vital that I found the right sangyum if I was to teach the Aro gTér in the West. They each gave instructions and predictions that proved accurate and immensely valuable.

I acknowledge all the Lamas with whom I have studied, met and conversed – but most of all: Kyabjé Düd'jom Rinpoche Jig'drèl Yeshé Dorje; Kyabjé Künzang Dorje Rinpoche and Jomo Sam'phel Déchen Rinpoche; and, 'Khordong gTérchen Tulku Chhi'mèd Rig'dzin Rinpoche.

Although I do not teach the Düd'jom gTér, it was the major part of my training as a Lama. I owe so much to the Düd'jom gTér and to the Lamas of that lineage I know and have known: Dung-sé Thrin-lé Norbu Rinpoche; Dung-sé Garab Dorje Rinpoche; Dung-sé Namgay Dawa Rinpoche; Chag'düd Tulku Rinpoche; and, Lama Tharchin Rinpoche.

It is not possible to function as a Nyingma Lama without being connected to the Nyingma Tradition through friendship, and for the kindest friendship I am grateful to Tulku Dakpa Rinpoche, and Wangchuk Rinzin Rinpoche and his son gTértön Drukdra Rinpoche.

I would like to thank all our students – without whom Khandro Déchen and I would not be teachers. Dung-sé Thrin-lé Norbu Rinpoche pointed out to us *It is students who make people teachers. If Lamas have no students – they are not teachers.' Goodbye Forever* has been edited and proofread by students. Rig'dzin Shérab checked the Tibetan spellings and it was finally brought to publication by the painstaking efforts of Ngakma Nor'dzin and Ngakpa 'ö-Dzin – the first two people to become my students in the early 1980s.

To those many people I have not acknowledged, I apologise – but to have acknowledged everyone would have taken another book.

Contents

Goodbye Forever

1

the white lady

1952–1957

Born 6th of June, 1952 in Hannover, Germany. Moved to Froggnal, Aldershot, Hampshire, England in 1953 – and thence Farnham Surrey in 1954.

What follows in italics may not make linear sense in terms of death and birth – but, I shall describe how it was in 1952, although the calendar year only came into the picture in unfathomable incremental phases.

White.

Terrifying white.

Howling cacophonous white.

White shining from the height of plummeting sky.

White hurtling through absolute zero at terminal velocity.

White noise. White silence.

White: before space; before dimensionality.

White before temporal continuity.

White before name and form; before cognition, comparison, or interpretation.

Then, black. Utter black. Inchoate velocity in which black and white have the same meaning.

Then, dawn. Spectral spacious heart of phenomena. Swirling blue, green, red, white, yellow – colour-names that are distant approximations. The 'terrible white' then seemed long distant.

Ubiquitous joyous luminosity pervaded sense fields. Colour-swirlings developing cohesive density, intricacy of texture – and, a quasi-perfection of pattern that gave birth to amorphous memory.

Then sound: visceral tintinnabulatory pulses. Nascent corporeal narrative coagulating in a ruby sea. Crimson and carmine pulsing with alternations and momentarily miraculous affiliations.

Then all faded into the mnemonics of memory – to be replaced by an infant quotidian kaleidoscope of bemusing gestures.

That is the only memory that remains of death and incarnation.

I was told by Kyabjé Düd'jom Rinpoche[1]—nineteen years later— that my predecessor, Aro Yeshé, had died in an avalanche.[2] This brought the sensory impressions of my infancy into focus.

Time—*in first few years of life*—is vague.

Time—*towards the end of life*—is vague.

What occurs between birth and death, isn't always as clear as might be wished.

The *theatrical stage of physical existence* hosts a surreal drama in which: scenes suddenly segue. Players enter sometimes simply to exit: stage left or stage right – either to re-enter, or not.

I never said *'Goodbye forever'* – there was no need. The world enunciated the phrase on my behalf, whenever anything became too comfortable, reliable, dependable, consistent, or coherent.

Everything historical is equivocal, unless there is nondual awareness. The alternative might be an *ever-present non-partisan biographer* capable of synthesising a narrative from the welter of impressions and erratic subjectivism that constitute life.

---

1   Kyabjé Düd'jom Rinpoche Jig'drèl Yeshé Dorje (1904-1987) was the Mind Incarnation of gTértön Düd'jom Lingpa (1835-1904). He was the Lineage Head of the Düd'jom gTér Lineage – and head of the Nyingma Tradition between 1960 and 1987.

2   Kyabjé Düd'jom Rinpoche informed me of a significant number of historical details – many of which are detailed in the concluding chapters of this volume of *Goodbye Forever*.

I do not have access to such a biographer. I do not rest continually in the nondual state. I can therefore only attempt to recall the sequences that still emerge, when I cast my erratic temporal-attention backwards.

At first, it's like trying to rewind a cassette tape which has accumulated too many ridges. The rate of re-wind fluctuates erratically between fast and slow – and occasionally jams. Sometimes you can get lucky and the tape frees itself—accelerates —and you find yourself rewinding as a '… *lover sighing like a furnace, with a woeful ballad, made to his mistress' eyebrow.'* Then as a '… *whining schoolboy, with his satchel and shining morning face, creeping like a snail unwillingly to school.'* Then as an '… *infant, mewling and puking in the nurse's arms.'* [3]

I cannot say at what age I first named her *The White Lady* – apart from the fact that I must have been able to articulate words. *The White Lady*, however, had always been there. She had been there between observation and inattention; between sensation and emotion; between darkness and light; and, between the infinite shades of dawn and dusk. I may as well say she was born with me – or that I was born into her presence.

I often gazed as a young boy—especially at dusk—attempting to catch the moments when *a greater shade* settled. It was almost as if I could catch one of those moments: if I gazed with sufficient stillness. It seemed that if I had *ideas* in my mind – they would cause me to miss the moment when the world darkened by a fraction. I sat and stared enough to know that the dimming-of-the-day was not gradual – but that the steps almost always occurred during moments of inattention.

The White Lady *almost* always appeared in my room at night. She appeared unless I was so tired that I fell asleep immediately.

---

3   Adapted from 'All the world's a stage' a monologue from William Shakespeare's *As You Like It*. It is spoken by Jaques in Act II, Scene vii. He compares the world to a stage and life to a play, and catalogues the seven stages of life. Here the first stages are given in reversed order.

I did not know it wasn't normal, to have ladies appearing in one's room at night. She was simply *part of my life,* as an infant-in-arms and thereafter.

Of course, I was said to be prone to see what *may, or may not, have been there to be seen.* I didn't know—as an infant—what the *boundaries of quotidian reality* were. That is normal of course—for an infant— but I would appear to have taken my infant's *imaginal world* further than allowed by those with a proper sense of English decorum. According to my own perception, however, I hadn't taken *anything* 'anywhere' – *it* had taken me. I was not creating my world – the world was creating me.

That I was abnormal—or something like it—was what I was given to believe by my father. He was the arbiter of appropriateness, custodian of the customary, and curator of the conventional. He meant well by it, of course. He meant no harm. He was born in 1902 – and was simply an elderly Edwardian.

There were 'rules of reality'—imposed by the adult world—which clashed with my experience. This proved increasingly disturbing to my father. It also became disturbing to my mother – but only to the extent that she had to deal with my elderly father's Edwardian English empiricism. So, I lived in *a world apart* from the conservative 1950s of my father; before the age of five. I then lived in a world apart, for as long as I could get away with it.

My mother wasn't given to visions – but neither was she disturbed by the fact that they occurred. She'd had her own unusual visionary experiences – but she never made an esoteric hobby out of them. She hardly ever talked about them – but she knew enough to know that there were *more things in heaven and earth, than were rationalised in her husband's philosophy.*[4] The fact that my imagination, daydreams, dreams, and visions intermingled seamlessly did not seem disastrous to her – but to my father it was the precursor to mental hospital admission.

---

4 Adapted from Shakespeare's *Hamlet,* Hamlet to Horatio: *'There are more things in heaven and earth, Horatio, than are dreamt of in your philosophy.'*

The *White Lady* often appeared in my room – and remained for varying periods of time; depending on my degree of tiredness. The words 'appeared' and 'remained' are only partial indications – as what occurred is difficult to relate in terms of conventional reality.

When she appeared – it was more that I suddenly became aware she was there. Then she remained – but I was never aware of her departure. Her appearances could not be codified in terms of time – because several hours or a fraction of a second could not be differentiated. At the time it was simply part of the fabric of experience – and only became incomprehensible when I tried to explain it to my mother.

The *White Lady* came in dreams as well – and, on rare occasions, in day-time reveries when I was on my own in the woods. Although I called her the 'White Lady' – she was not *actually* white. White was simply the closest I could come to describing her. She was actually every colour there ever was or ever would be – but somehow that only made sense as 'white'. Later, when I was at Junior School, I learned that every colour comes from white light. The teacher demonstrated this with a prism and I was amazed looking at the pure rainbow colour on the white wall. As soon as I saw that prismatic display, I knew what it meant: *white was all colours*. The White Lady had that ability to be all colours – but as a person, rather than as a glass prism.

My mother told me—once I was able to tell her about the experience—that the White Lady was a dream. That seemed peculiar to me – because I'd seen her quite clearly when I was lying awake in the dark. She didn't *seem* like a dream. My mother told me that dreams seemed real. I accepted her word for it – but the next time she appeared I reached over and took a drink from the glass that stood by my bed. The water was flavoured with a dash of rosehip syrup to make it palatable. I never enjoyed water on the basis that it was *somewhat less than ideal* to drink liquid that tasted like my mouth. I am still of the same opinion. Be that as it may, I knew I couldn't be asleep. I even spoke the words aloud *"Is this a dream?"* and heard my voice with my ears – or so it seemed to me.

My tongue had moved and the hiss of 'this' required my breath to gush past my teeth. The pronunciation was visceral. I looked around the bedroom. It was my bedroom. I looked at myself—or as much of myself as I could see—and spoke aloud again *"I feel as if I am awake and not dreaming."* The White Lady remained there simply gazing at me. *"Am I dreaming you?"* I asked – and, although she made no verbal answer, she intimated silently that I was not dreaming. I raised my hands and rubbed my eyes to make sure of what I was seeing – and she was still there.

"It's nice that you come to visit me" I said, addressing her one night *"but … who are you? Where do you come from?"* Again, as before, she made no verbal response – but I knew her answer. It wasn't a voice in my head. It wasn't even words that I *somehow detected*. I simply knew whom and whence – but sans conceptual linguistic information. It was non-verbal communication and non-verbal comprehension. This seemed fine to me – but I didn't understand how I could explain that to anyone else. How can one *know*, without – *knowing about*? What is knowledge without *things* that can be known in words – and thence communicated to others? How could I know *who* the White Lady was, without words to identify *how* I knew or *what* I knew?

This was puzzling to me during the day. The more I thought about it, the less clear it became – until after a while, I didn't know anything I'd known in the night. It was as if the night was a time when I understood everything quite easily – and then, when the sun rose, it was all gone – or almost all gone. There was still the memory of the White Lady, of course – but none of the *knowingness*. That *knowingness* would usually be there for a while after I woke up in the morning but would slowly drift away. It would vanish completely as soon as I became involved in the normal activities of the day. It seemed as if my night-state lasted until I had to speak to someone – and then it was as if I was being pulled into *some other world* which was different from what I had seen in the night. Sometimes I tried as hard as I could to remember—usually in the woods on my own —and there I had more success. I thought it might be because the ordinary everyday world didn't really exist in the woods either.

Maybe it was because my father never ventured into the woods – and so it seemed like a wild place where *the laws of normality* didn't apply.

I had the sense that the person who acted as if he was my father, was not my father at all. My idea of my father was of an old man with white hair and a wispy white beard. He was a slender man and quite unlike the person who appeared to be my mother's husband. He had a great love of birds and enjoyed feeding them. He was entirely gentle, kindly, and humorous.[5]

I used to wonder what had happened to my real father – but never asked my mother. I did not want to upset her. A peculiar aspect to all this was that I felt as if I had once been my father. I seemed to know him from knowing what it was like to be that person. These were all ideas that had no place at all in *the world to which I was being introduced*. The world to which I was being introduced seemed to be a dead world – dead in the sense of being arithmetically mechanical. It was a world in which trees had no feelings and could not communicate. In this respect it was a world in which water could not observe you. It was a world in which the sky and the eyes that saw the sky were cut off from each other. Cerebral impressions could not wander off into the clouds – and clear endless blueness could not invade the cranium.

One day, it occurred to me—out there in the woods—that the White Lady knew everything there was to know – or rather, she knew *how everything came to be* – and how *everything slipped back to where it was, before it was*. That's how I worded it to myself. Sometimes she wore white clothes and at others, coloured clothes. Sometimes she only wore white beads – and sometimes nothing at all. I remembered these different appearances – and was determined not to forget them when I returned to the house.

---

5 Kyabjé Düd'jom Rinpoche informed me that the father of my previous incarnation had been 'a-Shül Pema Legden. This was confirmed by 'Khordong gTérchen Tulku Chhi'mèd Rig'dzin Rinpoche whose previous incarnation—Khalden Lingpa—had been the Lama of 'a-Shül Pema Legden at 'Khordong Gompa in Tibet. 'a-Shül Pema Legden had been the visionary scribe and artist who recorded the visions of Khalden Lingpa.

Somehow, however, everything became vague as soon as I returned to *the rooms of routine* – and my father: the curator and custodian of customary quotidian concerns.

My mother said that I could have seen the White Lady in a film. She said that she often saw actors in different films – and knew she knew them from some other film but couldn't remember which film. I thought about this for a long while and decided that the White Lady could not have been in a film because she wasn't English or American – and those were the only people I ever saw in films—apart from the Black people I saw in *Gone with the Wind*— and the White Lady wasn't a Black Lady even though her skin had been the colour of night on one occasion. When I thought about it – I couldn't say what her colour was. It was as if it was no colour – so that other colours came through her. Sometimes it was as if black was shining through her and at other times other colours like blue, green, red, white, and yellow shone through her.

One night, I decided that I should be more active rather than just lying there being looked at by the White Lady – and so I got out of bed and went to her. She remained the same size however and I got no closer. As I reached the wall she disappeared. Then the strangest thing happened: as she disappeared, so too did the room– and, as my room dissolved, I found myself in Switzerland or somewhere like that. There were mountains and I was walking with two young women who were my friends. They were sisters. I was not their brother – but I seemed to be related to them. They were talking about going to visit a tiger's nest. I understood where they meant – but without *any understanding at all* of exactly what it was that I understood. It was as if *Tiger's Nest* [6] was some sort of name for somewhere that not everyone would know – because tigers did not live in nests, they lived in dens or lairs. It was important – and it was a long way away on the other side of the mountains perched on some precarious crag. Maybe it was a nest because it was like an eagles' eyrie.

---

6   Taktsang (*sTag tsham – Tiger's nest, lair or den*):

Then I woke up and I couldn't work out whether it had all been a dream – or whether I had simply gone to sleep in the mountains and mysteriously come back to my room again in the same inexplicable way that I'd left it.

The BBC serialisation of *The Lion the Witch and the Wardrobe* was on at that time and it seemed to me that my bedroom was like that wardrobe – but my mother said that was only a fairy story and that things like that did not exist in the real world. I asked why someone had made up that story and put it on television if things like that couldn't happen. She told me it was an entertainment for children – and that there were many stories like this because children liked them. I then asked why my father didn't like it when I mentioned the White Lady – because if it was normal for children to enjoy these stories, why was it bad when stories simply decided to happen? My mother had no immediate answer to that – but after a moment she commented that he didn't like the story on television either – so maybe that was why he didn't like me talking about my dreams.

But it wasn't a dream. I knew it wasn't a dream – or at least it wasn't all a dream. Some things were definitely dreams. I could tell they were dreams – but there were some occurrences that were real because I knew that I was awake. It was as if what happened crossed over between dreaming and waking. The part where I was in the mountains with the two girls was probably *the dream part* – but the other part where the White Lady was looking at me wasn't a dream because I knew I was not asleep. I was able to tell the difference between dream and waking because of the many different signs that existed that enabled me to distinguish between them. In the dream state I was very much a passive observer – and in the waking state I participated and used my mind in a more active and enquiring way. I described this to my mother by saying that dreams were like watching television and real waking life was a situation where the story was not fixed.

The next night when the White Lady looked at me – I sat up in bed to be sure that I wasn't asleep. At that moment, she looked at me in a way that made me understand that she had been my mother before my own German mother had been born – and that she would be my mother long after my own mother died.

Now this was something that I was able to remember and explain the next day. I told my mother – and she was kind. She told me that dreams were strange. She had dreamed about her brother dying. She found out later than he'd died at the same time that she'd had the dream.[7] My mother looked wistful. She turned her head away for a moment – and then gave me a concerned look, saying that I should not mention anything about our conversation to my father.

The whole subject of my dreams irritated my father. I was apparently supposed to dream something else – something apparently manlier. White Ladies who spoke gibberish had no place in a boy's dreams. My dreams were not a welcome subject with my father – and so I learned fairly quickly not to mention the White Lady who came to my room unless my father was somewhere out of hearing. I foolishly kept enquiring of my mother, why it was that my father didn't like to hear about the White Lady who came to my room. It seemed incomprehensible to me that he didn't think it was wonderful.

My mother explained—as best she could—that my father was a pragmatic man …. He was scientific and did not like anything paranormal or supernatural. How that worked with his belief in God she could never explain – but it seemed that he kept these ideas in two different boxes or on either side of a steel wall. Science and God were not on speaking terms in my father's head – or at least they were entirely unaware of each other.

---

7   My mother told me in later life that her experience of her brother's death had not been a dream – it had occurred when she fell unconscious during the day. She told me that she had had bruises in each place he had been wounded. She said that she had been reticent with her account in view of my father's position on paranormal phenomena.

My mother told me that she had tried to tell him that it was nice for me to have an imaginal world – but that he thought other boys would laugh at me if they heard me speaking of 'fairies' in my room. They'd think I was abnormal. My mother sighed and concluded that my father might be right about how other people would view me. She said that people were not always kind when others had unusual dreams and ideas.

So, that was the way life worked. One had to look normal. One had to speak normally about normal things. One had to think only what was normal. That was the rule – but … if you broke the rule … well … what happened? I asked my mother what happened if you broke that rule. She told me that you could give yourself a difficult life. I asked her if that was bad. She replied that it wasn't bad – just lonely. She told me that artists and musicians were not exactly normal, but they had friends – so maybe it wasn't completely lonely.

That was the thing then. I was to be an Artist. I was to paint. I was to write poetry – and perhaps compose music. Then I would be friends with all the other people who didn't want to *have* to appear to be acceptably normal. Maybe there would be other people who saw White Ladies in their rooms at night—or maybe marvellous animals in many colours—but I didn't ask about that. I had some-sort-of-answer – and that had to suffice: for the moment.

My father's verdict was that I was far too dreamy – too prone to fantasy. I had an *unhealthily* overactive imagination – with ideas so ridiculous that he had to question my sanity. To a certain extent, he did have cause to be concerned – because I didn't *always* hear people when they spoke to me. I was often lost in reverie – or sat staring into space for inordinate periods of time.

The White Lady just sat and stared into me or through me or into space – so it seemed to me like a thing I could do. I liked to sit and forget about the effort of making the world understandable. There were so many things about the way that the world worked—and the way people worked—that were so complicated that I thought adults must be extremely clever to understand it all.

However, having come to that conclusion, I wondered why—if they were so very clever—did they have terrible wars where hundreds of thousands of people had to die? That seemed terminally stupid – because the world went on after these wars as if the wars hadn't happened. Britain was at war with France and then Britain was on their side against Germany. Then I learnt that almost every country in Europe had been both the ally and enemy of every other European country. Was that clever? I thought not. In fact, it seemed far less sane than *I might be*.

Something was definitely wrong with something – and I had no idea how to untangle the problem. I asked the White Lady this question – but, as usual, there was no answer in words; just the understanding that *cleverness was not the answer*. It seemed that you could be as clever as you liked – but it wouldn't make you happy or stop wars. It seemed also that the adult world was not that different from the child's world. Children played their games – and adults just played a different kind of game. Children got angry with each other in the games and so did adults. The main difference seemed to be that the adults were in charge and so they were allowed to say that their game wasn't a game. This was a disturbing idea – and one that I didn't even think it was good to tell my mother.

I asked the White Lady many questions – and the answers, which were just gaps in time, made me feel that I needed to wait until I was old enough to play better games than adults played. It also occurred to me that it was better not to confuse *games* with *whatever the real world might be* – and not to tell lies about it. *Games* were not *reality*, however much fun such games might be. It seemed to me that adults needed to learn how to be adult – or maybe that kind of adulthood happened when adults were old. My German grandmother seemed completely sane. She was extremely kind and disapproved of many of the bad things in the world. She was strongly against any kind of racism, class elitism, or religious sectarian bigotry. She had to escape to Denmark in World War II because she had helped Jewish families.

Her whole family had been against Hitler – and suffered for it. It was good to know that there were people like my grandmother – and that gave me some sense of hope.

I had been thinking a great deal about *light* and 'how light *existed* in the dark'. It seemed to me that there was *normal light* that came in the day and electric light that enabled you to see at night – but then there was darkness. It seemed that there were different kinds of darkness. There was one kind of darkness where you could see nothing at all – and another where there seemed to be *light inside the darkness*. This *light inside the darkness* was a special kind of light that was not always easy to find – but when I found it, I was able to see my bedroom quite clearly without the electric light. It wasn't the light of the moon and there were no street lamps – because our house backed onto the woods.

I never really knew what I did to be able to see the light inside the dark – but sometimes it would happen. When it happened, I usually saw the White Lady. She was always full of light – but it was a different kind of light from the light inside the dark. If I was to put a name to it, her light was always multi-coloured – but the multi-colouredness of the light was not understandable in terms of colours that I could identify. I couldn't say I saw blue, green, red, and yellow – because the colours were all something else … colours I had never seen before. Every time I tried to understand a colour it would become white before I had worked out whether it was blue or green – so after a while I stopped trying to fix the colours. I tried explaining this problem to my mother. She said that people had all kinds of ideas in dreams and that it wasn't possible to understand them when you were awake. Some things made sense in dreams that made no sense at all when you were awake.

Eventually I stopped talking about the White Lady—even to my mother—because I could see that, even though she would listen, it seemed to trouble her. My mother was obviously worried about my annoying my father. He was easily annoyed – so I could understand her fears. I wondered whether I should try to stop seeing the White Lady – because maybe my mind would become sick.

My father had said that my mind would become sick *'if this sort of thing continued.'* That seemed terrible – because if your mind got sick they'd lock you up somewhere and never let you out again. That was something I'd avoid at all cost. It was bad enough having to act in the right way all the time in order not to anger my father – but what would it be like if he sent me to a mental hospital? I'd be made to wear a straitjacket and wouldn't be able to move my arms – and I'd have to sit all day long in a padded cell. Then they'd strap me into a chair and give me electric shocks to make me normal. That's what could happen – or that's what I overheard him telling my mother. My mother said little in response and so I believed that it must be true. Of course, my mother had no idea I was listening, otherwise she would have countered that idea – even at the expense of angering my father. He did not like being countered – by my mother, or by anyone. Major Ernest Mathers Simmerson was the sole arbiter of reality. And that's how it was. I was in danger of being sent to a mental hospital if I said anything about the White Lady or if anybody knew that I saw her. The worst thing I did— according to my father—was that I believed in what was conveyed to me by the White Lady – because, people who *heard voices* were insane. The thing was however, that I didn't hear her voice. I simply knew and believed what she divulged. There was some kind of communion that occurred – but I could not explain to my mother how it happened.

There was *some-sort-of subject matter* but it always vanished as soon as I entered into the flow of everyday life. It seemed to concern what I *was*, what everyone *was*, and what life *was*. There was however, no information – so there was nothing to remember. There was simply the sensation that there was nothing else to know. The central idea, or sensated impression, was of goodness and kindness. Everyone was good and kind. This *goodness* was *somewhere*, not exactly inside – but someplace that couldn't easily be found, as long as people were obsessed with being 'normal'.

One day I saw an avalanche. I don't know where in the world it was but it was there in front of me on the television. It was family viewing time and we all sat and watched.

My father, mother, and brother Græham each found it interesting in their own ways – but I was unusually affected by it. I said nothing because there was a relatively good family atmosphere at the time and I had no desire to upset the situation. I just sat there—vaguely horrified—and pulling back into my chair, as if to avoid the avalanche. The room was a reasonable temperature but I felt bitterly cold. It did not last long – but I remember sitting on my hands to keep them warm. The avalanche was filmed from a distance and it was not a situation in which lives were lost – but the sense of death stole over me. I had the ridiculous notion that I'd experienced an avalanche and that I'd died – but that made no sense to me. I'd never lived anywhere near mountains – and … I was still alive.

I lay in bed wondering how I could feel as if I'd died when I was still alive when I remembered my grandmother saying that some relatives thought I was the reincarnation of my German grandfather. My grandmother didn't set much store by that idea – but it caused me to ask about what reincarnation meant. My mother told me that it wasn't really a Christian idea – but that reincarnation meant that you had lived before in another life. I asked my mother whether she believed in reincarnation or not. She pondered for a moment and told me that she could say neither yes nor no. It was possible. She could not say it was not possible. Sometimes she thought that I was very much like her brother Bernt who'd died on the Russian Front in WWII. She had some of his clothes that she thought would fit me when I grew older. She could not say more than that – or if she did, I can no longer remember what it might have been.

Lying in bed after seeing that avalanche on television was strange – and stranger still when it occurred to me that I might have died in an avalanche in my past life. I didn't particularly care that it wasn't Christian to believe in past lives or future lives – because Christians didn't own everything in the world. There were many people in the world and they all had their own ideas. Even the Christians didn't all agree with each other. There were Roman Catholics and Protestants – and they even had wars; so who were they to lay down the law?

My mother was open to the idea – so, as far as I was concerned, it was possible.

I often lay in bed at night after that trying to remember – whilst being afraid of remembering. I wanted to know what happened before the avalanche. After some days or weeks of such pondering, it suddenly it dawned on me that I actually believed the avalanche had really happened – and that I'd died in it. The idea had moved from 'might have been' to 'it was' without my cognising the moment when certainty took hold. The *will to know* however, took me no further.

2

the thought-police, the woodland nymph, and the secret atheist

1957–1959

The White Lady remained a presence. She was a presence who intimated—ineffably—that there was something I should know: wordlessness. What was that?

As a child, I discovered the fact that there's a certain gustatory experience – that's not a taste. It's a feeling in the mouth as if the oral cavity were like an egg shell. This makes no sense – but along with that oral experience, there's a sense of something that is about to be known.[1] I have occasionally mentioned this experience to people throughout my life and a few people have said *"Oh yes ... I get that – but very rarely."*

It is like a name that's forgotten – but one has it *on the tip of one's tongue*. When it is a forgotten *name*, of course, one has clues. There were no clue other than the White Lady – and occasional unaccountable dreams. These dreams were unusual—I discovered much later—in being quite linear in their unfoldment. I saw scenes with large tents – unlike other tents I had seen. One tent seemed to be made of tiger hides. It would achieve nothing to itemise what I saw – other than everything seemed to be occurring in Switzerland. I saw huge white birds. I saw—and heard—large ravens, who appeared to have an extensive language that I couldn't fathom. There were two young girls who rode ferocious dogs. They seemed quite gleefully bereft of raiment under snow-capped mountains.

---

1   Kyabjé Düd jom Rinpoche told me that it was a nyam of the sense fields and occurred when one was not locked into concept consciousness. He said that it could happen to ordinary people who were not practitioners – because we all have moments when the realised state sparkles through and the psycho-physical elements begin to relax into their own condition.

I sometimes caught snatches of speech – but I could never recall what was said. Sometimes I would seem to wake up in the dream as 'someone who was at home in this environment' – but had forgotten who the little English boy was. I was a young man. I had white hair – whereas everyone else had much darker skin and almost black hair. Sometimes I would enter a large white tent and sit with the White Lady. It seemed that she was a Queen – but she didn't dress like a queen. She seemed to be a queen in terms of what she was – rather than how she dressed. She had no crown and no jewels – she was simply powerful without being frightening. It seemed that whatever she asked would be carried out – but she never appeared to request anything.

I had no comprehension as to *how* seeing such a wonderful being as the White Lady could lead to a person being sent to a mental hospital – but that is what my father had been saying for some time. Loud arguments between my mother and father occurred after I had gone to bed – and these worried me. His earlier intimations had become voluble exclamations. His force of expression started to make me anxious as well as distressing my mother.

My father had become increasingly belligerent in his vigilance concerning *what* I was thinking. He took to questioning me over meals. I tried to hide behind the toaster – but to no avail. Nothing deterred him. I tried to have food in my mouth as often as possible over meals – because it was known to be rude to speak with food in one's mouth. The problem was that I kept swallowing it and having to replace the food as quickly as possible. I started to put on weight at that point – and to develop a stammer.

Maybe there were just *too* many 'normal' people – and *too* many people who were *too* afraid of anything that was not sufficiently normal. Maybe it was these *normal people* who made the mental hospitals for people who were simply happy not to be normal. Maybe it was just too dangerous to live in a world where *not being normal* was reviled by most people. I'd heard about racism from my German grandmother – so maybe there were *thought-racists*.

My father was certainly an officer of the *thought-police*.[2] My mother would occasionally intervene when he questioned me too intensively – but it always led to arguments. The rows in the house seemed to increase and the situation started to feel like a pressure cooker; albeit lined with flock-wallpaper. I decided that I really might be bound for a mental hospital – and would therefore have to make some changes in order to save myself.

The change would be extremely sad – but there seemed no choice. I tried shaking my head violently when I saw the White Lady and eventually – I saw her more rarely. I was sad that I stopped seeing her every night – but I needed to avoid being sent to a mental hospital. The White Lady still appeared from time to time – but she appeared less and less, until she only appeared occasionally – and finally, only in dreams.

I was still a problem for my father in various ways. Apart from my stammer, I had an artistic bent – and that was always a worrying sign in a boy. I spent too much time drawing and painting and not enough time doing what boys were *supposed* to do. I showed no interest in sport; in fact I loathed it. I could not see any value in competition – and he therefore suspected that I was effete, effeminate, or homosexual. I had no idea what such words might mean – but worried in case they were further proof that I should be sent to a mental hospital.

Doctor Page—our family medical practitioner—thought I was 'an odd boy'. Whether he confided this to my parents, I do not know – but when medical records eventually became available for viewing in Britain – I discovered his remark in my medical notes: '… *an odd boy*, 8th of September, 1957'.

Doctor Page was a kindly fellow who reminded me somewhat of 'Mister Pastry', a television comedian of the time. He had wild white hair and round spectacles.

---

2   Thought-police was a term I dreamed up before I came across its use by George Orwell.

He gave me a series of physical tests which revealed that I was vaguely ambidextrous – or at least right handed and left footed. I was entirely inept at catching objects that were thrown toward me. Doctor Page suspected that I could have some visual problem – but this was never followed up.

No one explained why I was subject to these tests – and I never asked. I thought it was just the kind of thing that happened to all children – and thus never discovered what was deemed to be wrong with me. Maybe I was tested because my father had confided his fears as to my sanity or lack thereof.

Be that as it may, there were tests which involved choosing similar objects and placing them in groups. I was incapable of grouping objects however, because it always seemed to me that each object could belong in a group with each of the other objects. I was questioned on my conceptual difficulties with grouping objects. When it was suggested to me that there was an 'obvious' set of groups – I failed to see what was more or less obvious about other groupings. A wooden object could be placed with other wooden objects or it could be placed with smooth objects, dark objects, pale objects, heavy objects, or light objects. It was the same with the 'which one is the odd one out' test. I'd look at the pictures and could think of a reason why each depicted creature could be the odd one out. Then it would be explained that it was obvious that it was the goldfish because it was a fish and all the others were land animals. *"But … "* I'd ask *" … couldn't it be the bat because it only comes out at night? Or the beetle because it's the smallest? Or the wolf because it's dangerous? Or the horse because it runs fastest?"* Doctor Page did have the good grace to say that he could follow my thinking – but he still thought I ought to be able to see what was most obvious. No … I could not agree that one was more obvious that any of the others. I was *an odd boy.*

I'd had a string of childhood illnesses, probably a few more than anyone's fair share; *mumps, measles, whooping cough, scarlet fever,* and *chicken pox.*

I probably had *Poulet pox, goose pox, gander pox, turkey pox, duck pox, drake pox, mallard pox, grouse pox, pheasant pox, quail pox,* and every other kind of pox – so school was merely an intermittent irritation for a certain period of time. I used to think that it wasn't actually compulsory and that, one day, it would cease.

My frequent illnesses were another reason my father encouraged my rambling *"It will do the boy good to get some fresh air into his lungs."* He told my mother *"If he misses any more school – he will be good for nothing: if he is not good for nothing already."*

"Oh you must not—say—such things Ernest."

"I say it Renate, because it is true."

"But Ernest, Victor is just a little boy – many little boys are like this."

"Maybe in Germany, Renate – but this is England!" Pause. *"And ..."* in gentler tone *"... you do not know much of boys. I know—all—about boys, I can tell you."* There was some truth in this as he had had a son in a previous marriage – but whether this provided him with any great insight into boys must be left to be inferred. *"Boys can be a thoroughly bad lot if not watched. Boys need—strict—discipline, or they turn their lives to wrack and ruin. I know—all—about these things. I have seen a lot in the Army you know ... I have seen what happens when—boys—are not properly supervised and disciplined. They grow up to be depraved louts – criminals given to every type of depravity."*

That is how conversations often were with my father. He was right. Everyone else was wrong – and what's more; they all *knew* they were wrong and persisted in their wrongness despite that knowledge. I heard snippets of that kind of discussion throughout my childhood and was actually not terribly disturbed by it – in the end. I must have translated it in terms of the dreadful duo: my father and God.[3] I was not wildly impressed by either of them.

---

3   The author learned only later in life that the vision of God with which he was presented was a singular one – and bore little relation to Christianity as it was practised by those of a kindlier disposition.

They *did* call most of the shots in life – but they seemed to have no sanction or power of veto in Weyflood Woods, which was where I spent the bulk of my time. Rambling in the woods was, therefore, the perfect way of avoiding my father and allaying his anxieties about my … being odd.

I'd become aware of *the ominous brooding menace of 'God'* from an early age. He was responsible for all the misery on the planet, as far as I could see. 'God' was continually smiting people when they annoyed him – and my father had clearly taken a leaf out of God's book.

God smote the Assyrians – and most of the interesting people in the world seemed to be Assyrians. He also *worked in mysterious ways* to prevent enjoyment wherever he could ascertain its presence. My father was a staunch advocate of God and the normality he decreed *(in his mercy)*. My father did his level best to curtail deviations from normality whenever they manifested. My father—recognising me as a nascent Assyrian—started taking me to church in order to cure me of *the sin of being different.* It was there that I heard all kinds of gruesome facts about God:

Judah's firstborn, was wicked in his sight and God slew him – and the sons of Judah, Onan, and Shelah, who were born of the daughter of Shua of the Canaanites. And Er was evil in his sight and so he slew him too. Then he smote all the firstborn in the land of Egypt, from the firstborn of Pharaoh unto the firstborn of the captive that was in the dungeon; and all the firstborn of cattle.

And there went out a fire from God that devoured them – Nadab and Abihu died by fire. And when the people complained, it displeased God – and his anger was kindled and the fire burnt among them, and consumed them that were in the uttermost parts of the camp. And while the flesh was yet between their teeth—ere it was chewed—the wrath of God was kindled and he smote the people with a very great plague – and, behold Miriam became leprous, white as snow. And Aaron looked upon Miriam and, behold, she was leprous.

And God discomfited them and slew them with a great slaughter at Gibeon, and chased them along the way that goeth up to Beth-horon – where God smote them to Azekah, and unto Makkedah.

And God cast down great stones from heaven upon them unto Azekah and they died – and more died with hailstones than they whom the children of Israel slew with the sword. And God smote Benjamin and destroyed of the Benjamites that day twenty and five thousand and an hundred men.

Then he smote the men of Beth-shemesh, because they had looked into the ark of God. Then he smote fifty thousand and threescore and ten men – and the people lamented, because God had smitten many of the people with a great slaughter. And it came to pass ten days after, that God smote Nabal, that he died. Then the anger of God was kindled against Uzzah; and God smote him for his error; and there he died. And God struck the child that Uriah's wife bore unto David, and it was very sick.

And Elisha prayed unto God and said "Smite this people, I pray thee, with blindness!" And God smote them with blindness according to the word of Elisha.

And God smote the king, so that he was a leper unto the day of his death, and dwelt in a several house. And God sent lions among them, which slew some of them.

And it came to pass that night, that the angel of the Lord went out, and smote in the camp of the Assyrians an hundred fourscore and five thousand: and when they arose early in the morning, behold, they were all dead corpses. So Sennacherib—King of Assyria—departed, and went and returned, and dwelt at Nineveh.'[4]

After that hideous history of God's despicable conduct, I decided I'd better join Sennacherib in Nineveh – where God couldn't get at me. God was just too damn keen on smiting. He'd be after me next for certain … For yea, I'd be naughty in his sight – and he'd smite me *(in his mercy)*.

---

4   This passage – is a pastiche assembled from the Old Testament of the Bible. It is not intended in mockery—or a parody—but as a reflection of the impression the author received from his father and the church – as a five-year-old.

Enough with *mercy* already … I got it regularly from the lash of my father's Sam Browne[5] on my posterior – without need of God's mercy into the bargain. *'Spare the rod and spoil the child'*[6] was his motto. Somehow it never became plain to me, 'til much later in life, that my father was merely being a Victorian subsequent to Victoria's departure from the throne – and, somewhat later than her cultural bequest demanded. He was not the only such father, by any means. A Victorian father of a nascent hippie is going to be beset with causes for chastisement.

How was I to know that 1967 wasn't due to arrive for another decade? So, as 1967 had vexingly failed to arrive—and there was no 'happening' to attend—I roamed the fabulous spread of wilderness that began at the back of our garden. A lane—about ten to twelve feet wide—ran down the odd numbered side of Woodsfield Lane. You could follow it up – right into the woods. It was like a secret door to another dimension. The lane was an overgrown paradise where I could play before meals and my mother could call me quite easily. There were blackberries growing there and all manner of other small miracles.

On the other side of the lane lay the grounds of a deserted manor house. The house was supposed to be haunted and I always toyed with the idea of creeping over there to explore it—in the daytime of course—but severe warnings had been issued against that.

---

5   The Sam Browne army belt is a wide leather belt with a 2-prong buckle, supported by a diagonal strap crossing the right shoulder. Sam Browne was an officer who served in The British Raj in the 19th century. During the Indian Rebellion of 1857, Captain Sam Browne served with the 2nd Punjab Irregular Cavalry. In August 1858, Captain Browne fought at Seerporah where he received two sword wounds – one of which severed his left arm at the shoulder. He survived the injuries – but, deprived of a left arm he was now unable to control his sword. As a consequence, he invented the shoulder strap attachment which held the scabbard in place. Other cavalry officers in the Indian Army emulated him and it gradually became standard uniform.

6   A common phrase—before the late 20th Century—which refers to administering corporal punishment to children vis-à-vis discipline. The phrase 'spare the rod, spoil the child' means that if children are not punished when miscreant, they will be spoilt. It derives from the Bible Proverbs 13:24: 'He who withholds his rod hates his son, but he who loves him disciplines him diligently.'

The police would know about it and the culprit—meaning me—would be imprisoned for life and kept on a strict diet of bread and water. The police were everywhere as far as my father was concerned. They had eyes in the backs of their heads and—worst of all—radar. Radar was another of those sinister words my father used. The very sound of it made me feel queasy. They had radar—probably hidden in their pointed helmets—that would detect my slightest move. They'd see me from miles away – and then, they'd be down on me—at the speed of locomotives—with handcuffs and chains. They'd have truncheons, grunions, trunnions, and bunions – and who knows what other vindictive devices of moral order.

I was well accustomed to my route-of-escape. I more-or-less knew every tree – or at least every nut-bearing tree. There were hazel nuts and sweet chestnuts in season. There were acorns and horse chestnuts and all manner of delights. There were still a few red squirrels in those days – and I loved to catch a glimpse of them scurrying along the branches gathering provender for the Winter. So … up the brambled lane—along the path to the edge of the thicker woods—and across the stream into the really wild area where people—who were not backwoodsmen of my calibre—could become lost forever. Then I had some choices. I could range on up to the hills at the North end of the woods—if I had time—or I could turn South and find the largest path that ran through the middle of the woods. On this one particular day, I decided to turn South – and the result of that choice changed my life forever.

As I sauntered down the path, I wondered how far I would go and whether I'd come home by way of the road – or whether I'd retrace my steps. It was always a choice I'd have to make at some point. I was thus preoccupied when I caught sight of *something* flickering in the distant trees. I wondered if it was some kind of animal. It was too big for a badger. It was too small for a deer – and I knew there were no deer in the woods. It seemed colourful too – so I wondered if it could be a bird. A Woodpecker? A Kingfisher? It might be a Kingfisher because there was a small pond in that direction. I decided to explore. I quietened my tread and stole along the bank of the River Blackwater.

It was only a stream – but I'd been told it was once a river. I thought that if I walked as quietly as I was able—right next to the river— that the sound of it trickling would mask my footfall. I was right. Whatever it was that was flickering – kept flickering.

Then suddenly, the kaleidoscope image became a mosaic – and the mosaic became a sprite. A woodland nymph dressed in some kind of shimmering collection of colours – maroon, flame red, orange, yellow, and blue. I sat and watched the fairy on the edge of the stream as she leapt from one foot to another in some exotic and rarefied series of movements that almost resembled a dance. She was like a dragonfly—sometimes holding her arms high in the air like wings—and sometimes letting them trail. She pirouetted gracefully and twirled with surprising vigour – weaving her way amongst the entanglement of lithe young elm trees. I wondered whether she was the White Lady who used to come to visit me at night—and whether she'd decided to stay in the woods—but her face was different and she was much younger.

Then she saw me. She froze *"Why are you looking at me?"* she asked – but without any accusatory tone. She seemed innocently curious. I didn't answer immediately because I was still stunned by the fact that she wasn't from *the twilight world.* She was a real girl in the real normal world. She stood surprisingly still peering at me from behind a lattice of slender branches.

"Because … because you're beautiful." I replied, not knowing what else to say to a fairy.

"Am I?" she replied.

"Yes."

"How … do you know … ?"

"I don't know … it was in my mind – and that's why … and those words were just there, when you asked me why I was looking at you – and it's completely true."

"Yes … of course, yes …" she said as if in deep reverie *"… so what is—* your—*name?"*

"Victor."

"Where do you come from Victor?"

Suddenly I didn't know what to say. Where did I come from? I didn't know. I came from nowhere. *"I was just ... born ... and then ... and ... but now, I'm here."*

"No ..." she laughed *"I mean where do you live?"*

"I live on the other side of the woods from here – in Woodsfield Lane."

"Do you want to know my name?" she asked with a broad smile.

"Yes please – that would be very nice indeed."

"My name is Alice – Alice Rosalind Trevelyan – and that spells ART."

"That's the most wonderful name!" I replied – almost too loudly *"I've never heard any of those names before. I'd like to be called Alice."*

"No ..." she smiled *"You couldn't be called Alice – because Alice is a girl's name."* Pause. *"Didn't you know that?"*

"No ... well ... not exactly ..."

"Well I'll tell you then. There are girls' names and there are boys' names – and, Alice is a girl's name. You must know that girls and boys have different names."

"... yes ..." I responded *"... but I'd never really thought about it before."* Pause. *"I didn't really know about girls before you see. I mean ... I knew they were here – but I've never met a girl to talk to before."*

"You're funny." Alice laughed in a kindly way *"I like you."* Pause. *"You're not like a—*boy—*at all. Boys are horrid and kill insects and things like that."*

"That's horrible. I wouldn't want to kill anything. I love animals. I think animals are nicer than people – well nicer that a lot of people. My mother is very nice indeed – but ..." I ran out of steam.

"Isn't your father nice?"

"Well … sometimes …" Pause. *"I remember he did smile at me … once … a long time ago – so … I suppose he must be nice."* Pause. *"Maybe he smiled when we were on holiday in the Summer. He's nice when we're on holiday – so … I think he must be nice … really."*

"Well my father and mother are both—very—nice indeed. All the time too! And—they—are vegetarians."

"What's that?"

"That's when you don't eat animals or kill them."

"That's the very best thing to be! I hate lovely animals being killed," I announced with fervency.

"Now I really like you!"

"Can we be friends?"

"Yes!" Alice grinned *"Let's be friend forever!"* Pause. *"You can be my best friend! I've only just come here from London, you know, and I don't have any friends yet – well … I do know two girls in my road—they're sisters—and they're called Bethany and Gillian. They're my friends—sort of—but they don't play in the woods. My parents have all kinds of interesting things you know."* Pause. *"They have a cinematograph."*

Alice could talk at an amazing rate and I stood there almost hypnotised by her. If she'd started recounting her entire life history, I would have just stood there transfixed 'til she'd concluded. *"What's a cinemater … errrm … what kind of … thing … is that?"* I was hoping it wasn't like radar or one of those terrible machines my father knew about.

"It's a way of seeing films that aren't on television. You can see them with the cinematograph whenever it gets dark. There's a long—long—long number of pictures on a thing called a spool and it goes round and round past a light and the pictures go along the light. There's a screen you have to put up and you see the pictures moving on the screen. Then we all sit and watch! It's jolly fun!"

"That's fantastic! Will I be able to see that one day?"

"Yes! I should like that! It would be jolly fun to show you too."

"That's very kind of you. I would like that very much."

"Yes! And we have lots more interesting things too! You had better come with me and meet my parents – because … well … they don't like me to play with anyone they haven't met yet."

"Alright I'll come with you. Where do you live? Is it far away – because I have to go home before … before too long and my father will be angry if I'm late."

"No – I live just down the path, down the lane, and right by the main road at the bottom of the lane. It won't take us long especially if we run. Can you run? Boys usually run very fast."

"I don't 'run' very much at all" I replied sheepishly *"I'm not … very good at it – but I'll do my best to keep up with you … if you don't run too fast. I'm very slow at running."*

"Off we go then!" Alice beamed at me – and I followed. I'd never run as fast in my life – and, curiously, I seemed to be enjoying it. Maybe running wasn't so nasty after all ….

Soon we were at the bottom of the lane with houses on either side that ran up to the beginning of Weyflood Wood from the main road and there was Alice's house. I stood and gawped at it. I'd seen it before – but not from the standpoint of being invited inside. It was huge. There were large trees in the garden and two large cars stood in the large drive. We walked up to the rather large front door— which she pushed open—and walked through into the large hall. Everything was large and I felt rather small. *"What if they don't like me?"* I whispered *"My father said I was a duffer [7] – and maybe they will think the same and say you shouldn't play with me."*

"That's a bad thing to say about you – and it's not true. People shouldn't say bad things like that. My parents will like you because I like you and that will be an end of it."

Alice seemed rather firm and almost severe – and I felt slightly in awe of her. Still … she liked me and that was a marvellously good thing. I thought she was amazing in all possible ways. I had no idea of it at the time but I was seriously in love with Alice.

7 English slang term of the 1950s for someone who was intellectually slow – particularly of a child who failed to achieve at school.

All I knew was that life had just become better than I ever imagined it could be. This was better than the best thing there ever was – and Alice was the best friend I could ever imagine.

We passed along the hall and tried various rooms until we found Mrs Trevelyan in the front room reading a magazine. There was a delicious smell of cake coming from the kitchen and a lovely friendly atmosphere.

"Beverly!" Alice greeted her mother *"I just met Victor in the woods and he's my best friend. I think you will like him very much indeed. He's a lovely boy and he hates people being unkind to animals!"*

"Well that's a fine introduction Alice. How-d'you-do Victor." I shook hands with Mrs Trevelyan and for some unaccountable reason—I must have seen it in a film—I bowed to her.

"I am very well indeed thank you Mrs Trevelyan."

"My mother's name is Beverly you know – and my father's name is Clarence."

"Yes Victor – but you can call me Beverly or Mrs Trevelyan; whichever you like."

"Thank you … Mrs Trevelyan …" I blushed – not knowing what to say and suddenly realising I hadn't called her Beverly.

"Victor is probably used to calling parents by their surnames Alice – so we should not make him uncomfortable." Then she turned to me and asked *"Do you like fruit cake Victor? If you like you can stay for tea."*

"I love fruit cake Mrs Trevelyan – but … I'm expected home for tea … so …"

"Maybe another time then." Pause. *"Where do you live Victor?"*

"I live at number 17 Woodsfield Lane – just along the road."

"I'll tell you what, Victor … I have an idea." It having been established that my parents had no telephone [8] *"We could all drive over and ask your mother and father if it would be alright for you to stay to tea – then afterwards I could take you home in the car."*

---

8   It was not uncommon for people not to have a telephone in 1950s England – especially in the lower income brackets.

"Yes Beverly — that's the best idea ever!" Alice beamed.

So off we went in one of the amazing long cars with enormous leather seats. My parents' surname was ascertained and there we were outside my home. We all trooped out and approached the front door. My mother had spotted us and came to meet us. She was a little surprised — but gladly accepted the invitation to tea on my behalf. The two mothers conversed a little as I showed Alice the almond tree in the front garden. *"Is that really an almond tree!"* she whooped *"That's wonderful. When do the almonds grow?"*

"They start in the Summer."

"Are there blossoms in the Spring?"

"I expect so ..." I replied with uncertainty *"... but it's a long time ago — and I can't remember."*

"I expect so — I shall ask Beverly because she will know. Beverly knows all about trees and plants and all sorts of things."

At that point our respective mothers concluded their exchange and —as it turned out—the invitation extended to the evening. My bedtime was established and it was agreed that she would bring me home in good time to clean my teeth and depart into delirious oblivion. We trooped back to the enormous grey car and we drove to the top of Woodsfield Lane—rounded the turning circle at the top—and sailed sedately down. There were eyes upon the car as it glided down Woodsfield Lane and I found out later that a Bentley [9] had never before been seen in Woodsfield Lane. I was amazed at how easy it had been to secure my release. Mrs Trevelyan had obviously assumed it would be the simplest thing in the world to make such an arrangement — and had just done exactly what she'd set out to do. Even my father had agreed — although he never rose from his customary seat. He'd simply agreed and continued with his work. Wives were evidently of no great consequence — and the fact that she drove a Bentley was quite sufficient to ensure his son's encasement in a civilised setting.

9   It may have been a 1956 Bentley S1 Continental.

My father probably assumed Mr Trevelyan was a military type to whom one should defer – and he'd failed to grasp that my new friend was called Alice. He'd misheard her name as Alan from his distant position in the dining room – and when he learnt of his error, it was too late. He was slightly disconcerted about my having a girl as a friend – but on this occasion he got over his discomfiture quite quickly. There was no major explosion of annoyance – because … after all, a free meal was not to be sniffed at.

And so it came to pass that Victor Howard Simmerson *departed, and went and returned, and dwelt at Nineveh* – for an evening. This was more like it! This was life as it ought to be lived! For yea I had wandered in the wilderness and had arrived in the land of milk and honey – and, God had not smote me *(in his mercy)* after all. There were many such days – and in general my father seemed happy enough for me to be fed elsewhere. My brother Græham was still quite young[10] and required quite enough of my mother's attentions as far as my father was concerned.

"Do almond trees have blossoms Mrs Trevelyan?" I asked.

"Yes – they have lovely pink blossoms. I should imagine your almond tree is a gorgeous sight in the Spring."

"Yes—it is—I remember it now. I couldn't remember it at all 'til you told me the colour."

"That's interesting." Alice smiled.

"Yes." Mrs Trevelyan replied *"Memory can often be triggered by the senses. The sense of smell often brings back a memory more strongly than the other senses – but Victor obviously thinks in colours."* Pause. *"Do you dream in colour Victor?"*

"Yes Mrs Trevelyan – always. I used to have a dream where a White Lady came to visit me. She visited me every night – but my father said that people had to go to mental hospitals if they kept having dreams like that – so now she doesn't come to see me much anymore. I didn't know you could dream in black and white like the television."

---

10 Græham was born in 1955.

I noticed a change of expression in Mrs Trevelyan when I mentioned mental hospitals. It was brief and her expression returned to a smile again quite quickly, so I wasn't too worried by it.

"It's not so much that people dream in black and white – it's more that they don't really remember colour when they remember their dreams. But ... you know ... dreams are quite safe – so I don't think you need to worry. I don't think there's any likelihood of your going to a mental hospital. That only happens to people when terrible things happen to them. It's actually too complicated to think about at your age – so maybe it's better to forget the idea."

"Thank you Mrs Trevelyan – I won't think about it anymore then."

This was amazing to me. I was having an *actual* conversation with an adult. This was unprecedented – apart from my mother. My mother would talk with me – but there was always the sense in which she was disobeying the law-of-the-land. I knew the law quite well, not because it had been explained to me – but because it was a self-existent fact, learnt from bitter experience. The law stated that a child was forbidden to express any idea to an adult with the expectation that the adult would take it seriously in terms of giving a reply. If a reply was given it was only to be in such terms as 'don't talk nonsense' or at best 'never mind'.

Spending time in the Trevelyans' home was idyllic – and it was not long before Alice and I decided to get married; at some suitable future juncture when adulthood allowed. I was most enormously pleased. I'd got that worked out to my entire satisfaction. What could be better? What pleasure could come anywhere remotely close? I'd heard of luck – but I never thought it would come my way. Luck seemed to be what happened to other people – and now here I was with all the luck the world could possibly afford.

On special days like Halloween and Bonfire night—and other nights I cannot recollect—I was able to stay over with the Trevelyans. They had really nice beds there – apart from the sheets and blankets. I preferred the eiderdowns we had at home – at least when they'd aged a little. My mother was in the habit of starching the eiderdown covers and sheets and it took them a while to wear in.

My favourite phase came after a week – when they were comfortable for a while, until the next wash and starch. I told Alice about the eiderdown idea and she told her parents about them. *"That is what they have all over Europe."* said Mr Trevelyan *"I think they're a good idea – much better than sheets and blankets – and if I ever get the chance … I think we should make a change over. I slept under a continental quilt some years back when I was in Switzerland and I found them really far superior – so I've had it in mind since that time to obtain them for our own household."*

Then an amazing thing happened. Within a short time the Trevelyans had changed over to eiderdowns – or 'continental quilts' as they called them. It seemed almost shocking that I should have caused this to happen. Children were not supposed to do things like that. It made me a little nervous at first – because it seemed entirely against the natural order that I could have precipitated such a turn of events. I apologised to Alice for having mentioned it and hoped that her parents would not think that I'd complained about their sheets.

"Nonsense." said Alice *"My parents always like new ideas and what's wrong with you being able to tell them about a better idea?"*

"Oh …"

"And anyway – I like them far better than horrid sheets and blankets that get into stupid knots at night. It's really bad when you have to get out of bed and arrange them all again when it's cold. That's really horrible – but because of your good idea, it will never happen to me again. Clarence is really happy about that and so is Beverly."

"I think that it would have made my father angry. When I talk about my ideas at home, it makes him think that I will be a tramp when I grow up."

"That's also nonsense." Alice replied with a frown that was designed for my father rather than me – but the sight of Alice frowning was disturbing and my eyes moistened.

Alice detected my discomfiture and said *"I am not making my frowning-face at—*you*—Victor. My frowning-face is for your father – but—*he*—can't see it yet. When I'm older he will see my frowning-face – and I will make him stand in the garden in the rain for hours and hours. That will teach him not to be a bully."*

That made me smile – and I asked *"What—*is*—a tramp Alice? Do you know?"*

"I think it's – someone who doesn't have a house and has to sleep in hedges and things." Pause. *"But that will never happen to you because you're clever – and you love animals."*

"Sometimes …" I replied rather sadly *"I wouldn't mind sleeping in hedges rather than being at home. It's horrible when my father gets angry … he gets angry with my mother too … and I hate that even more than when he's angry with me – because my mother is kind and nice and takes the blame if I break something."*

"I like your mother – but your father is obviously a very bad pig!*"*

I was stunned by that. Could my father be called a 'very bad pig' without the police suddenly arriving and clapping the slanderer in irons? I thought the fabric of reality would be rent or something. I did agree with Alice—about my father—but remembered that he could also do good things. He went out to work every day so that we could eat – and he worked every evening too. He took on private estimating work in order to supplement his income. My mother had told me that – and she'd told me that his work was very hard indeed. That's what made him impatient and angry. I told Alice about that – and it made her quiet for a moment or two. *"I shall ask my father about that. He always knows about that kind of thing – and if it can be explained, he will explain it to me."*

"Will you tell me what he says?"

"Yes – and it will make you feel better! I don't want you to be sad ever again! Let's do something jolly now – and be happy as we should be."

Alice was remarkable. She seemed to be the fount of all wisdom – and if anything lay outside her comprehension she would simply ask her parents. If it could be explained to a child they'd explain it – and even if something was difficult to explain they'd try. This resulted in Alice being some kind of walking encyclopædia – as far as my perception could conceive of her. The thing that amazed me the most was that Alice's parents were atheists. That meant that they didn't believe in God – and that, was both frightening and exhilarating. I decided—within days of being made privy to this revelation—that I was also an atheist. The fact that God was an idea that people had invented, made complete sense to me. If God was supposed to be good—and if he had created the world—why would it contain so much pain? If there really was a God he could have stopped the World Wars and prevented the Nazis doing extremely terrible things to the Jews. My German grandmother had told me how frightening the Nazis were – and how they murdered millions of innocent people.

If there really was a God: *why* did he create people and animals only to have them die – and sometimes in great pain? Why was God always smiting people for no good reason other than they did things that didn't please him? When people were inventive and wanted to explore, he'd smite them for that too. The people who built the Tower of Babel seemed to want to know what was out there in space – and so God destroyed their tower. He made them all speak different languages so they couldn't start building another tower. Wasn't life often difficult enough without hundreds of different languages? I'd heard of spoilt children – and that's how God seemed. He'd have a temper tantrum whenever he couldn't get his own way – and we were all supposed to worship him for that. Not me.

I agreed with everything that Alice said and wondered why I had never questioned the existence of God before. This was something I would have to keep secret from my father – and probably *even* from my mother. I'd become a *secret atheist.*

I wished that I had never tried to force the White Lady from my mind – as I'd rather believe in the White Lady than a 'God' who really *wasn't* there. Unlike 'God', the White Lady really existed in my experience. 'God' had never visited me – and neither had he created the world. The world had created itself – and 'God' was just an invention of *the normal people*. It was my father who was insane for believing in an invisible 'God' who was supposed to have made everything – and *he* thought *I* was insane for seeing the White Lady. What sense did that make? The unfairness of this rankled with me – but Alice told me that most people believed in 'God' and *that* was why my father thought it was normal.

So, *that* was the way the world worked: the more people who believed in a thing, the truer it was. That was ridiculous. Alice told me that there was a time when everyone believed the wold was flat and that they had big nasty arguments about it – until the *flat earth idea* was finally proved to be stupid. It seemed that people were happy to believe in science – unless science said there was no proof of God – and then they'd decide science was wrong. It seemed that adults just made it all up as they went along – but had the cheek to tell children that *they* had silly ideas. I decided that if I ever had children, I would not tell them insane stories about reality. They'd be free to see whatever they saw without my telling them I'd have them locked away for it.

That was the last time I prayed – even though I went through the motions to please my mother. I sang Christmas carols with enthusiasm because I loved the melodies – and because I could ignore the meaning of the words. I generally preferred the one about the time that *good King Wensuss* [11] *last looked out.*

---

11 'Good King Wenceslas looked out' is a carol about a Bohemian king braving winter weather to give alms to a poor peasant on the Feast of Stephen. It is based on the life of Saint Wenceslaus I, Duke of Bohemia (907–935). Wenceslas is a Anglicised version of the old Czech 'Venceslav'. In 1853, English hymnwriter John Mason Neale wrote the 'Wenceslas' words, in collaboration with Thomas Helmore. It first appeared in *Carols for Christmas-Tide* (1853). The melody came from a 13th Century spring carol *Tempus Adest Floridum*—the time is near for flowering—published in the Finnish song collection *Piae Cantiones* (1582).

Much to my pleasure, the baby Jesus was absent in that carol – and *Good King Wensuss* sounded as if he was a person I'd like. He was thoroughly kind and generous – but without having to be pious or sanctimonious about it.

"You must think I'm really stupid and boring," I suggested one day.

"Why should I think that when you're my best friend ever – and forever?"

"Well … you know all kinds of things – and you're so much cleverer than I am. You play on the piano and all kinds of things like drawing, and painting, and singing, and embroidery as well."

"But you have a White Lady who appears in your room – and I've never seen anything like that ever in my whole life." I thought about this and had to agree that it was—or had been—a good thing. I explained to Alice that I'd been so frightened of being locked up in a mental hospital that I'd stopped myself seeing the White Lady. *"Then!"* Alice exclaimed *"You must try really hard to see her again – because I want to see her too."*

That seemed really exciting to me and quite astonishing, because if Alice believed it was possible – it must be possible. *"I will try as hard as I can and maybe one day when I stay at your house she will appear and we'll both see her!"*

"Yes!" Alice replied at tremendous volume and we both jumped around the garden in a state of advanced jubilation – as if we'd made some enormous discovery.

"But" Alice continued when we'd both calmed down *"beside the White Lady, your drawing and painting are lovelier than mine! And I know – because I know about that kind of thing and my mother said they were very good indeed!"*

"So … you don't mind when I don't know things?"

"Of course not – and anyway you know all the paths in the woods and there are thousands of them that I could never have found in a million years." Pause. *"And! That's how you found me there! And—that—was the cleverest of all!"*

3

the turquoise bee

1959

Alice never saw the White Lady – no matter how hard I tried to make it possible for her. This was disappointing – and more so because it was all my fault. I'd been the one who'd forced her out by shaking my head like an imbecile. It seemed extremely strange that I'd had to act like someone in a lunatic asylum to avoid being sent to such a place. The White Lady however, did start to appear again – just not every night and not as vividly. I wondered whether it was just a matter of time or whether she would never be vivid again. She never actually seemed to appear outside dreams. Alice was always extremely encouraging and seemed to have an absolute belief that the White Lady would return in her former glory – because "... *then she will be so glowing that I will be able to see her.*"

It was wonderful for me to have a friend with whom I could speak of the White Lady and of the scenes that I had witnessed in my dreams – or whatever they were. Alice had complete confidence in the fact that I'd seen sights that were somewhere other than England – and that I had seen the two young girls who rode on dogs in a mountainous landscape. I told her about the white tents and the caves that had doors that turned them into dwelling places. We would look at the huge encyclopaedia [1] in her home that had many volumes – to see whether we could find the place. We thought it might be Norway or Lapland. There were so many countries that had mountains and we tried to look at pictures of them all.

---

1 Most likely the Encyclopædia Britannica – a general knowledge encyclopaedia. It was written by over 100 full-time editors and 4,000 contributors. It was first published in 1768 in Edinburgh, Scotland, in three volumes. The 2nd edition was 10 volumes – and the 4th (1801–1810) had 20 volumes. Its stature as a scholarly work enabled the recruitment of eminent contributors, and the 9th (1875–1889) and 11th editions (1911) were regarded as landmark encyclopaedias in terms of scholarship and literary style.

The most likely place seemed to be Nepal – because the Himalayas were there, and on the other side was Tibet. I kept going back to the photographs of those mountains – and somehow there was always some strange feeling associated with them. I could not say *"Yes! This is the place!"* but neither were these mountains entirely unfamiliar.

The day arrived however when the Trevelyans' plan was announced. The family would be moving to Herefordshire. They wanted to live somewhere where there was a little more open countryside, and the Welsh borders looked ideal to them. I would be welcome to visit – but it was a long way away.

The weeks dissolved into each other – and then the days and hours. Then Alice was gone. *Gone, gone, gone beyond, gone completely beyond …* [2]

I didn't know it at the time – but the repetition of the word 'gone' that rang in my mind, was something that would recur. It would recur in different ways until it became something profound. [3]

Alice had been gone for a good six months – but the months were not good. I had been invited to visit, but my father would not hear of it – nor would he give me their address. Alice—*through the laissez-faire, eccentric, bohemian, vegetarian, nonconformist, and probably Marxist, influence of her parents*—was deemed 'a bad influence'. That was the end of the story. I was deeply unhappy about this [4] – but I was supposed to pull myself together and get over it. My father was at pains to make me understand that any sense of loss I felt was entirely self-inflicted and that he would not tolerate any moping.

---

2   *Gate, Gate, Paragate, Parasamgate Bodhi Svaha.* The mantra of the Heart Sutra.

3   The Heart Sutra *(Nying mDo / sNying mDo / Prajnaparamita Hrdaya Sutra / Wisdom-Heart Perfection)* is called the 'Mother of all Buddhas'. It is—with the Diamond Sutra—the most prominent text preserved in Tibetan, Mongolian, Chinese, and the Sanskrit language of Newari Buddhism. It exists in long and short versions. The earliest extant version is the short version. The Chinese Buddhist canon includes both long and short versions, and both versions also exist in Sanskrit. In the common Tibetan canon only the long version is preserved – although a Tibetan short version exists in small lineages such as the Aro gTér. This Tibetan short version has also been discovered in Dunhuang documents which contain material from the First Spread of Buddhism in Tibet.

4   See *'an odd boy'* Volume I by Doc Togden – ARO BOOKS WORLDWIDE.

I therefore kept my moping to myself and spent more time in the woods, where I was not visible. I spent long periods of time sitting on the branches of trees—vaguely obfuscated by foliage—trying to see the White Lady again. Try as I would she was as gone as Alice was gone. *Gone with the Wind.* I'd seen the film and there was the word 'gone' again. I didn't really understand the film that well – apart from the fact that Scarlett O'Hara was not kind to people especially Rhett Butler. I couldn't understand what he saw in her. She was nothing like the White Lady and nothing like Alice. Alice and I had been kind to each other and we had been good friends. Ideas of that kind often circled in my head.

On one occasion—nested in the branches of a willow tree—I encountered Mr Love. Mr Love lived at N° 5 Woodsfield Lane – and accidentally became my Blues tutor for a year or so. I'd been sitting on a branch in the willow tree at the juncture where his garden and the overgrown track at the back of Woodsfield Lane merged. I'd been listening to the Blues playing on his gramophone. I'd never heard anything like it before and was entirely captivated by it – as if I was listening to music from some other planet. As I sat there on that branch, Mr Love caught sight of me. He asked me what I was doing there in the tree – but in a welcoming way. *"I'm listening to your music Mr Love. I hope you don't mind. I don't know what sort of music that is – but it's jolly exciting. I've never heard music like that before and so I was listening to it. What kind of music is it, please?"*

He smiled *"It's … Blues. It's from America. That is why you have not heard it before."*

I asked him whether I'd be able to hear it somewhere and he replied *"We don't often listen to Blues in England,"* he laughed. *"It's a little too … exciting for average English tastes."*

"Can I stay in the tree and listen?" I asked

Mr Love laughed *"We can do better than that, Victor! You can come into the garden and I shall tell you about Blues, if you like."*

"Of all things in the world!" I exclaimed. *"Yes please, Mr Love! I would like that of all things."*

I descended from the willow and sat next to him, in a deck chair that had seen better days. The orange and blue striped canvas was sun-faded and the wooden frame had the marks of woodworm. It was there that I listened to the hiss-and-pop crackling 78rpm records of Big Bill Broonzy when Mrs Love suddenly appeared. She had long white hair curly hair. I was startled: not because she was unusually dressed for a woman at the end of the 1950s – but because she reminded me of the White Lady. The White Lady had not been old – but she'd not been young either. The White Lady had defied all concepts of age and so the elderly Mrs Love could have been the White Lady for all I knew. The closer she came, however, the more she looked like Mr Love's sister. She wore a white linen blouse decorated with elaborate lacework – and a long white Summer dress which swirled in the breeze. Although she soon ceased to be the White Lady – she brought her back to the forefront of my consciousness. I dreamt again of the White Lady that night – and understood something about Alice. It is not easy to explain what I understood – but I found myself with the conviction that Alice was necessary to my well being and to my artistic abilities. I also found myself with the understanding that this quality in Alice was there in every girl – or, at least in many girls.

This was simultaneously painful and propitious. I needed Alice – but Alice didn't have to be Alice. There would be other girls like Alice whom I could meet and would meet. Then eventually there would be one who was everything Alice had been and much more. But why couldn't she just be Alice? I didn't want to have to replace Alice no matter how much better another Alice might be. I didn't want a 'better Alice' – I just wanted Alice. Somehow, however—as I was having these thoughts—it occurred to me that the White Lady knew far better than I did what was wanted, what was needed, and what should happen. She knew the *when and where of everything* – but, to me, the future was a huge mystery. Becoming a teenager, let alone an adult, would bring changes that I couldn't imagine. I'd be driving a car perhaps. I'd have my own house. I'd be apart of an adult world that I could now only see as a spectator.

I'd earn my own money and spend it in whatever way seemed enjoyable. What would that be like? Who would I be? I knew that there had been huge changes already. I was no longer the baby or infant I had been. Would being a teenager or adult be as different as the difference between being a baby and becoming a boy? Maybe another Alice in the future would be perfect. There was no way I could know or even imagine.

In the middle of such a reverie, Mrs Love brought out glasses of delicious ginger beer. I'd never tasted ginger beer before – but it was provided whenever I visited. It somehow seemed to me like the thing Bluesmen drank.

Sitting relaxedly in Mr Love's impromptu school of Blues one day, I observed a bumble bee zim-zumming in the apple trees. *"That bee …"* I announced *"… is making a very strange sound."*

"Yes, he—is—indeed, Victor" Mr Love laughed *"He's a little tipsy, I think."*

"Tipsy?" I asked.

"Yes … he's been drinking the juice that forms in the little pockets on the apples where the birds pick at them. The juice turns into alcohol through contact with airborne yeasts and the apples ferment on the trees. It always happens at this time of year."

"That's very interesting – so … the bee is drunk?"

"Yes – as you would be from drinking too much wine."

"I have a small glass of wine for Sunday lunch" I ventured *"so … could that happen to me?"*

"Not on your mother's elderflower wine, young Victor. Delicious though it is – it does not contain much alcohol, so you would be quite safe to drink even a full glass of it."

"I have heard of being drunk – but I don't know what it means."

"Well … it's not a good thing Victor – and it should be avoided. It's like … not being able to walk properly. People can fall over when they're drunk or drop things because they have no proper control of themselves. They also wake up the next day feeling ill."

"Why do they do it then?"

"Well … at first … it makes them feel good – but then, if they have no self-control, they just keep wanting more … and that's what makes them ill."

"I never want to do that – that sounds awful."

"It is, young Victor – and I hope you will always feel the same. If you do – you will avoid it and have a better life for it. In moderation wine is a very pleasant thing – as you have seen with your mother's elderflower wine. Your mother was so kind as to send me a bottle – nay, several over the last few years and I am most partial to a sip of it." Pause. *"Speaking of bees however … I have a record I could play concerning bees."* He sorted through his box of records and pulled out one of the delicious looking brown-paper sleeves. *"You may have heard about the queen bee – but this song is about a king bee."* He placed the record on the turntable and carefully set the needle down. There followed the familiar hiss and crackle and then Slim Harpo broke out like Armageddon.

> *Well I'm a king bee buzzing around your hive*
> *Said I'm a king bee, baby buzzing around your hive*
> *Yeah I can make honey baby if you'll just let me come inside.'* [5]

"That harmonica playing is … like nothing I've ever heard before … I didn't know harmonicas could make sounds like that. The ones I've heard sound nothing like that at all. I've got one at home – but I've never made sounds like I heard on this record."

"Ah … I think I know why that may be Victor. Does your harmonica have a little silvery knob on one end that you can press to change pitch?"

"Yes!" I said amazed *"How did you know?"*

---

5   'King Bee' was written by Slim Harpo and first recorded in 1957 as the B-side to his debut record 'I Got Love if You Want It'.

"It's not secret Victor. Almost all the harmonicas in music shops are like that. They are called chromatic harmonicas because they can produce every note of the chromatic scale. The chromatic scale means all 12 notes with all the sharps and flats."

"Sharps and flats?"

"Yes ..." Pause. *"... do you have a piano at home?"* I replied that we had a piano and he asked me whether I ever played on it. I said that I had fun tinkling about on it. *"Well then – you will have noticed that there are black keys as well as white keys – and the sharps and flats are all the black keys. If you start on any note and play 12 notes one after another – you come back to the same note but a note that is higher in pitch. Have you noticed that when you've been exploring the instrument?"*

"Yes I have – it's interesting – that two notes sound the same but one's higher and the other is lower. It seems to go all the way up the piano."

"Yes it does Victor – well observed." Pause. *"That is called an octave ... I think this might be getting too complicated for you ..."*

"A little ... but maybe if you tell me again ... or if you tell me a few times, I'll remember."

"Good for you Victor – I am sure you will learn about this at school at some point – but there's no harm in getting started early is there?"

"No Mr Love – I really want to know as much as possible about music."

"Well then ... what next. Ah yes – we were talking about the chromatic harmonica. Now that is not what Slim Harpo is playing. Slim Harpo—and most Blues musicians—use the diatonic harmonica. In fact – they don't even call them harmonicas, they call them 'harps'—in the way that some people call the harmonica a 'mouth organ'—but most Blues musicians simply call them harps."

This was fascinating. I wished that school was like this. *"So!"* I smiled broadly *"That's why he's called Slim Harpo!"*

"Correct Victor! Top of the class!"

"I'm really glad to know all these things. Thank you very much for telling me. I do so like to hear all these things about Blues."

"Well to finish the lesson – I will tell you about the Blues harp." Pause. *"The Blues harp—I shall call them harps now that you know what I mean—is actually a cheaper instrument than the chromatic harmonica. The harp is called diatonic because it will only play in one key."* Pause. *"This is perhaps a little too complicated to explain all at once Victor – but think of it as an instrument that cannot play all 12 notes. It only plays notes that go together. There are always 8 of these notes in the 12-note chromatic scale. Those notes are called a 'key' and there is a different key—or set of 8 notes—for every note in the chromatic or 12 note scale."* I was utterly lost – yet riveted. Mr Love was explaining the secrets of the universe. I was amazed that music was made of so many different things and it all followed such an elaborate system. Although I couldn't really grasp it – it seemed highly graspable. I just needed to hear it enough times and maybe ask some questions.

"This means that you need 12 harps if you are a professional harp player. Are you still following my explanation … this is a little difficult, I know …"

"Yes – I will need 12 harps when I'm a professional Blues player."

"Yes indeed you will, young Victor!"

"There were some things that were a bit difficult though … would you mind explaining everything again on another day so that I will be able to understand a bit more?"

"Certainly Victor – just as long as you don't become bored by it."

"I will never become bored!" I squeaked. *"I want to know everything there is to know about Blues and all about music."*

Mr Love chuckled at my enthusiasm. *"Well … I'm not a music teacher … and we have no piano – so I can only go so far – but I shall do my best. Anyway Victor – you make teaching a pleasure – so I will always be happy to tell you as much as you want to know."* Pause. *"The other thing about the harp is that you can bend notes on them much more easily and powerfully than would be possible with a chromatic harmonica."*

Now I understood everything. My harmonica at home was a useless object that I would ignore in future. It hardly deserved the name of a musical instrument. *"I think I want to get a real harp one day."*

"I'm sure you will Victor. But now, I will tell you about Slim Harpo because I know a little about him. He was a real master of the Blues harp." Mr Love made himself comfortable in his seat – as he did whenever he intended to give me some information. *"He was born in the* 1920s *and his name by birth was James Moore. He came from Louisiana. He was an orphan and worked on the docks and as a building worker during the* 1940s. *He began his performing life in bars in Baton Rouge where he used the name Harmonica Slim accompanying his brother-in-law, Lightning Slim. He was named Slim Harpo by his producer JD Miller and started recording in* 1957. *Just think of that young Victor – just five years after you were born."*

"That is fantastic – it's so old but it's still in my life … Maybe that means it will always be part of my life."

"There is no reason why it should not be so Victor – because today there are still young Blues musicians in Chicago. Wonderful electric Blues musicians like Howling Wolf and Muddy Waters." [6]

"Those are marvellous names – I really like how they sound. How did they get names like this? Did they get them the way Slim Harpo got his name?" [7]

"Yes … either that way … or they were nicknames … You might be given a nickname at school by your friends …"

"Mmmm … what would that be?"

"Impossible to say … sometimes it's a shortening of your name. Victor—for example—would become Vic. Daniel would become Dan and Robert would become Rob or even Bob. Then there are names that change completely – John can become Jack and Margaret can become Maggie…" Pause.

---

6   *Howling Wolf* (Chester Arthur Burnett, 1910–1976) was an influential Blues vocalist, guitarist, and harp player and one of the best-known Chicago Blues artists. Some of his best known songs: *Smokestack Lightning, Back Door Man, Killing Floor,* and *Spoonful* became Blues standards. In 2004, ROLLING STONE magazine ranked him number 51 on their list of the *100 Greatest Artists of All Time. Muddy Waters* (McKinley Morganfield, 1913–1983), was an American Blues singer-songwriter and musician who is often cited as the *father of modern Chicago blues,* and an important figure on the post-war Blues scene. His style of playing has been described as *raining down Delta beatitude.*

7   Slim Harpo (James Isaac Moore, 1924–1970), was an American Blues musician, of the swamp Blues style, and master of the Blues harmonica: the harp.

"... but these are now really nicknames ... in the Army people used to get nicknames based on their surnames ... like Smudger Smith, Dusty Miller, Chalky White, or Nobby Clark."

"Those are interesting names – are there any others?"

"There are many – many more than I can remember ... but here are a few more: Pitchy Black, Dinger Bell, Bunny Warren, Swampy Marsh, Nosey Parker, and Spider Webb." Pause. *"... then ... there are nicknames which might come from some skill, personality trait, or idiosyncrasy ..."* He noticed my confusion at the word idiosyncrasy *"... idiosyncrasy means ..."* He looked slightly dreamy for a moment – then continued ... *"something you do, or say, that no one else would do or say – or maybe very few people would do it or say it."* Pause. *"For example ... my interest in Blues music would be regarded as eccentric for an Englishman."*

"Ah ... that is good – then I'm eccentric! I'm very pleased to be eccentric! Now we're both eccentric!"

"Indeed we are young Victor!" Mr Love laughed *"... but ... I would not say so to anyone else ... because ... well people don't tell others that they are eccentric ... It's hard to explain why ... so ... maybe you will just have to take my word for that. Maybe when you are older that will be easier to understand ..."* Pause. *"... anyway – enough of this chatter – let us listen to another song about bees. This one is called 'Queen Bee Blues' and it is by a gentleman called Bumble Bee Slim."*[8]

Mr Love sorted through his box of records and pulled out another brown-paper sleeve. He extracted the 78 record with great care and placed it on the turntable. He set the needle down and the hiss and crackle commenced.

'Queen bee, queen bee, queen bee, queen bee, please come back to me
'cause you got the best darn stinger – any queen bee I ever seen.'
Bumble Bee Slim, *Queen Bee Blues*, 1931

Mr Love noticed that I had tears in my eyes at the end of the song *"What is wrong Victor ... are you feeling alright?"* he asked in a gentle concerned tone *"Has something upset you?"*

---

8   Bumble Bee Slim (Admiral Amos Easton, 1905–1968), was an American Piedmont Blues singer and guitarist.

"*Sorry Mr Love … it's just that … that song made me think about Alice.*"
Mr Love said nothing – but simply nodded and waited for me to
continue. "*Well … Alice was my friend and now she's gone to Herefordshire
and I may never see her again.*" That was too much for me and I burst
into tears. Mr Love still nodded and I got over the upsurge of
emotion. When he could see I'd stabilised myself, Mr Love said
"*You see Victor … you have the blues … and … well … this is a large part
of Blues. This music comes from emotions … it comes from sadness … but …
it also comes from joy. Blues is sung to express human emotions and the stronger
the emotion the better the music – so …*"

"*So that would make me a good Blues singer Mr Love?*"

"*Yes Victor … although … I hope that your Blues will come more from joy
than from sadness…*" Pause. "*… but—some—sadness in life is important
… I think … maybe … if there is no sadness – there would be no joy …
but,*" he laughed "*I'm no philosopher – so I have nothing very profound to
say about joy and sorrow. All I can say is that you will learn about life from
living … and … you will be able to sing about what you feel. You will find –
that there are Blues songs to suit almost every circumstance.*" Pause. "*May I
ask, Victor—and please tell me if it is none of my business—but why would
you not be able to see Alice again? Herefordshire is not so—very—far away
…*"

"*Well …*" I felt that hot sensation again – but I got some kind of
spanner[9] from my *will-power bag* and tightened up my emotional
plumbing. "*… Alice's parents did tell me that they'd invite me to come and
stay … but …*"

"*Oh …*"

"*And … my mother told me that my father wouldn't allow me to go anyway –
so it's useless.*"

"*Oh …*"

"*So …*" I reached for the spanner again "*… that's why I will never see
Alice again … unless I can find her when I grow up.*"

9   Wrench in the USA.

"Well Victor ... that is not impossible. Maybe ... you should not give up hope. Who knows ... there may come a letter one day – or a Christmas card ... and who knows ... your father may not ... always feel the same way."

Yes, when pigs learn to fly. There was no way my father was ever going to change his mind about anything. My father was a huge fortress of law and rules – and everything was written down with the absolute agreement of God. There was no chance of anything changing about anything. The only freedom I had was in Weyflood Woods – where I hoped I would see the White Lady again. I'd sit in an old yew tree for hours trying to be silent enough to see her – but she never came other than in dreams.

There was another freedom – and that was Mr Love's garden. It was always pleasant, if ... slightly unkempt by conventional standards. The grass was always a little too long and there were no flower beds. There was just grass and trees and it felt much more natural there than in the brutally manicured gardens of other people in Woodsfield Lane. I liked the way that the grass 'round the base of the trees was longer than elsewhere. Mr Love told me that was because the lawnmower couldn't go right up to the trees. I told him I was glad of that because it looked much nicer with the small circle of long grass. *"Blues singer and landscape gardener!"* smiled Mr Love *"I am glad you approve of the arrangement. I'm afraid I don't mow the lawn as often as I should – nor do I mow it short enough ..."*

"It's perfect just as it is Mr Love – I like your garden best of all."

I also liked the way that the Loves' garden merged into the lane behind. There was no fence there. All the other gardens had fences at the back – but the wooden fence at the back of the Loves' residence had long since collapsed and they'd used it as firewood. The lack of fence made the Loves' garden appear much longer than the others – and I liked the sense of distance it gave.

It was always utterly delightful to sit in one of the Loves' ancient deckchairs; listening to Blues – and sipping the lovely ginger beer which was made by Mrs Love.

Mrs Love was *not* Mr Love's wife – she was his sister. The social etiquette of the day made her 'Mrs' Love even though she was a spinster. It seemed that all unmarried women over a certain age became 'Mrs' by default – unless they were school teachers and then then were called Miss even when they were married. The rules of the adult world were unbelievably complicated. The rules of music seemed so much simpler – at least they could be understood.

I must have been thinking about the inebriated bee – or at least the thought of the bee recurred intermittently. One night it recurred in a dream as a beautiful blue bee – a blue that was almost peacock blue but tinged with green. I described the colour of the bee to my mother who told me that this colour might be described as turquoise – but that she had never heard of bees being that colour. The word *turquoise bee* reminded with me as some sort of symbol. It sounded like a name I could call myself – The Scarlet Pimpernel.[10] Maybe I was The Turquoise Bee. There were words in the dream but I could not remember them exactly as they had been. It seemed as though I had spoken those words.

The flowers are all gone – but the turquoise bee isn't sad. I won't be sad either even though Alice has gone away.

That was a strange idea and strange words – but they stayed with me.

One thing that was not at all easy to understand was that Mr Love had 'queer turns'. It had something to do with WWII but no one wished to elucidate beyond a certain point. The intelligence from my parents was that he was 'shell shocked' – but the Loves never used that term. Mr Love himself told me that he had 'queer turns' and that if I ever found him ... '... *not being quite himself or talking strangely*' then it would be better not to try to talk to him that day.

"What would that sound like Mr Love?"

---

10 The Scarlet Pimpernel is the first novel in a historical fiction series written by Baroness Orczy and published in 1905.

"Oh … I don't know really young Victor … I can never remember what I sound like when I'm having a queer turn … but it doesn't make much sense – and you would not want to hear that kind of thing."

Mrs Love—who'd just brought out a lovely large tumbler of ginger beer—said *"I will let you know if it's not a good idea to come visiting – so there's no need to worry."* And that was it. That's all I ever knew. I did see Mr Love once or twice on Weyflood Road when he was absorbed and talking to himself. I bade him good day and he'd shaken his head. I took it as a sign that I'd better say no more – and that was it. My mother couldn't explain it to me – but assured me that Mr Love was a good man and never meant any harm even when he was talking nonsense. *"Some people have been offended by him and zay say he iss rude to zem – but he hass never been rude to me in all ze years vee have lived in ziss house."*

My father thought he would be better off in an institution – but my mother disagreed entirely. She never directly contradicted my father on this subject – but she told me what she thought. I only found out later, the grief I caused my mother by virtue of my Blues education. She'd had to bear the brunt of my father's consternation. Mr Love was not a safe person to be in the company of a child as far as he was concerned. The fact was however, that no harm had come to me during a dozen visits – and there was always Mrs Love at hand should anything 'worrying' occur. In the end my father had no obvious argument against that – apart from the fact that Blues was a 'depraved row'.

Life rolled on – and I learnt that I'd booked another *ticket to ride* on the desolation express. Alice had gone to some unknown location in Herefordshire – and soon Mr Love was to follow, not to Herefordshire, but to a place equally as obscure. Again someone I loved was to move beyond my reach. Mrs Love died without warning. There was no illness. She'd died in her sleep, of … nothing in particular. Her heart just stopped beating – and suddenly she wasn't there. Mr Love was badly shaken by the death of his sister and his 'queer turns' merged into something permanent.

Before I could understand what was happening, it wasn't – and Mr Love was gone. The house was sold and Mr Love had been taken to Brookwood, the mental hospital[11] where he died sometime later. It was the most dreadful misery that Mr Love was dead and that I would never see him again.

It was at that time that the White Lady came again – and she appeared every night for a while. When she was there, I came to feel that Mr Love had gone somewhere else – and that it wasn't maybe as sad as I thought. I knew there wasn't any heaven where God lived —or any nonsense of that sort—but it was good to know that death was not actually the ultimate end.

I didn't quite understand why I felt less miserable but, somehow, it seemed as if everything was understandable without actually being understood. The White Lady—as before—never spoke – so there was nothing to understand: she simply looked at me—or through me, or into me—and I understood things that I called 'sky' or 'clouds' or 'clouds made of sky'. These *skies* were ideas that hadn't appeared – but were always about to appear. They were like the experience of words on-the-tip-of-my-tongue. They were the moment before ideas happened. In one of these skies the idea appeared that the White Lady was looking at Mr Love – and that somehow, he would always be in my life somewhere.

The next day I translated this as Mr Love becoming an encouraging voice—albeit voiceless—who would always be there. I had the idea that he could become a baby again. He'd grow up in some happy place where he'd hear Blues again – but that was not something that came from the White Lady. That was just my wishful thinking. At that time I was aware of the light that emanated from the White Lady and began to feel that it could help people if that light shone on them.

---

11 Brookwood Hospital—Woking, Surrey—was founded on the 17th of June, 1867 by Surrey Quarter Sessions as the second County Asylum. The first was Springfield Asylum in Tooting. A third asylum was then established in 1882 at Cane Hill in Coulsdon. Brookwood Hospital was designed by Charles Henry Howell, the principal asylum architect of the Lunacy Commissioners from 1860–1893. The 'Brookwood Asylum' closed in 1994.

It would help people because the light was the White Lady – it didn't just come *from* her. It was then that I decided to picture Mr Love in my mind and see the light of the White Lady shining on him and through him. It seemed obvious to me that this would help Mr Love – but how this idea came into being, I have no idea. Ideas like this would appear in my mind from time to time – and I would have complete confidence in them.

Mr Love had promised he'd leave me his Blues records when he died – but the records vanished with the house. It was apparently illegal for a child to go to a mental hospital – so I could not visit him. I don't think my father ever said that – but he may as well have done. It simply wasn't possible – and I was a miscreant for even mentioning the possibility. *"The boy will probably end up in Brookwood himself if he doesn't learn some sense."*

Maybe I would. Maybe life would be better in Brookwood Mental Hospital. There'd be no laws about normality – because it would be normal for everyone to be abnormal. *Normal life* seemed terrible to me – and I wondered if you could go to other countries where there were no laws about normality. I remembered being in Germany one holiday when my father stayed at home. My uncles and aunts and older cousins asked 'me' what 'we' should all eat for dinner and I'd said 'cheese on toast.' Then—miracle of miracles—they made cheese on toast with tomatoes and onions just as I'd said it should be. What a wonder! Maybe I should go and live in Germany because it wasn't as normal there. I remembered that the houses in Ahlten— where Tante Rikchen and Onkel Arnold [12] lived—often had beautiful round paintings of animals on the outside wall. They were often paintings of stags [13] – and I loved to look at them. These round paintings were obviously extremely abnormal – because no one had pictures on their houses in England. They had really good bread there too – and marvellous cakes.

---

12 Aunt Rikchen and Uncle Arnold.

13 The round painted plaques on the walls of houses in Ahlten designated who had won the Schützenfest in any particular year. The Schützenfest (*Shooting Festival*) centred around a shooting competition.

They had delicious sausage and cheese – and real fruit juices made from blackberries and all kinds of berries. Yes – I'd have to go and live there … but then … how would I find Alice again?

That was life then. You loved people and they either died or went away. My grandmother—Clara Schubert—had died. I'd loved my grandmother. She was a fine old lady who knew a lot about music. She thought that black people were just as good as us—or better— and that people who thought otherwise were better placed in Brookwood than Mr Love. It was obvious that she was right about that – and I wondered why it was that most of the lunatics actually lived *outside* mental hospitals.

It was no use asking how to make sense of life – because *that* wasn't a sensible question. My mother had far more sympathy with the question than my father – but she said that questions like this couldn't easily be answered 'til I was an adult. When would *that* be I wondered – maybe when I went to junior school in September? That was to be a boys' school rather than the mixed-sex infant school I'd attended up to that point. My father had decided that I shouldn't go to the mixed-sex junior school because my association with Alice had made me even more abnormal than I was before. The Trevelyans had been *atheist naturist cranks* – and he suspected them of having communist sympathies. He wondered how they'd come by their money. They obviously had too much money for their own good – because they were prodigal in spending it. They had two cars when only one was required. Why should Mr Trevelyan's wife need a car of her own? Housewives didn't need cars. He'd never been able to ascertain the nature of Mr Trevelyan's employment – but as he'd never met him, he'd been unable to enquire. My mother thought he might be an architect as he had a room with a large table that could tilt – or something of the sort. My father was doubtful because architects were serious-minded people who were not prone to eccentric fads.

My time playing with Alice at the Trevelyans' home had also led me into *'disagreeable dalliance'* with two other girls—Bethany and Gillian —and that had obviously *'wrought havoc with my character'*.

My mother naturally thought this was overstating the case and she'd been glad that I'd had some friends of my own age locally. She's said *"In Germany it iss normal for little boys and girls to play as friends at ziss age."*

My father had harrumphed at that *"Maybe in Germany, Renate – but this is England. Here boys learn to enjoy sport and to take interest in manly pursuits."*

Sadly Bethany and Gillian had moved to Oxford six months after Alice had moved to Hereford – and as I'd only ever played with them at the Trevelyans' house – our contact was not the same. I did go to their house a few times – but their parents were not at all like the Trevelyans. They were kindly but seemed in some way to be of the same point of view as my father. A boy was somehow not quite appropriate as a friend for their daughters.

Hard on the heels of that piece of bad news, I would soon be moving up to the next school – which was West Street Boys' School in Farnham.

That was the next horror. I was to be subjected to the unremitting company of *boys*. There'd be 'sport' … How loathsome. My father told me about 'sport'. *"You should be really pleased."* I told him that I was really pleased – but I don't think he believed me. The picture became worse with everything he said. He may as well have said they'd strap a brace of rabid monitor lizards to my head and dunk me in liquefied dog-dung every day.

4

Frigg and White Tara

1960–1963

Having been condemned to the purgatorial penitentiary of West Street Boys' Junior School,[1] I found myself standing in the playground watching them. Boys … a repulsive spectacle: alien beings, whose enjoyments ranged from anomalous to abhorrent. They kicked and pursued perfectly innocent balls. They chased each other, yelling captions from boys' adventure comics – for purposes I could not comprehend.

Then there was their nauseating primitivism. The urinal—to the West of the playground—was an open-air situation: a free-standing wall facing a fivefold defæcatorium. On the playground side of the urinal-wall was a water-fountain at which one could drink – but there was always a risk involved in drinking from that water-fountain. If one didn't first check who was on the other side of the wall *(and purportedly micturating)* one could be subject to a malodorous drenching. One of the favourite tricks of the *fine young lower primates* was to stand in line at the urinal, applying pressure in order to prevent the discharge of urine. They'd wait 'til someone was taking a drink – and then let fly over the wall, to drench which ever unfortunate was taking a drink on the other side. Their degree of control and tolerance for pain had to be admired – but their wit and maturity placed them somewhat below the average invertebrate. I told my father about it – and, for once, he agreed with my dislike of immature male barbarism.

There were, of course other aspects to the barbarism. During my first days at Junior School, Adrian Parrott started picking on me – it went on all week until I finally hit him square on the nose.

---

1 The name changed later to Castle Primary School – but as of 2019 there appears to be no trace of the school.

I'd been amazed at how the boy simply fell to the ground with blood gushing from his nose. At first, I thought I had killed him and was horrified. I was still horrified when I realised, he wasn't dead. I'd not intended to hurt him that much and couldn't understand quite how I'd accomplished such a blow. I got into serious trouble over that at school even though a few other boys came to my defence. They all confirmed that Adrian Parrott had been bullying me and that he had started the fight – but the teachers deemed me to have hit back far too hard. How was I to know how hard to hit? I'd never hit anyone before. The teachers concluded that I was a thug. I told them that it was the first time I'd fought – but they didn't believe me. My parents received a severely worded letter – and I sat in a state of anxiety as my father read the letter aloud to me. By the time my father had read the letter and briefly questioned me – he seemed perplexingly pleased with me. He contacted the school to the effect that *I was not—and had never been—the type of boy to fight.* He told them I was not to be punished for defending myself against a bully when there were reliable witnesses who had observed the bullying. It was their responsibility to police the playground and if they were incapable of maintaining discipline, they had no business running a school. He read his letter to me – beaming. I was stunned by his approbation as I'd expected him to punish me. He must have concluded that I was a 'real boy' after all.

I was never bullied again and it wasn't long before I was talking to Adrian in a friendly way. The teachers observed this and I was taken aside to be informed that the school was now content with my playground behaviour. From that experience however, I knew I could hit someone hard enough to floor them – but it never enamoured me of pugilism.

One of the few things I liked about West Street School was the setting of the playground. The Victorian railings were magnificent – as was the rather splendid iron representation of cardinal directions, inset into the stone flagging near the entrance. Trees lined the playground on the sides which faced the two small streets on the North and East sides of the playground. I thought it was a wonderful idea to have planted them there.

At the Northern end of the playground, there was a smallish wilderness area—about three yards wide—which was full of all kinds of trees: a laburnum, silver birch, several willows and horse-chestnuts and sweet chestnuts, an oak, elder, hawthorn, crab-apple, and various beeches. They were identified for us in a nature-lesson and I suddenly felt as if the school wasn't so bad after all.

Then there was the music teacher—Mr Sharp—who actually *knew* something about music. He commenced to unravel the mysteries of notation – and I was fascinated. I sat next to a boy in the music class who seemed friendly. His name was Steve Bruce. He was a great help to me – because he seemed to know a great deal about musical notation. There was nothing Mr Sharp taught that Steve didn't already know – so Steve had plenty of time to provide me with extra tuition. I was always slow to learn anything – but once I'd learnt it, it was there for good.

Steve's parents were atheists. That was a pleasing piece of information. It gave me some degree of confidence in my association with him – as Alice Trevelyan's parents had been atheists. With any luck, they'd be as open minded and friendly as the Trevelyans had been. I talked with Steve about my fascination with the religion of the Vikings – and how I regretted that it was no longer available in the world. Of course, I knew almost nothing of ancient Norse mythology apart from what I gleaned from the television. I'd seen a few films—and read books by Henry Treece—but the rest was my fertile imagination.

"What d'you like about it?" asked Steve.

"I like it that there isn't a god who was supposed to have made it all. The Norse gods didn't make the world – they're just another part of it – a part that's mysterious."

"That's interesting ..." Steve replied *"... I suppose ... although it's a primitive religion – it's not as primitive as believing in an uncreated creator."*

Steve noticed he'd lost me with the words *'uncreated creator'* and explained in less arcane language. *"That's a god who made it all – but, with no one who made him."*

"Ah ..." I replied "That is obviously ridiculous. What I like is that there are things that happen that don't make sense in the ordinary world."

"What d'you mean ...?"

"Well ... it seems that teachers—and all those kind of people—think that everything works by rules and laws – but Thor and Odin don't obey those laws. That's what makes it impossible to have rules that work—all—the time." Pause. *"I think part of things in the world makes sense – and another part doesn't. Then ... the way the two are sort-of knitted together is what we see – y'know ... the universe."*

"I see ... " said Steve pensively *"... like ... how things are a mixture of patterns and accidents?"*

"Something like that – yes."

"My parents told me about how people try to make proofs of 'God' through examples of pattern and design. But there are equally examples where there's no pattern – or where the pattern is just something that's appeared for obvious reasons that have to do with things like climate changes – y'know like the things we've been learning about the Ice Age from that radio series 'How Things Began' ..." [2]

"I really like that series!" I grinned *"Apart from Music and Art – it's the only thing that makes school interesting."*

"Yes. But did you know, that there are some people who believe in 'God' who don't like what Darwin said about evolution – and say it's not true."

"Yes – my grandmother told me about that. They must be like Nazis ..." I added *"... she said that the Nazis in the war told my grandfather he wasn't allowed to teach evolution in his school. Just think of that! My mother was amazed when she saw her first dinosaur skeletons at the British Museum – because my grandparents didn't dare tell her about them."* Pause. *"They'd have been locked up if anyone found out – and my grandfather lost his job as headmaster anyway because he wouldn't teach what the Nazis were saying about that or about Jews."*

---

2 *How Things Began:* a BBC school radio series (1941–1968) which documented the prehistory and the evolution of life on the planet.

"Exactly." said Steve *"So if it's all God's plan ... then Hitler must have been God's plan too – and I'd like to know what wonderful kind of plan*—that —*was supposed to be."*

"Yes!" I almost shouted with the exhilaration of having something make sense *"And even if Hitler was the Devil's idea, you'd have thought that God would've been able to do something about him. After all God made the Devil in the first place."*

"Yes – the whole thing makes no sense." Steve responded emphatically *"So if you're going to have a mythology, it might as well be fun – like Valhalla. I could enjoy feasting in Valhalla."*

"Yes! And with beautiful Valkyries and all that!" I concluded.

Steve grinned at that. The idea that 'girlfriends' existed somewhere in the future, was a subject which was on our minds.

"Y'know—talking about Valhalla—makes me think of Freyja and Frigg the Norse Goddesses."[3]

"What are they like?"

"Freyja wears the necklace Brísingamen and a cloak of falcon feathers. She rides a chariot pulled by two cats and a wild boar called Hildisvíni runs along at her side. Frigg is white and shining – and I think I've seen her in my dreams since I was very young." As soon as the words were out of my mouth, I realised I'd said far more than I'd wanted to say – and said *"I hope you don't think I'm an idiot for seeing Frigg in my dreams."*

"No, Vic – it sounds fantastic! I wish I had dreams like that."

We were good friends from that day on. My father was pleased that I had a male friend – and one whose father was a Police Superintendent. He was surprisingly impressed. He seemed to get the idea that I had taken a better direction in life.

I was glad that I had been able to tell Steve about the White Lady – and that there was a way in which I could understand her through the Norse Goddesses. They were obviously real.

---

3   Freyja is the Norse goddess associated with love, sex, beauty, fertility, gold, and death. Frigg is the wife of Óðinn – and is associated with foreknowledge and wisdom.

They clearly still existed. How else was I dreaming about one of them? How else had *Frigg* appeared in my bedroom? Of course, Frigg's *actual appearance* in my bedroom had not recurred for a few years. I did wonder whether Frigg had *actually* appeared in my bedroom – or whether it was just a vivid dream as my mother had suggested. There was no way of knowing – but the feeling remained that her appearance *had* been real – even though she had been 'made of light'.

I still missed Alice. I didn't mention Alice to Steve straight away – because I didn't know what to say. He wasn't a *non-sapient sport-ape*— as most of the boys were—but I didn't know how he'd react to my mentioning Alice. Steve was a prolific reader and encouraged me to read. He said that people who didn't read were morons – and I was determined that Steve should not think me a moron. I'd enjoyed reading Henry Treece's Viking trilogy [4] but had found it hard to find anything else that was as interesting. Steve pointed out that the lack of good novels in the school library was little short of criminal. He was reading Guy De Maupassant [5] and thought that *The Famous Five* and *The Secret Seven* [6] were for infant school children. He told me about things which were much more interesting. They were harder to read – but they were much better, even if you had to use a dictionary a lot of the time.

---

4   The Viking Trilogy of novels by Henry Treece—*Viking's Dawn, The Road to Miklagard,* and *Viking's Sunset*—describe the life of Harald Sigurdson, a Norwegian Viking. He goes on three voyages, representative of those made by Vikings. Other books by Henry Treece were *Horned Hemet, Splintered Sword,* and *The Burning of Njal.*

5   Stephen Bruce was unusually precocious. He had read from an early age and his parents had encouraged his reading to the point at which he found no difficulties with most literature.

6   *The Famous Five* a series of children's novels by Enid Blyton. The first book, *Five on a Treasure Island,* was published in 1942. The novels chronicle the adventures of Julian, Dick, Anne, and Georgina (*George*) – and their dog Timmy. *The Secret Seven* is another series written by Enid Blyton. The seven are a group of child detectives consisting of Peter and his sister Janet, Jack, Barbara, George, Pam, and Colin. Jack's sister Susie and her best friend Binkie make appearances. They hate the Secret Seven and delight in attempting to humiliate them, due to their frustrated desire to belong to the society.

Steve had suffered a long childhood illness [7] which had adventitiously galvanised his enjoyment of literature. He'd had little to do but lie in bed reading whatever his parents thought he could manage – and what they thought would prove interesting and entertaining.

My interest in the Norse mythology led me to an extremely large book. It was an almost unreadable psychological portrait of the Norse gods. It took me almost a year to read halfway through it – and I can't say that I actually understood anything from it. It was one of those books where you forget what the words meant at the end of each sentence. You could understand the sentence word by word – but in the end … there'd be nothing there. I had to keep taking that wretched book back to Farnham Library to renew it every two weeks – and eventually someone else wanted it and I had to give up on the book.

Fortunately—around about that time—I was looking around the school library and I found two very interesting volumes on Tibet. They were written by two Czechoslovakian explorers – Vladimír Sís and Josef Vaniš. One was a book called *Tibetan Art* [8] and it contained surprisingly vivid images of … beings. Some were serene – but without the look of piousness with which I was familiar. The peaceful images didn't look holy or horribly humble. They didn't seem to need to grimace with the religious virtue I'd seen depicted elsewhere. There was no solemnity in them. They were joyful – but the joy was somehow at rest. I conceived of them as having all the energy they needed – but only when required. They looked as if they'd had a lot of fun and were now relaxing – looking out at the world with a sense of contentment – but magnificently alive to everything that was going on.

I read a great deal in those faces – mainly because I'd never seen such faces before. They seemed to be communicating with me personally.

7   Possibly glandular fever.

8   *Tibetan Art* (photographed by Vladimír Sís and Josef Vaniš) with text by Lumír Jisl – translated by Ilse Gottheiner. Spring Books, London.

They gazed out of the pages at me – saying something wordless that hovered just below or above the level of meaning. I had no idea what their message was – but I knew it was extremely important. Seeing these images—and wordlessly sensing what they conveyed—reminded me strongly of the White Lady. This was it! The same thing was happening – but now it was shining at me from the pages of a book. Somehow, I felt entirely validated. The White Lady had not been solely within my imagination. Here was a book with other people who were similar to the White Lady – and these pictures were in the real world. The book was complete evidence to me that the White Lady really existed. The faces I saw in the book were not quite as beautiful as the White Lady – but there was something about one of them—called Tara [9]—that seemed amazingly similar. The colours in the book were all a little muted – and so I supposed that Tara would be far more vivid and clear in real life.

The White Lady started appearing again after that – and it was wonderful to see her. When I thought back to her in the daytime, I wondered why she never spoke to me. I also wondered why I never asked her who she was. I decided that I would definitely ask her who she was – but somehow, I always forgot, or maybe the idea just refused to stay in my mind. She just looked at me and I was delightedly content to be looked at. I said nothing at all about it to anyone apart from Steve – because I had no wish to annoy anyone or have my father talking about mental hospitals again.

Then there were the fiery beings in the book. They were incredibly ferocious. They were also mysteriously well intentioned – as if they'd be good friends to have. Dogs could be like that, I thought: really savage when they were barking – but actually gentle and affectionate. I knew dogs like that, who'd bark until they recognised me – then they'd wag their tails and I'd stroke them. Somehow these fiery beings seemed as if they'd be like that in some obscure way.

---

9   White Tara *(Drölma / Jétsun Drölkar (rJe bTsun sGrol ma) / Sitatara / Mother of Liberation)* appears as a female bodhisattva in Sutrayana, and as a female Buddha in Vajrayana. She is visualised to develop understanding of outer, inner, secret, and ultimate teachings.

For some indecipherable reason I had some private delusion that Vikings were ferocious but kindly. I saw Vikings as having all the trappings of warfare – but merely as *some kind of personal style*. The huge two-handed swords and double-headed axes were simply amazing things that they carried. Their horned and winged helmets were the same – simply their style. Somehow, I'd devised my own Norse culture in which these warriors—men and women—simply roved around the sea in longships – and came home for fine roast dinners they'd cook with their beautiful golden-haired shield-maidens.

I knew it wasn't true, of course – but, it was what I'd have wanted if I could have created it myself. As I got older, my personal myth of the perfect Viking culture evaporated. It became increasingly difficult to maintain my naïve enthusiasm for a culture that never existed. So, when I saw these Tibetan beings who were both fierce and friendly – I felt as if I'd come home. Here was something very close to my Viking fantasy – but it was part of the real world. It was suddenly explosively obvious that I'd found my religion. I was a Vajrayana Buddhist. As soon as I could find my way to Tibet, I was going there – because *that* was where I belonged.

The other book in the school library, was called *On the Road Through Tibet*. Tibet wasn't exactly Norway—as it was landlocked—but it *did* have the most amazing mountains. The Himalayas were the highest mountains in the world and that—had—to be good. I looked at the photographs of the people in their huge dramatic landscapes. There were rushing torrents straddled by precarious rope bridges. They'd be exciting to cross! There were fantastic fortresses and places called gompas [10] that looked like the fortresses. They had dragon heads on the corners of the roofs which reminded me of the dragons on the prows of longships. I thought how much I'd like to live in one of those monasteries – although the idea of celibacy somehow failed to intrude on my idea of what life would be like in one of those wonderful buildings.

10 Gompa (*dGon pa* / *aranya* or *vihara* / remote place) are Vajrayana Buddhist religious enclaves which are common in Tibet, Bhutan, Sikkim, Nepal, and Ladakh. They can also be found in Mongolia, China, India, and Buryatia in southeastern Russia.

I'd seen long-haired Tibetans in stupendous costumes – so it was plain to me that shaving your head was only one way of doing things in Tibet.

As soon as I saw the beautiful Goddess called Tara, it struck me that it wasn't Frigg who was the White Lady who'd appeared in my bedroom. The White Lady was Tara. I wondered how I could find out more about Tara – but there was nothing further I could find out at that time.

There was also a huge dark blue yak-headed being with many arms and legs. This was certainly different from the imagery I'd seen in churches. There seemed to be no problem with nakedness in Tibetan culture either, because the huge dark blue yak-headed being with many arms and legs was naked – and moreover sported an erection. There seemed to be a huge problem with nakedness in England – and I remembered getting into trouble with my painting of naked dancing devils when I attended East Street infant school. My mother had had to come and hear all about it from the headmistress – who'd had some sort of anxiety attack about it. My mother had to explain to the headmistress that it was probably due to my father's bellicose reaction to the Trevelyans spraying me and three girls with a hose on a hot day one Summer. Alice and I—in the company of Bethany and Gillian—had leapt around naked in the spray enjoying the cool water and the rainbows caused by the mist.

The Trevelyans thought nothing of nudity for five-year-olds – but as far as my father had been concerned, it was the utmost depravity. I'd been forbidden to return to play with Alice and had to go there in secret after that. My mother colluded with me, so life went on as normal – apart from my naked devil paintings. I had a five-year-old fantasy that it was God who produced the nasty heat of Summer just to torment the happy fun-loving devils. My paintings therefore depicted devils dancing in cool sprays of water to thwart God's evil plan. It was the only way I could make sense of the world at the time – because no one would explain anything to me.

There were rules and morals – but where they came from or why they were there, was a mystery. According to my father it all came from God – and so God was obviously to blame for every imaginable evil.

As time went by, of course, my five-year-old imaginings revealed themselves as ridiculous. I still had a yearning for something that made sense of reality – and here it was! It was all happening in Tibet! Buddhism was all about kindness – but it was also exciting and colourful! Mr and Mrs Bruce—consequent to Steve having told them that I was a Buddhist—had observed that if they were to have followed any religion, it would be Buddhism. This was because there was no *uncreated creator God* in Buddhism – and, it was logical. 'Logical' meant that it made sense – and *that* made sense to me.

The Christianity on which I'd been raised made no sense whatsoever – and my father's view was reflected in what I heard at school. What a relief then, to find that there was a place in the world where people had rational notions of how to live! *On the Road through Tibet* had a photograph of a woman milking a dri.[11] She had a headdress that looked like something from a science fiction film – two huge circular ornaments which looked as if they'd come from another planet. So, it—was—possible to wear brightly coloured clothes! It was possible to be individual! Some of the ladies had their hair up in extraordinary horns made of wood with interestingly shaped objects hanging from them. It seemed as if you could dress any way you liked in Tibet! I decided that I would have to go and live there as soon as I was free to do so.

The White Lady began to appear again on most nights. My dreams began to burgeon with vertiginous vignettes: slightly unsettling, yet hypnotically fascinating. There were sensations that I likened to terrifying fairground rides – trepidation and exhilaration. The scenarios were entirely intriguing – and I seemed to segue between partial lucid dreaming and partial somnolent dreaming. I was never clear which was which.

11 Dri – the female of the yak.

Once I had seen the photographs in the books about Tibet, I was aware that the people in the dreams were Tibetan. The landscape however, was not like the landscapes I had seen in the photographic books. Tibet looked quite harsh in most of those photographs. There were a few photographs of mountains and a few alpine meadows at the beginning but the rest of the sepia-tone photographs looked quite barren. This did not dissuade me in respect of wanting to live there – but these images were not what I saw in my dreams. I saw no monasteries, temples, shrinerooms, or monks in my dreams – only a tent encampment in a high alpine valley where rather plainly dressed people either sat attentively or went about their quiet business. The women wore none of the fantastic costumes and headdresses I'd seen in the book – but seemed to dress in a similar style to the men. This was not vexatious to me – because it was obvious that there must be many different styles of dress in a country. Sometimes however people seemed to wrap themselves in colourful fabrics. Some wore hats that were vaguely like floral bishops' mitres – but not floral in the pallid pastel style with which I was familiar in ladies' dresses or sofas: they were deep colours. After what seemed to have been months of silence – I started to be aware of sounds. These people would sometimes sing in an eerie yet beautiful manner. These songs did not seem to be songs in the way I knew song to be. It was not because they were foreign: I'd heard songs from different parts of the world in school in the music lessons – and however foreign they sounded, they were still recognisable songs. What some of these people sang, were something else: they were using their voices to do something else – but what that might be I could not tell.

I began to look at these library books every day – and to copy the images in them. I drew them in the Art lessons and the teachers seemed to think that was an acceptable thing to do. The other boys seemed to prefer drawing æroplanes. They liked to draw air battles where the æroplanes gradually destroyed each other and their whole drawing turned into a mess. I thought that procedure was entirely asinine but never commented.

When my father and mother came to the parents' evening, they looked at my art work and at the art work of the other boys. There was a display of our work on the wall for the parents to see. My father asked about my paintings because they were so different from the work of the other boys and Mr Sharpe explained that I had been inspired by the two books on Tibet I had found in the library. My father was not well pleased that I was painting heathen gods and requested that I should have no further access to the books.

That was the end of a marvellous phase of time. It marked the beginning of the diminution of visits from the White Lady – apart from sporadic appearances that became increasingly vague. It seemed that the more I learned how to live unproblematically in the vicinity of my father—and authority figures in general—the less I was able to visit the Tibetan landscapes in my dream world.

A year passed – and, try as I would, my dream-world drifted into tepidity. There were still occasional journeys to somewhere or other —that may have been Tibet—but there was little vividness left. It gradually ceased to be a real place – and became a place that was merely a dream. After a year had passed my Tibetan dream-world seemed something of the remote past. All I remembered was that once *something luminous* used to occur. I described it as the sensation when one doesn't know whether one has dreamed something or whether it really happened – apart from the fact that I no longer knew whether I had dreamed these things or that I had merely *dreamed that I had dreamed.* This degree of illusion was too much or too little to retain, and after a while I spent months when the idea of the White Lady hardly entered my mind.

Steve had talked to his parents and they wrote to mine—we had no telephone—and it was thereafter arranged that I could stay at his house on occasional weekends. Fortunately, that turned out to be almost every other weekend – and … my father seemed happy about the arrangement. As Steve's father was a Police Superintendent, my father approved. *"The boy will be in a wholesome environment there …"* my father proclaimed *"… not an iniquitous den of nudist vegetarian fanatics!"*

I looked up the word 'fanatic' and it surprised me – as it was clearly my father who was the fanatic. The Trevelyans had been as far from fanatical as I could imagine. They had been friendly, open-minded, and inquisitive.

Weekends at Steve's place were times to learn about music; practise guitar; and, escape my father's surveillance. Steve seemed far ahead of the school's music lessons and so I could ask him questions. I taught Steve to sing some Blues numbers, which he enjoyed. He thought I had a good voice.

The Beatles were burgeoning in public consciousness—along with an ever-increasing number of Liverpool groups—and so the idea of starting a group ourselves seemed obvious. It seemed that Steve and I had the makings of a *group*. I was a nascent vocalist. I was loud and lacking in timidity – although given to tempo rubato that I often failed to pay back.[12] Steve was more than good with both rhythm and lead guitar. Steve's main love however, was bass. He planned to make the shift as soon as his hands were large enough; so, all we needed was a lead guitarist and a drummer – and we'd be primed for action.

I started thinking that I should write song lyrics rather than poetry and started looking at the Blues lyrics I knew. I played with ideas. I knew I couldn't write about things that happened in America – so I spent a lot of time thinking about what kind of language would work in England without sounding silly. Steve could read *and* write music – so he was able to collect our ideas and work on them.

Steve had a brother called Mark, who was three or four years older. Mark played bass guitar – and had started to give Steve some guidance on the instrument. The first time I heard the bass – I knew it was *my instrument*. It sounded as if it came out of the ground like an earthquake. The sound was substantial – and created shapes and colours in the room which were almost physical.

---

12 Tempo rubato means 'stolen time' and the idea is that if one extends a note one has to shorten another in order to pay back the time that was previously stolen – in order to stay within the time signature.

Mark let me play his bass one day and it loomed large in my mind ever after. In '64 Steve's uncle Stan drowned on a sailing holiday in the Mediterranean. Uncle Stan played in Mr Bruce's amateur Jazz band. He was the bass player and so all Uncle Stan's guitars ended up at the Bruce residence. He'd had a GIBSON EB0 [13] and a HAGSTROM CORONADO VI – a 6-string bass. The HAGSTROM was a marvellous instrument – but by no means attractive; to me at least. The manufacturer had obviously been unable to run to the production of all the required metal parts – and so the switching appeared to have been gleaned from domestic appliances. It therefore resembled a washing machine. Steve's æsthetics were entirely different from mine, so he saw none of the HAGSTROM's abominable qualities. *"See what you mean Vic … but the switches are all —so—crisp and definite. They're quick to find when you're playing too – because they're so large—and—it's—very—fine workmanship. Uncle Stan was a perfectionist, you know – and this was his favourite bass."*

"I prefer that GIBSON EB0 – it looks like the guitar Batman would've played – especially 'cause it's black! I love black guitars."

"I like black guitars too."

"Yes …" I pondered *"… they're all black aren't they … even your father's* RICKENBACKERs *and* FENDER PRECISION *bass …"* [14]

13 The 1961 GIBSON EB0 was a bass guitar with a mahogany body and a 30½ inch short-scale neck.

14 Mr Bruce had a 1957 RICKENBACKER Combo 450 – the tulip bodied 2 'toaster pickup' version of the COMBO 400. He also had a RICKENBACKER 365f deluxe with vibrato which was a thin—full body—model. The FENDER BASSMAN was introduced by FENDER in 1952. Steve's uncle had the model with a cabinet that contained two 15-inch speakers – and separate AB165 amplifier head unit. Steve Bruce had used a 1959 5F6-A BASSMAN with his 6 string HAGSTROM bass. The early FENDER PRECISION bass had a TELECASTER body-shape. Steve's was entirely black like the 6 string HAGSTROM bass he had also inherited from his uncle. The 1951 TELECASTER PRECISION BASS design with a large pickguard, small TELECASTER-shaped headstock, single pickup, and separate chrome control plate had a two-piece maple-capped neck with no skunk stripe on the back of the neck. They had silver FENDER script with the words TELECASTER BASS written in a sans-serif type underneath.

"That's because my dad's Jazz band is called 'The Dixons' you see.[15] *They were all policemen apart from Uncle Stan – and he had his bass guitars black too, so that he'd match."*

"They're called 'the Dixons' ...? ... like 'Dixon of Dock Green' ...?"

"Yes – it's a joke name."

"That's wonderful!" I chuckled *"Never thought I'd know a parent who'd use a joke name for something – although ... I think that the Trevelyans might have done something like that."*

"The Trevelyans ..."

Ah ... now I was in a slight fix. I'd not intended to refer to Alice – but ... I was suddenly stuck with having to explain myself. *"Yes ... I had a girlfriend called Alice Trevelyan when I was at infant school – but she moved to Herefordshire – and ... well ... I never saw her again after that."*

"You started early!" Steve grinned

"And finished early too ..."

"But Hereford's not Tasmania you know – why did moving to Hereford stop you seeing her?"

"... because ..." I began – with a lump in my throat even after the better part of half a decade *"... my father didn't want me having a girlfriend. Her parents said they'd invite me to stay – but it just never happened."*

"They never wrote."

"Not as far as I know ... they probably did but I was never told."

"The bastard ..." Steve groaned. That was extreme coming from Steve because he almost never swore. Steve had met my father and it was loathing at first sight.

15 The Dixons was a name humorously based on the Dixieland Jazz Steve's fathers band played and the BBC series Dixon of Dock Green. They were all policeman apart from Mr Bruce's brother and all the guitars were black as a tribute to police uniform. Dixon of Dock Green ran from 1955 to 1976. The series was set in a police station in the East End of London and concerned uniformed police engaged with routine and small-time crime. It focused less on police work than on the family life of the police station. Sergeant Dixon was portrayed as a paternal moral presence – who liked a tipple as much as his colleagues.

He stayed one weekend at my home but never wanted to repeat the experience. His parents understood the situation and were perfectly happy to have me stay there without return visits.

"*… the bloody bastard …*" Steve reiterated looking a little sheepish at the sudden intrusion of the idea that his parents might have overheard him.

"*Well … yes …*" Pause. "*My mother says that he had reasons that were … too complicated to explain but that he meant it for the best.*"

"*What!?*" Steve exclaimed with indignation "*What was—that—supposed to mean!?*"

"*… I think … it had something to do with the Trevelyans having money or something … or a lot more money than we have … and – I suppose there was some kind of problem about that.*" Pause. "*My mother said that she could understand his thinking and that I might have ended up being unhappy or something … but anyway …*" I interjected to dissemble "*… we were talking about the 'joke name' of your dad's Jazz band.*"

Steve detected that I'd rather not take the subject of Alice any further. "*Right … yes … it's a double joke too – and really quite clever. Apart from my uncle, they're all policemen—that's one part—and the other part is that they play Dixieland Jazz.*"

"*Even better!*" I laughed "*That's really good! I like that kind of thing with words. I try to double-up meanings when I write poetry. That's brilliant. It's like the Beatles which has the word 'beat' in it. I think all the best names are like that.*" Pause. "*You know …*" I continued as a non sequitur "*… I really like that* GIBSON EB0 *…*"

"*But it's only a single pickup bass … I mean … so was the* FENDER PRECISION *– that's why my father had it modified. Then after he'd modified it, he had it painted black, professionally. That* GIBSON EB0 *is a bit of a 'thumper' for Jazz which is why my uncle Stan got the* HAGSTROM. *My father did offer to modify it for him – but he said he'd rather have a long scale bass anyway.*"

"*Why's that …?*"

"Well you get far more 'sustain' with the long scale — it's much better … well, unless you want to bend notes and then the short scale is better."

"Ah … then it's the short scale I want — because there's a lot of note bending in Blues." Pause. *"You don't think … there's any chance of me … buying that EB0 …?"*

"I don't know … I can ask — but … it's probably not something my dad would sell because it belonged to his brother … and … well — he's not been … dead … that long."

Then Steve's brother Mark turned 17 and obtained his first car. He lost interest in music overnight. Motor car racing became his obsession — and Steve inherited all the bass guitars. Steve was enraptured—and so was I—even though I had no guitar myself. He'd suddenly got more guitars than you could shake a stick at.

The Bruces were a musical family. Mrs Bruce was more-or-less a concert pianist. She was mainly interested in Classical and Baroque and played all kinds of marvellous pieces. I wished my father had some interest in playing music. I thought it would have helped him be less angry about the world and everything in it. I knew he'd have been shocked if he'd known that Mr Bruce was a Jazz aficionado who played electric guitar — so I said nothing about it.

I had my eye glued on that GIBSON EB0. The idea of it dominated everything when I was in its vicinity — but Steve was not sure that buying it was possible. His parents would have to agree. We talked together about ways and means — including the idea of weekly payments. I chopped wood, mowed lawns, and ran errands for neighbours — so I knew I could earn at least a pound a week. It had been his uncle's guitar however — and Mr Bruce was very close to his brother. They'd shared an interest in Jazz that went back a long way. They'd even thought of turning professional at one time — but that was not the thing to do if you wanted a family life. It struck me then that sacrifice was required — if you wanted to be a Bluesman. I decided that I was up for that — and anyhow all that *work—a—day business* used up all the time you'd otherwise have for playing music.

Maybe if I found Alice again it would be different – but without Alice the idea of marriage made no emotional sense.

Steve eventually mentioned to his parents that I loved the GIBSON EB0 – and they surprised him by saying that they would be happy to sell it, as I was a friend and would be playing it with him. They said that I could have it—and the VOX[16] bass amplifier—for £50.00.[17] I thought of just about everything I could think of to enable me to take possession of that guitar. I'd considered the idea of having that EB0 stand in for every birthday and Christmas present for the rest of my life – but it was not to be. It proved impossible even though the Bruces were kind enough to offer to sell it for much less than it was worth.

After a weekend in which they observed me fooling around on the EB0, they could see I practically worshipped the thing. I was their son's best friend—and Steve preferred his father's FENDER PRECISION bass—so I think they felt moved to put me on par with Steve. It must have seemed as if I was always playing second fiddle – sans fiddle. They wrote a letter to my parents the Monday following that weekend to offer the guitar for sale – but my father wouldn't have an electric guitar in the house – even if I bought it in instalments with my own money.

My father eventually found out that Mr Bruce played guitar. He evidently found it perplexing that a policeman would play in a Jazz band—even as a recreational pursuit—but although he'd said nothing offensive about it, it didn't change his mind about anything. He must have slotted 'Mr Bruce' and 'Jazz' into two separate conceptual compartments – because I was still allowed to go and stay with the Bruces for weekends.

The Bruces grew more affectionate to me after that event – and went out of their way to make sure I had a good time. Being around guitars was *all* the good time I needed – and so I made the most of any musical opportunity that presented itself.

16 The VOX AC30 was introduced in 1958. It had a single 12-inch GOODMANS 60-watt speaker in a 'TV front' cabinet.

17 £50.00 in 1962 would be equivalent to roughly £500.00 in 2020.

Mr Bruce asked me what kind of music I liked and was surprised when I said *"Big Bill Broonzy, Robert Johnson, Lead Belly, Bessie Smith, Memphis Minnie, Ma Rainey, and Big Mamma Thornton."* He thought that music was quite old and was surprised that a young person would like that kind of music.

"It's my favourite music …" I explained *"… but, I also like Bach and the Beatles."* Mr Bruce found that an intriguing mixture.

The Bruces had a 'stereogram'—a six-foot cabinet with a speaker at each end—and whatever you played on that thing sounded better than anything I had ever heard before. On a thing like that, I could listen to 'Midnight in Moscow' and it became captivating even though I didn't particularly like the trumpet. I had trumpets pegged as 'military instruments'. My father liked military band music and so I had some degree of prejudice against anything of that nature. I did like the way the music swelled up in that number though – and told Mr Bruce that it was the best part of 'Midnight in Moscow'. I enjoyed hearing Mrs Bruce on piano – and wished that we still had a piano in our house. She played me Bach pieces – and modern composers like Eric Satie. It was amazing to me that such different kinds of music existed and that you could like them all. What my father had told me was definitely untrue. You *could* like Bach and Blues. Mrs Bruce appreciated that fact that I enjoyed Bach. She saw it as a good influence on Steve – because he was far more interested in his father's Jazz.

Having pestered for a guitar since the age of seven *(and having been denied an extremely reasonable deal on a* GIBSON EB0 *and amplifier at the age of nine)* the death of Mr Love—and the loss of his Blues bequest —finally prompted lenience toward a guitar entering the moral bastion of our home. I finally got a guitar for my 11th birthday. It was plastic. The neck and frets were mould-cast and it had four strings. The strings were tuned by pegs that slipped and the strings were not even strings – they were hollow lengths of plastic that didn't even sound like nylon strings. It was evidently made to make no sound – so that a child could pretend to be playing along with something without making the sound of the 'guitar' intruding.

It was a toy. It was called the 'Skiffle Junior' and had a picture of a fellow with a quiff who could have been modelled on Elvis Presley. The shape into which the paper illustration had been inserted showed other models boasting an image of Mickey Mouse. I was aghast – but had to look grateful and pleased. I had to look pleased even though the word 'Skiffle' meant 'watered down Blues' – but my father had no way of knowing that. 'Skiffle' was one of those attempts to repackage Black music for White audiences – and even at the age of seven I'd wanted no part of that. Whenever I touched that plastic guitar, I could see Big Bill Broonzy sneering at it, from wherever he was.

My future as a Bluesman was not looking wonderful. Steve Bruce had a real guitar. He'd received lessons since he was five. I'd have been content with the very worst second-hand low-end instrument. Naturally I wasn't inspired to play this plastic apology for a musical instrument and that was taken as sure proof that a real guitar would have been wasted on me. Steve was quite angry about the plastic guitar and told his parents about it. He told me they seemed a little upset on my behalf and that he'd heard them talking in the kitchen after he'd gone to bed. They'd talked about simply giving me the GIBSON EB0 – but they'd decided that they couldn't give it to me against my father's wishes. They'd then had—*another*—idea. They'd give it to me once I was 18 – because then, legally, I'd be an adult and there'd be no problem with their giving it to me as a birthday present. I was not supposed to know this – but the deal was sealed. Seven years and it would be mine! That didn't seem—*so*—far away. I'd be going to Netherfield Secondary School in a matter of months – and when that was over it would be well in sight.

5

oracles and demons

1964

Time passed. I'd been at Netherfield School for a year – and, was about to begin my 2nd year. The White Lady—or Tara—re-emerged not long after I found myself in a co-educational environment. The presence of girls was an explosive experience – albeit indefinable and intangible. I found them somewhat hypnotic in the way they moved and carried themselves. I'd obviously seen girls at infant school – but somehow my years at an all-boys primary school had made them seem distant. I'd also seen girls outside the primary school environment – but always at something of a distance. It had not been possible simply to sit and hear them talking to each other. It had never seemed possible to talk with girls as they wandered round Farnham or Aldershot – because … one didn't just walk up to people and start talking. That was unheard of in the 1950s.

I had missed Tara, almost without knowing that I missed her. I only knew that I had missed her when she re-appeared. I missed Alice too. In some strange way the White Lady, Alice, and Frigg had merged into White Tara. When she reappeared, I realised that she had been there all the time in the background as an indefinable feeling-tone. It was not possible to see or hear anything without being in her presence – and yet it was subliminal: something known without knowing that I knew it. Now she was back and I was both happy and bemused as to what part she might play for me as an aspiring Bluesman.

Much to the contempt of the boys, I made friends with most of the girls – particularly Lindsay Goulding. Romance however, was the last thing on my mind. It was more the fact that the girls were interested in poetry and art – and the boys were not. The girls would talk about art, nature, and anything interesting.

The boys seemed to be the same *fine young lower-primate sport-enthusiasts* I'd found at primary school. I tolerated them as best I could and tried to be friendly.

Girls had fascinated me from my earliest years – maybe because of the White Lady. The White Lady had in some oblique way appeared through Alice Trevelyan. Not that I ever thought that Alice *was* the White Lady – but there was a sense in which she inspirationally represented the White Lady as an adventitious poetic ambassador.

One night I remembered the time that the White Lady had mysteriously 'taken me to Switzerland'. I knew it wasn't Switzerland – but I had no idea where it was until I'd seen those photographs of Tibet at West Street Junior School. There were the two girls in that mountainous landscape who had seemed so incredibly familiar. I'd felt as if I *should* have known who they were. At one time I'd felt I might meet them in Farnham or Aldershot – but it had been a long time since I'd entertained such imponderable impossibilities. Meeting people seen in dreams was not something you could expect to happen unless you were insane. The fact remained however that it had felt extremely real: walking in those mountains in the rhapsodic company of … who were they? There was, nothing I could do with such a question. It just had to sit there at the *back of my mind* – whilst I pondered Blues with *the front of my mind.*

At the start of the 2nd year, an idea emerged. It was vague at first—flittering like a burlesque bat in the tonal ballet of twilight—barely within concept range. I remembered Mr Love and our many conversations about Blues. I remembered him telling me about a special place a person could go, to become a great Blues musician. It was *the crossroads* ….

The crossroads was the place you could meet Papa Legba.[1]

---

[1] Legba is the Djinn who comes to the crossroads and facilitates unprecedented skills on the musical instrument of your choice. Unfortunately, Papa Legba became identified—in societal Christian terms—with the Devil. As the devil, of course, he demands your soul in return for the skills bestowed. Legba is a contraction of Alegbara, a West Africa Djinn – who is both a trickster and an inspiration of music and language. Alegbara makes less demanding claims on aspirants than their putative 'souls'.

All you had to do—according to Blues folklore—was go to a crossroads at midnight. You'd have to sit there with your guitar. You'd have to play something—or at least sing something—and a large Black man, dressed like Abraham Lincoln, would come along. He'd put out his hand – gesture for you to pass your guitar over. You'd hand him your guitar—he'd tune it—and pass it back. You'd then play like Robert Johnson. That was how it could be – well … eventually … when I finally got a real guitar.

There were a few questions that troubled me. Was it alright for a Buddhist to have dealings with an African spirit? Having read the books on Tibet at Junior School—and partially recognised Tara as the White Lady—the fact that I was a Buddhist was something that had simply happened by itself. There was no moment when it had become apparent. I had not arrived at my 'conversion' by any process of thought. It was more a recognition of what I was – and what I had always been.

So, as a Buddhist, I wanted to know whether there was a difference between the oracles used in Tibet and Papa Legba? Was Papa Legba a Jigten Srungma?[2] I'd tried to read about these beings—and oracles —in a book by René De Nebesky-Wojkowitz.[3] The book was called *Oracles and Demons of Tibet*. I'd found that book in Farnham Library. Why did René De Nebesky-Wojkowitz have to write in such dense and complex manner? The book was a horribly turgid read. I had to plough my way through almost 700 pages without really understanding a great deal – other than: **a**. *there were Lamas who were able to summon beings – and, having summoned them, the Lama had the power to make demands of them;* **b**. *there were people (mainly monks) who could act as mediums. Their bodies were possessed by so-called demons who'd speak through them.*

---

2   Jigten Srungma *('jig rTen pa'i srung ma / lokapala)* a local protector – a spirit of the place.

3   René de Nebesky-Wojkowitz (1923–1959) was the Austrian Tibetologist who wrote *Oracles and Demons of Tibet* – published in 1956. The book was the first detailed account of Tibetan protector beings. In 1949 he published two articles on Bön and the state oracle. From 1949 to 1950 he studied in Italy under Giuseppe Tucci and Joseph Rock, and in London at the School of Oriental and African Studies. From 1950 to 1953 he resided in Sikkim researching texts on protector beings with the help of Tibetan scholars.

Right. Well, I wasn't up for being possessed by anything—or anyone —but a simple favour might not be out of the question. That *was* Papa Legba's *stock-in-trade*, when all was said and done. He surely liked people playing Blues – and why not open a franchise in Britain? It all started sounding perfectly reasonable to me – and I considered that it was fair enough to take my chance with Papa Legba.

There were some other writings by René De Nebesky-Wojkowitz— in journals—that I ordered through Farnham Library – much to the astonished disbelief of the librarian. *"What does a 12 year old boy want with anthropological articles from erudite ethnographic journals?"* I looked sheepish *"It's for a school essay"* I lied. I returned them all after two weeks without renewing them – because they were just too academically dense to comprehend. One book however, seemed more accessible—and humane—than the others. It was called *Where the Gods are Mountains*[4] and I devoured it voraciously.

There was no one I could ask as to whether my plan was feasible for a Buddhist or not. I decided to rush in—like a fool—where *angels feared to cycle*. But … would Papa Legba show for a plastic guitar? Could my prospective demonic assignation occur at any crossroads, anywhere? Could it be an English crossroads? I didn't know the answer to these questions. Lacking a local Hoodoo man or Hoodoo woman with whom I could enquire, it was all down to me. I rather feared it would have to be a crossroads in Mississippi somewhere. Probably somewhere obscure, down the Southern end of Highway 61. If that was the case however, there wasn't a hope in hell I'd meet Papa Legba. Nothing to do but give it a try.

---

4 *Where the Gods are Mountains: Three Years Among the People of the Himalayas*, René de Nebesky-Wojkowitz, Weidenfeld and Nicolson, London, 1956.

There was a crossroads down at Runfold[5] – just past Badshot Lea.[6] It wasn't Mississippi – but there *were* open fields. They spread out in *all four quadrants* of the crossroads just as I had in mind from my conversations with Mr Love.

Mr Love—because I'd asked him—painted a picture in words as to how the crossroads might appear. *"Mississippi is flat and the fields have no boundaries with roads"* he'd said. So … maybe this likeness was a point in favour of Runfold. Runfold lies on the Pilgrims' Way—an ancient track—and so it had some kind of magic about it.

I went down to the crossroads, after school, to check it out. Runfold was indeed as flat as anything realistically could be. The fields were unfenced around the crossroads – just as I'd remembered. It was in the obscure outskirts of Farnham in 1964. I'd known it vaguely from having once cycled up onto the Hogsback,[7] the long hilltop road to Guildford. Runfold was as balefully bucolic as a brussels sprout. So, the Runfold crossroads would have to be the place – but would Papa Legba deign to appear for a White English boy with a plastic guitar? Maybe. Maybe not – but … I wasn't the run-of-the-mill White boy, was I? No. Not by any means. I was a Bluesman – and had been since the age of eight. Well that was how I saw it. I could still sing those songs I'd learned from Mr Love at the age of eight. I was moreover, in line for a GIBSON EB0 bass and VOX amplifier on my 18th birthday. A mere six years.

---

5   Runfold, along with Alfold, Dunsfold, Durfold, Kingsfold, and Chiddingfold, comprise the 'Fold Villages'. The suffix relates to forest clearance for pasture and grazing land for sheep or cattle in Saxon England.

6   Badshot Lea dates back to the Mesolithic, Neolithic, and Iron Age. It is bounded by four bridges – three railway bridges and Pea Bridge over the uppermost part of the River Blackwater. There are remains in, or close to, the village from the Mesolithic, Neolithic, Iron Age, Roman, and medieval periods. In 1967 the Badshot Lea school master and amateur archæologist William Rankine discovered a Neolithic Long Barrow there.

7   The Hog's Back—as it is now called—is a narrow, elongated ridge along which the road to Guildford runs. Jane Austen, in a letter (dated Thursday the 20th May 1813) to her sister Cassandra wrote *'Upon the whole it was an excellent journey and very thoroughly enjoyed by me; the weather was delightful the greatest part of the day. Henry found it too warm, and talked of its being close sometimes, but to my capacity it was perfection. I never saw the country from the Hogsback so advantageously.'*

I was 12 – and champing at the bit to be on stage with Steve Bruce and whomsoever the other members of our Blues band would be. A Blues band … just to run those words through my mind was magical.

Then after Papa Legba had set me up – I'd get a Blues name. I'd be rid of 'Victor Howard Simmerson' for ever. Maybe I'd be STAMMERING STAN STRANGE …. 'Stammering' because a fair few of the best old Bluesmen were blind or crippled or something – and there was a pride in that. I could just come out and say *'I'm,* STAMMERING STAN STRANGE, *people – and I've got s-s-some s-s-stunning s-s-songs fer y'all.'* Why Stan? Because Steve's Uncle Stan had been a bass player. Eventually I'd inherit his GIBSON EB0 – and it seemed right that I should honour his name. Why *Strange*? Because there was a boy called *Gordon Strange* at school – and I'd always admired that name. As to the stammering however … I hoped that my speech therapy would get rid of that.

The nurse who saw me every Tuesday was robustly attractive – and so I had great enthusiasm for my speech exercises. I was told I'd get over it, if I worked at the exercises. I worked hard – and also took the nerve medicine that my grandmother brought from Germany. My Aunt Rikchen kept up the supply after my grandmother died. I don't know what it was – but it was green and suitably vile. My father had been told by the doctor that my stammer would be helped if I were able to feel more relaxed. He put it to him that a *gentler manner* might help. In fact, he insisted that corporal punishment was to be kept within reasonable limits or the authorities would have to be contacted. My father was furious—of course—but he was not a man to act obdurately. He was not an unkind man at heart – simply too military in his bearing and too draconian in his sense of appropriate punishment.

I did notice some greater sense of easiness around the house – but although my stammer lessened, it still remained an impediment to communication unless I was at Steve's house or talking with the girls in my class. I always stammered with teachers and lived in fear of reading aloud in the English classes.

I thought of asking Steve whether I could consult his parents on the idea of going to the crossroads – but decided against it. They were atheists, so they'd have no problem about Papa Legba – but they didn't walk on the wild side. Mr Bruce was—after all—a police superintendent. The Bruces wouldn't give me that GIBSON EB0 bass guitar against my father's wishes – so they'd certainly not approve of my cycling out to the Runfold crossroads at midnight.

I thought about it most of the Summer. I'd turned 12 and it seemed as if the midnight journey to the crossroads was something I needed to do *before* I turned 13. That was the magical year at which a person could officially be known as a teenager. As far as I was concerned I'd been a teenager since the age of 10 – after all, 10 was comprised of two digits and teen meant 10 – but not everyone went along with that idea. For me, that seemed to mean that 10 – 13 were the twilight years. Mr Love had told me that the crossroads were a twilight setting; like *the eaves of a wood*, or *intertidal zones* – the areas of sea shore that are alternately seabed and land.

So … the crossroads at Runfold. I'd have to sneak out of the house at a quarter of an hour before midnight; when I could be sure my parents would be asleep. I'd have to brave the squeaking stairs—I knew exactly which ones they were—and leave by the back door so they wouldn't hear anything. The back door had a key and so I could lock it behind me. I didn't want anyone to burgle the house whilst I was away and I wanted to leave the house looking normal. I'd put a coat in my bed to look as if someone was in it and … then I'd cycle to Runfold. So far so good with the plan – but as I pondered the fact that it still wasn't Mississippi, I started to feel as if I needed to do something more … more dangerous. What could I do to make the situation more dangerous? I could take the air-rifle – but no: that was locked away in my father's workshop and I had no idea where he kept the key. Then suddenly a ghastly idea arose – and I regretted its appearance as soon as it appeared. Of course—once the idea was there—there was nothing I could do about it. I was stuck with it. I'd have to cycle there naked.

The whole idea was deranged enough as it was – so *why* had I decided to make it all worse? Well … of course … I knew *why*. I had to do everything I could to make sure that Papa Legba showed up. I wasn't going to get any guitar lessons and I'd never get a real guitar anyway – so other than the occult intervention of Papa Legba I'd have to await my 18th birthday when the GIBSON EB0 bass and VOX amplifier would be mine. The next step was to name the day. If I named the day I would have to go through with the plan – so I spoke out the days *"Wednesday or Thursday."* Óðinn's day or Thor's day. They both seemed right for the adventure. I tossed a coin and got Thor's day. It was fixed.

When the day came, I felt a great wave of anxiety hit. I had to live with that all day – and, as the evening approached, I got decidedly edgy. I decided to go to bed early in order that it might hurry my parents to bed. The ploy failed and I lay in bed listening to them talking. I was glad that this was not one of those nights on which my father launched a row about something. Finally, they went to bed. Finally, their lights went out. Finally, my father commenced to snore. I had about half an hour to wait before I set out – so I crept downstairs and sat in the living room. I'd leave my pyjamas and slippers under the glass veranda where there was a small cupboard that housed gardening implements. They'd not be seen there. I got my bicycle out of the bicycle shed and took it to the front of the house. I opened the gates slowly and left my conveyance propped against the outside wall with my guitar. I then hurried back to the glass veranda and hid my pyjamas and slippers. It was deathly quiet and even my bare feet seemed to make an unnecessary noise.

I closed the gates—mounted my bicycle—and as I did so I realised that I'd not considered certain anatomical problems vis-à-vis naked cycling. The pedals were not comfortable – but the saddle was decidedly worse. Then of course the string by which my guitar was suspended across my back made its presence known. It cut into my shoulder and I knew I'd be rubbed raw by the time I got home – if I ever got home that night. What if a police car sailed by and I was arrested for indecent exposure? How would I explain that?

'Well Officer … I was going to meet Papa Legba at Runfold Crossroads so that I'd be able to play guitar like Robert Johnson.' They'd probably send me to Brookwood.

As I turned into the main road I was struck by another horror. What if *any* kind of car appeared? I'd have to nip into someone's drive as soon as I saw headlights. I'd have to keep my senses alert for any semblance of car headlights either in front or behind. I breathed a sigh of relief as I turned off the main road in the direction of Runfold. The streetlights were left behind and I sailed into the darkness. That of course, was another kind of problem – because I couldn't see where I was going. Dare I risk turning on my front light? There was no choice. However, I decided to switch it on for short intervals and cycle as far as I could see with each illumination. That went well until I hit the kerb where the road curved. I decided I'd have to risk the light – and, turn it off and stop, if I saw anything human anywhere. The ride didn't take long – and I was there sooner than I'd expected. My eyes had got used to the dark and soon I could make out the fields under the moon. This was the crossroads.

The string hadn't quite made me as sore as I feared – because I worked out a way of moving that didn't make it rock around too much. I laid my bicycle in one of the fields and sat at the edge of the road on an old milestone. There were no houses around – but the idea of singing suddenly made me anxious. How far would my voice carry? I started to sing Crossroads Blues—quietly at first—but then it occurred to me that there was no point in holding back. I'd got this far and it would be stupid to ruin everything having come so far with the plan. I let rip. Then I let rip again. I must have sung that song a dozen times. A dog moved across the field as I was singing – and gave me a start. It howled for a while. I wondered if it was Papa Legba's dog. Mr Love had told me that Papa Legba had a dog. I was suddenly gripped with fear. Was Legba actually going to appear? What had I done? Would I get out of this alive? What if it really was the devil and not Papa Legba? But I knew— fundamentally—that there was no God or Devil.

So, settling with that conviction, the panic quickly subsided and gave way to disappointment. I sat there for what seemed to be an hour or two getting increasingly cold. Papa Legba was obviously engaged in more serious matters in Mississippi – so, numbed with cold, I cycled home not even bothering about being arrested.

That was it. Back in bed. No one had heard or seen anything – so I was safe.

What a disgusting word … 'safe'. I resented the need to feel *safe* – but was glad that I had taken the risk. Maybe the safety that followed taking a risk was acceptable? Perhaps – but I was *wary* about feeling too relieved.

I'd succeeded and failed simultaneously. The failure? That was obvious – but what of the success? That comprised of my having had the single pointed intention to do what I had done. I'd carried through with a plan. I'd not given up. That was important for a Buddhist practitioner. The lengths to which obsession carries a person, in terms of activity, is the mark of someone who stands the chance of realising goals in Buddhism. It would probably not be 'enlightenment'—*I could not set my sight that far*—but it might be something worthwhile. It had to be something more than living an *average* life with *average* expectations in the *average* suburban acreage of apathy. I was determined not to fall prey to the inevitability of mediocrity. It did not have to be the inevitable fate of everyone raised in the Home Counties. I had observed the way in which everyone grew up like allotment vegetables – all in tidy rows. I did not wish to work in some dreary executive version of a factory merely to get a mortgage on a cloche.

It was an odd feeling – ruminant with ruminations.

In terms of how chilled I'd become, I was monstrously glad to be back in bed. The full moon was gawping through the window. At first, I didn't really notice how bright it was – but, when I noticed it, the moonlight seemed to illuminate the room. I wondered at first whether it was actually daylight – but the clock on the wall told me otherwise. It was just gone two o'clock in the morning.

I was still shivering – but not actually cold. Then I realised that the White Lady was there. She had evidently been there for some time – but I had not seen her as soon as she appeared. I lay there staring at her. Then, gradually, I stopped shivering and fell asleep.

6

the mother of invention

1964

The appearance of Tara after my naked ride to the crossroads had been a joyful shock. Papa Legba had not shown – but that was not too violently disappointing. It ceased to be disappointing as soon as Tara appeared. I hoped she would appear again after that night – but my hope was in vain. She made a solitary appearance – and then … the days and weeks passed. Nothing.

That wretched 'Skiffle Junior' plastic guitar felt like a synthetic albatross 'round my neck. I wanted to be rid of it – but … it had been a present. I felt that I couldn't throw it out with the rubbish. Although I was *not* too grateful – I did not wish to display ingratitude. My father had probably meant well – and he was not to know that I had any knowledge of guitars. He was not to know that I had actually played real guitars – and more. I'd played top-line GIBSON and FENDER guitars. All my father knew about FENDERS was they that sat in front of the fireplace. He had no idea that giving me a plastic guitar was like giving a cowboy a hobbyhorse.

My only alternative therefore, was to do something with it. The nauseating appellation 'Skiffle Junior' had to go. That was something, at least, that I could fix. I soaked it in a bath of hot water and was delighted by how easily the paper insert peeled away. An ominously recognisable shape remained, however. It had obviously been re-marketed as the 'Skiffle Junior' – as the initial design had evidently been intended to glorify Mickey Mouse. The cartoon mouse face outline was all too apparent. With the careful use of a chisel and some wet-and-dry abrasive paper however, I was left with a clean yet matted surface. I then painted the front of the guitar silver with paint designed for painting model aircraft.

It looked far better after about a dozen coats and some work with SOLVOL AUTOSOL[1] chrome polish to take away the brush marks. So much for æsthetics. Next, I attached steel strings – and hit a major problem immediately. The smooth aluminium tuning pegs provided no friction to hold a tuning, as they were turning against plastic. I'd used the lightest strings I could find. I even used a banjo string for the top string as there were no lightweight guitar strings around at that time – and the top string of a banjo provided a thinner gauge than the top string of a guitar. It was still no use. I thought about it for a while and eventually plucked up the courage to ask the woodwork teacher, Mr Reardon, whether I could make a project out of it in the woodwork lesson. The answer was yes: if wood was involved.

I took the guitar to school on the appointed day – and Mr Reardon helped me drill out the peg-holes to a much larger size. I then glued in four hardwood dowels. I'd got the dowelling—a mahogany Victorian curtain pole—from the local dump. I cut four sections to size – sanded and polished them. Once they were glued in—good and hard—I drilled four holes just large enough to ram in the aluminium pegs. Success! No … it *still* didn't work.

I took the 'guitar' home with a slight sense of dejection – but my father, having enquired about the project, surprised me by being helpful. He'd been pleased by my improvements in English at school. I'd risen from the bottom of the class to the higher bracket of my year – and wanted to acknowledge my efforts. He was impressed with the efforts I'd made with the Skiffle Junior and saw that I'd run into a wall with my project – despite having worked on it in the woodwork class. He seemed to recognise *(a little late, I thought)* that the thing was a toy – and that I was trying to make it into something real.

Being a belt-and-braces man—when it came to making anything— my father suggested that I drill four tiny lateral holes through the sides of the headstock and fit four thin brass screws.

---

1   SOLVOL AUTOSOL metal polish paste was founded in Solingen, Germany, in 1929.

These would prevent the hardwood dowels from moving – should the glue prove insufficient to the task.

I roughened the aluminium pegs with emery cloth and—lo and behold—it appeared to work, especially with the violin rosin from Onkel Bernt's violin. I could now tune the beast! Well no … I couldn't because the aluminium pegs *still* slipped.

My father was highly inventive with such practical problems and set about showing me how to make four larger pegs out of the mahogany curtain pole. There was plenty enough mahogany left. He looked at my Onkel Bernt's violin and copied the pattern with his table-top lathe. *"You see,"* he said *"the reason these aluminium pegs will not work is because they are not tapered. That means that you cannot get the required friction."* He'd showed me how the pegs on the violin worked and I saw immediately how the problem could be solved. The pegs we made were much bigger and looked serious. I was delighted. It still wasn't a *real guitar* – but it was no longer a toy. It was now something that I could hand over to Papa Legba without having him whack me over the head with it in sheer disgust.

I tuned it to a chord—I have no idea which it may have been—and proceeded to strum it whilst fretting alternate strings at the 3rd, 5th, and 12th frets. It sounded suitably like something from the Delta because the frets were never intended to represent anything close to correct intonation – and the off-pitch row it made sounded suitably mournful to my ear.

I showed it to Steve who was kind enough to say that it was a huge improvement. He tried to play it and pulled a face that made him appear as if he'd bitten into a citrus from hell. *"Vic … it's bloody horrible – almost every note's either sharp or flat of where it should be."*

"I thought it didn't sound quite right …"

"Not quite right?" Steve shook his head in dismay *"It's more that it's not quite entirely wrong."*

"So …" I ventured with desperate optimism dredged form the uttermost depths of wishful thinking *"… d'you think there's anything I could do to improve it?"*

95

Steve shook his head *"No Vic … that's impossible … unless you sanded down the neck and put new frets on it – and that would cost a fortune because you'd have to take it to a luthier – and I doubt whether a luthier would touch it."*

"A luthier?" I queried

"Yes … a luthier *is someone who makes and repairs guitars – but, as I said, even if you could find a luthier – a luthier wouldn't work on a plastic guitar."*

"Oh …"

Steve noticed my bereft look and said *"There might … be—one—way of changing it … I'll ask my dad and see what he says."*

Mr Bruce took a look at it and said *"The one thing you could do … and it might improve things … is to fit a tailpiece and a separate bridge. My brother Stan used to tinker with guitars and I have a box of guitar pieces in the attic that used to belong to him. I will see what I can find."*

"Thank you Mr Bruce, that is very kind of you."

"Think nothing of it Vic – I'm glad to help."

And so, Mr Bruce ventured into the attic – with Steve and me standing at the bottom of the pull-down ladder with hopeful expressions. Mr Bruce ascended. After a few minutes—filled with the creaking sound of boxes being moved here and there—he descended with two objects in his hands: a tailpiece and a bridge. *"The bridge is broken and the tailpiece is quite rusty – but if you work on it – these things should fit the bill."* Pause. *"The problem is going to be how to fit the tailpiece to the plastic body. I'm no good with this kind of thing – but what I imagine it needs is a piece of wood setting into the bottom of the lower bout."*

Mr Bruce noticed my confusion and continued *"The two bulges of the guitar are called 'bouts' – the upper bout is where the neck joins the body and the lower bout is the one where the tailpiece and bridge are situated."* Pause. *"Now … I wouldn't like to tell your father what to do – because it's not for me to make suggestions – but … if he were to find some way to put a wooden block into the lower bout – it would make it strong enough to hold the tailpiece."*

"Thank you very much indeed Mr Bruce! That's wonderful!"

"Don't be too happy about it yet *Vic – I have no way of knowing whether this will work. My idea is that by adjusting the position and angle of the bridge … you*—might—*be able to correct the intonation – but … it's something of a gamble. Don't be too disappointed if it doesn't work. The frets are … somewhat approximate – but you might be able to play something on it. You like that Delta Blues – so maybe the result will not be too far off. Some of those old Blues players used quite poor quality instruments."*

"Fantastic!" I beamed *"That will make it more authentic!"*

"I admire your enthusiasm Vic." He smiled and left Steve and me to examine the bridge and tailpiece. The bridge was broken at one end – but that was not a problem because my guitar only had four strings. I could simply cut it to size. I'd position the four-string remainder in the middle of the bridge-cradle between the bridge-height adjustment-wheels. We took the tailpiece to the kitchen and took turns rubbing it with SOLVOL AUTOSOL chrome cleaner. It took an hour but by the time we were finished – it gleamed.

"What you need to do," Steve told me *"is use the middle four holes. It will look much better with this tailpiece and a proper bridge – but the nut at the top is still plastic and that's part of what's muting the sound. It should be made of bone."*

"Right … I don't suppose your dad's got anything like that in the attic?"

Steve asked his father and his father dutifully investigated the attic again – but found nothing that could be of use. *"I'll just have to ask my father … and hope to find him in a good mood."*

When I got home, I showed my father the bridge and tailpiece and described how Steve and I had worked on them. My father looked at them for what seemed a long time and said *"Well … I think I may be able to work out a way to fit a wooden block into the base of this guitar – as Mr Bruce has been so obliging as to provide the pieces."*

We walked up to the garden shed that he called the 'workshop' and he proceeded to look around amongst the different pieces of wood he had stacked on a shelf.

There was a piece of dark red iroko wood —about 7 by 5 by 5 inches—that was left over from making the garden bench. He drew the curve of the lower bout and cut the block to shape – and planed it down so that it would be a tight fit inside the guitar. Then, horror-of-horrors, he proceeded to cut into the guitar. I watched with trepidation at the exposed hole – but soon he had that piece of wood in place. He pondered for a moment and said *"The problem is – that although this gives the tailpiece a secure mount – it has to rely on the strength of the rest of the guitar and there is no strength in plastic. I think we need a rod that connects the neck with the wooden anchor-piece."* My father then did something quite amazing – he *invented* the truss rod. He had no idea about truss rods—and of course this one would not be adjustable—but that's more-or-less what it was. It was an iron bar however; as it was all he had that would work – and my father was ever one for over-building. I remembered the time he'd repaired my Uncle Bert's leather motorcycle jacket but riveted a piece of linoleum to it. It was as ugly as hell but it served to keep the wind out and my uncle Bert was *as pleased as Punch.*[2] I was also as pleased as Punch because the iron bar quadrupled the weight of the guitar.

He then drilled tiny holes through the plastic into the wood and used a counter-sinking drill in order that the screwheads would not stand proud of the surface. He then made the block of wood secure with two dozen small brass screws.

"As the front is exposed—because I had to cut the plastic away—I've set the block of wood level with the face of the guitar. To overcome any weakness to the structure I am setting these screws into the bottom and sides ..." he told me *"... this is in order that the pull of the strings will be spread over the body as much as possible. That way the plastic will not give way under the strain."*

He then went on to set a small brass rod where the existing nut was situated. He made four grooves with a delicate file in which to set the strings and the job was complete.

---

2   As pleased as Punch is an expression dating to the 1700s. The idiom derives from Punch and Judy puppet shows. The character Punch derives from the puppet Polichinello, created in the sixteenth century by the Italian *Commedia Dell'arte*. Punch is depicted as evil. He beats his child, his wife, a policeman, and various other characters to death. After each murder, Punch—highly pleased with himself—declares *"That's the way to do it!"*

My father had been in the Royal Engineers in the Army and seemed to understand things like 'stress factors' and all kinds of mysteries. Suddenly there it was – and all I had to do was re-fit the strings and set them on the bridge. One weekend trip to Steve's house and his father set about placing the bridge in such a way as to make it sound like a musical instrument.

"Well Vic … your father can certainly set his hand to anything. I would never have credited it. This is now almost a real guitar. I cannot get the intonation accurate over the entire neck – but as long as you only play up to the 7th fret – it shouldn't sound too bad – not too bad at all."

I thanked Mr Bruce profusely and Steve and I went off to see what sort of sound we could get out of it. I loved the fact that it now had wooden parts. I loved the brass screw heads visible on the soundboard – and the brass nut. I loved the dull gleam of the steel tailpiece. The sound left a lot to be desired – but the improvement had been staggering. Somehow this was an instrument more likely to attract Papa Legba's attention. It was a poor man's guitar – but Bluesmen *were* poor – so that was a mark in its favour. Steve put the guitar into *open* E *tuning* for me – and gave me a set of pitch-pipes in order that I could tune it when it lost its tuning.

"I've tuned it to the top four strings of a guitar Vic – because that won't bow the neck. I've also tuned it down lower – so it isn't really E, it's D but the shape of the chord is still E." Pause. *"In this tuning … you could … do things like this."* Then he proceeded to show me strums where I fretted different strings to make a simple Blues. I got the idea readily enough and started messing around with it. I found an amazing trick after a while – where I could repeatedly hit one note before changing into a run of notes. I was slow at first but after an hour or two I worked out how to sing 'Crossroads Blues' but the repeat line foxed me until Steve made a suggestion.

"Sing it – and I'll see if I can show you where to finger it."

I sang the line and Steve tried a few things on his guitar *"Ah – it starts in D then the second line moves to G – so … if you fret the second string just there – that should give you a chord that works for G."*

We continued in this way 'til I had the song worked out. As soon as I got it, I started singing – and singing loudly enough to attract the attention of Mr Bruce.

"I sat down at the crossroads, with my gui-tar 'cross my knees / I sat down at the crossroads, with my gui-tar 'cross my knees / Papa Legba have some mercy, on this po' white boy – if you please." Not the original words, of course – but I'd never seen them written down and I'd swung my own change on what I remembered.

> *Going down to the crossroads, take my midnight ride, / Going down at the crossroads, take my midnight ride,/ Nobody gonna see me, so I'll just ride on by.*

> *Going down to Runfold, Gonna ride there by-an-by. Yeah going down to Runfold / I'm gonna ride there by-an-by. / Then I'll play that barrel-house baby, down by the riverside.*

> *I don't run, I can't run, tell my friend Stephen Bruce / Run, I can't run, yeah – tell my friend Stephen Bruce / That I'll be riding to the crossroads, Lawd I b'lieve I'm cuttin' loose.*

Mr Bruce had been standing in the doorways whilst I'd been singing and came in along with Mrs Bruce. They both had huge smiles on their faces as they gave me a round of applause.

"Delta Blues in Surrey, England eh! That is something I would never have imagined!" chuckled Mr Bruce. *"Where did you learn that? And how clever of you to change the words!"*

"It was on a record that Mr Love had – but the words are not the same – as you noticed. Mr Love said that Bluesmen always changed the words of songs to make them their own. He lived in our road – but he died ... He was going to leave me his records in his will – but then it never happened because he had to go to a mental hospital where I wasn't allowed to visit him."

That changed the Bruce's expressions *"I am so sorry Vic. It sounds as if ... as if you ... spent some happy times with him."*

"Yes Mrs Bruce ... I did ... and I will always remember him. He was very kind to me and so was his sister Mrs Love."

I got that stuck feeling and my eyes heated up. I did my best not to cry and succeeded – but Mrs Bruce noticed and said how sad it must have been.

"Yes ..." said Mr Bruce *"I was very sad when my brother Stan died – but I am happy that you have that tailpiece and bridge now. Stan would have liked to have heard you sing that song – and I must say, you have a very powerful voice for one so young."*

"Thank you Mr Bruce. I want to be a Bluesman one day and you have to have a powerful voice for that."

Mr Bruce had heard of Robert Johnson—who wrote Crossroads Blues—and we talked for a while about the different Bluesmen and Blueswomen I knew: Bessie Smith, Big Mama Thornton, Ma Rainey, Son House, Charlie Patton, Peetie Wheatstraw, Blind Lemon Jefferson, and of course Big Bill Broonzy. Mr Bruce liked Bessie Smith because her Blues was similar, in some ways, to Jazz. He pulled out his guitar and played one of her songs. It was very intricate and he didn't sing – but I recognised the song *"A Fo'd is a car ever'body wanna ride, jump on an' you will see – I got Fo'd engine moo'ments in ma heerps – it's un'er ma gua'antee"* I joined in.

"Of course ..." coughed Mr Bruce at the end of the song. *"This is not a song you could sing ... anywhere ... it's a trifle ..."*

"Risqué?" offered Mrs Bruce.

"Yes my dear – quite so. But I suppose one has to consider the historical context ... and ... perhaps Vic – you might be careful not to let your father hear you sing anything like this."

"I'm sorry Mr and Mrs Bruce – I didn't mean to ..."

"Think nothing of it Vic—think nothing of it—there are many things of great historical interest that aren't exactly proper and it would be a shame to lose such things. Anyway I started playing the song – so you were perfectly right to join in. It is entirely my responsibility – and you made a fine job of singing it."

Steve was in hysterics after his parents left the room *"You're a total maniac Vic!"* he laughed *"That really surprised my parents – but I think they enjoyed it. I could see my mother smiling – so it's not a problem."*

"Sorry Steve – I don't know what happened … I just got carried away by what your father said about my voice and then he started playing that Bessie Smith number and I was really excited because I knew the words." Pause. *"Maybe … you could tell your parents that I never sing anything like that at home – because I wouldn't like them to be worried about it or anything."* Pause. *"I won't sing anything like that again here either."*

"I think that might be better …" Steve laughed *"… or at least not when my parents are around. I don't think they mind – but they probably feel responsible and they wouldn't want your father hearing that my dad had accompanied you singing that Bessie Smith song. He'd probably go through the roof."*

I was happy with having turned a stupid piece of nonsense into a workable guitar – but in some way I was happier about the inventiveness of it all. It was thrilling that such things were possible. At one moment there's nothing: a worthless object. Then there's an idea – and that idea can be followed. It takes hard work and perseverance – but then something real happens. It seemed fascinating the way in which other people would help once they saw that you were serious and working hard to make something happen. Who'd have thought that Mr Bruce and my father would *almost* have cooperated in putting me on the road to the Mississippi Delta.

I pondered the question of *invention* and *inventiveness* – and concluded that inventiveness must be important in Buddhism. It must be important because ideas come out of nowhere. Ideas come out of emptiness – as everything comes out of emptiness.[3] You could just be sitting there and an idea would spring into existence. I'd read the term 'plenum-void'. It was in one of the Buddhist books with which I'd struggled and come away with a greater sense of how the universe functioned. The 'plenum-void' was the *nothingness* that was continually giving rise to *somethingness*.

In terms of science, there was voidness – and then suddenly there were atoms. Then the atoms—in their endless trillions—became solidness.

---

3   Emptiness – tongpa nyid (*sTong pa nyid / shunyata*) and tongpa'i ting-ngé'dzin (*sTong pa'i ting nge 'dzin / shunyata samadhi*) meditative absorption in emptiness.

Then that solidness exploded into suns that flew off in every direction – some with orbiting planets and some of those planets with orbiting moons. I'd gained that simplistic notion in the science lessons at Junior School from the 'How Things Began' series on BBC radio.

Apart from *nondual awareness*,[4] it seemed that science and Buddhism were quite similar in how they saw existence. Everything came out of nothing: protons, neutrons, and electrons. The protons and the neutrons are the centre of the atom and the electrons fly around above them. The ideas were the same. They just came out of *the state without thoughts* – and inventions happened that way. So, if you were creative and inventive, then you were simply doing what the universe did.

Buddhists were natural inventors … and Tara was *the Mother of Invention!*

What a thought!

---

4   Rigpa *(rig pa / vidya).*

7

euphoria

1964–66

Although I'd failed to meet Papa Legba at the crossroads in Runfold in the September of 1964 – the year was not a total loss in terms of what was important to me. Tara had appeared—if only once—and I'd become a member of the Buddhist Society [1] and received their quarterly magazine *The Middle Way*. [2]

1964 saw my acquisition of the book *Experiment in Mindfulness* by Rear Admiral EH Shattock. [3] I'd heard about the book through the Buddhist Society in London – and thought it sounded interesting. It was described as a meditation manual from which anyone could learn to meditate. I was not disappointed. I began to meditate as Rear Admiral EH Shattock meditated, before I was more than a few chapters into the book. At that point the White Lady began to appear in my dreams again – and I began to feel an intense sense of loss. It seemed to me that she had been so much more vivid when I was a young child. My tactile memory of her vividness was far more vibrant than my dreams – and it occurred to me that my sitting meditation practice might restore that vibrancy.

---

1   The Buddhist Society was inaugurated by Christmas Humphreys, a British High Court judge, in London in 1924. Originally a branch of a Theosophical Lodge – it became independent in 1926; Christmas Humphreys remaining its president until his death in 1983. The Buddhist Society was one of the first Buddhist organisations outside Asia. It is situated at 58 Eccleston Square in South-West London. The library has a collection in excess of 4,500 volumes. It has a lecture hall and two shrinerooms.

2   *The Middle Way* is The Buddhist Society's quarterly journal. It contains articles by Buddhist teachers and scholars Each issue includes book reviews, the Society's programme, and Buddhist news from the Society, Great Britain, and around the world.

3   The book, *An Experiment in Mindfulness: an English Admiral's Experiences in a Buddhist Monastery,* was published in 1958. It is a highly literate account which deals with the problems of daily living – and conveys a serious and moving religious experience.

This provided me with the willpower to sit every day for as long as I could. It began with quarter hour sessions and increased as I got used to it. 1964 had also seen the release of *House of the Rising Sun* – by the Animals. Then there was *Good Morning Little Schoolgirl* by the Yardbirds, and *Little Red Rooster* by the Rolling Stones. I was delighted by *Little Red Rooster* because it really *was* Blues rather than Rhythm *&* Blues. The Stones took it slow, too—which was exactly how Blues should be—and from there on, Buddhism and Blues ran parallel in my life; almost like emptiness and form. Buddhism was the empty aspect because almost no one was aware of my interest, apart from Steve. My mother noticed the arrival of *The Middle Way* once a quarter and was worried about what my father would say if he ever caught wind of it – but when he eventually found out about it, the fact that its president was a British High Court judge, seemed to make it acceptable in his eyes. He cast an eye over it once and found it so intellectually impenetrable that he didn't scrutinise it any further than a paragraph. My mother told me later that he considered it valuable for my education to be challenged by such academic writing and that anything that would improve my English results at school could only be good. Fortunately my English results improved and so he looked on *The Middle Way* with an approving eye.

1965 saw my first try out with a band. Percy Gordon, a lad from St Mary's *(a school between my home and Netherfield)*, had got a group together. They called themselves 'The Applause'. Percy had ideas about changing the name to Percy's Applause and wasn't shy of telling me about the idea. He'd taken to talking to me if he espied me passing his school on the way home. He was somehow impressed that I knew a verse that wasn't on the single brought out by the Animals.

Percy's group needed a vocalist because none of them could sing – and there was no one around whose voice had broken for long enough to be able to sound plausible. I reluctantly let Percy persuade me to try out with them as a vocalist. The reason for my reluctance was that I didn't want to be part of any band of which my friend Steve was not a member.

I mentioned it to Steve and he surprised me by encouraging me to try out. He told me it would be good experience – especially as the Applause had a microphone. He appreciated my loyalty but said that he didn't view it as any threat to our long term goal. So … I went to the try-out with The Applause and we had equally low opinions of each other. I was a baritone who sang with Black intonation, syncopation, and rubato. They were a musically infantile Pop group spawned by parental indulgence—sour grapes on my part, of course, with regard to their instruments—and they needed a vocalist. My voice had broken whilst I was still at Junior School – and so I was now well settled into my adult voice.

If I'd been a tenor – it wouldn't have been a problem – but they were unable to transpose their songs. The rhythm guitarist was a four-chord wonder. The lead and bass must have played at least six different notes between them. Percy was the drummer – and perhaps the best of the four group members. They played Pop music and hated almost all the music I liked. Percy Gordon turned out to be a racist and—a few days after the disastrous try-out— threatened me with a fight for having the audacity to like Black music. I'd apparently shown him up in front of his friends—who were all 'fine young racists' like himself—so … I was going to pay for my near-criminal impudence.

"I'm not interested in fighting you Percy." I said as calmly as I could – but Percy, red with rage, shouted *"I'm not frightened of you – you shit-faced Nazi!"* Percy knew my mother was German. *"I'm going to fight you whether you like it or not, you coward! You'll wish you were never born when I've finished with you!"*

I sighed *"Percy … if you start … I—will—have to hit you back."* Percy continued to assail me with foul language – and I was surprised by his inventiveness. I was also horrified by the fact that I was about to enter into some sort of violence. How had that happened? I really did not want to hit Percy – but I wasn't going to let him hit me either. This 'turning the other cheek' was fine for Christians – but it took no account of allowing others to reinforce their own bellicosity.

I decided I'd better try to say something that might deter him. *"Y'know Percy, the last time I hit someone was at Junior School – and I didn't want to do it then either – but that boy didn't get up straight away. I really don't want to hit you ... but ... if you try to hit me, I'll have to protect myself – which means I'll have to hit you as hard as I can. I really don't think this is a good idea. Maybe just take my apology for not being the vocalist you wanted. It's up to you."* I moved one foot back and clenched my fists – prepared to go straight for his nose. Percy just stood there looking faintly confused – so I said *"Well ... are we going to forget about it?"*

I stood there breathing. Breathing as I breathed when meditating – simply staring in Percy's direction, without looking at him. Suddenly Percy burst into tears and walked away. I was astonished. How had *that* happened? What had Percy had in mind? Did he think I'd run away – or what? Maybe he was used to intimidating people – but entirely unused to the reality of belligerent contact. I was extremely glad that I had not had to hit him – because I found the whole idea of fighting to be primitive and abhorrent.

That was the last I saw of Percy Gordon.[4] I was sorry it ended so badly – but glad that I didn't have to hit him. I told Steve about the incident and he pondered for a moment. *"Y'know ... it might have been better if you had hit him – because now you've humiliated him and that's worse. Maybe if you'd had a fight you could have made friends afterwards – but ... you wouldn't want to be friends with a racist anyway, so I suppose nothing's lost."*

"Interesting perspective Steve ..." I replied – feeling foolish *"I hadn't considered the humiliation he might have felt – but yes, you're right ..."* Pause. *"Although ... what else could I have done?"*

"Walked away?"

"Yes ... of course. Now ... why didn't I think of that? That would have been so easy."

---

4   The author did see him again in the Summer of 1968 when Percy attended the first gig Savage Cabbage gave in Weyflood Village Hall – but he did not seem to recognise the author and there was no communication between them.

"Well ... maybe not." Steve offered *"He might have tried jumping you from behind or something."*

"Possible ... whatever – but the thing that annoys me about myself is that I should have a better sense of situations. I mean ... I'm trying to act appropriately in terms of wisdom and compassion – and then the best I can do is to humiliate someone."

"Remember ..." Steve cut in *"... that I'm only guessing. Percy's probably forgotten about it already. He doesn't seem the kind to remember something long if it's not to his advantage."*

And so we talked – looking at the thing from various angles. Steve was always good at that – and he always kept my involvement with Buddhism in mind. It was sometimes as if he took it as a duty to keep me on track. I was always grateful for Steve's observations and he seemed pleased that I took him seriously. I always felt that Steve was a fine example of what a good friend should be.

1965 also saw the arrival of the fabulous Miss Elphinstone – the new drama teacher at Netherfield. She wore floor-length homemade dresses, scandalous Moroccan sandals, and highly unusual jewellery. She wore octagonal spectacles with a blue tint which I thought amazing. I had to start wearing spectacles at that time – so I chose to adopt my father's old British Army issue spectacles. They were like the National Health spectacles but were of better manufacture: nickel-plated with strong spring-back side arms that were flat rather than the thin wire of the National Health type. I asked for a blue tint. My father didn't seem to notice the pale blue tint and I was amazed to have slipped by undetected. My father was usually hot on deviations from the norm – so ... maybe blue tints were fairly normal.

Miss Elphinstone got us to recite a poem called 'The Congo' which swang as Blues swings, if you hit the words right. That was something I could do with no difficulty at all.

Wild crap-shooters with a whoop and a call / Danced the juba in their gambling-hall / And laughed fit to kill, and shook the town, / And guyed the policemen and laughed them down / With a boomlay, boomlay, boomlay, boom / Then I saw the Congo, creeping through the black, / Cutting through the jungle with a golden track. Vachel Lindsay, *The Congo*, 1914

Even when it came my turn to read on my own I was fine – in fact I was better than fine because the rest of the class didn't hold me back. I was free to let rip as if I was singing Robert Johnson – and I almost did sing. The wonder of it was that my stammer disappeared and I read well beyond what I'd been asked to read. Miss Elphinstone was obviously both enraptured and startled . *"Have you done this kind of thing before?"* she smiled. *"Not exactly—Miss Elphinstone —but it's like Blues and I sing Blues and so ... I just read it like that."*

Miss Elphinstone decided I should recite solo where Blues rhythm was the operative mode. I thought it worked and had the whole class clapping in time. Even the males of the class were impressed.

The ebony palace soared on high / Through the blossoming trees to the evening sky. / The inlaid porches and casements shone / With gold and ivory and elephant-bone. / And the black crowd laughed till their sides were sore / At the baboon butler in the agate door, / And the well-known tunes of the parrot band / That trilled on the bushes of that magic land. Vachel Lindsay, *The Congo*, 1914

I was sitting on the low wall at the girls' end of the school playground with Lindsay Goulding. She'd become a good friend of mine since the first year—as had several of the girls—and we often sat and talked together. We both wrote poetry and so there was always something to talk about.

"Y'know ..." I said to Lindsay *"I've dreamed of doing something like this."*

"Bet you're pleased" she replied with a broad grin. *"That was the most fun I've had in a school lesson."* Pause. *"I was surprised ... well ... you didn't ..."*

I finished her sentence *"... stammer? No ... didn't stammer at all. Never —do—when I sing."*

A troupe of skull-faced witch-men came, / Through the agate doorway in suits of flame, / Yea, long-tailed coats with a gold-leaf crust / And hats that were covered with diamond-dust. / And the crowd in the court gave a whoop and a call / And danced the juba from wall to wall. / But the witch-men suddenly stilled the throng / With a stern cold glare, and a stern old song. Vachel Lindsay, *The Congo,* 1914

There was to be a performance of 'The Congo' that would be open to parents and friends, and I was to be the star of the show – but the Drama class came to an unexpected end. Mr Davies and the startlingly voluptuous Miss Elphinstone were caught *in flagrante*[5] in the chemistry laboratory one lunch time and both were dismissed. I couldn't see what all the fuss was about, as neither were married to anyone else. The Drama classes weren't replaced by another English language subject. I regretted that as I'd enjoyed the Drama classes.

Miss Elphinstone's planned recital of 'The Congo' was abandoned consequent to her florid departure. A school performance—hard on the heels of licentious conduct—was unthinkable. Censure rained down on the poem as a work of unsound morals.

Lindsay told me she was very upset that I wouldn't be able to perform. *"It's bloody unfair"* she said with some obvious heat.

I'd not heard a girl swear before – but I appreciated her empathy with my loss. *"Yes … I'd been getting myself ready for being on stage. I could see it – the lights and everything … but that'll have to wait until Steve and I get our Blues band organised."*

"You don't need big-bum Elphinstone to sing Blues, Vic. You can sing any time you like. Still … I'm really annoyed with her for spoiling everything for you. And anyway, what—flaming idiot—has sex in the chemistry lab in the lunch hour?"

I wanted to reply that I'd have been eager—*anywhere*—with Miss Elphinstone – but … some things are best left unsaid.

5   In flagrante delicto (*in blazing offence*) or in flagrante (*in blazing*). The Latin term is used colloquially as a euphemism for someone being caught in the act of sexual intercourse

Miss Elphinstone was a sad loss – but Ron Larkin appeared right out of the pages of legend: Mr Lightning. Ron was a new friend of Steve.

Ron lived in Farnham but attended Grayshot Grange boarding school as a day student. Steve had met him at a guitar seminar and introduced me. We played some Blues – and as soon as he started playing I knew we had a band. We had more than a band because Ron wasn't just good – he was a staggering musical phenomenon. If Eric Clapton was God—as some were saying—then Ron Larkin had the GCMG as a guitarist: GOD CALLS ME GOD.[6] He seemed to play as if he was hardly trying – and his riffs weren't tight little patterns high up the neck. Ron employed the entire length of the neck – and he riffed as fast at the low end as he did at the high end.

Ron abjured grimacing as 'infantile posturing' – although he made an exception for the Black American performers. He just stood there firmly planted with his feet about a stride apart – and commanded the entire stage with his presence. We soon learnt that one did not sit as a Blues player – unless one was a pianist. One also had to practice as if one were on stage. Ron delivered all this as ultimate fact. Steve and I accepted Ron's word as *wisdom from on high*. What else would one do when faced with a prodigy—a virtuoso—a genius. We never sat whilst playing again.

It was immediately clear to Steve that Ron was his musical superior. Ron had taken 'O' level music when he was 12 and 'A' level music when he was 13. He'd also taken musical grades outside school and could have got a university place easily but for his age. His understanding of music theory was 'terrifying' according to Steve.

6 'GOD CALLS ME GOD' is an Army joke concerning honours – that the author learned from his father, a major in the British Army. It is based on the initials of the public service honour *Grand Cross Michael George* (GCMG). The most Distinguished Order of Saint Michael and Saint George is an order of chivalry. It was inaugurated by King George IV, named in honour of two military saints, Saint Michael and Saint George. The Order has three classes: the lowest is *Companion Michael George* (CMG) nicknamed 'CALL ME GOD'; the next class is *Knight Commander Michael George* (KCMG) nicknamed 'KINDLY CALL ME GOD', or *Dame Commander Michael George* (DCMG) nicknamed 'DO CALL ME GOD', and the highest class is *Grand Cross Michael George* (GCMG), nicknamed 'GOD CALLS ME GOD'.

Ron could see Steve's efforts were well in advance of anyone else he'd met – but was evidently unsure if I was worth the effort.

Knowing I was a vocalist Ron asked me to sing – so I obliged—unaccompanied—with 'In My Time of Dying'. Steve grinned the following day *"Ron said he never heard a voice like yours that wasn't from Chicago."*

I was surprised. *"I know I can sing – but I can't play anything other than harp – and that's still a bit basic."*

"Well … Ron's ambition's an electric Chicago Blues band" Steve replied. *"He said that it doesn't matter how good he is on guitar—or I am on bass—we have to have a vocalist who can sing Hoochie Coochie Man – and mean it. He said …"* Steve laughed *"… some wimpy white wanker from the Home Counties who sounded like a choir boy just wouldn't cut it."*

I was emotionally perplexed. *"I know I'm not a choir boy—and I do make a fair stab with Black Southern States accent—but there are other people who sing much better …"*

"There may be – but Ron's not met them yet. And those he's heard are all at least ten years older than you."

"Yes … I suppose we couldn't exactly get Jack Bruce could we."

"No – but Ron's not as keen on Jack Bruce as you are. He says that he's more of a Jazz vocalist – and that he prefers your voice."

"Right … well, that's novel – but … I suppose I should be delighted. I can't see it myself. I think Jack Bruce is the state-of-the-Art."

And so, we met up every week—sometimes several times a week—and practised. We were a band. Ron had made that happen, almost overnight. I was immensely grateful – because the dream was no longer a dream. It was reality – and a vast shining reality.

I was also grateful for Mr Preece the English teacher – even though he was strict, sarcastic, and slightly severe. He was an old-fashioned teacher even though he was a relatively young man. He was a good man however, with a strong sense of diligence and integrity.

He was intelligent, philosophical, intellectual – and his sarcasm didn't worry me. I saw the wit of his remarks – and, in some way, enjoyed them; even when applied to me. I wanted his approval – and, unlike the approval of my father, there was a direct way to obtain it: hard unremitting work. Mr Preece's class seating-arrangement was based on end-of-term marks. I started more-or-less at the bottom of the class and rose to the top table alongside Lindsay Goulding. Mr Preece warmed to me considerably as I rose and it obviously pleased him to see me rising. He took to smiling at me as I sat down – and to greeting me if I met him walking to school.

One day I plucked up the courage to show him my poetry – and, although he wasn't impressed, he took the time to show me the failings of what I'd written. He didn't believe in giving praise as encouragement – but he was more than willing to help me. *"Free verse is all very well ..."* he said *"... but if you wish to break rules, you will have to be able to write fluently within the rules you wish to break. Any fool can throw jumbled words onto paper and call them poetry."* He showed me the works of great poets and expected me to write essays on them.[7]

I wrote poetry essays in the mathematics class – and threw down a smattering of numbers to make it look as if I'd been working at the assigned tasks. It didn't take long before the mathematics teacher gave up on me as a lost cause. *"Simmerson is numerically retarded and there is no purpose in him being in this class."* He told the headmaster – and thus, I was allowed to use the time for additional English. It was deemed that it would be a waste of school money to allow me to sit 'O' level Mathematics.

I used to time my walk to school deliberately to coincide with Mr Preece. He was a tall thin man and keeping up with him was not easy. Everything about him seemed designed to make me work hard – but I was amply rewarded by his attention.

7   Harriet Arbuthnot, William Blake, Rupert Brooke, Robert Bridges, Elizabeth Browning, Byron, Chaucer, Samuel Coleridge, Robert Graves, Thomas Gray, John Keats, Christopher Marlowe, John Masefield, William Shakespeare, Percy Bysshe Shelley, Alfred Lord Tennyson, Willoughby Weaving, and Mary Wollstonecraft.

He wasn't keen on the Beat Poets – but he gave his subjective opinions no excessive objective weight. I was to learn the rules and structure of poetry – and *master the English language*. Only then could I experiment.

I began reading the Penguin Classics Series. It was a revelation – a new horizon peopled with intriguing personalities and their Artistic philosophies. I read: Nikolai Vasilievich Gogol; Honoré de Balzac; Gustave Flaubert; François-Marie Arouet whose *nom de plume* was Voltaire; Jean Paul Sartre; Albert Camus; Jean Genet; Franz Kafka; and, generally *anyone* with an interesting non-English name.

1966 was the year in which a strange and disturbing event occurred in the Summer. A young man called James Kirkpatrick—who'd previously attended Netherfield—was wanted by the police. We discovered this on the news the day after a local drama occurred. I was sitting in the living room one evening watching Patrick McGoohan's television series The Prisoner.[8] The Surrealism of the series appealed to me – but not to my father. The Surrealism was heightened on this particular evening when I heard a car crash at the bottom of our road. *"There's just been a car crash at the bottom of our road, Dad."*

My father—somewhat taken aback by my apparent nonchalance— leapt up from his chair. I made for the door to see whether I was accurate in my assessment of the sound I'd heard. And my father followed me out into the street to join me – where we stood vaguely bewildered as a young man legged it past us at a speed that seemed almost super-human. *"After him!"* my father cried out and I ran off up the road wondering exactly what I was supposed to do if I caught up with him. The chances of success were utterly remote as I've never been a runner. The police soon passed me and asked me what I was doing. *"My father told me to chase him."*

---

8   Patrick Joseph McGoohan (1928–2009) was an American-born actor, who grew up in Ireland and later England, where he established his stage and film career. His most notable rôle was in the two 60's television series *Danger Man* and *The Prisoner*. Patrick McGoohan co-created *The Prisoner* as well as writing and directing several episodes. The Prisoner was a surreal series which became increasingly surreal – the last episode being a landmark in surrealist television.

The policeman shook his head as if he'd never heard anything so absurd and replied *"Go home lad—good try—but we shall take care of this."* Then he ran to catch the other police who were attempting to gain on James Kirkpatrick.

The next day the incident was reported on the news and it appeared that James Kirkpatrick was wanted for armed robbery. The police had not caught him that night and he was said to be lying low somewhere – maybe in the woods or somewhere further afield. My father admitted that he should not have sent me after the fellow – but he'd thought—from my nonchalance in reporting the car crash —that I'd be up for such an exploit. He was genuinely horrified when he discovered that James Kirkpatrick was wanted for armed robbery and that he may have been armed at the time I went chasing up the road after him. I told my father I'd been happy to chase him—armed or not—and if the police hadn't turned me back I'd have continued. This was all entirely bravado—of course—but my father then surprised me by beaming at me as if I was the apple of his eye. Wonders would never cease.

Later that day I was sitting with my guitar in the garden—up under the apple tree at the top end near the lane—reading a book of WWI War Poetry which I was studying at school. I was trying to memorise Rupert Brooke's [9] poem 'The Soldier'. My father thought it right and proper that I was studying such work – even though he would have not approved of the satirical anti-war sentiments of some of the war poets.

> *If I should die, think only this of me: / That there's some corner of a foreign field / That is for ever England. There shall be / In that rich earth a richer dust concealed; / A dust whom England bore, shaped, made aware, / Gave, once, her flowers to love, her ways to roam …*
> Rupert Brooke, *The Soldier*, 1914

Græham—my brother—suddenly hailed me *"Vic – Mum wants you in the house."*

---

9 Rupert Chaucer Brooke (1887–1915) an English poet known for his war sonnets written during WWI.

I went to see what was wanted and my mother asked me where I wanted the legs of my Levi's hemmed. They hadn't had a pair in my leg length and so they needed to be shortened. I've always had slightly short legs in relation to my waist size – so this happened from time to time. After trying the Levi's on—and having the legs tucked up to the right length—I returned to my War Poets and … where was the guitar? I stared stupidly for a moment or two and then scanned the area quickly. The guitar was gone. My father was in his workshop and I wondered if he'd taken it in there. He hadn't. Græham hadn't taken it either. Just as I was asking Græham about it however, my father came storming into the house in full rage – but this time not with me. *"It will have been that criminal the police are hunting! They said that he could still be hiding in the woods! He'll be the one to have stolen the guitar!"* And with that he marched down the road to the public call box and telephoned the police.

I lived in hope of two things after that. One was that the guitar would be found. The other greater hope was that my father would buy me a replacement. The guitar never came to light even though James Kirkpatrick was captured and imprisoned. My father never mentioned the loss of my guitar again. It wasn't that it had been such a wonderful instrument – but it was unique. After all the work that had gone into it, I found that I missed it more than I would have imagined. And still four years before I'd be 18 and receiving the much dreamed-of GIBSON EB0.

1966 was the Autumn when I met Anelie Mandelbaum, a 22-year-old Swiss au pair, at the 'Euphoria' discothèque. There was something about her that gave me a subcutaneous flashback to the White Lady who had appeared in my room or my dreams—or whichever it was—when I was a child. She seemed to glow in some preternatural manner for which words were useless. I'd noticed that about ladies in general – but some glowed more than others. It had nothing to do with beauty, so it was not the effect of attraction. The elderly Mrs Love had glowed too. It had nothing to do with friendship either – because Steve didn't glow. I had never seen that glow emanating from men.

I cast my mind back and it seemed to me that the presence of girls or women, was always magical in some way that I could not define. It was almost as if having seen the White Lady had done something to my brain. Maybe now I just saw in a different way – the way that insects see ultraviolet and beyond.

I'd read in one of Steve's nature journals that trichromatic insects—such as bees—have three types of pigment receptors, like humans. They distinguish a wider spectrum of colours than other insects – but their pigment receptors don't coincide with those of human beings. The spectrum of colours visible to insects is a little higher in frequency than humans see. The lowest frequency we see is red – which is invisible to insects. Conversely, while violet is the highest frequency humans detect, many insects see ultraviolet and even higher frequencies. Maybe something like that had happened to me – and now ladies simply sparkled and glowed.

I was not so rapt in conjecture as to fail to notice one young lady intermittently glancing in my direction as I danced. There was something unusual about her, other than how incandescently beautiful she was. There was something in her expression that reminded me of Alice. It was as if Alice had somehow grown up to be a few years older than me. It was also as if Tara had manifested from the pages of the book on Tibet I'd seen at Primary School – because there was something about her that wasn't exactly English. Was it her clothes? Was it her way of sitting or her projected personality?

I started to feel as if I was performing for her. I also took care not to look obvious, as I inched—by what I hoped would be imperceptible increments—in her direction. Suddenly she was grinning broadly and clapping. No one ever clapped at the 'Euphoria' discothèque and so we became the entire centre of attention. Feeling gauche, I bowed and offered her my hand. I must have seen that in a movie. She seemed to find my gesture charming and joined me on the floor.

We danced for an hour before she said *"I am a little tired now and it has become the time I must leave."* My disappointment was transparent – because she offered *"If you vould—like—to come home vith me?"*

"Of all things" I replied (I'd like nothing better).

Somehow, she had the impression that I was 16 or so – and, to my shame, I did nothing to disabuse her of that error. Then, when I found out she was 22, I decided that honesty was definitely *not* the best policy. What were a few years here or there?[10]

From that day I moved from early adolescence into the glorious vistas of adulthood – and never looked back. Meeting Anelie signalled the return of Tara. From that point I started having dreams again. The vividness returned – and with it a sexual dimension that had not previously existed. The sexuality was not connected with Tara – but with two girls, who may have been her daughters. At first, I thought I was dreaming of Anelie – but she was pale blonde, almost white, and the girls were so dark haired that their tresses could have been black.

---

10 I was unaware that I was potentially placing Anelie in a criminal context – as the age of consent in Britain is 16.

8

the five precepts

february 1968

"Your parents'll—kill—you if they ever find out about Anelie – 'specially your father." Steve remarked with a curious mixture of grave concern and undisguised glee.

"Don't think I can be killed much more than—dead—Steve."

"Very funny Vic—but you know what I mean—they'd go crazy … and you'd —never—hear the end of it. They'd never let you go out anywhere ever again."

"In that case Steve …" I sighed *"… they'd better not find out."* Pause. *"I mean … what would—you—do? Would you've bailed out just because your parents would go spare if they found out?"*

"I don't know—I really don't know—but … I suppose … I—am—as envious as hell … and I suppose … I have to say … that … yeah alright … I'd probably do the same – Anelie is fierce, I mean—really—fierce."[1]

"Yes." Pause. *"You see … I didn't exactly—plan—to have a relationship with a 22-year-old au pair girl, did I?"*

"No – but you made a very good job of it as an accident, nonetheless" Steve laughed.

"Anyway Steve – look at it this way. № 1 – there's no telephone at home. № 2 – my parents are hardly going to walk down the road to the public call box just to chat with me at your house, are they? № 3 – they don't even know your telephone number. № 4 – well … maybe three's enough."

"They have my address though …"

---

1 The word 'fierce' at that time was a slang superlative.

"Yes ..." I groaned with slight impatience *"... so my father's going to drive out here just to check that I'm not homesick or whatever? I really don't think so. I've been coming to stay at your house since I was 8 years old and I haven't died of anything yet. Nothing's blown up or got flooded or whatever – so, as far as they're concerned, there's nothing to worry about."* Pause. *"'sides which ... your father's a—police inspector—so, as far as my father's concerned this is the next best place for me outside prison – like a maximum security wing or something."*

"Alright—alright—you've got me convinced ... It's just – what would happen if they did find out – I mean, with my parents?"

"As far as I'm concerned Steve ... when I leave here ... you think I'm going home. I never told you anything. You know nothing."

"Mmmm ... I'm not trying to get out of it or anything – but I don't feel—too —good about lying to my parents."

"No ... I can see that. I like your parents—as you know—but you did winkle it out of me didn't you? I did say that it was better that you didn't know where I went – didn't I?"

"Yeah ... you did ..." Pause. *"... yeah ... and ... I know it's not your fault – I did keep on at you 'til you told me."*

"Think of it like this Steve ... you're not lying in the—usual—way. You're not lying to stop your parents finding out what—you've—done. You're not lying to stop your parents finding out that you're doing something they wouldn't want—you—to do. You're not making up stories – you're just failing to tell them that I'm not—actually—going home ... when I leave here."

"Yes ... well ... that does make it sound better than lying."

"And anyway Steve ... this has been going on since ... February 1966 – and you've known since ... March last year ... and Anelie's going home to Switzerland for good in April – that's a month away so it's a bit late to start feeling anxious about it – or start worrying about being dishonest. The time for that was a year ago."

"You're right ... of course. I think I just got into some sort of panic about it when my father asked if you had a girlfriend – y'know when I got keen on Susan French and it didn't work out. He was suggesting I talked to you about it and ... that's when it came up as to whether you had a girlfriend."

"Ah ... right ... I see ... I can see how that would have been tricky." Pause. *"So you said no?"*

"Yes – I mean, yes I said 'no' ..."

"Well you were more-or-less honest then – because although a 22-year-old might just about be called a girl – a 24-year-old, is definitely a woman."

"Jesus, Vic! You're a total maniac!" Steve laughed *"... but ... I suppose you're theoretically correct. It's more a question of the fact that I thought I was lying. Whether I was lying because whether Anelie counts as a girl or as a woman is just splitting hairs."*

"Yes ... can't deny it Steve ... All I can do is try to make you feel better about it." Pause. *"I could just stop coming 'round on weekends ... if that would make it all easier."*

"No ... that wouldn't work either—because my parents would wonder why— and anyhow, that wouldn't be good would it? We've got all this music to work on and plans for our Blues band."

"I know that Steve ... I wouldn't want to miss our music time—you're my best friend in any case—so it would be a bad idea all round."

"Yeah ... it would ..." Steve shook his head. *"There are no other dark secrets are there?"*

"Well ... there was one thing I did when I was 12 that would probably make your hair stand on end."

I told Steve about my naked jaunt at the Runfold crossroads to meet Papa Legba and he laughed 'til he had tears in his eyes. I was glad of that because it seemed to make him feel much better about my trysts with Anelie. I told him that I'd told Anelie about it and that it had made her laugh as well.

"Well ..." Steve laughed *"if you can get away with that – you can probably get away with anything. However – there's been something that I've been meaning to ask you ... How does 'not telling the truth' fit with Buddhist ethics ... I mean isn't it one of the Buddhist commandments or rules or – what are they called?"*

"Precepts. Yes ... it's one of the Five Precepts."[2]

"... and ... they're things you take like vows?"

"Yes ..."

"So ... what are they – I mean can you tell me what the five are?"

"No killing or murdering; no theft or taking what's not freely given; no sexual misconduct; no dishonesty; and not getting drunk."[3]

"So ..." Steve began – but went no further.

"So, not being dishonest ... Yes ... I don't exactly feel—good—about it. I'd —rather—be open and honest about everything ... but ... I'm in a situation where my life isn't my own. My parents rule the house. They rule my life to a large extent. Now ... I didn't ever—agree—to that. It wasn't—my—idea. I didn't ask them to be my parents – well ... not consciously. So ... I find myself here—with them—or, more particularly with my father – because he's the one who makes all the rules. As you know, my mother's fine and massively more easy-going. Are you with me so far?"

"Yes ... but truth is still truth ..."

2   The five precepts (*bsLab lNga / panchasiksapada*) are a moral-ethical system of Buddhism which applies to celibate and non-celibate ordainees – and to the laity. They are sometimes referred to as the shravakayana precepts in the Mahayana tradition in contrast with the bodhisattva precepts.

3   1. Srog gCod songwa (*srog gCod song ba*) – avoidance of killing. Literally 'to cut the life force' – the motivation to terminate a being's existence through obliterating being. 'Causing death' and 'cutting the srog' are therefore not identical. The meaning of this 'difference' is easily misinterpreted. For example, the yogi who dispatched various other 'loser yogis' through 'phowa and who was on the verge of 'killing' Milarépa (*before realising that Milarépa was going to attain realisation*) was not in breakage of this vow. To be in breakage of this vow one has to intend to 'obliterate a being entirely', or to 'terminate sentience'. 2. Ma-chin pongwa (*ma byin sPong ba*) – avoidance of theft. 3. 'död-pé lo-par gempa pongwa *('dod pas log par gem pa sPong ba)* avoidance of sexual exploitation. 4. Dzundu ma pongwa (*brDzun du dMra sPong ba*) – avoidance of manipulative speech. 5. Yö-pé 'gyürwa'i tungwa (*mYos pas 'gyur ba'i bTung ba*) – avoiding deliberate loss of awareness.

"Yes – I'm not trying to tell you I'm not lying – even though I'm mainly lying by omission. That's not quite the point I'm trying to make."

"So let's hear the point then – not that I'm trying to criticise you or anything: I just want to know how you see it."

"Right ... well ... I think that I'm going to have to use an extreme example to show you how I see things. Say ... ... If you lived in Nazi Germany – and say you were sheltering a Jewish family who were trying to escape from Germany. Then say that the Gestapo or SS knock on your door and say 'We're looking for a Jewish family who are trying to escape to England. Have you any information that would lead to their capture?' What do you answer? Do you say 'Yes officers – they are upstairs hiding in our attic.' Or do you lie?"

"Right – well ... of course, I'd lie – but that is an extreme example."

"Yes—I did say it would be an extreme example—but the point is that truthfulness isn't 'an ultimate stance'. Once there is an exception – the law, or rule, or ethic has to be seen as flexible."

"I thought it was the exception that proved the rule?"

"Here—for once—Steve ..." I laughed *"I may know something about language that you don't know. The word 'prove'—in this saying—means 'test' as in 'gun proofing' or the 'alcohol proofing'. So this saying is misunderstood. It really means 'it's the exception that tests the rule'."*

"Right ... that makes far more sense. I wonder why I'd never thought of that. It's obvious now you explain it."

"So anyhow ... once there's an exception – you have to ask what other exceptions there could be. So ... for me ... being truthful with my parents would impinge on my freedom – and as far as I'm concerned, I'm not doing anyone any harm. *I never consented to obey my parents and I don't agree with how* they *see the world – particularly my father. He's in favour of the death penalty – and he'd hang homosexuals, on principle."*

"See your point ..." Steve groaned.

"*So, they do have power over me without being entirely right-minded. My father would be in favour of putting people in the stocks – he's a strong supporter of hanging and flogging. So, the thing about lying—as far as I see it—is that if you aren't lying to get an unfair advantage, or to hurt someone, it's not the same as if you* were. *It's still not* good *to be devious – but when it's a matter of freedom: I'm choosing personal freedom over unnecessary honesty.*"

"*Right ... I sort of see that ... or at least I can see that honesty isn't a simple matter.*"

"*That's how I see it – and, in terms of Buddhism, there are no 'absolutes' in terms of ethics. What is more important than* what *you do – is* why *you do it. Buddhism is more concerned with motivation. So ... I don't have any harmful motivation in what I'm doing. I'm not hurting anyone. I'm not depriving anyone of anything.*" Pause. "*That's it. I'm sorry I have to do it. I'd rather be honest – but: who would it help if I were honest? Who would it harm? Being secretive or merely withholding information is not breaking the precept, if no one is hurt – and no one loses anything.*"

"*Yeah ... It makes perfect sense. I'm just glad that I can be open with my parents.*"

"*So ... don't take this the wrong way – but d'you tell them every time you have an erotic dream?*"

"*Oh ...*" Steve shook his head "*... it looks as if my idea that I'm open with my parents has just been shot down in flames ...*"

"*Sorry. That wasn't my intention Steve – I just wanted to explain my situation and explain that I really do take the five precepts seriously ... while ... living as I live with what's important to me.*"

"*Yes ... I can see that your father's made it hard or even impossible to be honest with him – so ... he's obviously responsible for your having to hide things from him.*" Pause. "*It's been so much easier for me ... apart from ... well ...*"

I decided not to fill in the words 'erotic dreams' because I'd obviously embarrassed Steve with the way I'd applied logic in such a persistent manner.

126

"Good of you to see it that way." Pause. *"And … that's why* I *always come here – and* you *never come to* my *home. I don't blame you in the slightest – because I'd rather be here than at home anyway."*

"So—right—there are all kinds of dishonesty, aren't there" Steve pondered. *"I mean my parents didn't tell your father what they thought of him over not letting you have the* EB0 *bass … I know they've never met him – but …"*

"Yes …"

"And … they planned to give it to you on your 18th *birthday – knowing that he still wouldn't like it."*

"Glad you see the point Steve …" I sighed: not in exasperation with Steve – but exasperated with the situation in which I found myself. It pained me to have to break a precept, even though I was not breaking it to cause harm or give myself an unfair advantage over someone else. *"And of course – I don't see your parents as being anything other than honourable. My father's giving them no choice if they want to do something kind for me."*

"True." Pause. *"So what about the 'sexual misconduct' – does that mean the same as in the Ten Commandments, like not committing adultery?"*

"Yes … but it means more than that. It means men or women not seeing each other as stereotypical or treating each other according to ideas that squeeze them into boxes."

"Right …" Steve enquired *"… I think I understand what you mean, but could you give me an example of what that would look like?"*

"Well – that's easier than the first answer. It means that your girlfriend would be a real friend and not just a 'girl' who would be some sort of hobby or pastime. You'd have intelligent conversations – not much different from the one we're having."

Steve grinned *"And that's how it is with Anelie?"*

"That's exactly how it is with Anelie. There's passion – and, there's conversation. We respect each other's opinions – even when we don't agree. When we don't agree we talk about our different points of view – and there's always something to learn that is interesting. We discuss ideas – and ... we're good friends."

"Yes – I see that." Steve nodded. *"I think my father and mother are friends. They talk to each other a lot. He respects her Classical music—she respects his Jazz—and they both listen and enjoy it. They obviously have preferences – but they don't have to see each other's music as inferior or boring."* Pause. *"And ... that's Buddhism?"*

"Yes – that's Buddhism—as far as I understand it—but that doesn't mean that these ideas can't come about naturally, if people are open minded – and, if they avoid the standard indoctrination." Pause. *"Then of course there's not killing."*

"That's fairly black and white isn't it – or ..."

"No—you should know that Steve—don't you remember about my Uncle Bernt being part of the Brandenburg Company's plot to assassinate Hitler?"

"Sorry—yes—that had slipped my mind. I remember you telling me about that and how he and his whole division got sent to the Russian front and wiped out in seconds."

"Yes ... so with Uncle Bernt that would have been killing based on the motivation to end WWII. This is quite a valuable history for me because it's modern and because it happened in my own family history. There is a story about a sea captain who confesses to the Buddha that he's committed murder – he killed a robber on board his ship. The Buddha asked him about the circumstances – and the sea captain tells him that the robber was going to sink the ship in order that five hundred merchants would drown and he'd be able to salvage their gold. The Buddha tells him that his act was not a bad act— because although he killed the robber—he had no hatred in his mind. His intention had been to save lives."

"That's really interesting … right. I prefer the story about your uncle because it's real … not that the story of the Buddha and the sea captain isn't real – but it's so far away from anything that could happen now. So are all the precepts like this? I mean, are they all more like … guidelines?"

"Precisely Steve, they're guidelines rather than absolute laws."

"I don't think my father would like that idea … being in the Police, laws aren't really adaptable."

"They are if there's a war. Killing your neighbours is against the law … but, killing enemy soldiers wasn't against the law in the World Wars – and all those soldiers were someone's *neighbours. I don't know how many were killed in Hiroshima and Nagasaki – but there must have been hundreds of thousands who died. Then there was the British fire-bombing of Dresden. Dresden wasn't a military target, it was a pottery town. So that should have been a war crime – but somehow … it wasn't because Britain won the war. So … what's legal and what's not legal become vague depending on the circumstances."*

"And not everyone accepts that killing is alright in war, do they, like conscientious objectors … so, this is obviously quite a big question."

"Yes … like the death penalty … It's legal to kill people who kill people – but not legal to kill the people who pass the death sentence or take the prisoner to the gallows."

And so we talked through the evening until it was time to sleep.

We left the subject of Anelie with Steve deciding he'd just have to grin and bear it. And he did. It didn't take long for Steve to relax about the idea – and fortunately nothing was ever mentioned again as to *whether Vic had a girlfriend.* What the eye did not see … or the brain cognise … was of no great consequence. Be that as it may, neither of us realised that I'd placed Anelie in a criminal context, in terms of her having a sexual relationship with a minor. Perhaps that was just as well, as Steve would have found that an impossible situation.

Time was ticking by. I did occasionally still wander back in my mind – and, images of the White Lady morphing with Alice Rosalind Trevelyan would appear … flitting amongst the trees.

It would have all been so easy if she had not departed for the Welsh borderlands. We'd be practically married by now … I'd long since stopped feeling guilty about Anelie in respect of Alice … after all … I would not have expected her to become an old maid on the basis of our having once been childhood sweethearts. That would have been entirely unreasonable. The same then had to apply to me – and yet *that* was still a line of logic that I had to apply to myself periodically.

Memory of Alice was a strange thing – and that memory became increasingly strange as time went by. I found that I was confusing my visual memory of Alice with Tara. In some vague way, they had become the same person or two manifestations of the same person. Tara had never spoken to me and so the ideas that entered my mind *(when I encountered Tara)* I remembered as being spoken with Alice's voice. When I remembered Alice, she was rarely a young girl – but rather someone of indefinable age. I had no photograph of Alice – and so time allowed her to blur into powerful yet fragmented *dream-memories*.[4]

Although Steve was almost two years older than me, I was tall for my age. I'd grown to full adult height—five-foot-11—by the age of 11. My voice broke at 10 and the first traces of a moustache started appearing at the age of 12. I met Anelie when I was 14½ – and was more-or-less a believable 16-year-old. I was somehow expecting to be six-foot-tall or more but once I reached five-foot-11 nothing further happened. My father put it down to 'self-abuse'. I overheard that one night after cleaning my teeth. I had to research the term – and once I'd discovered it meant masturbation, I felt like telling my father *"Don't worry Dad! Those days are over! I've got this really lovely lady friend, see – so the days of self-abuse are over! No need to buy me a wrist brace! I'm saved!"* No … life imprisonment and penal servitude in Tasmania would have resulted from that. My mother simply told my father that they should be grateful that I was the height I was – and my father, for once, said no more on the subject.

---

4   A photograph appeared many years later. It had been in the possession of my mother – and she gave it to me when I was 51 years old.

He was five-foot-two and—although a vociferous arguer—had the grace to know when he was beaten. It was rare for my mother to get the better of him – but that was one occasion when I had to stuff an entire handkerchief in my mouth to quell my laughter. My father was practically a dwarf – and with that thought 'Grumpy' came to mind from *Snow White and the Seven Dwarfs*.[5]

It occurred to me—in terms of self-abuse—that maybe my father, being short, knew about the effects of self-abuse first hand, as it were. My father had been a boy, after all, and Alice had been right about boys in general. Most of them were inveterate insecticides as well as maniacal masturbators. They seemed to love nothing more than stamping on anything that lived. It was hideous. No wonder there'd been Nazis. My German grandmother had told me about the horrors of the Nazi regime in Germany and as I looked at boys of my age I could see that another generation of Nazis were rising all around me. I was somewhat alarmist on the subject – but my mother told me that I was a little too extreme in my view. *"Zees boys vill not always be like ziss. Zay vill learn of kindness later – but I can understand very vell, vhy you like girls better at ziss time. Just—please—do not mention ziss to your farzer because he vill not understand and vill become angry viz you again."*

I was lucky my mother understood the world and could explain it to me. My father just seemed to make everything incomprehensible. According to his reasoning the problem was all to do with being a fool. He thought that somehow, I had wilfully decided to have senseless notions. My likes and dislikes had all been created in order to irritate him. I'd developed a stammer for the same reason. I'd known it would infuriate him and I'd started stammering deliberately. My mother told me that the doctor had said this was impossible – and that the doctor had had 'words' with my father. After that my father seemed to calm down a little and life became less imbued with his unaccountable rage. That was a decade in the past now – and my stammer had receded somewhat.

5   The seven dwarfs were Doc, Dopey, Bashful, Grumpy, Sneezy, Sleepy, and Happy.

It was completely absent with Anelie – and so I gained the sense of having transcended both childhood and adolescence.

I'd be 16 in June – which was the age I was supposed to have been when I'd met Anelie. By that reckoning I should now be 18 … and … slightly beyond skulduggery vis-à-vis secret assignations. Maybe things were different in Switzerland and 18-year-olds were still under the parental wing. Maybe I was fortunate that Anelie wasn't au fait with the differences between our cultural mores.

I often talked with Steve about the knife-edge of my home situation and so he was naturally edgy about what my father might do – especially with regard to Anelie, should I ever be found out.

I departed from Steve's house and—there right on cue—was Anelie, waiting just at the turning to the avenue on which Steve lived. *"Veek … 'allo I voz just laughing to myself about the 'Dong vith the Luminous Nose' from Edvard Lear – and the poem you read to me. I have the copy in my handbag."* Anelie called out to me from the car window. *"Vhen vee get back I still have the one duty of piano – then I vill be free: All-day and all-of-the-night!"* she laughed – quoting the Kinks song.

> *I'm not content to be with you in the daytime / Girl, I want to be with you all of the time / The only time I feel alright is by your side / Girl, I want to be with you all of the time / All day and all of the night.*
> Kinks, Ray Davies, *All Day and All of the Night*, 1965

"Nice one Anelie – you're getting the idea really well." Anelie had picked up my habit of quoting Rock songs. She enjoyed it because it helped her with her vernacular English – and she was getting quick at it.

"Maybe vee listen to Bob Dylan again – and you help me understanding the vords?"

"With pleasure—anything to make a lady happy—you know me."

Anelie laughed and poked me in the ribs in that way she had. *"Happy comes later after Bob Dylan!"* she laughed and I reclined in the passenger seat with a millionaire's grin.

We got back to the house and I was whisked into the granny annexe – and, as usual, no one seemed to notice me. It was the blind side of the main house and someone would have had to have been keeping watch for me to have been seen. Of course – there was no problem with Anelie having guests. It was just a matter of when they left – and so come Monday morning I'd have to lie low on the back seat with my coat over as much of me as could be managed. It always felt a little like those WWII movies where someone's being smuggled past the Nazi guards on their way to the Swiss border or wherever. I told Anelie about that and the image made her laugh. It occurred to me that she was being as dishonest as I was; me about my age – and her about her overnight guest. So ... in that we were equal. She never questioned me about my parents and I never questioned her about her employers. There were better things to talk about – such as *"Stuck inside of Mobile with the Memphis Blues again."*

"Why not – put it on and I'll scribble the words down – then you can ask me about the things that don't make sense to you."

We listened to the song—several times—whilst I wrote as rapidly as I was able.

"So ... first is this '... the post office has been stolen – and the mail box is locked' ..."

"Mmmm ... well ... the first thing that comes to mind about that ... is ..." I stretched my legs out to get comfortable *"... is that communication is impossible. Letters can't be sent and they can't be handled or delivered."*

"Yes – I see this – but ... how is the post office stolen?"

"Well it's impossible to steal a post office – so ... that probably suggests that things have got as bad as they can get if not worse." Pause. *"Of course he tells you the post office has been stolen first – so adding that the mail box is locked is almost superfluous ... but ... it adds the final seal to ... stuck inside of Mobile."*

"Yes ... and then can I ask ... why 'inside of' Mobile rather than just 'in Mobile' ... ?"

"There you've got me … Maybe it was just a matter of what would scan … but … 'inside of' does sound more trapped than 'in' … It sounds as if Mobile might even be like an engine or something – y'know, a car is an automobile – so maybe Mobile feels like some huge horrible machine." Pause. *"Also … 'Mobile' is probably just the city name he's using because of how that name sounds. The song might have nothing to do with Mobile – but with a state of mind."*

Anelie was busy making notes – and as always it made me grin and remind her that it felt strange that she was taking what I said so seriously. *"You make me feel like some kind of college professor – which is really quite … well … as long as you're happy I'll do my best. Just remember that Dylan might not mean anything like how I'm interpreting him."*

"… all the railroad men – drink your blood like wine" Anelie commenced. *"This seems simple – it seems to mean that they vill exploit you?"*

"Yes – that works."

"… but then … he just smoked my eyelids – and punched my cigarette … ?"

"That's really beyond me I think … although … if you reversed it '… he just punched my eyelids – and smoked my cigarette …' that could then mean … being beaten up and robbed – but I think that would be taking it a bit too far." Pause. *"Y'know Anelie … sometimes this stuff is just surreal … and I know that because when I write … sometimes I just get a line that works and I have no idea why."*

"Ah yes … this you see in Surrealist paintings. I always forget that it can be the same vay vith vords." Pause. *"Maybe you just tell me ven you think it is surreal?"*

"That would make it easier … I'll try my best with interpretation though – when it seems as if I can do that … or have a stab at it at least."

"Have a stab at it?" Anelie questioned

"That means trying—going for it—giving it my best shot."

"Ah – yes." Pause. *"So … then … '… he built a fire on Main Street – and shot it full of holes.' … ?"*

"I love that image ... I imagine some frontier town ... a place where you could drag some wood and build a fire before anyone got 'round to stopping you. Then you'd stand there with a crazed look on your face emptying your gun into it." Pause. *"It's a powerful image – and I guess grandpa's lost control ... Maybe there you have to look at the whole verse about people being shocked and of course grandpa's already buried in the rock ... so maybe this is some really tough old timer – railing against trespasses on his freedom. I think there's a lot of empathy for the Old West – and maybe grandpa's some hippie from the end of the 1800s and he's become a symbol of something that's happening now."*

"... and then—the next verse does not seem so difficult—but then ... here '... the preacher looked so baffled - when I asked him why he dressed with twenty pounds of headlines – stapled to his chest ...' "

That sounded fairly simple to me so I ploughed right in. *"I'd say 'twenty pounds of headlines – stapled to his chest' was just another way of saying that the preacher was crippled by the indoctrination he'd accepted."*

"Ah ... yes ... I can see this now – so twenty *pounds of headlines ... is the newspapers and the misinformation they often have? And stapled means that he can't get it out of his mind?"*

"That's what I'd say ..."

"Good ... so '... the rainman gave men two cures' ... 'Texas medicine and ... railroad gin ... and he mixed them ... his mind is strangled ... and people get uglier ... and he has no sense of time."

I burst out laughing at that point. *"Sorry Anelie – I have to give up on that one. I have no idea what a 'rainman' might be ... I hear him singing 'ragman' which might be another word for a hobo or tramp ... but Texas medicine and railroad gin ... no idea other than that he had two extremely bad alternatives and made the mistake of trying them both at the same time ..."*[6]

"... so again—the next verse is not so hard—but then '... you must know about my debutante – and she says 'Your debutante knows just what you need – but I know what you want ...'"?"

---

6   *Texas medicine* is slang for mescaline. *Railroad gin* is slang for brake fluid.

"Mmmm … well … you know what a debutante is …" I asked and Anelie nodded. *"So it seems unlikely that he's in a position to know one of those … so maybe it's simply a reversal of images – as a debutante would probably be more inclined to want than need. When you're poor you usually need rather than want – wanting tends to come later."*

"Ja!" Anelie laughed *"Soon we are finished! Then needing and wanting can all happen!"* Pause. *"… so … who are the neon madmen? The rest is simple."*

"… the neon madmen … no idea … Y'know Anelie – I think Dylan sometimes just throws these images in for the colour and for their … incongruity … Then … there's simply the sound of the words – and, of course, that probably applies to a lot of the phrases that I've interpreted …"

Anelie finished writing her notes on Bob Dylan's song and we tumbled into the night.

The days and weeks rolled by – and then suddenly, as if it were entirely unexpected, Anelie was gone. *Gone, gone, gone beyond, gone completely beyond.* She was gone permanently sans address. That's the way she wanted it. I could see the sense of it from her point of view. Anelie was a strange mixture of romanticism and pragmatism. She was evidently sad to leave me behind – but … she knew that our lives could no longer coincide. She had career plans in Switzerland. I had Art School ahead – even though it was two years later than she imagined. I also had a Blues band who relied on me for vocals – and so there was no realistic space for trips to Switzerland. That was how it had been arranged from the beginning – and there was no way to change what we'd arranged. I'd agreed to the temporary nature of our liaison – and it would have been both doltish and churlish to complain when the end became a reality. I'd been an adult … and now … I was something else – with two months wanting for my 16th birthday.

Steve and Ron had mentioned the need of a percussionist. I was less bothered – but happy to go along with the idea; as long as it didn't intrude into the ethos we had evolved as a trio.

I'd hardly settled to the idea that we needed a percussionist when Jack Hackman turned up. He'd entered Farnham Grammar School that year – because his parents had moved from Wiltshire. Steve came to know Jack was a drummer in the usual way – as music was everyday conversation in the 1960s. Jack could perform fancy drum rolls on the school desk with improvised drumsticks and Steve concluded he was worthy of an introduction. *"Jack has a … weird hairstyle* [7] *– but he seems competent. I think we should try him out."*

I thought that was good – but Ron was wary *"I … hope he didn't get the idea we'll take him on just like that. We need to be able to tell him if he's not good enough."*

Steve looked a little put out *"Well—naturally—Ron. He knows he's coming for a try-out."*

"Well …" I chimed in *"… when do we put Jack to the rack?"*

Jack came. We launched into Rolling and Tumbling. Jack played along. Ron frowned. Steve and I looked sheepish when we noticed Ron's expression. Ron—with the expression of an exasperated parent—motioned for Jack to leave his drums. Ron motioned Steve and I to play – so I hit out a simple 12 bar on Ron's Telecaster. Ron then proceeded to show Jack how to play Blues percussion. After a few rounds of 12 bar Ron handed the drumsticks back to Jack asking *"Can you do that?"* Jack nodded and complied. He stumbled a few times but after a couple of minutes he had it down. It was an arduously difficult audition for Jack—who looked highly anxious throughout—but Ron accepted him in the end, on the condition that he put in a great deal of serious practice.

Suddenly, we were a band. Suddenly we needed a name. We spent an evening brainstorming it and we ended up with The Savage Cabbage Blues Band. Then—unexpectedly—I was also named. Farquhar Arbuthnot. Who'd ever heard of such a name?

---

7   Jack had a mullet. The 6th Century Byzantine scholar Procopius observed that some young male factions wore their hair long at the back and sides and short over the forehead. This non-Roman style was termed 'Hunnic'. The mullet began to be worn in the mid to late 1960s, but became highly popular in the 1970s – favoured by performers such as Paul McCartney, Rod Stewart, and David Bowie.

However, Steve Bruce, Ron Larkin, and Jack Hackman were all good Blues Band names – but Victor Howard Simmerson … was deemed docile. I either had to sound dangerous – or weird. I put in a bid for Frank Schubert – but although Ron liked it, Jack didn't – and, as I'd come up with Savage Cabbage, he thought it only fair that I should accept my new name gracefully. I accepted gracefully – as who was I to be *self*-protective?

9

like seeing angels

1967

Back in '65, Steve and I noticed that the world was changing. We were both changing. Our hair had started to cover our ears – and certain care had to be taken, both at school and with parents. We'd have to position ourselves front-ways as much as possible so that the length of our hair was not as obvious from the back or sides. The military 'short back and sides' was long gone for us – and we intended it should remain long gone. I might be a Buddhist – but the celibate-crop, although somehow perfect for Tibetan monastics, was not a workable arrangement for a Buddhist Bluesman. I knew that Son House[1] had once been a preacher – and so there was obviously a respectable tradition of religion and Blues. Son House had sung *John the Revelator* – and it occurred to me that maybe I'd do the same one day when the right Buddhist theme caught my attention.

> *You know Christ had twelve apostles and three he laid away* / *He said "Watch with me one hour, 'til I go yonder and pray." / Tell me who's that writing: John the Revelator. / Tell me who's that writing: John the Revelator. / Who's that writing: John the Revelator. / Wrote the book of the seven seals.* Son House, *John the Revelator*

---

1 Eddie James 'Son' House, Junior (1902–1988) was a Blues musician—noted for slide guitar—with a highly emotional singing style. Initially a preacher and church pastor he was hostile to Blues, but he turned to Blues performance at the age of 25. He quickly developed a unique style by applying the rhythmic drive, vocal power ,and emotional intensity of his preaching to the newly learned idiom. In a short career interrupted by a spell in Parchman Farm penitentiary, he developed to the point that Charley Patton invited him to share engagements, and to accompany him to a 1930 recording session for Paramount Records.

Steve thought that was quite possible because George Harrison had written songs with a Hindustani Classical Music slant on the Beatles' *Revolver.*[2]

"I think you could do something like that – because you have a style when you experiment with riffing that sounds kind of Eastern, y'know."

I pondered it for a while – and put something together. The problem was that it was far more difficult than I imagined – and it was clunky, and somehow silly. It seemed that Vajrayana didn't really suit itself to this song form – well, not in this way. I would have to look for some other way of approaching it.

> *Pema Jung-né had twenty five disciples / And he told 'em all where to stay / Said "Climb up to those caves and practise – you'll hear me teach again someday." / Tell me who's that flying: Lady Yeshé Tsogyel. / Tell me who's that flying: Lady Yeshé Tsogyel. Tell me who's that flying: Lady Yeshé Tsogyel./ Wrote the texts that'd be revealed.*
> Vic Simmerson – Padmasambhava and Yeshé Tsogyel

Steve nodded *"Maybe you could accompany it with that wild thing you made – that massive great sitar thing."*

"Oh that …" I groaned *"That was a disaster. It was never any use for anything. It was just a plank of wood with an entirely useless attempt at a sound-box."*

"It had 16 strings didn't it?"

---

2 *Love You To* was George Harrison's first venture into Hindustani classical music and is set in the scale of C minor, in Dorian mode. George Harrison recorded the track with musicians from the London Asian Music Circle, who provided instrumentation such as tabla, swarmandal, and tambura – with George Harrison on sitar.
Within You Without You was an essay in cross-cultural fusion: rock music and meditative philosophy. The track features tempo rubato which is without precedent in the Beatles' material. The key in which it is set is Khamaj, which is similar to the Mixolydian mode. The track ends with laughter – on which George Harrison commented *"… It's a release after five minutes of sad music ... You were supposed to hear the audience anyway, as they listen to Sergeant Pepper's Show – and that was the style of the album."*

"Yeah … 28 if you count the 12 sympathetic strings – and all with the clunky steel tuning rods I made in the metalwork class. The problem was that it would have made a better contraption for Robin Hood – as the strain of the strings practically bent it double. It would have been easier to fire arrows with it than play music on it."

The sun was slanting in erratic cascades through the window of Steve's living room. It was an eerie effect because it intermittently transformed the room visually. It expanded and contracted. The light shrank the space and the sudden absence of sunlight seemed to make the room grow in size. As these impressions were fizzing between my ears the White Lady appeared and I sat there staring for a moment – and then she was gone.

"Vic?" Steve had been repeating *"Vic – are you alright?"*

"Fine Steve" and my voice sounded as if it had come from some great distance. I could hear myself speaking but it was as if I was not there in the room with Steve – and yet I was.

"What happened?" Steve enquired *"Your eyes looked as if … as if you weren't seeing anything."*

I really didn't know what to say. I didn't want to have to explain – but neither did I want to shut Steve out.

"This is going to sound weird Steve – but … I feel that I ought to tell you …"

"You suffer from epilepsy …" Steve asked in apparent anxiety. He'd had a cousin who had epilepsy and so he'd heard things about it from his parents.

"No Steve" I laughed *"Nothing like that – well, not as far as I know. It's just that there's this White Lady … I've been seeing her since I was … since I was a baby I suppose. She used to appear in dreams every night at one time – and sometimes outside dreams."*

"Daydreams?"

"No … I suppose I'd have to call them visions … or something."

"Like Christian saints seeing angels?" Steve asked – but not in a mocking way.

141

"I really don't know, Steve … I can't say what happens – because I've never talked with anyone about them. If I was a Christian … I could talk to the vicar, or Bishop, or whatever – but there's no one I can go to with this. I'd have to go to Tibet—and I'd have to learn Tibetan—and that would all be years away …" Pause. *"… I used to talk to my mother about them a long time ago."*

"What did she say?"

"Y'know … I really can't remember too well. I think she thought they were dreams. Well … some of them were – but some of them were definitely not dreams. I made the mistake of telling my father and he thought I'd end up in the mental hospital. It was really quite a bad time – because I was too young to deal with him being the thought police or whatever."

"So does she speak to you?"

"No …" I shook my head *"I don't 'hear voices' or anything like that. She doesn't speak – but she … she seems to—and this will sound totally weird— she seems to operate like some sort of television transmitter – and … I seem to receive what she transmits – but it's never in words. I just know certain things – but there are no words for it. It's like knowing that you feel happy or sad or relaxed."* Pause. *"I mean, how would you explain 'feeling happy' if there wasn't anything you were happy about?"*

Steve admitted that he didn't know. He'd just have to say that he felt happy and had nothing he could add. *"So … was she there, just then?"*

I became silent at that point because I felt rather strange about the answer I was going to give *"Yes … but only for a moment … and then she was gone."*

"It wasn't a moment Vic – you were gone somewhere for a few minutes."

I told Steve that it hadn't felt longer then a moment – but that time did tend to lose its usual linear form when I had visions. Steve sat silently for some moments and said *"Y'know … if anyone else had told me that, I wouldn't have believed it – but I can tell that this is not made up and it's not insane either … I just don't know what it is."*

"I'm glad we can talk about it – or I'd have no one at all to talk to about it. I don't think you should mention it to your parents or anyone else – because … it's just not understandable. Even I don't understand it and it happens to me."

"No, Vic …. I won't mention it. I can see that wouldn't be … that wouldn't be such a good idea – but you'll tell me if it happens again?"

"Yes. I'll tell you whatever you want to know – but it might not make sense. It doesn't make sense to me in everyday words. A lot of the time, I just have no words for it. I can tell you what I see – but I can't tell you about the sense of 'meaning' that happens. I mean … when I seem to know something – but don't know what it is that I know." This was sounding increasingly ridiculous and Steve had shrugged in complete incomprehension – so I said *"Maybe it's better to put it like this: why do you like Camembert?"*

"Because it tastes good."

"Alright – what is it that tastes good about it?"

Suddenly there was a look in Steve's face that told me he'd understood something *"Right … now I think I understand. I just can't say why I like Camembert – all I can say is that I like it. I could say its creamy – but so is Brie. I could say all kinds of things but they wouldn't really explain anything. I don't think my father could explain why he likes Jazz—and the same for my mother with Classical music—or you with Blues."*

"That's right. I just heard it one day and liked it. I could say that it was different and exciting because it was different – but now there's plenty of Blues around and I still like it. I also know that I always—will—like Blues. "

Some weeks later, I heard Mike Cooper[3] play at the Farnham Blues Festival at the Bush Hotel – and I tried to emulate what I remembered of his style.

---

3   Mike Cooper was born in Reading, England in 1942. He began playing guitar in Skiffle bands at the age of 16. His style changed in 1961 on seeing Sonny Terry and Brownie McGhee at Reading Town Hall. He co-founded the *Blues Committee* and played Country Blues as a solo artist – opening for many American Blues Artists. He met Ian A. Anderson in 1967 and recorded three EPs for the SayDisc label – released later as an LP entitled *The Inverted World*. He associated with many British Blues musicians, including Michael Chapman, John Martyn, Ralph McTell, Roy Harper, and the young Ngakpa Chögyam (*Victor Howard Simmerson*) – then performing as Frank Schubert.

He'd come on stage with two National ResoPhonic guitars [4]– a Tricone and a Style 'O'. I'd been hypnotised both by the way they looked and the way they sounded. This was music from s*omewhere else entirely* – Africa and the Mississippi Delta, or from some distant galaxy where guitars were made of steel, and cars were made of pressed flowers. The reversal was amazing to me. These were guitars as guitars *should* be. I told Steve about it and he was intrigued. We asked his father about them and he knew enough to tell us that we'd be unlikely to find them in Britain.

I decided I'd have to make my own National ResoPhonic guitar. I was given to entertaining entirely impossible projects – like being a solitary Buddhist in the Home Counties … So I found a wreck of a Spanish guitar that was going for a pittance because it was in such bad condition. I bought it from a bric-a-brac shop called *Dawn's Bargains*. I knew enough about guitars to talk Dawn down by one pound and ten shillings. I pointed out the bowed neck and shocking condition of the varnish. I pointed out the serious cracks in the soundboard and the dents in the sides where it had obviously taken knocks.

I worked on it for three months and by the end of that time the beat-out old nylon strung guitar became something of a wonder. It wasn't fit for playing conventionally – but it was *just-about-suitable* for playing lap slide vaguely like Mike Cooper. I decided to call it the Debil after the way 'Devil' was sometimes pronounced in Blues songs. The Debil was a *diabolical* creation—not, perhaps in the infernal sense—but musically. It was like a cross between a hurdy-gurdy and a dustbin. It did have, however, a body that was almost as perfect as a vintage Rolls Royce or Bentley. This was due to the effort I'd put into burnishing the silver car enamel with which I'd coated the body.

---

4   The resonator guitar was invented by John Dopyera (1893–1988) born in Dolna Krupa, Slovakia. His father Joseph Dopyera was a violin maker. On the approach of WWI, the family emigrated to California. Arriving in LA, he began to make and repair violins. A local vaudeville promoter—George Beauchamp—asked him if he could create a louder guitar to be heard against brass Jazz instruments. The solution was a metal bodied guitar with three aluminium-alloy cones that acoustically amplified the strings. He and his brothers set up the National Stringed Instrument Corp. in 1927.

The paint killed the sound but that was compensated by the rattling of the contents – and the shock of its visual appearance. The inside of the DEBIL was crammed with ferrotype diaphragms which buzz-crackled like crazy at anything above 60° Fahrenheit. That was important because without activating those ferrotype diaphragms – the DEBIL was somewhat restrained. It weighed about 11 lbs when it was all put together with the aluminium cover-plate and perforated zinc. I drilled several hundred holes in concentric rings. The central sound hole was backed with a piece of perforated zinc – and the result was visually magnificent.

The word DEBIL was etched into a copper plate—through which the tuning heads emerged—and the lettering, filled with emerald-green gloss-paint, was partially rubbed away. The result therefore looked a little like verdigris – and gave it an air of … mysteriousness. DEBIL was also etched into the tailpiece and into the brace on the back so that it all looked as if it had actually been manufactured – well at least to anyone who was not too familiar with guitars.

My father had helped me – because he'd caught me in mid-manufacture. I'd been working on the project in secret in the bicycle shed – and he'd taken pity on me, as he had done with the Skiffle Junior back in '64. If I wanted a guitar *that* badly … then he may as well help me make the best job I could. He was good too—brilliant in fact—and he seemed to know everything there was to know about tools and abrasives. He'd been in the Royal Engineers and had a great deal of experience working with all manner of materials. For once he found a good student in me and I'd worked on my guitar project for untold hours.

I bought a tailpiece and a bridge to replace the combined unit that was stuck to the body. Even though steel-strung guitars had similar bridge-tailpiece assemblies – I wanted to create as much distance as I could from the reviled nylon-strung guitar it once had been.

The neck was bowed so I made a brace for it to take the strain of steel strings. Then I replaced the nut to increase the height of the action right down the neck.

Once that was done, I could use my section of chromium bath-towel rail to slide up those strings as if I'd been born in the Mississippi Delta.

I took to playing harp as well and started collecting what would be the complete set of 12 – so I'd have them in all keys.[5] Again I had to listen to albums to copy the style – but I was determined to be a Blues musician at any cost. I listened to Little Walter and Big Walter Horton. They were so interestingly different – and what amazed me was that I found harp much easier to play than guitar. I could actually get somewhere on an instrument like this. After some months of practice, I asked Steve to play a Blues in D in order that I could accompany him on my G harp.[6]

"Where did you learn to do – that!" Steve asked in vague astonishment. "You're not Little Walter – but you're not very far away either."

"Thank you" I grinned "I'm Vicariously Vic Something-or-other!"

"Whatever something-or-other you are – Ron's got to hear this!"

And so he did. It seemed that I'd be playing harp with THE SAVAGE CABBAGE BLUES BAND.

5   As explained by Mr Love, a Blues harp player needs 12 harps to cover every key in the chromatic range.

6   This is called 'cross harp' i.e. when the harp chosen is a fourth above the key of the song. This means that although the harp is in a major key – it hits minor notes in the key of the song.

10

it's like being a hermit

june 1968

I'd gained familiarity with the wrathful awareness beings and protectors of Vajrayana, and wouldn't have describe my father as an ogre [1] – even though Lindsay and her friend Sandra described him thus. The older I became, the more sadness I sensed behind his anger. He was not a bad man at all – simply a man who had made some unfortunate choices. He'd had unrealistic expectations of his promotion in the Army – and was too proud to accept his lot as a working-class officer. The situation was not fair – but neither are many other forms of elitism, chauvinism, and racism. One can fight these things—and it is good to fight them—but the consequences of fighting need to be accepted. It seems there was no one to tell him how to play the game. Maybe there were. Maybe he didn't listen. I would never know – because it was not possible to have a conversation with him. I had to guess at the source of his bitterness from the clues he threw out from time to time.

I tried to be *as good a Buddhist as I could be* in terms of how I thought of him – and I knew that trying to understand his background was the best way to go about it. It's not easy to understand a working-class Tory – who has occasional unexpected bouts of socialism. He exclaimed several times on the unfairness of a furrier's employee never being able to buy his wife a coat such as the ones he had made. There were many aspects of life that he could not reconcile with being a working-class Tory. There were many aspects of life that he could not fathom at all. I was one of them.

---

1   Nod-zhin (*gNod sByin*) ogre, troll, goblin, or hobgoblin.

Sandra lived up the road from where Alice used to live – the last house on the left before Weyflood Woods. Sandra's parents owned an MG MGB GT.[2] It was a thing of wonder. It seemed marvellous that a car could be named after a series of initials like that – and being able to reel them off gave me some bizarre credit with the boys in my class. Lindsay had wanted to call on my father and give him a piece of her mind – but Sandra thought that would be unwise. She thought it would get me into even more trouble. Lindsay and Sandra could only compare him with their own fathers – who were considerably younger.

My father was bent out of shape by being an Edwardian—with a strong dose of Victorian morality—in post WWII England. He was born in 1902 and so he was probably more-or-less a fair man – for the time and culture with which he was familiar. Genghis Khan[3] was a fair man for his time too. He'd ride up to a city with his army and give the populace three choices. The first choice was that the populace could stay and life would go on exactly as it did before – only they'd become part of Genghis Khan's growing empire. The second choice was that they could all leave – and they'd not be hindered. They could take what they needed and hit the road. The third choice was that they could attempt to defend their city – but if they did that and lost, every last inhabitant would be put to the sword. They all went for the first choice – and ... life simply continued, but with the added safety of Genghis Khan's rule. Now if you look at Genghis Khan and judge him by modern criteria – he was an imperialist warlord bent on world dominion. Now ... my father wasn't exactly Genghis Khan – but there *were* certain similarities. Things would have been better if I'd taken option one.

---

2   MG MGB. The MGB is a two-door sports car manufactured by the British Motor Corporation as a four-cylinder, soft-top roadster from 1962 until 1980. Variants include the MG MGB GT three-door 2+2 coupé (1965–1980).

3   Genghis Khan (1162–1227) was the founder of the Mongol Empire, which became the largest contiguous empire in history after his death. He came to power by uniting the nomadic tribes of northeast Asia. After founding the Mongol Empire, he commenced the invasions which resulted in the conquest of most of Eurasia. By the time of his death his empire covered a huge portion of Central Asia and China.

My memories of early childhood are what they are. It's important to state that my father could often be generous. He built a climbing frame on which Græham and I enjoyed many hours of amusement. He was actually pleased with me when I learnt how to hang upside-down in that thing. It was only *sport* I disliked – and it came as a relief to him whenever I did anything that made it look as if I was a normal boy. My father sometimes came home with special gastronomic treats such as gammon. Then we'd have a feast with chips and fried eggs.

It's hard to frame a realistic picture of Major Ernest Mathers Simmerson – Royal Engineers, Retired. His generosity tended to be eclipsed—in my young mind—by his rule-of-iron. He was an old-fashioned martinet. His anger was his own problem – and he suffered from it probably more than I ever did. He had a sense of moral order which was at odds with society. The social order—as it was—enraged him on a daily basis. Edwardian England had vanished and he seemed unprepared to accept the fact. Britain had won the war and lost the peace – in terms, at least, of the societal mores he valued. The end of the war was to have betokened the beginning of a life that he was to have enjoyed – but as soon as the war was over, the rules started changing. The social mores became increasingly mutable. People kissed on television and there was no public outrage. Brief glimpses of bosoms had appeared in films – and no one was imprisoned for the offence.

He'd lived in a time when *Lady Chatterley's Lover*[4] had been a scandal. – and when public outrage was roused at Rhett Butler telling Scarlett O'Hara *'Quite frankly my dear, I don't—give—a damn.'*[5]

4   *Lady Chatterley's Lover* by DH Lawrence was published privately in Florence in 1928. It could not be published openly in Britain 'til 1960. It was notorious for its narrative which concerned: the physical relationship between a working-class man and an aristocratic woman; its descriptions of sexuality; and use of censorable language.

5   A quotation from the 1939 film *'Gone with the Wind'* starring Clark Gable and Vivien Leigh – as Rhett Butler and Scarlett O'Hara. These are Rhett Butler's last words to Scarlett O'Hara when she asks him *'Where shall I go? What shall I do?'* The line contains the profanity 'damn' which was generally not allowed in films of that time period. Prior to the film's release, censors objected to the use of the word 'damn' as the word had been prohibited by the 1930 Motion Picture Association's Production Code of 1934.

He raged alone and unheard. My mother would agree with him to keep the peace – but I knew she had a far broader mind. If I'd understood his pain, I would have cried for him – but I had no concept as to why his jaw stiffened every time he heard the news.

By 1968 he was 66 years old and had already begun a decline in which he incrementally mellowed. My father had always seemed old. He was 22 years older than my mother – and sadly he made her older, rather than she making him younger. The year 1968 turned out to be the last year of my father's reign as Monarch of 17 Woodsfield Lane, as far as my life went – because *the times they were a-changing.*

Shortly after my sixteenth birthday my father threw down the gauntlet. The ultimatum was in respect of the length of my hair. I had to get a 'conventional haircut'—by which he meant a military 'short back and sides'—or leave home. I took Genghis Khan's Option 2. Option 3—fighting—was a dishonourable option for me. It was his house and he was working to pay the mortgage, pay the bills, and put food on the table.

"Alright Dad, I'll leave." I sighed. *"I understand your position – and I bear you no ill will."*

I extended my arm—to shake hands—as if I was a character from *Jeeves and Wooster*.[6] He took my hand with a look of eerie bafflement on his face. We shook hands. I went off to pack. Thinking these would be the last words I would ever exchange with my father, I'd wanted the words that I used to be good words rather than words I'd regret. Strangely I felt no anger and no resentment toward my father. I simply felt like an independent adult. It was somehow nobler to be polite. It would have been ignoble—and actually childish, from my point of view—to have had some sort of altercation.

---

6   *'Jeeves and Wooster'* was a British comedy series adapted from PG Wodehouse's 'Jeeves' stories. Bertie Wooster, is a young bachelor and minor aristocrat (*a blend of nonchalant naïveté and refined discombobulation*) and Jeeves is his ingenious quick-witted valet. The stories are set in the 1920s and 1930s.

This came as a complete surprise to my father. My wishing to shake his hand on being cast from the parental home had clearly thrown him. It must have seemed the most unlikely response. What I failed to cognise was that when I'd extended my hand, I'd given him no choice but to accept it. He was an Edwardian Major, after all.

The last thing he could have imagined was that I'd willingly head off into nowhere – with the possibility of no roof over my head and nowhere to sleep other than some hostel for the destitute or an obliging tree. I'd have chosen any field or hedgerow rather than an institution – but I had no idea where I'd go.

My mother was horrified – and, entirely at a loss for how to handle the situation. Her husband was obdurate – but so was her son. Neither would listen to reason. Well, that's not entirely true. I did *listen* to reason—I would never have refused to *listen* to my mother —I just failed to agree with the nature of her reasoning. It suggested compromise – but the time for compromise was over. It had been over since the Beatles' *Revolver* album in '66. I'd had one haircut too many. I presented my Mother with my reasoning *"I'm sorry mum – but I'm 16. No one owns my body but me. I own my hair. No one else owns any part of me. No one has the right to alter any part of my body without my agreement."*

I imagine I may have been the person who invented the broken record technique in terms of that argument.[7] Whatever was said it came back to the fact that I had to have the final choice of anything that concerned my body. No one owned me. I was not breaking any law. I was just demanding the right to sole control of my appearance. My father had to accept that—as far as my body was concerned—I was *beyond his command*. I'd not exactly become rebellious. Far from it. I just insisted on governing my own appearance.

---

7   After 1970 assertiveness came to be viewed as a behavioural skill and was taught by personal development experts, behaviour therapists, and cognitive behavioural therapists. The term and concept was popularised to the general public by books such as *Your Perfect Right: A Guide to Assertive Behaviour* published in 1970 by Robert E. Alberti, and *When I Say No, I Feel Guilty: How To Cope Using the Skills of Systematic Assertiveness Therapy* (1975) by Manuel J Smith.

I was quite willing to acquiesce in all other areas – such as the volume I played music and the tidiness of my room. This was no problem for me because I was never a head-banger in terms of volume. I was also naturally, or perhaps unnaturally, tidy.

The strangest event then transpired. My father conceded. He told me I was free to look as I chose – but warned me that my choice would damage my chances of any decent livelihood. I told him I understood – but I was willing to take that risk. That was then the end of the matter. It was never discussed again.

After the brief but intense hair debacle, my father and I entered a new phase of relationship in which I became *the good son* – the son who never argued or took issue with his political views. My father was a staunch Conservative – which was difficult for me because I found myself with decidedly Marxist Anarchist leanings. It was my brother Græham who suddenly rose up to champion the cause of youth-rebelliousness in the house and challenged my father whenever he said anything too absurdly right-wing.

Steve had been there every step of the way on my *road to freedom* – because I'd given him a running commentary on the state of play with my father. Steve never came round to my house because he found my father too unlike his own to connect in any way. My father was like something out of Charles Dickens as far as Steve was concerned. He could talk with his own father—and mother— almost adult-to-adult – but my father would not allow any such relationship. I could understand Steve's reaction entirely.

"How d'you stand it?" Steve asked *"I mean … you're Lieutenant Loony – how can you—not—go crazy? It must be like being a hermit …"*

"Well I may be Field Marshall Mayhem; General Disorder; Brigadier Bizarre; Major Débâcle; Captain Chaos; Warrant-officer Weird; Sergeant Surreal; or, even Private Parts …" I added – interrupting Steve's flow *"… but I am also some kind of hermit. A Buddhist is always—some kind —of hermit."*

"… very funny—but seriously—how can you have any kind of conversation with him?"

"I can't."

"But does that ... isn't that like ..."

"Like being a hermit" I interjected – finishing Steve's sentence for him. *"Yes – it's like being a hermit."*

"But you're free-thinking ... You've got more far-out ideas than a deck of cards – and you reshuffle them and deal them on the spur of the moment, as if there was no tomorrow – and you like to talk about all that."

"I like to talk about ideas, Steve – but it's not compulsory. I don't explode or implode if I can't talk."

"I'm amazed you can switch on and off like that ..."

"Well ... I've had some training in it."

"Training?" Steve laughed in surprise.

"Silent sitting meditation." Steve looked perplexed – so I explained. *"In silent sitting meditation you let go of thoughts. You let go of everything that comes up: all the ideas; all the plans; everything. You remain uninvolved – so, when I'm at home I can remain uninvolved with the need to express myself."*

"That's ..." Pause. *"... quite a thing ... you must have a hell of a lot of self-control."*

"Kind of you to say, Steve – but 'self' control isn't so much of an issue when you're trying to let go of the idea of 'self' – you only have to control the 'self' when 'self' is a big deal."

Steve laughed *"But your 'long-haired self' was an extremely big deal—if I'm not mistaken—or is there some fine point of logic I'm not understanding?"*

"Good point, Steve – you've got me there" I grinned *"I'll have to think about that ..."* Almost a minute passed. *"Well ... you're right, of course – and theoretically it should not matter how I look. I should not have made my mother unhappy ... that was selfish of me – and I should have ... Hell, I don't know how I could have done it any differently."* Pause. *"I'm not 'enlightened'—you see—I'm nowhere near ... I'm nowhere near even being able to say 'I'm nowhere near'. I may never get anywhere – so I do my best to let go of 'self' when that sense of 'self' would exist purely to be embattled against something ... where there doesn't* need *to be a battle.*

"So … my hair's part of my creative life as a Bluesman – and that's something that would affect you when you're on stage with me."

"Yeah – I can see that … that does makes sense."

"But more than that, it's part of my sense of appreciation – and so I need to be able to let my appreciation expand." Pause. *"And anyway – how would you and Ron like a vocalist with a short back and sides?"*

"Jesus no! That would ruin our image completely! No one would take us seriously if you looked like a squaddie."[8]

"Exactly." Pause. *"So … this 'self' thing … it's a knotty problem … in terms of my understanding of Buddhism …"* and there words failed me. *"You see … because I'm still trying to make 'lack of self' fit with compassion … because compassion includes everyone and everything, everywhere – and that includes 'me' – whatever 'that' might be. And compassion is also appreciation. So, I can't just brutalise myself because that would be 'the selfless thing to do'. That wouldn't be good for my father in the long run. All I'd do then, would be to help him make me miserable and spoil things for you and Ron and Savage Cabbage."*

"Yeah … I can see that too – but what have compassion and appreciation got to do with each other?"

"Well … compassion—in the Buddhist sense—can't be divided from appreciation – or from love, desire, passion, and lust …"

"That makes compassion sound a lot more interesting than religion usually makes it – not that I'd like to be uncompassionate – but it's always seemed a bit too 'holy' for me."

"Exactly, Steve. Compassion is massively appreciative *rather than being 'holy' – and you know me – I'm not exactly holy, am I?"*

Steve chuckled at this *"Not exactly – no. I can't see you being holy where Anelie's concerned – so it's just as well there's lust involved with Buddhist compassion."*

---

8   1960's British slang for soldier.

"Well … it's not exactly 'lust' as we usually understand it – it's the …" Pause. *"… it's lust without labels … lust without any idea of dividing lines between the one who's lusting and what is being lusted after. It's when everything is happening simultaneously – and there's no observer in your head watching it all and making a documentary out of it. It's extremely hard to explain."* Pause. *"But anyway … that's why it's such a knotty problem for me when that runs into not taking my mother into consideration when I was prepared to leave home."*

"You didn't think about what she was feeling at all?" Steve asked in a slightly horrified voice.

"Yes … I did, Steve." Pause. *"That was, what was extremely difficult about it. It was painful – but, there seemed no choice. I mean, even if I'd backed down it would have pained my mother to see me unhappy. More than that – my mother and father would have had rows about it. I thought of—*all of that—*when I made my choice."* Pause. *"You see … I haven't quite found an answer yet in terms of how to act for the best in every situation – but I will find an answer one day. I just have to keep sitting and it'll come to me."*

Steve looked quizzical *"So how does the 'lack-of-self' work with it being alright not to be able to have conversations with your father? Isn't that … horrible?"*

*"No … it's just what it is. You see … my father is empty—*as far as I can see—*of anything that would interest me. He has been to India and China and I have asked him about that – but he has nothing interesting to say about it. He does tell stories – but they're all about Army life and the complex problems he had dealing with people who couldn't complete work on time. He never explored Indian or Chinese culture – so questions got nowhere."* Pause. *"Anyway … we don't have conversations when my father's around. He talks and expects us to listen – but that's no problem to me, as I can just sit and listen. There's no need to say anything – and y'know, as long as he leaves my appearance alone – it's actually perfect."*

"Perfect!" Steve spluttered.

"Yes. Perfect. My mother's happy now – especially as I'm always polite to my father. I always defer to his opinion. I can let him rant on about hanging and flogging—and the evils of Communism, and glories of the British Empire—and everything else …"

"So you just agree with him?"

"Yes – or, at least, I appear to agree with him. I don't really agree with him – but as I can't change him by disagreeing with him, there's nothing to be gained by it. So it's perfect. It's also perfect because I don't have to cut my hair again— ever—and … now … I wear what I like … and … what more *could I want. I can talk with you. I can talk with my brother Græham. I can talk with my mother—and—I can talk enough with your parents. Your father and mother are brilliant – and so I don't think I miss out on anything. I get to talk with Mr Preece the English teacher on the way to school – and … well, it's all fine."*

"It's fine that Anelie's gone back to Switzerland?"

"No Steve … 'fine' is what it's—not—but …" Pause. *"Yeah … I know what you mean."* I sighed *"I'm in a ridiculous situation now – and … really I should have known all along that I'd end up in a ludicrous situation."*

"What's ludicrous about it? You had a fantastic clear run – and, came though without being caught! I think that's totally brilliant!"

"Yes … if you look at it like that." Pause. *"… but that's not what I'm saying … My situation is ridiculous because I've turned into Doctor Who.[9] I've time travelled to my own future – or what might be my own future. I've had two years of … completely adult relationship with Anelie – and now I'm back in the present without an adjectival time machine."*

"Oh … right … yeah … I see … but at least you've time travelled – you should be grateful. I'd swap lives with you any day!"

"With my father and a stammer?"

---

9   Doctor Who is a British science-fiction BBC television programme which began in 1963. It depicts the adventures of a Time Lord called 'the Doctor' from the planet Gallifrey. He explores the universe in a time-machine called the TARDIS which resembles a police telephone box. Having gained a cult following Doctor Who became part of British popular culture.

"Alright—point taken—but I think you need to be grateful for the good time you've had."

"Yes Steve … I am. I know what you mean. I am grateful. I'm enormously grateful – but I'm also quite sad y'know."

"Yes … I can understand that. I think I'd be sad too – but, as I said, at least your father never caught up with you on that. He'd have hit the ceiling."

That made me grin. *"Difficult at his height, weight, and age, Steve."* Steve howled with laughter – and when he'd got over it I continued *"But … y'know … I have the feeling that my father could've coped with it. My mother certainly would've coped with it – and … my father might even've been relieved to have definitive proof that I'm not homosexual."*

"What!?" Steve exclaimed staring in disbelief.

"Didn't I ever tell you about that?"

Steve shook his head. *"No. I mean how …?"*

"Because I hate sport and … because I'm artistic … I write poetry – and preferred the company of girls when I was young."

"Yeah really that makes a lot of sense—that—does!" Steve laughed *"I've never heard that liking girls makes you a homosexual!"*

"As Hamlet said … '… therefore, as a stranger, give it welcome. There are more things in heaven and earth, Horatio, than are dreamt of in your philosophy …' [10] *So, although his suspicions were something I found uncomfortable … they did at least make it less likely that he'd ever suspect me of having a 22 year old Swiss girlfriend."*

"Very funny – but seriously, that's the looniest thing I ever heard."

"The funniest thing is actually the fact that our *being such good friends put his mind at ease – I mean … we could have been sodomising each other senseless for all he knew."*

"Buggered if that appeals to me!" Steve laughed.

"Quite so." Pause. *"Of course – there were other things that my father suspected."*

10 William Shakespeare, Hamlet Act I, Scene v.

"Such as?"

"Such as my having some kind of mental condition – on the basis that he sometimes found me meditating. Of course, what he saw was me sitting there motionless."

"Did you have to do that when he was around – I mean, couldn't you have been more secretive about it?"

"I tried y'know, I'd only ever meditate in my bedroom – but he had a habit of walking into my bedroom unexpectedly and asking me why I was sitting on the floor doing nothing. Of course I tried to explain that I was doing—something— but that it involved keeping still. I tried to keep it simple and strictly non-Eastern."

"How the hell did you manage that?" Steve asked with incredulity.

"Well, that wasn't so hard. I just told him it was a method of mental discipline that I learned from a book by Rear Admiral EH Shattock."[11]

"And he believed that?"

"I showed him the book cover and he seemed satisfied – because he saw the title and the author's name. My father knew his name because he spent a lot of time in the army out-East. He said that the name was often quoted in news reports concerning the progress of the war – so my father being in China as well as India – was quite familiar with his high reputation."

"Lucky coincidence eh … ?"

"Exactly!"

"So … did you plan it like that?"

"No!" I laughed *"That would have been a brilliant move – but I'm not that clever. The book was called 'An Experiment in Mindfulness' and I read a review which described the book as an excellent meditation manual that anyone could follow.*

---

11 Rear Admiral E H Shattock was a commanding officer in the British Pacific Fleet – a Royal Navy formation which saw action against Japan during WWII. Instituted in 1944, its main base was Sydney, Australia, with an action-base at Manus Island. One of the largest fleets assembled by the Royal Navy, it had four battleships and six fleet aircraft carriers, 15 smaller aircraft carriers, 11 cruisers, numerous smaller warships, and submarines.

"Nothing more to it than that. I told him he could read it if he wanted to know more – but he said it was acceptable being that it was written by the illustrious Rear Admiral EH Shattock! It did seem to bewilder him a little that a rear admiral would advocate 'sitting in silence for periods of time' – but concluded that there was something scientific about it. Anyhow … I was the sort of died-in-the-wool eccentric who'd be attracted to something like that. I suggested that it would help me concentrate at school – and so he felt that it couldn't do any harm: as long as I didn't do too much of it."

"So he was alright about it in the end?"

"More-or-less – but he'd always ask 'How long have you been sitting there?' and I'd have to say 'Oh not long – no more than five minutes.' Then he'd say 'Well that's probably long enough' and I'd have to stand up and do something different. Then I'd usually take a walk and sit in the woods."

"How long d'you sit now – as a matter of interest?"

"Oh … about half an hour a day on average – longer if I can manage. Sometimes an hour – but not at home."

"So, is it working?"

"That's hard to answer Steve." I laughed *"You're not supposed to look at it in terms of anything happening – but I'd say that it helps me a lot – y'know dealing with* what *happens: like with Anelie. If I find myself thinking about her too much – I can decide only to be in the present and just* see *what I see and* hear *what I hear. That gives me some kind of freedom from feeling too … sad or whatever."*

"That sounds useful – but I don't think I could do something like that. Doesn't it get really boring just sitting there and not thinking?"

"No Steve …" I laughed *"It can't be boring if there are no 'thoughts' – it's only boring when there—are— 'thoughts'; I mean, 'thoughts' that I don't want to be having. As soon as I find myself able to drop the 'thoughts' there's nothing to be bored about. You need 'thoughts' to feel bored. Boredom's made of 'thoughts', you see."*

"That's a bit profound for me Vic – I suppose we're all different."

"That's a fact."

159

"So ..." continued Steve *"... is meditation different from when you were having those visions? I mean ... are you still having those visions?"*

"My visions of the White Lady ... yes ... I still have those visions ... but no – what seems to happen now is that the space that's left when thought isn't there – seems to be ... somehow ... what she is ... and ..." I ran out of words at that point and sat staring.

"So ..." Steve enquired *"What's going on now? It's a little eerie when you do that."* By 'that', Steve was referring to my staring for periods of time without speaking – and, in his words, *'looking as if I'd died or something'.*

"Waiting for words, Steve. It's a little hard to find the words for this – but ... when I'm here at your house, you know I'm here. If I go to the loo and this armchair's empty – you know I'm still here in the house – but you probably aren't continually telling yourself that I'm here. In fact, you're probably not thinking about me at all – but the sense that I'm here is just there – and unspoken. Does that make any sense?"

Steve nodded. *"Yes ... kind of strange – but that describes it. I'd never thought of it like that."*

"Well, you wouldn't. I mean – there's no need to put that kind of thing into words."

"Maybe that's what philosophers do" Steve suggested.

"Maybe ... but I think I'll stick to the Buddhist books. They're difficult enough as it is without adding philosophy to it. I tried to read Wittgenstein[12] *and it was diabolical. Anyhow, if you leave out the 'armchair example' ... the White Lady and the space where there's no thought seem to have become the same."*

"D'you think I should practise meditation?"

---

12 Ludwig Josef Johann Wittgenstein (1889–1951) was an Austrian-British philosopher who specialised in logic, the philosophy of mind, language, and mathematics. During his lifetime he published Tractatus Logico-Philosophicus. His personal manuscripts were edited and published posthumously as Philosophical Investigations in 1953 and credited with being one of the most important works of philosophy in the 20th century.

"If you really wanted to ... yes ... but somehow ... I'd rather you practised bass. That's also meditation—as far as I can see—if you don't think of anything when you're playing. If you just play." Pause. *"So ... when's Ron due over?"*

"Not for an hour yet ... I wish it was sooner because I'd like to get down to practising the set we're finally going to play when we play at Weyflood Village Hall."

"Yeah ..." I sighed with a huge grin *"... that'll be ... the beginning of the best time of my life."*

"Better than Anelie?"

"... in some ways, yes ... Anelie always was ... temporary, you see – and so ... although it was wonderful ... it was also ..."

"Temporary ..." Steve interrupted.

"Yes – and—this—is ... permanent ... 'til death do us part – as it were."

"You think we'll actually get somewhere?"

"With you and Ron!? No doubt about it! We'll make Cream look like Skimmed Milk by the time we're through ... Seriously—you two—are unbeatable."

"Well ... Ron's a world-class musician—I know that—but I still have a way to go."

"Maybe Steve – but you're getting there quite fast as far as I can hear. I know that Ron's some kind of Bach-of-Blues, Mozart-of-Mojo, and Beethoven-of-Boogie combined – but you've changed so much over the last three years. You're really fast and smooth now – and you can bend those strings even on a long-scale bass."

"Alight – I have got a lot better Vic ... but maybe that's just because of Ron. I get a lot of help from him you know. It's like having a master-class all the time when he's around."

Steve picked up his TELECASTER-shaped FENDER PRECISION bass and threw his fingers up and down the neck in a series of highly extended twiddles that left me wide-eyed.

"I worked out this series of riffs last night. It's to go with Rolling and Tumbling *and I want to see what Ron thinks of it."*

"It sounds—and looks—brilliant! Plug in and let me hear it properly."

Steve plugged in as requested and began to boom with subtle dexterity. Steve got to the end of the riffs and I requested he just kept repeating it for a while. After a dozen or so repetitions Steve decided he'd better save his fingers for later.

"I think that Ron will really like that ... I mean, I really like it a lot ... It's like nothing I've heard before – and I can see how it's going to turn Rolling and Tumbling *into something quite different ... it's got some Jazz accents to it that'll ... really do something interesting."* Pause. *"It'll make the vocal line more of a challenge because I'll be tempted to sing what you're playing rather than the line I'm supposed to be singing."*

"That'll be good for you though ... because if you ever want to play back-up bass – you'll need to be able to sing over the bass line."

"Good point ... but maybe I'd better get myself a bass first ... I know that your parents'll be giving me that GIBSON EB0 *on my* 18th *birthday – but that's rather a long way away ... D'you think'd they mind you loaning me that* DANELECTRO?*"*

"Mmmm ... I don't see why not ... and ... there's a spare amplifier you could use. It's not great, not very loud that is – but you wouldn't want to be too loud at first."

"Right ... don't mention this to Ron yet ... because I want to bring the subject up with him ... at some point when I think he might go for it."

"Wise move, Vic – wise move."

There was suddenly the sound of the doorbell – and Ron had arrived. He stood at the door waiting with his TELECASTER case resting on his left foot and his hands resting on the top. Ron always looked and acted the epitome of cool. *"Ready to make history?"* he chuckled.

"Ready as ever" Steve replied and Ron strode in – opened his case and plugged into the amplifier that Steve's father used.

162

It was a FENDER amplifier and Ron liked it almost as much as his MARSHALL. It was a 1963 FENDER VIBROVERB.[13]

"Y'know … I can never quite decide which is better – my MARSHALL or your dad's FENDER … maybe one day I'll have to have both and use them for different numbers."

"Good idea Ron … it does have a sound of its own."

"Y'know … Steve … these things are starting to get a little hard to find now … FENDER revamped their amps in 1963 and this is from that year – a blackface … a SUPER REVERB with 2 ten-inch speakers! Shame they were discontinued in 1964. Your dad must've got one of the last ones! If he ever wants to part with it – I'd snap it up in a minute."

"Can't see that happening – but you never know. If he ever shows any signs of giving up playing with The Dixons *I'll mention it to him. He might not want to do it for ever, I suppose – although he'd always want to play at home."*

"Yeah … he might want a smaller amplifier then … eh?" Ron grinned as devilishly as was his custom. *"So … anyway …"* he let fly a stream of notes that came from nowhere – but were as perfect as anyone could wish *"… you said you had a new bass line for this!"* and he launched into Rolling and Tumbling. Fortunately I'd already plugged my microphone into the PA system that belonged to The Dixons and we were away.

"Errrm … Ron … Steve … do you—mind—if we take that at half the speed?"

"Half!?" Steve croaked with incredulity.

"Half" I stated flatly. *"I know everyone gallops it but we don't—have—to do that do we?"*

"Vic has a point Steve" Ron advised *"Y'know … it could be much better adagio … not quite … molto grave … that would give us far more room for improvisations and high speed riffs."*

13 The 1963 FENDER VIBROVERB—a 40-watt combo amplifier—was the first FENDER amplifier to incorporate reverb and vibrato.

Lawd I was rolling and tumbling – God the whole night long / Said I was rolling and tumbling – god the whole night long / But when I woke up in the morning – all I had was gone / Well y'know my little baby – she gonna jump and shout / Yes you know my little baby – she gonna jump and shout / When that train come rolling in – and I come walking out. / Well you see my little baby – she got her red dress on / Said you see my little baby – she got her red dress on / and when that sun go sinking down – it won't be —on—for long.[14]

Steve nodded his assent and we took it from the top. Ron chose the tempo and he hit it perfectly. I was able to put more passion into the vocal line – and also to throw in some vocal acrobatics to boot. We sat chatting after our practice – when Ron suddenly narrowed his eyes *"D'you smell that, either of you?"*

"Smell what?" asked Steve.

I knew what Ron could smell – but said nothing.

"Smells like … like vomit …"

Ron could smell my right boot. My brother Græham had been to a party and come home by the prescribed time – but had gone straight to bed. I'd come home several hours later and he'd been asleep when I got in. I did notice some sort of smell in the room – but I'd been dog-tired and fallen asleep as soon as my head hit the pillow. Then—on waking—I discovered the ugly truth. Græham had vomited in my boot. I emptied it out and filled it with cold water several times before trying hot soapy water. I left the boot to dry in the garden – but to no avail. It stank of vomit still. My mother tried to help out and did everything imaginable, including tipping Eau De Cologne into it. Nothing worked.

---

14 *Rolling and Tumbling Blues* is usually credited as 'traditional' and has been recorded countless times with differing lyrics and titles. The song may have some connection to *Minglewood Blues*, recorded in 1928 by Gus Cannon's Jug Stompers. The earliest recorded version is *Roll and Tumble Blues* by Hambone Willie Newbern in 1929. Other Blues artists have recorded their own versions, such as Robert Johnson's *If I Had Possession Over Judgment Day* recorded in 1936. The best-known version was Muddy Waters' *Rolling and Tumbling*, produced by Chess in 1950. The version given here is a mixture of several different versions.

There was always the slight smell of vomit that arose from the boot whenever they warmed up beyond a certain point. I admitted the situation to Steve and Ron who fell about laughing 'til tears ran down their faces.

"Well ..." I said with a wan smile *"I'm glad I've given you two such a good time."*

"Vic ..." Ron cackled *"I know you miss Anelie – but aren't there better ways to avoid getting another girlfriend than wearing a boot that smells of vomit?"*

They both fell about laughing again – and this time I joined them. *"Right ... the boots are going to the Oxfam Shop ... maybe their next owner will think they're tanned in some special way that makes them smell like that."*

Jack was away on holiday with his parents – and somehow I enjoyed the lack of drums. Ron always said they were absolutely necessary – but Steve and I could have lived without them. It was easier to have practice sessions without drums because we could go to Steve's house and use Dixon equipment. The three of us had to carry the show – at least as far as Jack's percussion went for the time being. Ron had given him a fairly serious talk about improving and he'd promised to practise more – and listen to Ginger Baker as much as he could. Jack had improved—there was no doubt—but Ron felt he still had a long way to go.

I liked Jack and felt that I wanted to give him as much of a chance as possible. I felt I'd been given a chance – and that I was lucky that neither Steve nor Ron could sing. I felt that I could be replaced at any time—as could Jack—but somehow I'd found myself in some sort of special category with Ron. Steve and I had been friends from way back – but Ron was new on the scene; new and radically talented.

I was lucky that Ron liked my voice and the way I *tortured* the vocal line. I was lucky in a lot of different ways – and that fact never escaped me.

11

Ich bin ein Dichter

1968

Emptiness happens. That was how I saw situations. Having read and re-read articles on emptiness in the Buddhist Society magazine – it had become a fact of life.

A kyil'khor[1] can be created from coloured chalk dust. Unexpectedly the wind blows – and the pattern is no longer what it was. One can grieve the lost pattern – or enjoy the mingling of colours and the strange shapes created by the staggered disintegration. One can try to create a social milieu by inviting the appropriate friends to the perfect place at the right time – then, one small aspect shifts and the situation randomises. Life appeared to be some sort of existential kaleidoscope in which *the meaning* could only be in *the moment*. If one tried to extend the meaning beyond the moment – the meaning could become increasingly meaningless.

The Savage Cabbage Blues Band had two successful gigs and then we took a holiday. Ron and Steve had family obligations. I couldn't visit Jack. Jack's house was out of bounds by order of his parents. I was a deranged working-class subversive as far as they were concerned. I had hair that was far longer than they could endure. I dressed too unconventionally. I went to Secondary School rather than a Grammar School. The deepest horror, was that I was planning on going to Art School – the very pit of iniquity and depravity. The worst thing about me—according to Jack—was my vocabulary. It was significantly larger than theirs.

---

1 Kyil'khor (*dKyil 'khor / mandala*) centre and periphery; sun and moon disc; sphere; entirety, sacred place; visionary dimension circumference; the context of a yidam (*yi dam / deva / awareness being*); esoteric diagram. A kyil'khor is usually a yidam and surrounding environment. A kyil'khor is a symbolic representation of a yidam's dimension, a profferment visualised as the universe, or the arrangement of profferments in tantric symbolic enactment.

His parents had said *'He gives himself airs, speaking in that pretentious literary manner.'* The working classes should obviously know their place. I obviously didn't understand that there was a place I should be other than where I was.

Although they accepted that Jack had to associate with me in the context of the Savage Cabbage Blues Band, they wouldn't have me in their house – or even telephoning their house. Jack couldn't telephone me because we had no telephone – and so … Jack may as well have been living in Lithuania.

I would miss the music – but there'd be more time for silent sitting meditation and reading whatever I could lay my hands on vis-à-vis Tibet and Vajrayana. There were not that many books available – so I kept re-reading them. The books were mainly academic—and viciously difficult to read—so the more times I read them, the better.

I had a fine motorcycle – bought with several years of weekend work cleaning the floors at Farnham Hospital. There were untold miles of country road. The 500cc BSA pulsated like a sabre-toothed tiger with mean things on its mind. *'I got—*mean—*things – I got mean things on my mind'*[2] I sang as I roared sedately down Crondal Lane. It was curious that I could sing about *having mean things on my mind* without any sense of those words reflecting *anything* about me. I had no 'mean things' on my mind – but singing the words had a meaning of its own. I was a Buddhist – but I sang hymns every morning at the school assembly and thoroughly enjoyed singing most of them. I was an atheist – but I could sing praises to God with great gusto. I simply loved singing. In that sense, Blues and hymns were like plays – and I was an actor in those plays. Opera singers could play villains – so I could sing anything just for the sheer enjoyment of the sounds and the abstract poetry of *meanings* sans *meanness*.

There was something about being seated on a motorcycle that fitted both Buddhism and Blues – especially a chopped easy-rider motorcycle.

2   From Robert Johnson's *Rambling on my Mind,* May 1937.

I had to concentrate in a relaxed manner – alert, yet not anxiously alert. Being aware of the manœuvres of other motorists—which were not always precise—was a form of open-ended vigilance. It was delightful that anything could be meditation if one was open to that dimension of experience.

Riding out, anywhere at all, was almost unsurpassable – when lady friends and Savage Cabbage were absent. It took me to places where I could sit and stare at the sky. I'd read about staring at the sky as a meditation practice – but it was a mere reference and no details were given. So, I simply sat with my eyes open—looking out into the sky—and letting go of thoughts when they arose.[3] It was unusual to sit with wide-open eyes – but I found that I was far less prone to thought than when sitting with eyes partially open.

My brother Græham, for some unaccountable reason, was in Germany – staying with the family of a young cousin. She'd spent some time with us the year previously, to improve her English. My father seemed to think that the favour should be returned – and so Græham was packed off to Germany. I could never quite figure why – as Græham's grasp of the German language was slim even in comparison with mine. He'd been gone for some days—and had another three weeks' sojourn there—when my mother said *"Veector … I have just received ziss sad letter from your bruzzer Græham."*

"What does he say?" I nodded – splaying my fingers out in a slight flourish that said 'let's hear about it'. My mother laughed a quiet laugh *"Your farzer never vozz able to stop you gesticulating. He blames it on me"* she chuckled. *"He says ze English do not gesticulate."*

"Well …" I grinned *"I'm only half English – and … as I masticate, postulate, recapitulate, prognosticate, and enunciate, I may as well gesticulate for good measure."* Pause. *"So … anyhow, what does Græham have to say?"*

"Ja—ja—ja … he says he is not happy with Wilhelmina Rübenhacker and family. And … zay write and say zay they find him … phlegmatisch – how is that word in Englisch?"

---

3   Namkha Ar-tè (*nam kha ar gTad*) Dzogchen sky-direct mediation.

"Phlegmatic ... ?" I laughed *"Græham's not phlegmatic – he's English."* I stated—in mock upper-class accent—with a touch of exasperation at people who make myopic subjective value judgements *"I think there's a subtle difference. Græham's composed, calm, and unflappable – and that could be seen as phlegmatic to someone who's excitable, febrile, or emotionally incontinent. I've never met Wilhelmina ... is she anything like that?"*

"Yah ... zat iss vott I have been sinking ... she laughs all the time, when zair iss nussing to laugh about." Pause. *"So ... he vonts to come home ... but ... your farzer vill not hear of it. He says zat Græham must not be a child – he must learn to grow up and be an adult."*

"Well yes ... but I've never seen Græham as immature ... he's really pretty level and independent. I mean, he works up at the Black Prince making hors d'oeuvres – and earns a tidy sum at it too." Pause. *"Y'know Mum ... it's quite a thing to be trapped in a place where you're not enjoying yourself – especially if you can't really speak the language."* Pause. *"I wish my German was better and ... I wish you'd been able to bring us up to be bilingual – but I think I'd have found it easier than Græham to spend three weeks on my own in Germany."*

"Yes, I know ziss iss true" my mother stated quite emphatically. *"Ziss iz just vhat I am sinking."* Pause. *"And ziss, is vhy I am vondering about some-sing I vont to ask of you."*

I raised my eyebrows in token of asking what she was wondering *"Ask away – I'd be happy to oblige if it's at all possible."*

"I am vondering ... Veector ... vezzer you vould like to go to Germany to keep Græham company." Pause. *"I am also sinking zatt you might like to go and stay with Onkel Arnold and Tante Rikchen – and maybe go to visit Tante Ruth and Onkel Otto. You know their daughters. Maren is more your age and Antge is more Græham's age – so maybe it might be nicer for both of you zan viz Wilhelmina. Wilhelmina's husband ... Ja., Horst ... iss sometimes a funny man – I sink ... ze Vorr ... Ja ... zer Vorr has affected him you know – like Mr Love ... he sometimes does not always have his right mind."* Pause. *"Not so much as Mr Love – but like ziss in some vay ... he has moods and becomes angry easily."*

My mother continued after a pause *"I know Mr Love woz alvays kind – but Horst iss alvays … a little too practical and that makes him … severe and hard."*

"Certainly … we can't have Græham sitting out a prison sentence." I nodded my general approval of the idea. *"I'll just have to get an international driving licence – but that shouldn't take more than a few days."* There was nothing I wouldn't do to please my mother. She'd been so kind to me all my life that I took it as given, that I'd comply – besides which I felt sorry for Græham living in a house where people evidently hung from the rafters and grazed on the lawn.

Oh Polly love, oh Polly, the rout has now begun / We must go a-marching to the beating of the drum / Dress yourself all in your best and come along with me / I'll take you to the fol-de-rols in High Germany.[4]

"So Veector … I have a little money I have saved."

"Don't worry about that Mum – I can manage the petrol."

"But zair iss zer ferry crossing to pay – so I vill give vhat iss necessary wiz petrol too. You must—not—pay for ziss."

"Well … if you insist, Mum … consider it agreed. I'll get my continental driving licence and insurance fixed tomorrow – it shouldn't take long and the GB stickers[5] *aren't hard to come by."*

"No … not so soon, Veector. First … I must speak vizz your farzer – and, I must write letters. I sink zat if you say zat you want to go … your farzer vill see no problem. Nussing you now do iss a problem – because always you are so polite viz him." My mother looked a little sad for a moment and added *"But … Veector vott of your Savage Cabbage? Vill it not make difficulties for Stephen and Ronald?"*

---

4 High Germany refers to mountainous southern Germany. In medieval Latin—in chapter 23 of *Imago Mundi of Honorius Augustodunensis*—the term can be found in the definition '… Ab Danubio usque ad Alpes est Germania Superior …' which means 'From the Danube to the Alps is High Germany'. In German, the term Hochdeutschland to mean Alpine Germany was common in the 16th century, and used by the Brothers Grimm in the 1 century. The term is found in the English folk song of the late 1600s about the 'Thirty Years' War' entitled 'High Germany'.

5 In Europe cars have to identify their nationality with a sticker applied to the vehicle. In the case of Britain the sticker was GB for Great Britain.

"Not at all Mum – they're gone for three weeks anyway – and actually … I'm at something of a loose-end. I've got books to read and guitar to practise, but that can happen in Germany as well as here – and, it'll be good to see Græham. He's turning into a rare young devil."

"… Teufel …" My mother shook her head and clucked at the word 'devil' but smiled broadly at me nonetheless. My mother had a tendency to literalism with words and couldn't see how anything to do with the Devil could be good – likewise fierce, cool, heavy,[6] or a host of other slang usages.

I felt really glad to be able to do something for her. I also felt that heading out on the highway was what I ought to be doing on my chopped BSA. All seemed to work out with my father. He appeared highly appreciative of the fact that I was obliging my mother to such an extent. He knew quite clearly that I had my own life to live. He witnessed my schedule on a day-by-day basis – and so he was aware that I was always busy; always having appointments to keep. Times had changed and it seemed that I was always 'doing the right thing' in my father's eyes. Emptiness Happens. The embattled father and son scenario of 16 years had evaporated.

It was organised that I'd bring Græham home on my motorcycle and that would save the rearrangement of his travel home. Wilhelmina's husband had picked him up and was to have brought him home. He often had work in Britain connected with refrigeration, or some such thing – and so his business trips marked the start and finish of Græham's incarceration in a slightly more commodious version of Colditz.

And so my journey was planned. I'd spend a night with my Aunt Ivy in Gillingham – and call in on Uncle Bert and Aunt Elsie. Uncle Bert had been a keen motorcyclist in his younger days and had a remarkable pair of WWII military leather motorcycle panniers. My uncle chuckled about my strange motorcycle *"We're going to have to make up some special brackets for your 'creation' …"* Pause. *"… I think … I may have some brass doorstep edging and stair-rods that might serve."*

---

6   The slang word 'heavy' meant good in 1968 – but turned to mean the opposite by 1970.

It turned out that my uncle was also something of an engineer. He'd not taken the same academic route in the Army as my father – and had remained at the tooling-shop end of engineering. My father was always fairly nifty as a handyman – but Uncle Bert was a genius. He examined my motorcycle and made a few drawings with precise measurements and within three hours I had a robust yet elegant set of brackets. As he finished each piece, I set to work with wet and dry abrasive papers, SOLVOL AUTOSOL chrome polish, and finally BRASSO – and the brackets gleamed in the evening sun. Uncle Bert was as impressed with my polishing as I was with his engineering prowess.

I was always amazed with the way that phenomena could be brought into being. Even when I was part of the act of creation – the creation was still some kind of miracle. There was no God – but every creative human being—every artist—was some kind of god. Creativity was a natural phenomenon that pulsed in us all – and our rôle as beings was to allow that to surface from the primal ocean of existence.

Uncle Bert and I had a fine conversation whilst working – and then, he and Aunt Elsie joined me at Aunt Ivy's for a dinner of roast lamb with all the trimmings. I needed the panniers in order to bring Græham home from Germany – as I had to be able to stow my own baggage in them and attach his suitcase to the sissy bars. Those panniers came in extremely useful over the years and I made sure to lavish great attention on them whenever they got wet. The leather from which they were constructed was amazing stuff: ¼ inch thick —at least—with a deep grain and a wonderful patina. I have always taken great care of leather – remembering that it was once the skin of an animal. I have always had the impulse to respect that and to make sure that it endures. Were everyone to take adequate care of leather goods they would last for generations.[7]

---

7 I owned those panniers for 40 years and finally gave them to a young motorcyclist on the condition that he took care always to oil them.

The journey to Hannover was easy for the most part. I enjoyed the ferry crossing from Dover to Ostend. Belgium assailed me with fæcal aromas that nearly made me cross-eyed with their intensity. The stench changed every few miles and I was aghast at how many different versions of *vile* there could be. I was not unhappy when I left that olfactory version of hell behind.

In terms of getting to Germany, I had some insane idea of riding through the night in order to arrive for breakfast – but my concept of my own stamina and endurance proved to be a trifle exaggerated. I'd been purring along the Autobahn at a pleasant 70mph when I dreamed that I was in Farnham Park. I'd tripped over something or other – and was falling in slow motion toward the ground. When I hit the ground, it was surprisingly soft and I bounced back up again – but very slowly. When I'd bounced up to approximately 30°, I started to drift back in the direction of the ground again. Then I'd bounce up again – and the pattern repeated. I was just enjoying this amusing aspect of the dream when my visual field ignited. There was a flash of intense light in which the White Lady appeared. She was there for a fraction of a second. I'd opened my eyes immediately I saw that light because it felt as if I was staring into the headlights of an on-coming car. But as soon as I opened my eyes, the White Lady was the first image I saw. Then she was gone and there was an empty Autobahn. Maybe it had been a car's headlights I'd seen. I realised—when I opened my eyes—that I'd been drifting into the central reservation of the Autobahn, clipping the kerb with a soft thud and then drifting out again. It was the sudden vision of the White Lady—or the headlights of a car—that had woken me. There was no sign of a car in the distance behind me – but I could not be sure. It could have been traveling at high speed – but would I not have heard it in the distance? It would have to remain a mystery. I'd been asleep for maybe four or five brushes with the central reservation. This was obviously not a desirable situation; so—still partially asleep—I pulled my motorcycle onto the grassy strip in the middle of the Autobahn. When I stopped in the central reservation it was utterly dark and silent.

Being discombobulated by tiredness I mistook the central reservation for the left-hand verge – as it would have been on a British motorway. I just about managed to pull the machine onto its stand and unwind my father's old army sleeping bag from the sissy bars. I'd only brought the thing to protect the DEBIL from the elements – but I was grateful to buckle the thing around me and lose consciousness.

I awoke in a different setting altogether. Cars were flashing by on either side of me and a member of the Deutsche Polizei was demanding *"Aufwachen! Aufwachen! Was machen Sie hier !?"* I smiled sheepishly and replied in faltering German *"Entschuldigung, aber ich war zu müde um weiter zu fahren."*[8] The motorcycle policeman was a kind fellow however. He simply shook his head as if to say *'Idiot'* and said *"Ja … Engländer …"* Pause. *"… Ja, na klar … wer auch sonst …"*[9] He checked my passport, driving licence, and insurance papers. Then he stopped the traffic 'til I got to the other side of the road. He waited 'til I'd wrapped the DEBIL in the army sleeping bag and secured it to the sissy bars before slowing the traffic so I could head out on the Autobahn again. I was touched by the kindness of the German policeman – as he could have fined me or whatever happens to a person who sleeps in the central reservation on the Autobahn. The incident reminded me of the inherent goodness of human beings – the primal goodness that is the basis of sentience.[10]

After only a few miles I came upon an Autobahnraststätte [11] and ate two hearty breakfasts and drank a pint of coffee. I was now feeling fit to ride through Germany, Poland, and on through Russia into Mongolia – but then, I never had much sense when it came to limitations.

---

8 *"Wake up! Wake up! What are you doing here?!"* – *"I'm sorry I was too tired to drive on any further."*

9 *"Right – an Englishman – what else would you expect?"*

10 Död-né zangwa (*gdDod nas bZang ba*) – basic goodness, a term often employed by Chögyam Trungpa Rinpoche.

11 'Motorway services' in British and 'rest stop' in the USA.

The interlude in which I fell asleep at 70mph on my motorcycle made me ponder on the nature of Dream Yoga. I'd read the Evans-Wentz book on Tibetan Yogas [12] and was familiar with the idea of mi-lam or dream yoga [13]– so I wondered about my state of consciousness. Was I only partially asleep—or partially awake—or fluctuating between sleep and wakefulness? What was that? Did the dream become a dream in which I had awareness – or what happened? I'd seen the White Lady. She kept appearing at different points in my life. It had occurred to me years earlier that she must have some sort of existence outside my imagination. Was it possible that she had appeared in order to protect me? Was that possible? Was she some sort of Buddhist guardian angel? Were there Buddhist guardian angels? There *were* protectors – but they had to be invoked … and one had to be a Lama to invoke them. Any Tobgyal, Dé-kyi, or Tashi couldn't summon them. [14] I would need to ask someone about this at some point – but there were no Tibetan Lamas in Britain as far as I knew; even at the Buddhist Society in London. [15] This was a notion that I was going to have to put on one side and return to it if I ever manged to get out to the Himalayas.

The question I could more realistically ponder, was how I'd managed to remain seated on a two-wheeled vehicle in the sleep state? I had tried to apply something of what I had read about mi-lam – but met with a little success. I'd had many moments of clarity within dreams when I knew I was dreaming – but these experiences were scattered and of no great duration.

12 Walter Yeeling Evans-Wentz (1878–1965) was an American anthropologist, writer, and pioneer in the study of Tibetan Buddhism. He translated and published four Tibetan texts: *The Tibetan Book of the Dead* (1927); *Tibetan Yoga and Secret Doctrines* (1935); *The Tibetan Book of the Great Liberation* (1954); and *Tibet's Great Yogi: Milarépa* (1928).

13 Mi-lam (*rMi lam / svapnadarsana*). Dream Yoga is a tantric practice linked with the bardos of sleep, clear light, and dreaming. In the bardo of dreams (*as well as the bardo of death*) one exists—in terms of perception—in yi-lü (*yid lus*) as a subtle cognate appearance.

14 Tobgyal, Dé-kyi, or Tashi are common Tibetan names like Tom, Dick or Harry.

15 I did not know about the Kagyüd Lamas who had arrived in Britain at that point – but Lama Chime Yönten Rinpoche, Lama Akong Rinpoche, Lama Ato Rinpoche, and Chögyam Trungpa Rinpoche were all in Britain at that time. I was to meet Lama Chime Yönten when I went to Farnham Art School in 1970.

Three or four nights a month was the best I ever achieved at that time. I had struggled through other books by Evans-Wentz but found them all to be rather hard work.[16] I decided that such books required at least a dozen readings each, to glean anything from them. Still—in for a penny, in for a pound—I was determined to penetrate these texts and develop my understanding of Vajrayana.

The idea of mi-lam moved through my mind as I rode. The time passed surprisingly quickly – but when I arrived in Ahlten in the early evening I was no closer to an understanding of my dream experience.

Ahlten was a large village near Hannover where my uncle and aunt —Rikchen and Arnold Rathmann—lived. Græham was to arrive two days later as Horst Rübenhacker—Wilhelmina's cranky husband —could not arrange to take him to Ahlten any earlier. That was a nuisance – but Tante Rikchen advised me that the length of my hair would be a problem with Herr Horst Rübenhacker. He was politically slightly right of Goebbels and wouldn't allow Græham to ride on the back of a motorcycle with a hippie – even though I was his brother and was taking him home. Nothing had been said to Herr Rübenhacker of the plan for me to take him home on my motorcycle, or Græham would have had to have seen out the duration of his confinement. Herr Rübenhacker's opinion of me— having seen a photograph—was that I should be in prison hanging chained to a wall. A year previously I suppose, my father would have been of the same opinion – but … times had changed.

All was well however – and Herr Rübenhacker knew nothing of my presence in Ahlten. Tante Rikchen and Onkel Arnold thought Horst Rübenhacker was insane – and so they kept schtum.[17] They were monumentally kind and easy going – and, even though they were ever-so-slightly fearful lest I was arrested for being long-haired, they made no mention of my shocking appearance.

16 *The Tibetan Book of the Dead* published by Oxford University Press in 1927; *Tibet's Great Yogi Milarépa* published by Oxford University Press in 1951; *The Tibetan Book of the Great Liberation* published by New York, Oxford University Press in 1954.

17 'Schminglish' – British slang that resembles Yiddish. Keeping schtumm mean to keep something quiet or secret.

I was Renate's elder son and as far as they were concerned – that made me a fine fellow. My mother evidently thought I was a fine fellow in spite of my hair and outlandish clothing – so they accepted the package with apparent ease.

There was magnificent sausage to eat and utterly wonderful coffee to drink. There was also Dagmar Strauß to visit. Dagmar was a girl a year older than me who was in some way connected to my aunt and uncle – but I never found out in what way. Nevertheless, I was introduced and she turned out to be extremely pleasant and bright. She seemed fascinated by the fact that I was 'more-or-less famous'. I was up there with her British Rock music heroes and—it shames me to admit this—I didn't try too hard to rid her of that impression. I told no lies – but somehow failed to undermine her imagination. That's not too arduous when your German is rudimentary. In our few days together her mother had bounded up with a copy of HÖRZU – a television guide magazine. There was a pop song competition and it was deemed appropriate that I should enter it. After all I was some kind of pop star—so why not—and anyway it would make a good translation exercise for her daughter. How could I say no? How could I explain that I hated pop music and that entering competitions was anathema to me? No … I couldn't do that. I had to agree and before much time had passed I started really enjoying the process.

I had to put my mind to reconstructing one of the songs I'd written, 'Dead Man's Hand' – but that proved less easy than I anticipated. Dagmar found the English utterly incomprehensible and I had to explain that it wasn't normal English. It was poetry – and more-than-that, it was poetry with a Black American slant. I had to go through a process that reminded me of explaining Bob Dylan to Anelie Mandelbaum. Just before Græham arrived we'd got the thing in shape and sent it off to HÖRZU.

I look at the deal – but can't understand, / Dealer's lookin' through me at the piana–man, / The clothes I'm wearin's all contraband, / Seems like I'm lookin' at the dead man's hand.[18]

In the evenings we watched the German television production of 'Der Abenteuerliche Simplicissimus'[19] which I managed to follow—more-or-less—as the story made itself clear as it went along. Dagmar would interpret the complicated parts and kept me abreast with what was unfolding. 'Der Abenteuerliche Simplicissimus' follows the ups and downs of a boy—Simplicissimus—the son of a peasant family from Spessart. He is separated from his home by foraging dragoons – escapes from them and is adopted by a forest hermit. Set to live the life of a hermit, he is conscripted again into military service. Having reached maturity in a depraved environment, he adventitiously joins the armies of both warring sides – switching allegiances purely on chance circumstances. His story is one of continual alternation: wealth and poverty; triumph and defeat; romance and depravity. Sick at heart with the ways of the world he returns to the forest hermit – who has since died. He takes over the hermitage and lives the rest of his life in tranquillity.

As I watched Der Abenteuerliche Simplicissimus, it occurred to me that my life was not so entirely dissimilar to his – except that my life was one of *emotional rags* to *emotional riches*. Would I end up as a hermit? I was a Buddhist after all and there were Buddhist hermits in Tibet. It might make sense at some point – but I was far from *sick of the world*, even though it had its lows as well as its highs. I was currently riding pretty high – and although I was aware that I needed to find *the one taste* of pleasure and pain, I had no objection at all to pleasure. Maybe I'd just have to accept that you had to choose both from the menu at *Restaurant Reality*. Would I ever be able to do that? I both wanted it and feared it.

18 The 'Dead Man's Hand' is the hand that Wild Bill Hickok was holding when he was killed: aces over eights. The lyrics were written by the author and Steve Bruce.

19 *Der Abenteuerliche Simplicissimus* is a Baroque novel written by Hans Jakob Christoffel von Grimmelshausen and published in 1669. It was inspired by the 30 Years' War which had thrown Germany into turmoil between 1618 and 1648. Der Abenteuerliche Simplicissimus is regarded as the first adventure novel in the German language.

Still – I had a lifetime to reach the point where I'd meet hope and fear and *treat the two imposters just the same.* Some fragment of Rudyard Kipling's poetry came to mind. They were from a piece called *If.*

> *If you can dream – and not make dreams your master;*
> *If you can think – and not make thoughts your aim;*
> *If you can meet with triumph and disaster*
> *And treat those two impostors just the same …*

Profound words. And yes, that's what I wanted – or at least that was the state to which I aspired. Rudyard Kipling's 'two imposters' brought to mind the 'eight imposters' designated by Buddhism. One had to find their sameness of flavour.[20] Triumph and disaster had to be experienced—along with praise and blame—as having the same taste. The idea that they were 'imposters' was interesting – they were merely public opinion posing as reality. Wearing a certain item of clothing could be cause for applause or ridicule – but neither response was real. The world was thick with meaningless opinions – and one could either be a slave to those opinions or not.

> *If you can make one heap of all your winnings*
> *And risk it on one turn of pitch-and-toss,*
> *And lose, and start again at your beginnings*
> *And never breathe a word about your loss …*

Well … I never breathed a word about the loss of Alice or the loss of Mr Love – or Anelie. Steve had pried a few words out of me – but I'd been fairly scant in what I'd said. I was used to losing it all and starting again. That was the shape of it—in terms of life—as far as I could see; so, maybe I could make a partially decent sort of Buddhist out of myself.

I was sad to bid farewell to Dagmar because … well … I think we'd both been getting interested in each other. I'd learnt my lesson with Anelie however – and wasn't up for another relationship with a lady from another country.

---

20 Chö-gyèd ro-nyom (*chos brGyad ro sNyoms*): the equal taste of the eight mundane concerns. The eight mundane concerns are: hope and fear; praise and blame (alternatively fame and shame); gain and loss; meeting and parting.

I was married to the Savage Cabbage Blues Band in any case – and couldn't go forming liaisons that would take me away.

Græham was obviously overjoyed to see me and we talked away half the night. Græham was downing English by the pint – as if he'd been dying of thirst. We had hilarious discussions in which he described Horst Rübenhacker as a cross between Herman Munster and Lamburger Gestler. [21]

We spent some splendid days with our Tante Rikchen and Onkel Arnold – eating excellent Mettwurst, Jagdwurst, Bratwurst, and Bockwurst. We drank the most wonderful coffee and ate bread rolls with the most excruciatingly exquisite cherry jam. We spent an afternoon helping Tante Rikchen pick those sour cherries in her allotment—an allotment that would have made Chekhov envious [22] —so eating the jam made from last year's cherries was made all the more delicious. We checked out the Schützenfest [23] at which I won several hundred screwdrivers, by shooting sections of chalk on wires. Every five sections of chalk I shattered won me a screwdriver.

---

21 *Herman Munster* is a character in *The Munsters* – an American television comedy series— a satire on monster movies and popular family entertainment—which ran concurrently with The Addams Family. The family of monsters consider themselves fairly typical working-class Americans of the era. Herman Munster—the father—is modelled on Frankenstein's monster. *Lamburger Gestler* is a character in *The Adventures of William Tell* – a British adventure series, first broadcast in 1958, with Conrad Phillips as William Tell and Willoughby Goddard as Landburgher Gestler. Most people pronounced the name 'Lamburger Gestler'. His real name—in Schiller's 'Wilhelm Tell'—was Landvogt Geßler. His legend is recorded in a late 15th Century Swiss chronicle – as set in the Old Swiss Confederacy of the early 14th Century. William Tell—a brilliant shot with crossbow— saved his son by shooting an apple from the top of his head – and eventually assassinated Landvogt Geßler, a tyrannical reeve of Habsburg Österreich.

22 *The Cherry Orchard* is a play by Anton Chekhov in which a Russian aristocrat returns to her family estate (*which includes a large cherry orchard*) just before it is auctioned to pay the mortgage.

23 A Schützenfest is a traditional festival or fair featuring target shooting competitions. Schützenfest contestants compete based on shooting abilities – with side stalls set up for youths and the inexperienced. The winner of the competition becomes the Schützenkönig —shooting king—for the following year – and has a permanent large circular painted plaque to honour his or her home.

They asked me if I didn't want to shoot at the target to win better prizes—because I was evidently some kind of sharp shooter—but I said I was happy to shoot chalk and win screwdrivers. In the end I cleared them out of screwdrivers and they offered to trade them back for a radio. I accepted the radio gladly and gave it to Tante Rikchen and Onkel Arnold as a present. They were delighted with it and told me they were proud of me – despite my hair. Word had already got back to them about the English hippie who was resident in their home. *'Er sieht fürchterlich aus, aber er ist höflich und er kann gut schießen'*—in spite of being a Struwwelpeter [24] —who could shoot like whomever the German version of Annie Oakley might be.

I owed whatever prowess I had, to my mother. She was an excellent shot. She had a fine row of rifle-shooting medals she'd won as a teenager. We had a couple of .177 air-rifles at home – purchased by my father to encourage 'manliness'. To his delight – I took to the art and seemed to excel, with a little help from my mother. She could swing one of those things up to her shoulder with one hand and hit the *bull's eye* dead centre after not more than a split second's aim. She'd done that once when my father had claimed the sights were out. She'd asked to give it a try and shot through the dining room window – rifle in one hand and the teacloth in the other. *"Zeese sights are correct"* she commented, handed the gun back to my father, and returned to cooking Sunday lunch. My father was good enough to say that he'd better work on his marksmanship. He was never vain, self-enamoured, pompous, petulant, or unjust – even though he could be exceedingly overbearing.

The last two days we spent with aunt Ruth and her daughters. What nice young ladies—*they*—were! They both spoke remarkably good English and played musical instruments: flute and piano. They were amazed by the DEBIL and amazed to hear Blues. I played a fair few numbers for them and wrote down the words so that they could sing with me. They loved to sing and found it great fun – trying to pronounce English with a Delta accent, or my version of it at least.

---

24 *'He looks frightful – but he has good manners and shoots well.' Der Struwwelpeter* (Shockheaded Peter) by Heinrich Hoffman is a children's book published in 1845.

The Kogelheide family were charming, gracious, generous, and monumentally hospitable. They made a punch one evening with pink champagne and more strawberries than the mind can comfortably conceive. The champagne was diluted with sparkling water in deference to the ages of their daughters and of Græham – but that didn't detract in any way from the sumptuousness of it.

And then it was all in the past. The long ride home and giving our parents an account that evidently pleased them. Then a week later a tie arrived. It was from HÖRZU magazine. It was a runner-up prize. It was deep sky blue with deep rose clouds – and was emblazoned with the glorious words *'Ich bin ein Dichter.'*[25] Well … I knew that. My mother was mightily proud of my achievement and so— strangely—was my father. I was ever-so-slightly disappointed at not having won first prize. I caught myself *feeling disappointed* and felt like an utter dolt. Did I actually—*want*—to win a pop song competition? No. What did it signify? Nothing. What did a Vajrayana Buddhist care about winning or losing competitions? I didn't have to reject the *'Ich bin ein Dichter'* tie because it was an illusion. That would just be another illusion. I didn't have to run in illusory circles trying to escape the illusion of the popular media. I creased up laughing.

"What's so funny Vic?" asked Græham

In answer I held up the tie and announced with mock hauteur *"Ich bin ein Berliner!"*[26]

"Nein …" Græham laughed *"Du bist ein Hamburger!"*

---

25 *'I am a poet.'*

26 *'I am a Berliner'* – or *'I am a doughnut'*. From a 1963 speech by President JF Kennedy in West Berlin. The word Berliner means both *citizen of Berlin* and doughnut. The *Berliner Pfannkuchen* is mainly referred to as a Berliner, in the same style as a Frankfurter, Hamburger, or Wiener. This follows the German-speaking tradition of naming food specialities after the towns that made them famous. A *Berliner* is a traditional German pastry similar to a doughnut with no central hole, made from sweet yeast dough and fried.

12

the Buddhist and the Bluesman

september 1968

There was little time left before the new phase of my life was to begin at a different school. It was another interlude bardo – an intermediate phase between this and that, in which I was not defined.[1] The definition would arise as new patterns coalesced.

I'd returned 'triumphant' from Germany – and a short hiatus ensued in which I spent time with Steve and Ron. We had a few Savage Cabbage rehearsals. The rest of the time I devoted to hours of silent sitting. My father applauded my zest for woodland walking – and, as he never walked in the woods, there was no chance of him ever discovering that I spent my time sitting in the branches of an old yew tree.

I was sitting for an hour a day at that point – and periods of thought-free presence had begun to occur more frequently. I was far from stable in terms of silent sitting – but I had the sense that I had a direction and a destination. The sensation that a previous version of 'me' had died—and was dying all the time—was increasingly present in terms of the sense of *what it was that was moving through life*. *What it was* that was *moving through life* could be abbreviated to 'me' and what 'I' was experiencing. The 'me' and 'I' however, had become ideas which were becoming decreasingly reliable. I was aware that there was a perceptual locus that changed in a chameleoid manner according to where I happened to be – and with whom.

---

1 Bardo (*bar do / antarabhava*) intermediate state or interval – most commonly understood as being between death and rebirth but actually between any two areas of experience such as being awake and sleeping. This teaching comes from the Bardo Thödröl (*bar do thos grol*), commonly—and incorrectly—known as *The Tibetan Book of the Dead*. It is from the Zhitrö Gongpa Rangdröl (*zhi khro dGongs pa rang grol*) revealed by the gTértön, Karma Lingpa.

With Savage Cabbage the locus looked and sensated like a Bluesman with friends. We inhabited a world that made sense of itself. I did not feel moved to question *that* world – but then, later, I'd be at home and re-defined as a son and brother. There'd be my father and mother—and Græham—and then I'd be *some other form of perceiving* in which the Bluesman was a memory. I was aware that I never really wished too much to be elsewhere – and this provided some kind of smoothness to every transition. Then the Monday arrived at which I was to set out for Virginia Water School – some 12 miles away.

My acceptance in the 6th year had been set in motion by Miss Sparshott, the Headmistress of Farnham Girls Grammar School. I'd committed an act of mild insanity by applying to Farnham Girls Grammar School for a place in their 6th year. Why? Well … Netherfield School concluded with the 5th year and anyone wishing to go on for another two years to take 'A' levels had to apply either to Farnham Boys' Grammar School or to one of the two Technical Colleges – Farnborough or Guildford. There was a problem however – you needed five 'O' levels to be accepted at Farnham Boys' Grammar School and four 'O' levels at each of the Technical Colleges. I had three 'O' levels … English Language, English Literature, and Geography. I'd have had History too but the teacher had left and was not replaced. The same was true of Drama, Art, and Music – but those subjects ended in the 3rd year. Finally, I *should* have had Religious Education 'O' level but for the teacher having had an 86 percent failure record. No one passed the examination in my year. I was somewhat shocked because I'd been obtaining marks in excess of 70 percent on a regular basis. Still … I'd gained 'A' grades in English Language and English Literature; so, I thought my three 'O' levels were relatively worthy – and as Farnham Girls' Grammar School only required three 'O' levels, I thought I may as well apply.

I took the precaution of only giving my first initial with my surname and was duly called to an interview.[2]

2   The interview with Miss Sparshott is given in detail in *'good morning little school girl'*, chapter 11, *'an odd boy'* Volume I by Doc Togden – ARO BOOKS WORLDWIDE.

After some consternation Miss Sparshott's annoyance with my foolishness became good humoured. She understood the situation vis-à-vis the Religious Education teacher because she'd heard the same complaint from all the Netherfield girls who had taken the subject. She had also heard of the libidinous horror that had taken place – of Mr Davies and Miss Elphinstone being caught *in flagrante* one lunchtime in the Chemistry laboratory. They'd been dismissed in disgrace. The Drama classes were not replaced by another English language subject – and I failed to obtain the 'O' level in Drama that I could easily have obtained. The upshot was that Miss Sparshott took pity on me. Although I was not accepted at Farnham Girls Grammar School – she wrote a letter to Mr Ironsides the headmaster of Virginia Water Comprehensive School. And so it was that I attended an interview and was accepted for the 6th year there.

Having eaten breakfast and filled my satchel with the required books (I'd read them all in the Summer) I rode off in the direction of the Farnborough Road which I took 'til it intersected with the London Road. I had directions and they were easy enough to follow. I arrived early and without problem—parked my motorcycle in the school car park—and went to find my class room. There was no one there. Observed on my own, I was told by a helpful teacher that the rest of the sixth-years would be in the 6th Form Common-room. I strolled over to a small building—separate from the main school buildings—and entered.

"Hello" I began *I'm Vic – I'm joining the 6th year here."*

The person I addressed turned out to be Pete Bridgewater – and he turned out to be a good friend.

"Welcome to hell" Pete laughed.

"You made the deal with Legba too?" I asked.

"Legba?" Pete enquired and I told him about the crossroads. As we were talking, Greg Ford joined the conversation and it was clear I'd hit the right note. Virginia Water School was Bluesville. Greg Ford was a Rocker who looked every inch the Rocker.

He had a fine suitably aged back leather jacket, black zip-up winklepicker boots,[3] and long dark hair. His repartee took no prisoners. Once it was understood that I was a member of the Savage Cabbage Blues Band – my credentials were established and everything else followed easily. I was introduced to the other Blues aficionados and the school day began.

I never knew quite what to make of two things in life: *the scene* – and *who* I *was in 'the scene'*. Clearly being *in the scene* was better than being *out of the scene*—as I'd been at Netherfield—but both had to be regarded as illusion if one were a serious Buddhist. I was trying hard to be a serious Buddhist. I was also trying hard as a serious Bluesman. I had no doubts that I was a Bluesman – but was not quite as confident that I could be a real Buddhist. If I was a serious Buddhist, would I not drop everything and hightail it to the Himalayas? Yes … but with what money? I could quit school and work on building sites – but then Id have to abandon Savage Cabbage. I had a debt of loyalty to Steve—and to Ron—and it was not a debt that I resented. I was a mixed bag of identities – and there was no separating them.

The nature of reality—whatever it was—was in the habit of changing. This was the latest in a series of cameos – and, whatever 'I' might be, was walking around in it smiling and being greeted with approval. I smiled back in return. I knew I could never explain such thoughts to anyone around me; other than Steve – and he had his limits when it came to discussing emptiness. The idea that reality was not *this*, not *that*, not *this and that*, and not *neither this nor that*. He'd just say *"Isn't it just there as it is"* and I'd reply *"Yes! Exactly—and that's what Dharma means—'as it is'."* And that would end the conversation with a gale of laughter.

---

3   Winklepickers were a style of shoe or boot in the late 1950s and early 1960s. Rockers continued to wear them after they fell out of general youth culture fashion. The pointed winklepicker toe was so-named because in Britain periwinkles or winkles were a popular seaside snack – eaten using a pin to extract the soft parts out of the coiled shell.

One of the first things I learnt was that there was a heavyweight party-scene in the area and that parties were regularly tracked down as far away as Camberley, Frimley, Woking, Bracknell, Slough, and Farnborough. The whole area around Virginia Water was a warren of suburban residential streets and so there were *always* parties. At that time, there seemed to be a culture which allowed people to show up at anyone's party as long as they had bottles of wine under their arms – and, although I wasn't a ferocious party-animal, I hit the party scene as part of the Virginia Water induction process. Lucky for me that I plunged in – because that is how I came to meet one of the loves of my life: Lindie Dale.

They said of John the Baptist—in the Gospel of St Matthew—that he was *Elijah come again*.[4] When I met Lindie it was as if she was both Alice and Anelie come again. It was love at first sight for both of us – and from that point it grew exponentially.[5] We had everything imaginable in common apart from academic prowess – and the ability to learn foreign languages. Lindie was a thoroughgoing culturally encyclopædic, massively well-read polymath. She was also the most beautiful being I had *ever* beheld. She had brilliant ginger hair and blue-green eyes that were like search lights. She seemed to sparkle with life from head to foot. Her smile made me dizzy. I'd suddenly become the happiest creature on the planet. I was definitely not a monastic type. That seemed to settle the issue in relation to quitting school and heading for the Himalayas – but it threw me into a bedazzlement of conflicting notions in which I lost track of personal identity. I seemed to be *whatever happened* or *whatever was unfolding*. It was not unpleasant – but it had certain resonances with what I'd heard about acid trips. It was as if I was *hallucinating life* – and the only solid ground I had was silent sitting; a state in which there was no ground.

---

4   *'For all the prophets and the law prophesied until John. And if ye will receive, this is Elias, which was for to come.'* King James Bible (11:13–11:14).

5   This first meeting is described in *'easy rider'*, chapter 1, *'an odd boy'* Volume I by Doc Togden – ARO BOOKS WORLDWIDE.

Virginia Water School was pleasant enough – but suddenly it became an immense pleasure. I was fortunate in having only a few subjects. I only needed five 'O' levels and two 'A' levels for Art School and so I was not hard pressed. I didn't need wonderful grades in the 'O' levels – so they were no great problem. Sociology and History were interesting and gave me somewhat more of a political sense than I'd had before. Art was brilliant and I had some fine teachers. Mr Havilland, the English teacher however, was a disappointment. Although he was as old fashioned as Mr Preece he entirely lacked his spark or literary authority. Mr Havilland was pedantic – a stickler for petty rules. He took objection to my lack of school uniform – even though the headmaster had told me that wearing my Uncle Charles' dark grey woollen three piece herringbone suit would be fine – as long as it bore the school badge. It bore the school badge – so what was the problem? Mr Ironsides, the headmaster, considered it to be an unnecessary expense to purchase a uniform for two years. He thought the suit rather smart. To his mind 'smartness' was the issue rather than the exact rule. Mr Havilland complained and was overruled – but that caused him to treat me with a certain severity. Still, my work was always handed in on time and my marks were always in the 70s and 80s – so he had no grounds for having me flogged or keel-hauled. Not that anyone was flogged—or even whacked with a plimsoll—at that school, but I could see there was a certain look in his eye that bespoke a desire for retribution. Fortunately he was fundamentally an honourable man – and so apart from viewing my appearance with continued displeasure he did nothing to penalise me for it.

I'd inherited a substantial wardrobe from my uncle Charles subsequent to his sad demise. He'd had cancer of the throat and had died in his 50s. He was a cavalry officer and a rather snappy dresser. I therefore inherited a white three-piece suit, velvet smoking jacket, and all manner of Edwardian clothes. The smoking jacket had a satin collar and wonderful frogging closures. Jack always said I should wear it on stage – but that wasn't my image as a Bluesman. It might work for Jimi Hendrix – but I felt that a honky Bluesman should be understated.

Black American Blues performers could *Put on the Ritz* with outrageous ostentation – and look *just the part*. Honkies however, just looked ridiculous when attempting it.[6]

My idea of Bluesman appearance was: Levi 501s, collarless shirt, and de-mob suit waistcoat. It was a workingman's look. Blues was a working-class métier – and so that's exactly what I wore the first time we played the Queen's Oak.[7] Steve and Ron followed suit – but Jack came on as he always did, looking every inch the Burlesque Vaudeville Cabaret Showman in silk floral shirt and velvet loon pants.[8]

There'd been quite a rumble of interest about my being in a Blues Band at school – and so when the weekend arrived a lot of people showed up to see what Savage Cabbage would be like. As Steve, Ron, Jack, and I mounted the stage there were hoots and whoops and we all felt we were starting on the right note. The audience had taken in the MARSHALL amplifiers and LUDWIG traps[9] – and now they took in the guitars: Ron on FENDER TELECASTER; Steve on FENDER PRECISION bass and 6-string HAGSTROM bass; and me on GIBSON EB3. The GIBSON EB3 belonged to Ron – but he'd let me borrow it for gigs. He'd let Steve talk him into the idea that back-up bass was a creative vector that would make us different from every other band. All I had to do was play the simplest riffs and leave Steve free to roam the fretboard in an extravagant manner. Steve tuned high and I tuned low. He played loud and I played a little less loud – so that errors would not be too horribly obvious. I was playing backing-bass and learning to play bass whilst singing. That wasn't always easy—especially with *Born Under a Bad Sign*—and so Steve always took over the bass line when I was singing.

6   This was obviously racist – but as long as it favoured African Americans, I found it acceptable.

7   I also inherited my uncle's Cavalry frock coat which I wore in the colder weather in unheated venues.

8   From 1966 bell-bottoms became increasingly fashionable. They were flared below the knee, with bottoms sometimes matching the waist measurement. Loon pants were a variant, with an increased flare – sans pockets and waistband.

9   *Traps* is a contraction of 'contraptions' and refers to drums.

My time came in the improvisational instrumental sections when Steve took off into flights of rhapsodic bass virtuosity – leaving me to provide a simple pulse.

So there we were. We launched in with *Rolling and Tumbling* which was an exciting piece with Steve playing slide on bass and me wailing on harp. The audience were almost all grinning at us and we knew that this was how it was going to be in most places. Ron—as ever—was the star and when he took off people started yelling occasional ecstatic fragments of language that I never quite caught. It's an amazing thing to see an audience enjoying what you're playing. It's also surreal – because somehow, you can't quite believe it. I could believe it of Ron and Steve – because although they were under 18, they were entirely professional. Ron had been a world-class player at the age of 11 – and he was now 16. Steve—almost 18—was moving steadily in that direction, having advanced rapidly since meeting Ron. Playing next to Ron was an inspiration for us all – because he was Bach, Mozart, and Paganini rolled into one. He was all four Kings: BB, Albert, Freddie, and Earl. He was Robert Johnson, Muddy Waters, and Buddy Guy. There was almost nothing that he wasn't when it came to music. He played piano too – and often played piano riffs on guitar and guitar riffs on piano.

Between songs, it occurred to me that it was just as well that I was not convinced by the illusion of what I could have taken myself to be. I was a focus of attention because of Ron and Steve. I might have a voice – but I'd be nobody without them. This was not 'Buddhist humility'. I never went in for humility—Buddhist or otherwise—it was simply my own take on realism. I did not feel unworthy – or as if Savage Cabbage could get a better vocalist. I was happy to be exactly where I was – but had no sense of the applause having anything to do with me.

Cries of execration would have been upsetting. I'd never had to deal with execration since being hit almost weekly when I was young at Netherfield, on the basis that I had a German mother. I was once so badly beaten up that the police had to be called in. Then the assaults came to an end.

So what was this all about? Who was I? I had no idea apart from the subjects that obsessed me: Buddhism, Blues, and the Arts. Meditation would eventually reveal the nature of *what looked out of the senses* to witness these phenomena – but in the meantime …
where was the reality behind the characters who inhabited my name:

> *The failure at mathematics and sport; the Buddhist and the Bluesman; the Realist explorer and the Surrealist poet? The stammerer and the fellow quick with linguistics? Mr English and Herr German? The quasi-early 20th Century English gentleman and the hippy with starched and ironed Levi's? The fellow with the Edwardian smoking-jacket; and, the Man in the White Suit?*

I was an *empty space* who inhabited images – that were both *what I was,* and somehow extraneous in terms of a *space* that was fundamental. This description could sound like a person with an identity crisis—if you were to analyse it in *that way*—but I had no sense of crisis. I was as happy as I could ever remember being – but it felt like being in an *unstructured play* in a *theatre shaped like the world.*

There was no visceral paucity in my passions – but somehow my passions never defined me too severely outside the moment. Whatever the passion in the moment, it soared like a dragon – maybe because I was born in the Water Dragon Year of the Tibetan calendar. Passion was always contextual and there never seemed to be any conflict between passions. Whether being with Lindie, riding my chopped BSA, playing bass, walking in the woods, writing poetry, painting, drawing, or sitting silently in the branches of a yew tree – I was always utterly absorbed.

So much for stream-of-consciousness pontification … Passion is all well and good when everything seems well and good – but what of tragedy? I'd seen *that* – or whatever seemed tragic to a child: the departure of Alice for Herefordshire; the death of Mr Love; and, the departure of Anelie for Switzerland.

I'm not sure whether I thought that I was *Dr Blues the survivor—or the nascent Buddhist attempting to take impermanence in his stride*—but, standing on stage that night, I had no idea that the locomotive of lacerating loss and lachrymose lamentation was hurtling down the tracks behind me.

Brigadier Dale and his good lady wife wished to know who was courting their daughter Lindie. They called her Linda and I was to call her Linda in their hearing. They did not approve of having their daughter's name abbreviated – even though she'd abbreviated her name herself. That should have been a warning. I was invited for afternoon tea and cake. I went. I ate. The next day my relationship with Lindie was over. I was deemed an entirely inappropriate liaison. I was a long-haired lout, an irredeemable drug-ingesting pervert – and, probably, a depraved criminal. They took no account of my suit or polite speech. They took no account of anything other than an appearance they instinctively loathed.[10] Lindie was commanded not even to speak with me at school – but on that point she rebelled. Lindie did continue to speak with me – but meetings beyond the school gate ceased.

So why did I think *impermanence* was such a wonderful notion? Everything and everyone came and went – wasn't *that* the idea? And I was supposed to sit back and see it all as illusion? Brilliant Buddhist I turned out to be. Still ... no one told me I was supposed to like it. It's just how it was – and how it always would be. *You* got attached to some aspect of *reality* – and then, sooner or later, *reality* detached *you*. When I sat in silence and let go of thought, it was fine – and I could often be happy simply enjoying the colours and sounds of the world. I could laugh too – because I could easily find myself amused by a variety of phenomena. Still, taking up a positivist-eternalist religion would do nothing to change the fact that Lindie was lost as a romantic partner.

---

10 The meeting with Lindie's parents is detailed in chapter 5, *'an odd boy'* Volume II by Doc Togden – ARO BOOKS WORLDWIDE. Lindie is also mentioned in chapter 9 of the same book.

I was no goddamn Gottfried Leibniz.[11] Thinking that *'everything is for the best in the best of all possible worlds'* was deranged. Gottfried Leibniz was an idiot. Hardly surprising that Voltaire lampooned his philosophy in *Candide*.[12] So this was the suffering of which Shakyamuni Buddha spoke[13] ... Well ... I'd been there before – and here I was again; apart from the fact that the musical part of my life was better than it had ever been. I decided that it would be an act of imbecility to let the tragedy of my love-life prove detrimental to Savage Cabbage – so whenever I got to feeling too miserable about the loss of Lindie, I sat, or I sang.

I sat and repeatedly let go of *the Lindie-thoughts*. Then I let go of them again. And again. And again – until occasionally I succeeded. And then, of course, there were the times when music functioned as sitting meditation functioned: when music was all that existed *in the moment*. The moments when I was on stage singing – or during rehearsals when I let rip with *Born Under a Bad Sign*: *'... if it wasn't for bad luck – I wouldn't*—have—*no luck at all.'* Not true for me of course —Lindie notwithstanding—but the words of the song went beyond what they meant. Blues was always like that for me. I could sing any line and mean it in a way quite other than the *words as normally defined*. Blues was a medium through which I could simply *be the sound of what I was singing*.

---

11 The phrase 'the best of all possible worlds'—'Die beste aller möglichen Welten'—was coined by the German polymath Gottfried Leibniz in 1710 in the essay *'Essais de Théodicée sur la bonté de Dieu, la liberté de l'homme et l'origine du mal' – 'Essays on the Goodness of God, the Freedom of Man and the Origin of Evil'*. The claim that the actual world is the best of all possible worlds is the central argument in Leibniz's theodicy, or his attempt to solve the problem of evil.

12 *Candide, ou l'Optimisme* is a French satire published in 1759 by Voltaire. It follows the life of a young man, Candide, who is living a sheltered life in pleasant surroundings where he is indoctrinated with Leibnizian optimism by his mentor, Pangloss. The book recounts the abrupt end of Candide's lifestyle, followed by his gradual disillusionment as he witnesses the suffering of the world. In the end Candide doesn't completely reject positivism – but advocates practical realism.

13 Dug-ngal (*sDug bsNgal / dukkha / unsatisfactoriness*) is usually translated as 'suffering'- but it is actually the entire spectrum of unsatisfactoriness from the slightest irritation to the most extreme anguish.

Ron and Steve told me that the loss of Lindie had given my vocals an extra edge – and that I had developed from that point to delivering a vocal line that was vaguely shocking.

"I don't know how you did it, Vic …" Ron commented with a puzzled shake of his head *"… but your vocals have got lethal."*

"Thanks Ron – but I don't sound any different in my own ears."

"Maybe – but I can see it in the faces of the audience when you start torturing the vocal line the way you do. It's like when I play a long howling bend – the audiences respond to your voice in the same way. It's like you're playing guitar with those notes sometimes."

"Well … I'm glad it sounds good."

"What d'you think made the difference?" asked Ron

"Beats me …"

Steve moved his hands—looking at Ron—in a way that betokened that perhaps this was not a happy subject to raise with me – even though it was complimentary. Ron failed to pick up on Steve's cue and said *"I suppose it could be Lindie …"*

"I suppose it could …" I replied and changed the subject *"… but – I think I'm mainly responding to what you and Steve are playing. You two are a huge inspiration – it's as if I was up there with Cream."*

"Yeah …" laughed Ron *"… apart from the lack of Ginger Baker."*

"Yes … well …" I grinned rather faintly *"… alright – but Jack's improving, isn't he."*

"A little …" Ron replied with some exasperation *"Y'know … you always defend him – but he always complains about us having to be led by your tempo rubato."*

"Maybe he has a point" I offered.

"Crap" Ron scoffed. *"And you know it."*

"Yeah, Vic …" Steve shrugged with a grin *"… Ron and I have no problems with your vocal line – 'cause there's a logic to it that we follow. What Ron's saying's basically that Jack doesn't really deserve your support."*

"Maybe not …" I mused *"… but I don't see it in terms of fairness or whatever. I wouldn't like to get into making what he says affect what I say – and anyway I don't see drums as being that significant. I could do without drums altogether – so I don't mind that he's simple or rudimentary or whatever."*

Ron and Steve both laughed – and Steve said *"So – in the same breath you've defended Jack and written him off altogether."*

"Right …" I laughed *"… never said I wasn't paradoxical – but … what I'm saying about drums, isn't personal about Jack – it's just that I tend to feel that percussion is superfluous. With most bands they're just too loud. What I want to hear is the music rather than the banging. I feel it gets in the way of the melody."*

"But the melody line needs punctuation" Ron explained.

So I replied clapping my hands loudly between quiet words *"Yes*—**clap clap**—*Ron*—**clap clap**—*I*—**clap clap**—*see*—**clap clap clap**—*what*—**clap**—*you*—**clap clap clap**—*mean."*

Ron and Steve both doubled up laughing. *"There's no winning with you is there"* Ron hooted.

"Sorry …" I responded – and actually was sorry *"… I really shouldn't try to tell you two anything about music. As you know*—*I have a lot of my own weird ideas*—*so don't take any of it as if I think I know what I'm talking about."*

"Yeah well …" Ron grinned *"… we know you're the kind of bloody saint who never gets shirty about anything – but we do take what you say seriously; even though you've never been able to study music. You live music though – and that's the thing that makes the difference. So what you say always interests me. Maybe we should play one number a set without drums? What d'you think Steve?"*

"Yeah—*why not*—*it could be interesting – but what would Jack do?"*

"Bugger Jack!" Ron laughed

"You first" I quipped – at which Ron rolled onto his side almost in tears of mirth.

"But seriously …" I continued *"… he'd need to have a rôle – maybe I could play a harp duo with him; a Train Time,*[14] *where I let him lead. He could call all the shots then – and I'd just follow whatever rhythms he played."*

And so we talked on into the evening—brimming with the ideas—each bouncing them off each other – and, for a stretch of time, there were no thoughts of Lindie.

I thought about that on the ride home. It seemed peculiar that I could be free of thoughts of Lindie for periods of time – and feel quite light hearted. Maybe meditation made that possible. Was this some sort of sign of success; however small? I wished there was someone I could ask. Certainly, I couldn't judge. I realised that I was seriously in need of a teacher. Ron and Steve could tell me where I was musically – but there was no one who could tell me where I was with Buddhism. The need of advice from a Lama—a Buddhist teacher—became ever more obvious.

---

14 *Train Time* was a duo played by Ginger Baker on percussion and Jack Bruce on Blues harp and vocals on the *Wheels of Fire* album.

13

It feels like 'this'

november 1968

I shook my head in disbelief at the article in MELODY MAKER. *"I've no idea why anyone wants to read about other people's lives ..."* I sighed with some degree of chagrin *"... unless those lives are glorious."*

"Good f'ra laugh I s'pose" offered Jack.

"Yes ... I suppose it can be amusing to hear about fascists getting the comeuppance" Ron chipped in, in an offhand way *"but I think Vic's on his way to philosophising about it. I can tell – he's got that weird look in his eyes."*

"As usual" I laughed. *"It's just this—rancid offal—they print about the private lives of musicians. I really don't need to know about it."* Pause. *"Take a dekko[1] at this adjectival drivel."* I passed Jack the MELODY MAKER in which some journalist had expressed an unsavoury opinion.

"Well ... it's reality isn't it" Jack commented.

"Well—if—it's all true, yes – but even if it—is—true, who cares? It's only part of a story anyway. People's lives are mixed aren't they – and mostly, the press either want to make fun of something or give it a nasty slant. They only adulate what's on the agenda for adulation – like who's the latest tunelessly-fast guitar hero or whatever."

"True" Steve said with a strong affirmative nod of his head – before standing up to continue. Steve often stood up when he had something serious to say. *"I mean – what would the press have made of Vic and Anelie? I mean – can you imagine. 'Underage sex scandal discovered in the murky past of Savage Cabbage vocalist Farquhar Arbuthnot'. That's how they'd present it – and it would be one way to look at it."*

---

1   Dekko: English slang derived from Hindi. Dekho means 'look' and dekhnā means 'see'. The term was imported by soldiers stationed in India during the British Raj.

"Yeah but it would be fantastic for publicity – that stuff never hurt the Stones did it?" Jack chuckled *"That whole story about Mick Jagger and Marianne Faithful with the Mars Bar was wild."*[2]

"The point Steve's making, Jack …" Ron said – rolling his eyes up a little in exasperation *"… is that it wouldn't be a realistic picture of Vic, would it?"* Pause. *"I mean Vic's a dyed-in-the-wool romantic who doesn't like girls being called birds."*

"Not even chicks?" asked Jack, addressing me.

"No Jack …" I replied with a grin *"… chicks are fowl."*

"Thought you absolutely loved'em?" Jack laughed.

"Jack …" Ron said rolling his eyes—yet again—and shaking his head in exasperation. *"Use your brain you gnome … Vic is joking. A chick is a baby chicken and chickens are fowl."* Then—seeing Jack's slightly dazed expression—Ron spelt it out *"F—O—W—L. As in ducks, geese, turkeys, grouse, and pheasants – y'docile peasant."*

"Ah … right … yeah—the penny bloody drops—very bloody funny Mister Arbuthnot, I'm sure."

"Anyhow …" continued Ron *"… the point is that the bloody press distort everything and whether Mars Bars make good publicity or not – they just might have nothing to do with what actually happened."*

"Yeah, alright then" Jack conceded. Jack always conceded when Ron stepped in. Jack would argue the toss with me all night—or for twenty minutes with Steve—but Ron almost had parental status with Jack. That was just as well as far as I could see because Jack sometimes needed keeping in line. Ron turned to me at that point and gave me the 'come on say your piece' movement of his head – accompanied as always by a slight narrowing of his eyes.

---

2 A bogus story of the time that can be obtained from the internet should the reader wish to do so

"Well ... the press seem to love flinging people into the gutter – after having raised them to demigod status. They feed on that polarity. I have the sense that he quickest way to become indentured to bestial banality, is to become a journalist – or worse, a newspaper reporter. People who start out as normal humane people with a desire to write, can end up as perverted manipulators of public opinion – without even knowing how it happened."

"Yeah ..." nodded Ron with a sigh *"... but ... the poxy perverted press wouldn't exist without its pox-ridden prurient audience. As long as people want to read about who got a leg over whom – they'll keep printing it."*

Steve shook his head *"Yes Ron – but it's an alligator and egg argument isn't it. People want bad news because they've grown up with it. Maybe people only think they like reading bad news because it is always there. Newspapers are for sale – so people buy them. They buy them – because that's what people do."*

"Can't deny that" Ron conceded.

"So ..." I ventured *"Society's indoctrinated into thinking that 'news' is necessary. People have asked me 'How d'you know what's going on if you don't read the newspapers or listen to the news?' and I reply 'I—always—know what's going on: someone, somewhere, is lying, cheating, or exploiting someone else.' Wonderful exciting things must also be happening – but the press hardly ever cover those stories – unless it's the local paper reporting the local bring-and-buy sale. Otherwise positive news is limited to football and who won the match."* Pause. *"Y'know – somebody asked me if I'd seen the match on the weekend and I said 'Yes—it was a Swan Vesta[3]—and it flared up nicely."*

Ron and Steve guffawed at that – but Jack had become a little removed, sensing that his contributions to the conversation had not been hugely welcomed. He was a keen football supporter and I realised I should have known better than to have made that remark.

3 Swan Vestas are the most popular brand of matches currently available in Britain that will strike on any rough surface. They date back to 1883 when the Collard and Kendall match company in Bootle-on-Merseyside, Liverpool introduced 'Swan Wax Matches'. These were superseded by 'Swan White Pine Vestas' made by the Diamond Match Company, which were made of wooden splints soaked in wax. In 1906 they were named 'Swan Vestas' when the Diamond Match Company merged with Bryant and May and promoted the Swan brand – and by the 1930s 'Swan Vestas' became the best-selling match in Britain.

What was I to do though? I couldn't pretend to be other than I was. I'd have to make a point of supporting Jack at some point on the next likely occasion.

"This place would turn into Nazi Germany in two shakes of a lamb's tail" Steve opined. *"My father worries about attitudes in the police force sometimes. He says that nationalism can be problematic when people get over excited."*

"Yeah …" Jack laughed *"… shouting hallelujah because Britain sends in the bloody gunboats to quell insurrections in some place we shouldn't even be. Then the tabloids print jingoistic headlines and everyone and his uncle gets 'Rule Britannia' tattooed on his penis to pretend that y'c'ld spell out bloody 'Land of Hope and Glory' if he had an erection."*

"That's about the way of it Jack" I commented – glad to be able to support one of Jack's statements, even though *Rule Britannia* and the *Land of Hope and Glory* were different compositions.

"Listening to 'the news' equates with accepting indoctrination as far as I'm concerned" Ron stated. *"My father's always on at me to read the papers – as if that's a mark of bloody adulthood."*

"It used to be the same with my father – but he's given up now. I think he accepts that I'm an anomaly and that there's nothing that can be done with me."

"Well he's right about that" announced Jack with a chuckle.

"Yes Jack" I smiled *"you're absolutely correct – I'm an enigma with variations."* Pause. *"I hear what goes on in the world without needing to read about it. Someone I trust—like you three—usually tells me what I need to know – but as I am not a politician there's nothing I can do with the information."*

"But I thought you were a political man – and that you practised what you preached?" laughed Jack, quoting the Jack Bruce song.

"Yeah so don't decry me Jacko – not when I'm tryin' to teach" I replied in parody, getting a round of applause from Ron and Steve.

"But, apart from that …" I continued *"… what use is information you can't use? It's only value is to give people the false sense of thinking they know what's happening in the world."*

"You have to read what the press want you to read" Steve added. *"And one event can be portrayed in many different ways—even without actually lying— how does anyone know what really happens? Lies are easily managed through what's left out – and the way the 'facts' are described."*

"The 'facts' of the press" I stated with heavy emphasis on each word *"are mainly the semantic sophistry of sensationalism."*

"Fine alliteration!" laughed Steve.

"I get what you're saying" Jack offered. *"… must admit that I don't like it when the bloody* MELODY MAKER *makes snide remarks about people I like."*

"Quite right Jack – that's exactly what I'm saying. I mean – what you told us about Jimi Hendrix the other day was interesting. That's the kind of thing that would make me want to read news."

That convulsed Jack. *"Yeah – right!"*

I got the sense that Jack felt he'd won his way back into favour and was glad to see his expression change. *"The thing is … ingesting 'the news' equates with accepting the pill of repressive tolerance."*

"Interesting term" Steve mused. *"What's repressive tolerance?"*

"It's useful" I replied *"to understand 'repressive tolerance' – because it's the rubber dummy that society shoves into everyone's mouth. It prevents us from having tantrums that disturb the status quo – or changing society. Repressive tolerance is often a tool to keep people from revolution."*

"So …" queried Ron *"… what's tolerated that allows the repression? How does that work?"*

"The idea's that if you throw the serfs a biscuit from time to time, they'll not attack your castle. So, 'The News' is one of the biscuits they throw to the peasants – but it's an insidious biscuit. It gives people just enough to keep them quiet. People are conned into thinking that reading 'The News' keeps them informed – and therefore somehow they have some sort of power."

"Yeah …" chuckled Ron. *"That's a bloody illusion for a start."*

"Right, and I was introduced to the idea of 'repressive tolerance' by my history teacher. He was one of the few good teachers at Netherfield. The idea comes from a book by Herbert Marcuse – called 'Repressive Tolerance'. I've not read the book – but the history teacher summarised it well enough. I don't see myself as a political revolutionary, so I didn't take it any further."

"Yeah ..." Ron sighed *"I've got a lot of sympathy with radical socialist political ideals – but ... I think socialism turns into tyranny as well once the wrong people take over ... and ... the wrong people always do seem to take over."*

Jack, by this time, had wearied somewhat of our philosophising – and decided that he'd get an early night. *"Unlike you two geniuses ..."* he addressed Ron and Steve *"... I have school work to catch up on. Mr Arbuthnot here ..."* he chuckled *"... doesn't have to do anything but paint pictures and write poetry – so he can stay up all night long."*

At that point I burst into song: Steve and Ron, surprisingly joining me *"We gonna pitch a wang dang doodle all night long, All night long—all night long—all night long."*[4]

Then I continued *"Tell Automatic Slim , tell Razor-toting Jim, Tell Butcher-knife Toting Annie, tell Fast-talking Fanny, We gonna pitch it all, down that union hall, We gonna romp and tromp 'til midnight, We gonna fuse the lights at daylight, We gonna pitch a wang dang doodle all night long."*

It was good of Jack to laugh. *"I see you're going to have a knees-up. You'll have to tell me what I missed."* And then he took off for home.

Once Jack had left Ron asked *"So ... Vic ... I've been thinking ... You seem to have got something going with philosophy or something. D'you read Aristotle or something?"*

"No Ron – that's all Greek to me" I laughed.

"Where's it come from then?"

---

4   *Wang Dang Doodle* was written by Willie Dixon and first recorded by Howling Wolf in 1960. It was released by Chess Records in 1961. In 1965, Willie Dixon and Leonard Chess persuaded Koko Taylor to record it for Checker Records, a Chess subsidiary – and Koko Taylor's version became a hit, reaching number thirteen in the Billboard R&B chart as well as number 58 in the pop chart. Wang Dang Doodle then became a blues standard.

"You may as well own up" Steve suggested with a shrug – as if prompting me was something he just had to do.

"Well ..." I commenced *"It's no big secret – it's just that I don't tend to talk about it much."*

"Vic's a Buddhist" Steve added – because he detected that I was going to continue to dissemble.

"What? Lobsang Rampa[5] and all that stuff?"

"That's why I don't talk about it much" I smiled. *"But no, it's nothing at all to do with Lobsang Rampa. He's a plumber from Devon somewhere, who read a lot of Theosophy [6]—y'know all that Western occultist twaddle—and decided to pretend he was a Tibetan Lama – or rather that some Tibetan Lama had taken over his body because Cyril Hoskins—that was his name—was tired of life, or some such thing."*

"Sorry Vic—I shouldn't have been facetious—I was just kind of, taken aback."

"No offense taken Ron – but I suppose you can see why I don't talk about it: not that I won't talk about it if you want. Just don't let me bore you with it."

"So ... how does that work then I mean ... with austerity and all that? I mean you seem pretty normal ..." Ron laughed *"... apart from being the raving lunatic we all know and love?"*

"Well austerity is only part of the picture—and really only for monks and nuns —and I've got no inclination in that direction."

"That's clear enough ..." laughed Ron *"... from your scene with that Swiss au pair girl!"*

5   Cyril Henry Hoskin (1910 –1981) was the British author of *The Third Eye* (1956), written under the pseudonym Lobsang Rampa. Despite exposure as a fraud—whose books had scant reference to Tibetan Buddhism—he published a further 20 books as Lobsang Rampa. Heinrich Harrer hired private detective Clifford Burgess to investigate him. His report was published in the Daily Mail in 1958.

6   Theosophy (*Greek – from theos:* God – and *sophia:* wisdom. Literally: *God's wisdom*) refers to an elaborate esoterically structured philosophy of the mysteries of life with regard to divinity. Theosophists seek to understand the mysteries of the universe and what it is that unites the universe, humanity, and the divine. The goal is to explore the origin of divinity and humanity, and the world. From such an hoc investigation, theosophists try to discover a coherent description of the purpose and origin of the universe.

"Hit the nail on the head there, Ron" I smiled. *"For me … it's about understanding the nature of reality."*

"Sort of scientific, then?" Ron mused.

"Yes … scientific – but also psychological. And … I'm also interested in Tibetan culture – the religious art. The paintings are fantastic – and I'm interested in the way that Art's part of it. So … I suppose … it's like science and psychology as seen through Art and music – and, well, through all the Arts."

"Yeah …" mused Ron *"I can see how that'd suit you."* Pause. *"So … Blues, then? That can just be part of it without any problem I suppose."*

It wasn't a question – but a statement, so I nodded *"It's not a heavyweight moral-ethical approach like Christianity – so there's no emphasis other than … compassion – which, mainly just looks like acting decently – y'know, being: open-minded, tolerant, generous, honest … and … not to get hooked into thinking I am the best thing in the universe."* Pause. *"Something like that."*

"Vic …" Ron stated with a mock-stern expression *"… you don't have to give me the children's version y'know."*

"Alright …" I laughed *"… but don't say I didn't warn you."*

"Fire away Vic."

"To begin with – Buddhism is atheistic."

"That's good to know" Ron grinned.

"Yeah – but Vic's been an atheist since he was five" Steve said.

"How's that then?" Ron cackled.

"Well …" I was wondering exactly how much to say. *"My girlfriend …"*

"You had a girlfriend when you were five!?" Ron laughed. *"Jesus – you started young."*

"Always have liked ladies Ron – but anyway, her parents were atheists, and Christianity didn't make sense to me – well … as my father interpreted it. God, for him, was an autocrat – besides which, there were too many illogicalities even for a five-year-old."

"True enough … but anyway—sorry to interrupt—tell me more" Ron encouraged.

"Right … so … Firstly, reality is self-creating. There's no concept of a creator-god. Secondly there's no soul – but that isn't quite as bleak as it might sound. It's simply that there is nothing that continues; which can be identified. If it can be identified, it's impermanent – and therefore cannot be a continuum."

"So … what continues then?" asked Ron *"I suppose something continues – unless we just vanish when we die, which is normal if you're an atheist."*

"Exactly, Ron" I smiled. *"Buddhism is only atheistic inasmuch as it denies God. It doesn't deny 'the continuity of being' – it just defines that 'continuity' as emptiness: an uncharacterised stream that carries patterns from one life to another – but those patterns are not fixed. It's not really so much different to what happens in life. For example – when you look back at who you were as a five-year-old – can you really say that you're still the same?"*

"Yeah …" Ron mused *"… but there's my memory – that's still there."*

"Yes – but can you feel as if you were still that five-year-old?"

Ron shook his head *"Got me there."*

"I could say a lot more – but maybe we should leave it there for now. I could go on for hours y'know."

"Thanks Vic – good of you to tell me … maybe, yeah … we'll talk again sometime. This is stuff I need to think about."

Steve—who sat silently while I held forth—said *"See, Vic: I told you, you should talk about it."*

"Yeah" added Ron. *"Just maybe not when Jack's there – because … well I don't think I need to say why."*

Ron and Steve burst out laughing at that point – and Ron commented *"He's not the brightest spark I ever met."*

Somehow—although I agreed—I didn't feel comfortable about laughing at Jack. I said nothing because I felt somehow protective of my religion. I didn't want to give the impression that it made you sanctimonious, pious, or self-righteous. I detested that kind of thing – but I also felt sorry for Jack. Ron put on a Howling Wolf album – because he wanted to listen to Wang Dang Doodle.

"Yes … Ron …" I smiled a little sadly *"… but there's something else I bear in mind in terms of Buddhism … kindness. I think we need to give Jack the support that will help him stand up to his parents. If we're all on his side encouraging him – he might well pluck up the courage to tell them that he's old enough now to live a little more of his own adjectival life."*

"That's logical – I suppose" laughed Ron. *"Can't argue with the Lama."*

"But is that the 'one l' or the 'two l' variety" I laughed. *"I think I'm more the latter than the former."*

Ron looked vaguely bemused so I quoted Ogden Nash *"The 'One L' Lama, he's a priest; The 'Two L' Llama, he's a beast; but I will bet my silk pyjama there isn't any 'Three L' Lllama."*

Ron guffawed at that – but went on to ask *"So … how does 'realism' work with 'kindness' then – in terms of Buddhism?"*

"Mmmm …" I pondered *"… that's not so easy to answer – because there's the question of subjectivity and objectivity. Many things we imagine are objective are actually subjective – and so there's no absolute answer outside the realisation of nonduality that allows pure appropriateness …"* Pause. *"… but, now you're going to want me to explain nonduality – and that's beyond me. I can try – but it's outside my experience and so all I can do is fumble with the principles I've tried to study. Y'know that dictum 'Read, learn, and inwardly digest'?"* Ron nodded. He'd heard it. *"Well … I've read. I've tried to learn – but I've got a case of indigestion at the moment."*

"Alright" laughed Ron. *"Groan it to me then."*

"Give it to us – like Sepulchrave"[7] Steve jested.

"Not if it means being eaten alive by owls" I replied – knowing that Steve was referring to Mervyn Peak's Gormenghast trilogy. *"Anyhow … where to begin? Well … there are two technical terms that have to be explained:* 'emptiness' *and* 'form'. 'Form' *is everything that can be sensed – including thought.* 'Emptiness' *is the complete absence of* 'form' *– but emptiness has the potential to allow form to appear."*

"Like … silence and sound?" Ron suggested.

"Exactly – and then, the same would hold true for all the senses including thinking. That's why one of the main practices is to sit in silence in order to discover the quality or experience of mind where there is no thought."

"So … what's the benefit of that then?" asked Ron.

"The benefit, is you can rid yourself of 'addiction to thought'. *I mean, for example, I'll bet you're not thinking of anything when you get into one of your amazingly long riffs."*

Ron pondered for a while and replied *"Never thought about it in those terms … but …"*

"Well—put it like this—you're probably not planning the next note or the next series of notes – are you? I mean I'm no more than mediocre on a musical instrument – but even I don't think when I play harp. Even on bass I can get carried away sometimes – now that I've got the idea of the way certain bass riffs work."

"Yeah …" Pause. *"Yeah … Yeah, I can see that"* Ron grinned in recognition. *"So … I can see that you have to be able to let your fingers live a life of their own because they move faster than thought in any case."*

"Exactly. However – there's still nonduality to explain … and I'm not quite sure how I'm going to move into that idea. Basically, of course, it's when emptiness and form are no longer separate – but beyond saying that … it's not something I have experienced yet – so I don't really know how to talk about it."

7   Sepulchrave Groan is the 76th Earl of Groan and Lord of Gormenghast, the citadel-state which forms the otherworld setting for the novels of Mervyn Peake. Sepulchrave is Titus Groan and Fuchsia Groan's father and estranged husband of Countess Gertrude. He is afflicted with intense claustrophobia because his every waking hour is dictated by the rites mandated by hereditary law.

"What does it look like though?" asked Steve. *"You told me this a while back – but the idea was too slippery to remember."*

"Right ... yes ... it's slippery for me too – and I probably don't explain it very well." Pause. *"I don't know ..."* Pause. *"...Y'see ... I only have an intellectual idea – but here it goes. It's when things are no longer polarised: like hope and fear; security and insecurity; knowing and not-knowing. The problem is that these words are meaningless without the experience – and you have to remember that I've really only just started out into this. It's almost as new to me as it is to you – but ... I hope—as time goes on—that I'll have more real experience. Before then – my explanations will be pretty tepid."*

Ron and Steve sat and stared at me – and for a moment I thought I had either bored or annoyed them in some way – but Ron eventually broke the silence. *"That's ... important stuff. I don't know quite what I understood from what you said – but ... yeah ... it's important stuff."*

"And ... you could apply that to guitar?" Steve asked Ron.

"Too right mate ..." Ron almost whispered *"... too right ..."*

The next day, Steve told me that he and Ron been quite amazed by what I'd said the night before. *"You must have read a hell of a lot to be able to talk about Buddhism like you did last night ... I mean, it's like you're some sort of Buddhist professor or something."*

I didn't know how to answer that – and Steve sat patiently while I considered how I would respond. He was used to my silences – and so I knew I'd have time to turn the thing over in my mind.

"Thing is, Steve – that I'm more aware of how little I know. There's so much to know – and there's so much that's outside my experience."

"But" interjected Steve *"when you explain something like you did last night, you sound completely authoritative."*

I paused for a moment before answering. *"Thing is, Steve – when I'm talking like that I sometimes say things ... that I don't know I knew ... I just speak and find myself explaining – and my explanations are ideas that seem to have come from nowhere – but ... it's as if those answers were always there ... buried in my mind. I couldn't plan it or anything. I wouldn't know where to start. It's as if it's 'the explaining' that makes the explanation possible."*

Steve was silent for a moment *"Like those visions you have?"*

I shrugged.

"Y'know" he continued *"you told me that this white figure—like Frigga or Tara—communicates without words and you know that you know something – but you don't know what it is."*

Steve's words had more of an impact on me than he had imagined. *"Steve …"* I began after a long silence *"I feel you're right about that – but … I still really don't know what's happening. I don't know how 'wordlessness' becomes 'words' – but it only happens when I have to explain something. That has happened a few times now with you and with Ron – but, never …"*

"… when Jack's around" Steve completed my sentence.

"No …" I sighed *"… you're right … but, I don't do that on purpose. It's probably because Jack's not interested – and, when Jack's around, the conversation never moves in that direction."*

When I was on my way home from Steve's, I pondered the question. I couldn't recall reading about nonduality. I'd seen the word—I was sure—but nothing much was said in terms of explanation. It was there in the *Heart Sutra*—I knew that—but there was no intelligible extrapolation in the book I'd read;[8] or at least, none that I could comprehend. These Buddhist academics seemed to give no quarter to the average reader – and I had to struggle to understand anything from their paragraph-long sentences. Every sentence read like a 'life sentence' that left me feeling brain-dead. There had to be a way to absorb Buddhism without having to struggle though the horrendous tomes I tried to read. Even *The Middle Way*—The Journal of the British Buddhist Society—was heavy going. If Steve was right, however, and it was possible to learn directly from Tara *(if she actually was Tara)* then maybe it could all be simple.

The visions did occur from time to time, as well as the dreams in which I felt as if I was awake in the dream. Every time Tara appeared it was the same – whilst not being entirely the same.

8   *The Diamond Sutra and Heart Sutra*, translated and explained by Edward Conze – 1958.

I could not tell whether it was because I was in a different frame of mind, or whether it was because the *texture* of what she communicated was different. I told myself repeatedly to ask, in the dream or vision: What is *inside* this experience of communication? What words *are* there? What *ideas* are there? What is the *meaning*? Somehow, I could never remember to ask the question – even as a 'wordless sense of questioning'. It occurred to me later, that when you're in the sea, the idea of asking *'What does this seawater-wetness feel like?'* is somehow meaningless.

All one could say would be:

"It feels like this."

14

bardo thödröl

In 1970 Ron and Steve died. Ron died of a heart attack. None of us knew he had a weak heart. Steve followed a month later in a car crash – with his father at the wheel. Multiple collision. They took out three lampposts.

Suddenly I found myself in the final week of the Summer term – and the end of my school days. There was a coach trip. The last event of the year. We went *somewhere* for *some* purpose which now entirely eludes me. At that time I was complicit, in life eluding me. I'd ingested a massive dose of LSD: **L**eaden **S**adness and **D**espair. I drifted in a marginal zone – mortality-jagged by loss. Death hung over me. It seemed impossible not to *want* death hanging over me. The deaths of Ron and Steve were incomprehensible.[1]

Sometimes I'd wake up in the morning – and it was as if Ron and Steve were still alive. Then I'd go through another bereavement as reality descended on me, as a gargantuan Jurassic winged reptile.

The Savage Cabbage Blues Band was a memory. Lindie Dale was a memory. She'd been there every day at school – but her presence merely served to remind me that she wasn't available beyond the school precincts. We talked. We were friends. We still had everything in common we'd always had in common – but she was terminally unavailable in any other way than pseudo-platonic friendship. Romance was still there. We still sparkled at each other – doomed to torture ourselves with what couldn't be. We were living in a world where parents held the trump cards – and the fact that I'd broken free, merely made me an isolated anomaly. What kind of freedom is *freedom owned in isolation*? Apart from long hair and liberty to dress as I pleased, I was as free as *the other captives* – at least as far as ladies of my own age were concerned.

---

1   See chapter 10, *'an odd boy'* Volume II by Doc Togden – ARO BOOKS WORLDWIDE.

It was like renting a room in a prison, where I was free to leave – but only if I left everyone else behind.

I had a considerable swathe of time to think about death. We all have to die – but that's a platitude uttered when death's not on the doorstep.

In terms of Buddhism, I'd studied the right material. It should have prepared me. I'd read about impermanence: old age, sickness, and death. I'd read about them as *facts to contemplate*. I'd contemplated. I thought I'd reflected on them religiously – but realised that my contemplation had been facile. Old age, sickness, and death had been conveniently far off. My contemplations had been expediently abstract. Now that I faced *real contemplation*, I found I resented it. I couldn't relate to it as meaningful. If there was meaning, it was bleak. If there was no meaning, it was bleak. If meaning and meaninglessness had the same taste – that too, seemed bleak. I had no way of knowing. The one taste of pleasure and pain? The one taste of success and failure? The one taste of hope and fear? The one taste of emptiness and form?

That was the goal – but would I ever reach that goal? Did I actually want to reach that goal? There were two answers. The first answer was affirmative. Yes – I wanted to taste that one taste. Then there was the honest answer – no … what I really wanted was hope, success, and pleasure. The problem was that *what I really wanted* was suspect. It was not attainable. I knew that – but I only knew it intellectually. I'd only known *the inevitability of death* intellectually – and now I was faced with reality.

People had been dying for almost 2 million years. In all that time— and amongst the countless millions who had died—I was an invisible cypher. I was so far to the right of the decimal point that it would have taken a radio-telescope to catch a glimpse of it. I was utterly insignificant. My *being insignificant* didn't worry me – but Ron and Steve could not be relegated to somewhere out of sight at the end of a series of zeros.

My contemplation did help me see that I could not indulge in *any* sense that *anything* was unfair. 'Unfair' was a word for idiots. People had experienced far greater loss. Britain had just come through two World Wars. My mother had lost her brother. Probably every family in Britain and Germany had lost someone. What was I to make of any of that – apart from seeing that life was in the moment?

I couldn't base happiness on the guarantee that no one would die – or, that Lindie's parents would finally relent. No.

Happiness can only be in the moment – with exactly what the moment contains. I have to keep coming back to that moment. When I do, everything is fine – for a moment. The moment is a gap between history and temporal prognosis. There is a future that is forming itself out of everything that has happened and is currently happening. That future is, as yet, simply empty potential. The future is empty potential unless it becomes inevitable due to habits and causes that are being set in motion and maintained by habit. If there is no habit, however – what then? I have the sense that a habit-free moment could expand into all moments. They would all still be that one moment – but it would be a vast moment that contained all moments: each separate – yet inseparable in their momentary quality. I have no idea how such a configuration has arisen. I wish I could ask a Lama about these things.[2]

I decided that the answer must lie in the Bardo Thödröl: *The Tibetan Book of the Dead* and so I opened it and read. I continued to read until the end – but was none the wiser. The problem was that Evans-Wentz—despite his fascination with Vajrayana—remained a Theosophist. Theosophy is based largely on Hinduism [3] – so his presentation of the Bardo Thödröl was somewhat skewed. His Biblical *thee* and *thou* were annoying too – but they were nothing in comparison with his fascination with comparative religion that intruded in such a way as to make the book heavy going.

2   This paragraph came from notes that were written at the time. The notebook was lost – but found by a friend at that time, Patricia Jenkinson, when she investigated her art folder. It had slipped down to the bottom and had lain there for thirty years.

3   His last months of life were spent at Yogananda's Self-Realisation Fellowship in California.

I was going to have to learn Tibetan and read the original text – or, hope that someone else would translate it. I was thrown back on personal resources, yet again.

I drove home from Steve's funeral riddled with purposelessness: machine-gunned by the Thompson-of-tragedy.[4] Life had emptied the whole circular ammunition-case into me – and it felt as if it would have killed a rampant triceratops.

It was bad enough losing my two best friends – but there was the *guilt* as well. The *guilt* was due to the fact that I should—*not*—be grieving the loss of my Blues future. I had no business mourning anyone but Steve and Ron. Whenever I started feeling bad that *the main musical chance of my life* had also died, I'd feel some kind of inhuman monster. The only thing that made it any better was the knowledge that I'd have traded my Blues future to have them both back again, even if we'd had to have stayed as a strictly nowhere-band.

I wondered, in spite of this, if I'd ever really be free to mourn the loss of being the vocalist of the *best Blues band there* **ever** *was*. Savage Cabbage was now *the best Blues Band there* **never** *was*. Then there was the loss of Lindie. Somehow Savage Cabbage had cushioned me. There'd been pleasure in my life—great pleasure—and I could forget about Lindie, on stage. I could forget about Lindie in rehearsals. I could forget about Lindie when wrapped in musical discussion with Ron and Steve. I could forget about Lindie when I sat in silence and let go of thought. But Lindie was there—in being 'not there'—in almost every other moment. And now … there was *nothing at all*, other than the promise of Art School in mid-September. I knew I should be grateful for that. I had to keep reminding myself however, that I *should be grateful* – because there wasn't really *nothing at all*. It just felt like that. I was a failure as a Bluesman. I was a failure as a Buddhist.

---

4   The *Thompson* is an American submachine gun invented by John T Thompson in 1918 and known colloquially as the *Tommy Gun*, *Chicago Typewriter*, or simply the *Thompson*.

Only rarely did the slightest of grins cross my face – and that was when I considered the fact that I'd been born in West*phalia* – and therefore *failure* should be no surprise to me.

I got home in the twilight and parked my motorcycle at the bottom of Woodsfield Lane. I sat on that glorious chopped 500 BSA— leaning back on the sissy bars—staring into the indeterminate dusk. I'd not decided I *didn't* want to go home – but the feeling had settled on me just as I turned into the Lane. I would have preferred to have kept riding. I could have ridden down to Cadgwith [5] – or anywhere just in order not to deal with anything but the open road. I didn't want to have to talk to anyone or answer anyone's questions. I didn't want to do anything or plan anything – or *exist anymore than was absolutely necessary*. Motorcycle riding was perfect for that – because it gave me an occupation. It demanded attention – but nothing else. Sitting in the dark was better than arriving at home – but it didn't last long. My father suddenly made his turn into Woodsfield Lane and his headlights were full on me. He knew where I'd been. He parked and came over to me. He asked me if I was alright and I said *"Yes … Dad … I'm fine"* but there were tears running down my face. That's why going home was something I didn't want to do. It was easier somehow to sit in the dark.

"Come home, when you can, Victor."

I nodded. He left me there – got in his car and drove the remaining 200 yards. I saw him reverse into the drive. The lights went out. I knew I'd have to go home sooner rather than later. Dragging it out wouldn't help. It actually made me smile to think of my father being so sensitive concerning the death of Steve. In previous times he would have barked at me for sitting at the side of the road in the dark – but, since the hair debacle of '68, all that had changed.

---

5 Cadgwith (*Porthkajwydh 'cove of the thicket' in Cornish*) is a small independent fishing village on the Lizard Peninsula of Cornwall between Lizard Village and Coverack. Cadgwith has existed since medieval times as a collection of fish cellars in a sheltered south-east facing coastal valley with two shingle coves divided by a spit of rock called the Todden. Ngak'chang Rinpoche's family went there for holidays for a number of years – and he grew extremely fond of it.

It suddenly occurred to me that it wouldn't be generous of me to sit there more than five minutes – as he and my mother might be worried. I dismounted, toed-up the stand—kick-started—and puttered quietly up the road. My father had left the gates open. I noted it with gratitude.

I walked into the house and smiled at them – just to let them know I was alright. My mother told me that we were having Welsh Rarebit for dinner[6] and I smiled at her *"That'll be perfect – I'll just go up and change."* When I came down the television was on—as usual—so I sat down to watch with Græham. I don't remember what programme was showing. I didn't look at it. I simply used it as a means of remaining silent. The table had already been laid, so there was nothing for me to do in any case. By the time I was called to dinner – everything *was* more-or-less fine. No one asked anything of me – and my mother and father did what they always did, talked about his day at work. The following day both told me of those they'd lost in WWII and told me they knew how I felt. I thanked them—and meant it—and spent some time dwelling on the fact that bereavement was a universal experience—like Donovan's *Universal Soldier*—and its *orders came from far away no more …*[7]

Images of Savage Cabbage arose from time to time – but vivid memory was fading fast. I kept thinking about the possibility of getting the tapes from Ron's parents. I asked my mother what she thought and she said it was probably a little too soon. Maybe at the end of the Summer. So I waited.

Jack Hackman had vanished – sold his drums and gone to work at the Midland Bank. I dropped him a line. It wasn't answered. What did I expect? I don't think Jack ever considered me a friend. I was Jack's friend because of Ron, Steve, and Savage Cabbage.

---

6   This was Major Simmerson's Welsh Rarebit—which is not Welsh Rarebit—but that is how it was known to the author at the time. It was multiple layers of boiled onions and cheddar cheese – topped with sliced tomatoes and garnished with whisked eggs. The whole being salted and peppered and cooked until the cheese liquefied.

7   *Universal Soldier* by Buffy Sainte-Marie was released in 1964. It was not popular at the time but by 1965 the song was covered by Donovan and reached № 5 in the British charts.

Jack's parents considered me *Public Enemy* № 1[8] – just as Lindie Dale's parents had done. There was no point in calling. I was probably relieved, to be frank. I never did warm to Jack's scatological homophobic racist humour. He wasn't actually rabidly homophobic or racist – but his sense of humour tended toward those topics. He meant no great harm by it. He was merely unconsidered. He had no interest in philosophy or examining his ethical structures. I decided he wasn't to be blamed too much for that – as his parents were deeply ignorant people. My father may have been a 'working-class Tory' – but he was no racist. My father must have provided me with some moral ethical sense. Jack's parents on the other hand were greedy, upwardly-mobile, and fairly moronic. Not a flattering picture – but that is how they were. They in turn must have had origins which failed to provide them with religious virtues.

Could I spend a pleasant evening with Jack? Probably not – he'd probably got back together with Synthetic Cynthia, his calamitous cara sposa.[9] 'Synthetic Cynthia' was the name Ron and Steve coined for Jack's girlfriend. She was a connoisseur of Benny Hill, Harry Worth, and Norman Wisdom.[10] I smiled grimly at the memory of Steve's description of her: *'She's not exactly stupid – but she's extremely dull ... she doesn't comprehend Monty Python. She finds it irritating. I think Jack would make a better looking girl. She looks like a water buffalo, laughs like a hyena, and prattles like a parrot.'*

8   The actual name of the movie was *The Public Enemy* – but it is popularly misremembered as *Public Enemy* № 1. It was a 1931 Warner Brothers film directed by William Wellman, starring James Cagney, Jean Harlow, Edward Woods, and Joan Blondell. It details a young man's rise in the criminal underworld of the Prohibition era.

9   Cara sposa – Italian for 'dear wife'. Reference: *Cara sposa, amante cara,* Act I, Scene ii of *Rinaldo* by George Frideric Händel.

10 Benny Hill (1924–1992) was an English comedian known for mildly sexist humour and slapstick. He is famous for his long-running television programme *The Benny Hill Show*. Harry Worth (1917–1989, Hertfordshire) was an English comedian. His usual rôle was a harmless lower-middleclass, middle-aged fool from the North of England. He confused and frustrated people and was the bane of shopkeepers. Norman Wisdom (1915–2010) was an English slapstick comedian best known for a series of comedy films (1953–1966) in which he played a pathetic infantile character called Norman Pitkin.

Without the lads to back him up, Jack would have submitted to his parents' will and Cynthia would have him on her romantic-rotisserie before long – with a toffee-apple in his mouth … She'd crocheted him a hideous woolly bobble-hat the Christmas before last that caused Steve and Ron to laugh 'til the tears ran down their faces. Ron had asked him *"So Jack … is that part of the anti-sex league uniform or something?"*[11] and then they both howled with laughter again. Jack probably had a whole range of those hats by now.

My 18th birthday came and went. I got a card from Mrs Bruce and was touched that she'd remembered. The thing she'd forgotten however was that she and her late husband had told Steve they would give me his uncle's GIBSON EB0 and BASSMAN amplifier for my 18th birthday. It was to have been the cheaper VOX – but they'd decided to be even more generous. I wasn't supposed to know – but Steve had told me. Again I felt torn. How could I grieve the death of my friend and the loss of the EB0 and BASSMAN at the same time – especially as now I couldn't do much with the equipment? I still had my amplifier, microphone, and stand to show that I'd once stood on stage – but there was no EB0 to remind me of my musical ambitions. There was no EB3 either. I'd been on the cusp of buying Ron's EB3—the one I'd used with Savage Cabbage—but that bass and accompanying MARSHALL JTM-45 amplifier were now sitting silent in the music room in The Bourne.[12]

I remembered that music room well – because I'd spent many hours there either talking with Ron, listening to Ron play, or having Ron give me lessons on his EB3.

---

11 *Nineteen Eighty-Four* by George Orwell (1949) is a novel about dictatorship, pervasive government surveillance, and mind-control. The *Anti-Sex-League* encouraged the elimination of personal sexual attachments because they diminished political loyalty. The government neurologists were therefore working on a means to terminate orgasm in human beings.

12 In 1750 the Bourne was the Common of the Manor of Farnham with about 20 families in residence. By the enclosure of the Common in 1861, there were nearly 600 residents, the majority engaged in agricultural work. The Farnham-Guildford-London railway line, constructed in 1849, made the West Surrey Hills a favoured location for the wealthy eager to leave the pollution of London. The Bourne thus grew to become the most prestigious locale of Farnham.

There was a Steinway in the music room and sometimes Ron would play some Boogie, JS Bach, or weird and wonderful mixtures of the two. And now my two friends had gone – and their Blues was the blue of the sky. They were both dead, and … so was I – the only difference being the fact that I was ambulant.

That being the case – why not take the free school coach trip? I could do that on auto-pilot and maybe I'd be able to forget Lindie, Steve, Ron, and Savage Cabbage … for a while.

The only reason I remember that wretched school coach trip, is because a girl—whose name I cannot remember—decided to put the make on me in a manner that was both abrupt and entirely unlikely. It was thought—for some unaccountable reason—that I was about to buy Greg Ford's Beach Buggy. This made me— suddenly—an alarmingly attractive romantic prospect to the young lady in question. It was fine weather for adventures with a Beach Buggy – and I'd certainly not have objected to having such a vehicle, if I'd had a great deal more money to spare. As it was, I was more than content with my motorcycle.

The young lady—awash with the prospective thrills of Greg Ford's Beach Buggy—swung her way up the aisle of the coach and loomed across the top of the seat at me.

"Viiiiic …" she grinned vivaciously—and decidedly flirtatiously— drawing out my name into a long loquacious drawl *"… your hair's grown*—really—*long."* Then she plonked herself down in the seat next to me and proceeded to conduct herself in a manner that left little to the imagination. A hot tongue in the ear tends to leave one in little doubt as to the nature of a situation. Torridity erupted out of nowhere – like a hot sand-viper out [13]of a Schwarzwälder Kirschtorte.[14]

---

13 *Sand viper (Avicenna)* is a venomous viper found in the deserts of North Africa.

14 *Schwarzwälder Kirschtorte* is named after the Black Forest in South-eastern Germany. It is known outside the German-speaking countries as *Gateau Forêt-Noire, Black Forest Gâteaux,* or *Black Forest Cherry Cake.*

I was still mourning Lindie—not to mention Ron and Steve—and, although I knew I had to move on at some point, I'd not yet developed any enthusiasm for dalliance, however delightful. Still, there she *was* – and there I *was*. I didn't consider the situation in elaborate detail. It must have occurred to me that this represented a time to change – or simply an opportunity to see what might happen next. She wasn't exactly the kind of lady I'd seek out – but she seemed to want to make an effort to find Son House and NATIONAL RESOPHONIC guitars interesting.

"I remember you singing that—wiiiiild—Blues song in morning assembly in the first year 6th. I thought half the teachers were going to die or something. What was that? I always meant to ask you – but we were never in the same classes."

"That was 'John the Revelator' by Son House."

"Sun House? Sounds like a conservatory – is that a person's—real—name?"

"Yeah ... it's his real name or rather Eddie James House. But he was 'Son' – y'know, like 'Sonnyboy' like Sonnyboy Williamson." I gave too much detail – but she stayed with me. I asked her what music she liked and she named a few bands. *"I'm mainly into Pink Floyd, King Crimson, Deep Purple, Black Sabbath, and ... oh yeah, Led Zeppelin too."*

"Cream?" I asked

"Yeah ... them too – but they've split now and ... there's a lot of new stuff now that's really exciting."

I wasn't sure how to respond to that. Cream weren't exactly archaic. I liked some numbers by the bands she mentioned – but ... they weren't Blues Bands. Led Zeppelin had started out as a fine experimental Blues band – but they'd drifted into Progressive Rock. I liked some of the Progressive Rock well enough – but it wasn't Blues ... and somehow ... I couldn't get quite as excited about anything that wasn't Blues – unless it was JS Bach.

"Bach?" she uttered in amazement – as if I'd said Engelbert Humperdinck[15] *"How can you like Blues and Bach?"*

"I don't know … how exactly …" I replied – being deliberately literalist in my answer *"… maybe it just happens?"*

"No, I mean – they're so different."

"Did you ever hear Savage Cabbage play?"

"Yeah—brilliant—so sad about Ron and Steve … heard you three or four times, at least, up the Queen's Oak."

"Well if you liked how we sounded … Steve and Ron were always incorporating fragments of Bach into their improvisations."

"Really?"

"Really" I smiled. *"It would have been hard to tell, of course – but Ron always used to say that if you played any of Bach's piano pieces on baritone and soprano sax – you'd have Avant-garde Jazz."*

"You like Jazz?" she asked again with some degree of incredulity.

"Certainly – but mainly Avant-garde Jazz." Pause. *"Led Zeppelin used to play Blues / Avant-garde Jazz fusion material – but that was way back when they weren't the big deal they are now."*

"Didn't know that …"

There was much she didn't know – but that was hardly a matter for blame. The more we talked the more I knew she wasn't remotely like Lindie Dale. With Lindie, I would have been able to mention the pieces of Bach in question and to have talked about anything in riotous detail – but … with 'Miss Anonymous', I could only skim the surface of *any* subject. She didn't have that much to say about music – but we managed to keep ourselves occupied, especially when she slid a hand inside my shirt. That was a novel experience after five minutes' association – but who was I to object?

---

15 Engelbert Humperdinck (born Arnold Dorsey May 1936) is a British pop singer, best known for his 1967 № 1 hit *Please Release Me* which kept the Beatles' *Strawberry Fields Forever/ Penny Lane* from № 1 position in Britain. It lasted 56 weeks in the Top 50 single chart – selling 85,000 copies a day at the height of its fame. This was a fact that disgusted anyone who enjoyed Blues or Progressive Rock.

Then she took my hand and insinuated it into her brassiere. Alright – I wasn't going to object to that either. Celibacy had never suited me in any case – but I still felt vaguely … emotionally anæsthetised. It was as if someone had thrown on the *do all the things you're supposed to do* switch and I was … *doing all the things I was supposed to be doing* – but without any sense of pleasure. I was some sort of amorous robot, programmed to do what was expected. Maybe I'd just died with Ron and Steve – but my body was somehow just carrying on, as if it was alive, with a minute version of me inside it. The robot had to watch everything when it really just wanted to be switched off and put back in the shed where the sensual-robots were kept.

The coach deposited us somewhere—picked us up again—and in the time we'd seen *wherever it was or whatever it was*, she'd discovered that some *other* fellow was buying Greg Ford's Beach Buggy. I was jettisoned. I hardly noticed – but various people I didn't know seemed to find it hysterically funny. I was an object of comical derision – the more so, because I inadvertently failed to find myself risible. I mean – it wasn't as if I'd made a move and been repulsed. I felt about as repulsed as the coach seat on which I was sitting. The coach seat wasn't going to mourn the absence of my posterior and I wasn't going to mourn being thrown over by … what *was* her name?

When I got back to School, I went to the Art room to do something or other. I actually had no idea why I went there when I could have gone home. I liked the Art room. It was a place I could simply sit and smell the oil paint. My painting was there and I might even add a few brush strokes to it. Why not? Maybe my sense of existential surrealism would inspire something. The Art room was not empty. I'd expected it to be empty – but there was Peter Bridgewater. Pete had been a school friend—as had Greg Ford—from my first day at Virginia Water School. Pete had been accepted at Farnham Art School for the Foundation Year – and so we had plenty to discuss.

Pete was aghast when I told him about it. *"Wouldn't have thought she was—your—type at all mate."*

"Well … no … she wasn't." Pause. *"In fact … she reminded me a little of Synthetic Cynthia – or at least how she was described to me by Steve."*

224

"Jesus man! I met—her—once! I met Jack at a party in Frimley and she was with him … bloody frightening mate! I hope this bird wasn't as poxy as her."

"Couldn't comment Pete—never saw Cynthia—I was commenting more on her —personality—y'know … she thought Son House was a conservatory …"

"So … why did you go along with her?" Pete laughed in a haphazard manner – entirely perplexed by what I'd just told him.

"Well Pete … I suppose … I find it hard to say 'no' – and … well … it always seems so—courageous—to make moves like that. I would've felt bad telling her I wasn't interested."

Pete nodded *"So you just went along with the idea 'cause you felt bad about saying 'no'?"*

"Yeah … I … do that kind of thing …" I shrugged.

"So … is that a Buddhist thing, then?"

"No …" I laughed. *"Or maybe 'yes' – I don't know. As I said … it seems so … generous and vulnerable when ladies approach me romantically that … I've never been able to say 'no'."*

Pete told me I was crazy *"… you do have some … unique ideas."*

"Weird thing was …" I laughed *"… she quit me in the middle of 'Hello Goodbye'. It was playing on the coach radio. That seemed poetic … somehow – and … I was actually—grateful—to escape so lightly."*

I say high, you say low—you say why—and I say I don't know. Oh, no - you say goodbye and I say hello. Lennon-McCartney, *Hello Goodbye*, 1967

"You're a total maniac Vic!" Pete laughed. *"There's no other word for it – only you could think about the poetry of what song was playing when some bird walks out on you."*

"Well Pete" I mused *"that's the thing isn't it …"* Pause. *"… that's what Art's for … that's what Art is. And …"* Pause. *"… And that's why … I mean, Art isn't just painting and music as objects we create. It's life; or that's what life is, if you're a Vajrayana Buddhist."*

"Life is Art ...?" Pete queried. *"... yeah ... well ... I can see that in a way ... but isn't that a bit freaky ... I mean, isn't that like living in your own version of reality?"*

"Of course it is!" I laughed *"But that's where we all—are—anyway. How much common-reality d'you think there is?"*

"Well ... there's 1066 and all that."[16]

"Yes ... but history is always written by the winners – and so, how much reality do you think there is in that?"

"Fair enough ... but, I mean, we come to this School—we got our 'A' levels— and we're going to Art School in September. That's all reality."

"Yes. That's all reality – but the reality of that 'reality' is different for each of us. I mean, I'm happy about going to Art School – but that's against a background of ... well ... I don't think the word 'misery' is out of place – so 'my reality' isn't 'your reality' apart from the bare facts."

Pete shrugged – but also smiled to show he empathised with the monstrous loss I'd endured. For some reason I decided to continue *"I mean, the adjectival Dales—Lindie's parents—what would you say about their reality? They live in their own version of reality – it's just a long way removed from Art."*

"Good point mate" Pete nodded. *"You're going to fit right in at Art School —I can see that—and thinking like that does seem to keep you cheerful, no matter what life throws at you. Buddhism's obviously good for you – but I'd be buggered if I'd want to sit trying not to think for hours on end."*

"Yes ..." I grinned a trifle wanly *"but I'm looking forward to life throwing a bit less at me – or at least being able to duck out of the way when it comes."*

"Good luck" Pete called over his shoulder as he set off home.

---

16 1066 *And All That* by WC Sellar and R J Yeatman—illustrated by John Reynolds—first appeared serially in Punch magazine. It was later published in book form by Methuen & Co. Ltd. in 1930. It is a History of England, comprising: '103 Good Things, 5 Bad Kings and 2 Genuine Dates'. It is a tongue-in-cheek revamp of English history.

Ten minutes later Pete was back again because he'd forgotten his sketch book *"I'll be needing this tonight – as I want to draw some of the old cars down the dump. There are some interesting shapes amongst all that stuff."* Pause. *"I'm looking forward to telling Greg about the rumpus his Beach Buggy caused. I didn't even know he was selling it."*

"Maybe Greg doesn't know either" I laughed. *"Sometimes some fairly bizarre ideas get circulated; especially now we're all leaving."*

"Yeah ... 'spose you're right. Maybe we should start a few of our own."

"I'll spread one for you if you spread one for me."

"Sure – what's yours to be?"

"Tell 'em I'm going off to be a camel driver in the Gobi Desert."

"Y'know ... from—you—Vic ... that's almost believable..." Pause. *"... although Buddhist monk is probably more your forté dontcha think."*

"You have a point there Pete ... although I've never been attracted to celibacy." Pause. *"At the moment, however—after Lindie—it seems a workable option."*

"You're not serious!"

"No Pete. I'm not serious. Maybe 'Tantric hermit' would come closer to the mark. I'd kind of like to live in a cave for a while – and just not-have-to-deal-with-anything.*"*

"That's ... a bit depressing ..." Pete commented with something of a wistful expression *"... if you don't mind my saying."*

"Not at all – but it's not as depressing as it might sound to you" I smiled. *"I'd be able to concentrate on Buddhist practice and maybe get somewhere with it."*

"Alight ..." Pete nodded *"... I can see that ... But you'd leave the cave eventually?"*

"Sure!" I laughed. *"Can't be greedy – can you."*

"You always were a weirdo" Pete laughed. *"Anyhow – you can tell people I'm going out with Picasso's granddaughter – and she's given me one of his paintings."*

"That'll get'em talking – I'll slip it into the next likely conversation."

I sat in the Art studio looking out at a thin rain. The clouds had come in from somewhere and I had little inclination to drive home 'til it dried up. Being at a loose end was a novelty. I'd had every hour plotted since—since the dawn of time it seemed—and now … I could just sit in the school's Art studio on my own, looking at drizzle. Not that the drizzle wasn't interesting—I could invariably find interest in anything—but it made a strange mystery of life. It didn't matter where I was anymore. I could be anywhere. It wasn't one of those pointless / purposeless feelings – because I was headed to Art School and that was a massive festival of purposeful, meaningful, brilliance. I was just … on holiday without being on holiday. I had a job lined up with the Army Removals at Cavan's Road – and so there was nothing that needed my attention. There was a painting on which I was working – but it was almost completed, so it demanded little more application on my part. I contemplated it. There was Mr Love in his garden – and there was me. We were sitting in deckchairs. I'd worked hard to reproduce the delicate tracery of woodworm and the faded stripes in the fabric of the deckchairs. Deckchairs … I'd never thought about the word before – but they must have first been used on passenger ships. Then there was the NATIONAL TRICONE – the 12-string model that no one had ever made. I'd placed it there like a wish-fulfilling hoodoo charm that would get me the guitar on which I'd become Robert Johnson.

I'd depicted myself more-or-less as I was—rather than as an eight-year-old boy—because, I kept growing older and Mr Love was dead. He'd always be as I remembered him and I'd keep changing into new versions of … whatever. I was somehow *an empty space* sequentially inhabited by people who remembered something of the past manifestations of what was actually an *empty continuum*.

Was this a Buddhist realisation? Or was this merely maudlin? If it was a 'Buddhist realisation' I should feel cheerful about it – so maybe it was just *me being a woebegone wimp*.

I wondered at what stage I'd actually embody some degree of Buddhism as a *lived reality* rather than a *theological thespianism*. I didn't want to use Buddhism as a patch, prop, buttress, brace, or crutch. That approach seemed lame. I wanted to *be it* rather than *think it* or *apply it as a conceptual ointment.* Maybe that would evolve slowly over time; the more I sat in silence. No time like the present. I sat in silence. I sat for an hour or more. The rain ceased. I ceased too – but rode home nonetheless: Easy Rider.

15

a diminutive demon

august 1970

The last family holiday. Moving into a different phase of life. I'd left the standard educational system and was bound for Art School in September. *Going somewhere—Newquay—to do nothing in particular,* no longer seemed viable.[1] So why did I go? Well, we'd not had a family holiday for three years. My mother wanted me to go. Græham—my brother—wanted me to go. My father was keen that I should go.

I was not violently disinclined to go. I could sit and stare at the sea. It could approximate a meditation retreat. I would rather have gone to Cadgwith on the Lizard Peninsula, where we used to go as children – but …

Not long after we arrived, Græham drew my attention to a Folk and Blues Club poster giving details of a concert by Ralph McTell. It was a month old – but a telephone number was there to provide a strong secondary cause.[2] It didn't take much of a secondary cause for Blues to be provoked.

I called the number. *"Hello there, I'm passing through—name's Frank Schubert—acoustic Blues. I'd be happy to sit in if you've got any spots."*

---

1   Newquay (*Cornish: Tewynblustri*) is on the North Coast of Cornwall. It is holiday resort town, 12 miles north of Truro, 20 miles west of Bodmin. It is bounded to the South by the River Gannel and salt marshes, and to the North-East by the Porth Valley. The Western end opens to Atlantic Ocean at Fistral Bay. It has expanded inland since the fishing village of Newquay began to grow at the end of the 19th century – and is attractive only to those who enjoy holiday resorts.

2   Kyen-la rag-lé pa (*rKyen la rag las pa / pratyaya / dependent upon circumstances*) Karmic cycles can be compared with plants – in terms of seeds being primary causes (*because they are capable of reproducing the same species of plant*) which require secondary causes such as light, moisture, and air in order to mature. In this way primary karmic causes remain as the traces of past perceptions and intentions in each individual until they meet with the secondary causes presented adventitiously by life.

I said in as off-hand a way as I could. You had to be *Mister Blasé* to be believed in the performance game.

"Warm up? Don't do that often – but why not. Sure." It wasn't a falsehood exactly—I didn't often play warm-ups—but it wasn't horribly accurate. I'd warmed up for Jo Ann Kelly on two occasions—Mike Cooper once—but I wasn't on-the-books to be called up as a warm-up player. *"Sure—yeah—I'll take a stroll up there now. Be with you in ten minutes or so."*

I wasn't *mad keen* on dissimulation – but it was de rigueur in the music business unless you were famous. I'd been *Mister Big* in the Savage Cabbage Blues Band – but that was gone. I was now ... I was *Mister Nowhere Man* – but, that is how I got to converse with John Martyn.[3]

I turned up at the run-down church hall boasting the name of Newquay Folk and Blues Club – and there he was. John Martyn just sat there on the wall – waiting for Andy Polliter, who was conspicuous mainly in his paucity of politesse. John Martyn however, saved the day by seeming to know me. We'd been sitting on a low wall together chatting. I had no idea who he was – and so, for all I knew, he was just another small-time musician on the pub scene. He'd asked most of the questions and seemed intrigued by what I told him about the Savage Cabbage Blues Band and its sad demise. He seemed genuinely touched by the tragedy and genuinely interested in our two-bass line-up. Therefore, when Andy Polliter asked *"So, who are you?"* in a vaguely sneering manner, John Martyn answered for me – repeating what I'd told him as we sat chatting. Coming from John Martyn, this was received as an unquestionable recommendation. So it was that I was booked for Saturday night as warm-up for John Martyn. The world is illusion.

---

3   John Martyn OBE (1948–2009) was a Scottish guitarist, singer, and songwriter. Over 40 years he released 22 studio albums which received high critical acclaim. He was admired by players such as Eric Clapton. He began playing professionally at 17 in the British folk music scene and signed with Island Records. By the early 1970s he was incorporating Blues, Jazz, and Rock on albums such as Solid Air and One World. He experimented with guitar effects – particularly Echoplex, and was known for blurring the boundaries between Folk, Blues, Jazz, and Rock.

Being booked as *Frank Schubert, warm-up for John Martyn*, would have been wonderful – but as it happened Andy Polliter failed to inform either John Martyn or myself that I was merely to play *warm-up for the warm-up*. The official *warm-up* was the resident act: the Bodmin Blues Band. They were actually a Rock&Roll band—like many others who called themselves Blues bands—but I had my own reasons for not warming to them. They did their level best to humiliate me when they came on after my short set. My set had—not—been the best I'd ever played, for various reasons. My harp was blown on one vital note and was therefore unplayable. I was using my new 12 string EKO. Lovely guitar—not a MARTIN, GIBSON, or GUILD—but it had a fine full tone, deep bass, and ringing treble. The problem was not the guitar – it was the player. I'd only just started to play regular guitar in regular tuning. Before that my main instrument had been the DEBIL – the partially home-made guitar on which I played lap-slide in open tunings. Playing lap-slide—across the knees—with a length of chromium bath-towel rail is about as different as you can get from playing chords and riffing on a regular guitar. I was thus rather unsophisticated. No … I was primitive – but I had the voice for it and … I figured that if Son House could *play rudimentary* guitar and carry the day with his voice – then … maybe I could do the same. I was nothing if not well equipped with boldness, nerve, bravado, chutzpa, audacity, gall, impudence, and colossal naïveté – when it came to Blues. The problem with my limited musical capacity was that: I was not Son House; I was not American; I was not born in the Mississippi Delta; and, I wasn't old. I wasn't Black either – well … not on the *outside* a least.

The Bodmin Blues Band came and went. I was as impressed with them as they were with me – but they had clout as the resident band, and so their put-down vis-à-vis 'Blues clichés' was greeted with mirth. I almost went back to the hotel – but decided it would be viciously ungrateful to miss John Martyn's set. We'd had a fine conversation backstage before I went on and he'd been most friendly and generous. So … when the second half of the concert was about to start, I went in and took my seat next to my brother Græham, who'd come to hear me perform.

John Martyn strode on stage—almost with a swagger—but with a sense of ease that was electric. The crowd gave him a substantial round of applause. They'd obviously been looking forward to hearing him and were definitively excited. He approached the trestle table on which sat an array of effect-pedals. There was an ECHOPLEX and various other devices. He fiddled with them for a while as he tested the sound and suddenly bellowed *"They call me 'Buttons McGegghy'."* [4]

The words were followed by a manic laugh that shook the room *"Ha – ha! Jus' gimme a button! Ha—ha—ha—ha!"* He finished fiddling and turned to the audience *"Soume people! Yeah soume people—not so very foukin' far from here—as I hear it ... are not—s'very fond—of a Blues cliché! Ha—ha—ha!"* He waved his head from side to side in mock disbelief *"But I louve a Blues cliché more thæn foukin' life itself!"* The crowd loved his raving style and erupted into gales of laughter. *"So ... goud people Ha—ha—ha! I'm going to start oout with a—goud—old—clichéd—number—y'll—all—know ... only—tooooo—foukin'—well!"*

I couldn't believe my ears! I was on the verge of tears. John Martyn had overheard the musical assassination of Frank Schubert and he was coming out in my defence – *all* barrels blazing. He launched into Skip James' *'I'd Rather be the Devil'* and the audience was spell-bound.

> *Well, I laid down last night and I was trying to take my rest, / But my mind starts a-rambling like the wild geese in the West.*
> Skip James, *I'd Rather be the Devil*, 1931 / John Martyn, *Solid Air*, 1973

John Martyn was so obviously a world-class player that having chatted with him for so long discombobulated me. If I'd known who he was when I was chatting with him – I would probably have come across like an idiot. I might have been too much in awe of him to have a realistic conversation. Anyhow, if the Bodmin Blues Band were in the audience they must have felt about as bad as I'd previously felt. The song ended and the applause was furious.

---

4   'McGegghy' – John Martyn was born 'Iain David McGeachy' but the author was unaware of this at the time of writing – so the spelling has been left as it was remembered to reflect that.

Then just as the applause was receding John Martyn motioned me to stand. He had to beckon me a few times before I understood his intention. I stood ... feeling somewhat gauche – and John Martyn bellowed *"Song's f'm'friend here! M'friend Frrrrrrrrrrank Schubert! Big hand! Big hand now for Frank Schubert!"*

The hall erupted with applause. It took me a while to understand what was happening. I thought *'Didn't these people snigger at me earlier – at the instigation of the Bodmin Blues Band?'* It made no obvious sense. Then suddenly John Martyn was speaking again *"He played some fouking fine down-home Blues f'ya earlier—real honest Delta—big hand now! Big hand! Big hand for Frank Schubert!"*

The Hall erupted. I looked around and there they were – the audience for whom I'd been a joke an hour earlier. *"Ha—ha—yer-reet! Ha—ha! Up'n'coming Bluesman!—Frrrrrrrrrrank—Schubert!—Big hand! Big hand now! Y'll be hearin' from this man in the future – yoou jus' watch oout! Ha—ha—ha—ha! Frrrrrrrrrrank—Schubert!"* John Martyn's voice trailed into slurred Glaswegian and the audience continued to applaud.

'Up'n'coming Blues man' eh ... How outrageously kind. It's what I'd always wanted – but it was entirely unreal. How massively kind and generous of John Martyn to say that – but there was no more to it than that. I was, in reality, *down'n'going*. There were a few thousand school boys who could play what I'd played – and played it better. As soon as John Martyn's performance was over, I walked back to the hotel with Græham. I said goodnight. I went to bed. I lay there faced with the illusion John Martyn had created. I was no *Up'n'coming Bluesman.* It was a sad realisation. I did, however, belong to the tradition. I'd invested enough to say that. I wasn't good – but I did belong.

This wasn't a doleful thought—or even a state of sensible resignation—it was simply the recognition that most of life, if not all of it, was illusory. I could either buy into the illusion or see it for what it was. Sometimes illusion is joyous. Sometimes it's tragic– and sometimes it's simply undesignated.

I stared into the dark room for some uncharted time and realised after whatever time had passed that I was wide awake and thought-free. Then, of course, I congratulated myself on being thought-free and the whole baleful blancmange of concept filled what had been a most welcome space of being.

There was always something to be learned – either from formal meditation, or from the meditation that simply happened by accident. It had been obvious to me for a few years that meditation wasn't merely what you did – it was what you could become at any moment when you weren't manically conceptualising everything that registered with the senses. I realised then, something that I had occasionally realised before: that if I could actually give up all ambition, whilst simply jumping into whatever presented itself next, I'd be free.

That was the thing: to be free, to attain liberation. That's what the books conveyed – but sometimes, I felt as if I was just along for the ride. Naturally I wanted to catch a glimpse of the goal—in terms of Vajrayana—but I knew that: just as I wasn't a Blues hero, I wasn't a Buddhist hero either. I was content to play Blues as a Vajrayana Buddhist and to live my life from that perspective – whatever came along. Whether I was to be a musician or not was somehow not within my control. There was what I wanted to accomplish – and what the world would allow me to accomplish. All I could do was dance with whatever occurred – and remember not to take myself too seriously as being *whatever kind of something I might sporadically appear to be*. Then I fell asleep.

Then I woke suddenly from sleep—wide awake—but immersed in a realm of light that that burst into existence; presided over by Tara; or whomever she might be. There was suddenly no problem with anything. I wordlessly knew that Steve and Ron were dead. I knew Lindie was gone forever. I knew everything I knew without formulating anything semantically. I was the mere awareness of everything I felt and had ever felt – but oppressed by nothing; identified by nothing.

There was no sadness concerning anything – because I knew something incomprehensible that made sense of everything without any *sense of sense-making*. There was no answer – but there was also no question; no uncertainty. Joy and sorrow were two aspects of the same sensation – and time had no linear meaning. There was simply space. Then I fell asleep.

I was hoping that I'd re-enter this experience on the following night – but nothing occurred. Nothing recurred for the rest of the holiday. I did meet a lady called Helen Smith – and I spent some happy time together with her before we each went home. Goodbye Forever. Somehow we never saw each other again. I have no idea why.

After our unlikely meeting in Newquay, John Martyn went on to perform with some big names.[5] I pondered what might have happened if I'd had the DEBIL with me that night, and wondered how it would have been if we'd remained in touch – but I'd made myself look silly with my primitive efforts on the EKO. At the end of the evening I'd decided discretion was the better part of valour. I had no cause to take up John Martyn's time. What would I say anyway? *"Fantastic set John!"* He'd heard me at my worst. There was no way I could say anything to him that would not sound stupid. *"I'm really much better on lap-slide. In fact I'm really quite good ... you'd be impressed if you heard me on the* DEBIL. *I lay 'em low with*—that—*device."* No ... it was better that I should walk back to the hotel and go to bed. In any case there was Græham. I stood *in loco parentis* – being that he wasn't yet 16 and our parents were back at the hotel.

"That was—great—*what he said about you Vic!"* Græham exclaimed—sitting next to me on the back seat of our parent's car—driving home to Farnham.

"Yes. It was. John Martyn's a gentleman – and a genius."

5 Paul Kossoff, Richard Thompson, Steve Winwood, Phil Collins, and Eric Clapton. In 1973 he released *Solid Air* with Jazz bassist Danny Thompson – who also featured on *Road to Ruin* which was released Nov 1970 and on *Bless the Weather*. From *Bless the Weather* onward John Martyn inaugurated the slurred vocals which gave him the sound of a mythical wind instrument. He followed *Bless the Weather* with *Solid Air, Inside Out, Sunday's Child, Live at Leeds, One World*, and many other albums.

"Are you going to meet him again?"

"Who knows ..." Pause. *"... anything's possible though, I suppose – it's just a question of what's likely."* Pause. *"No ... I don't think it's likely. We're not exactly on the same planet musically – and so ... there's no reason for him to want to hear from—me—again."*

"After what he said about you?" Græham said indignantly. *"How can you say that!?"*

"I'm just being realistic, Græham ... John Martyn was just being kind to me – he wasn't seriously acclaiming me. I think he'd just been irked by the Bodmin Blues Band being hoity-toity—and trying to get a rise out of me—when they're fairly mediocre. They're better than I am – but that's not saying a great deal." As I spoke, I gazed at Cornwall passing by. The gorgeous green of it was restful on my eyes – and it was good to enjoy that colour whilst discussing a somewhat sombre topic. *"I'm going to have to improve radically if I'm going to get anywhere as a professional musician ... unless I can find another band as a vocalist. John Martyn, as I said, was extremely kind to me back there – but that gives me no opening, unless he knows someone who wants a vocalist. I wouldn't want to push it in any case. It would be embarrassing – and ... I've got no interest in being an embarrassment."*

The family drove back to Farnham after a holiday I'd never forget. I had mixed feelings – a storm of polarised notions lashed my sense of *who I was* and *where I was going*. I sat staring out the window trying to settle back to the preferable sense of *being nobody, going nowhere*.

"You're unusually quiet" Græham commented.

"Thinking, Græham ..."

"Thinking?" he naturally enquired – and I replied *"Y'know ... I have no idea ... there aren't any words to it – I'm just remembering things that have happened and seeing what sense there is when I put them all together."* Pause. *"So far ... well ... I haven't got very far."*

"Tell me where you've got then."

*"Well … good things have happened: successful pub gigs and a few clubs …
Then there was the Farnham Folk and Blues Festival."* I laughed *"Tore the
house down there!"*

"I wish I'd come along to that."

*"So do I. I'd rather you'd have been—there—than at that … grim
performance I just gave …"*

"You sang 'Sitting on Top of the World' really well though."

*"Yeah … well enough … I've sung it better though. I got thrown by that
audience right at the start. I'm used to laying out some lunatic line and having
the audience laugh – but when they just sat there like a load of lunch-pack
lemmings in a tepidarium … it kind of … crimped me. I've—never—had
—that—happen before. That Newquay audience was the adjectival end."*

"They cheered you at the end though."

"Yeah …" I laughed *"they did – but only because John Martyn gave 'em no
alternative. They'd have cheered a kangaroo from Kalamazoo if he'd said 'Up
and coming—Blues player—Mister Mephistopheles Marsupial!' … I mean –
just think about it."*

"I s'pose so … but – it must have been fierce meeting John Martyn though."

"Yeah – that was brilliant" I smiled. *"He's something else … he's a genius –
like Ron in a way … and he's really got such an open-hearted view of life. He
was extremely kind—and—generous – but … I'll need to develop my style
and technique a lot before I risk contacting him. I wouldn't ask him to stake his
reputation on me anywhere else. That would be the most pitiful behaviour …"*

"You could look up that bass player – you know Gaslight something-or-other?"
Græham asked.

"Gazzer Mitchell?"

"Yeah—Gazzer—that's right."

"No … probably not … for various … sensible reasons." Pause *"I'll tell you
about him some time."* I was aware of the parental ears in the front
seats of the car.[6]

---

6   Gazzer Mitchel had been apprehended by the police, in possession of heroin.

"He's—very—very—far from being Steve on bass anyhow. He's more than a hop and a skip in advance of me – but not anywhere near improvising as Steve did." Pause. *"And even if we did get together we'd have sounded …"* I whispered *"… muddy …"* Pause. *"That's what Ron worried about when I first suggested the two bass line-up."* Pause. *"Y'see … Steve had a thorough background in music theory – and Gazzer's like me … he can't read a note. Steve and Ron could—understand—what Jack Bruce was playing in a technical sense – and that made—all—the difference between Savage Cabbage and the average belt-it-out Blues-cum-Rock&Roller band."* Pause. *"Y'see … Steve and Ron played in counterpoint to each other – like the two hands of a piano piece – but somehow more than that."* Pause. *"Have you ever listened to Bach?"*

"No … not really. I don't really go for classical that much."

"You only hear the popular classics, Græham—when Dad plays his favourites —but …" I whispered *"There's a lot more than Tchaikovsky's Swan Lake you know …"*

"Like what?" Græham asked.

"Well … Johann Sebastian Bach for a start – Dieterich Buxtehude, Luigi Boccherini, Georg Philipp Telemann, Domenico Scarlatti, Arcangelo Corelli, Antonio Vivaldi … Y'know Ron used to say that if you played the two hands of any Bach piano piece on four saxophones—with just a slight change of timing—you'd have modern Jazz." Pause. *"I think people get put off Baroque music because of the people who tell you that it's real music and Blues isn't. It makes people reject Bach and the other amazing Baroque composers – and, that's a real pity. I know a lot about this because I sat in while Ron convinced Steve that he should be playing the Bach 'cello suites. He took a bit of convincing but as soon as he did – his improvisation skills improved in leaps and bounds!"*

"You'll have to play some for me."

"I will – I've got the 'cello suites. I borrowed the album from Steve – and … well … it's one of those things that never got returned. I … mentioned it to his mother when I went to the funeral – but she told me to keep it." Pause.

"So Steve's mother had him listening to Johann Hindle and Giovanni Bottesini.[7] She bought him scores for the Bach 'cello suites and he was beginning to play them as fluently as Ron had played them in '68. Steve progressed like a missile and I started gazing at him – as if through an acoustic telescope."

"Fierce! I'd really like to hear that" Pause. *"So what did you play on bass while Steve was being like Jack Bruce?"*

"Well ... I provided the background pulse. I was reliable—even passionate— but ... primitive. I plucked the simple patterns that Ron worked out for each piece. I'd thud out the 1st, 3rd, and 5th notes of the dominant chord-structures. Anyhow, when I'd feel despondent about being primitive – Ron would remind me: 'It was the so-called 'primitives' who walloped Custer!' D'you know about 'Custer's Last Stand', Graeham?"

"Not really."

"Well ... he was this young lunatic Northern general. They called him 'the boy general' in the War Between the States in that book Little Big Man that I was reading.[8] Ron lent me that – and it was really interesting. It tells about how Crazy Horse—this amazing Indian warrior who was the first Indian ever to employ tactics—completely annihilated Custer and his army. So anyway ... Ron told me that all I needed to be was primitive – as we couldn't have two lead-bassists in the band."

"Yes ... that makes sense."

"Ron told me my rôle was vital – even if I never got to be able to play the bass-line and sing at the same time."

"That's hard then?"

---

7 Johann Hindle (1792–1862) composed concertos for double bass, and pioneered bass tuning in fourths. Giovanni Bottesini (1821–1899) conductor, composer, and bassist – called the 'Paganini of the double bass'. He played double bass as never seen before – with leaps from the lowest to highest registers. His compositions were considered unplayable in the early part of the 20th century – but are now performed regularly. From BBC Music Magazine and The Grove Concise Dictionary of Music published by MacMillan.

8 *Little Big Man* by Thomas Berger was made into a movie starring Dustin Hoffman, Chief Dan George, and Faye Dunaway – released in December 1970.

"Yes ... there aren't many people who do that. I can only think of Jack Bruce and Paul McCartney off-hand. There must be others – but I know there can't be many."

Ron had noticed me getting adventurous in the long improvisations and had squinted at me occasionally in mock disapproval. I made sure I never got too wild or ventured too high up the neck as to clatter against Steve – so there were never any complaints from Ron.

We arrived home. I unpacked. I was still ruminating – to my own chagrin. I was a goddamn Buddhist ruminant. My whole sense of a band was built on playing music with my earliest friends. I'd known Steve since the age of 8, Ron since 13, and Jack since 15. They'd all accepted me for what I was – but what *was* I? I was an anomaly: a riotously rubato vocalist; harp player; bass player with extremely modest skills; Surrealist poet; and Psychedelic lyricist whose lyrics were too dense: too rococo; too complicated; too many adjectives...

I answered advertisements in the NEW MUSICAL EXPRESS and MELODY MAKER – but no one wanted a rhythm-bass vocalist and harp player. They either wanted a bass vocalist or a lead vocalist. No one was bothered about harp. There seemed to be no Blues bands in the area.

But what of Psychedelic-Blues song-writing? Jimi Hendrix was in full flight and it seemed only a matter of time before my *penchant for the peculiar* would be in demand. There was bound to be a growing need for Dylan-length lyrics. Very few people could write lyrics anywhere near the standard of Bob Dylan – and most were *a thousand miles behind*.[9] Most lyrics were a smattering of words – and the song was over. I'd be coming out of left field with my background of ingenious permutations of literature and poetry. I'd read widely *and* wildly. I'd explored Surrealist poets [10] – and had more ideas than I could contain.

---

9   Bob Dylan, *One Too Many Mornings, The Times They Are A-Changing*, 1964

10 Louis Aragon, Andre Breton, Robert Desnos, Paul Éluard, Nikos Engonopoulos, David Gascoyne, Aimé Césaire, and Pierre Reverdy.

My Psychedelic lyrics—as I saw them—were entirely different from the run-of-the-mill 'mind-blowing' ditties. They'd surely be welcome at some point in time – maybe just 'round the corner. The métier had to evolve artistically – and therefore well-crafted lyrics would be de rigueur for serious bands. I had all those psychedelic Savage Cabbage numbers in a file – with a shoal of ideas for further songs. I'd have liked to have played those songs myself – but lacking the musical annotations made by Steve and Ron, I was a little stuck in terms of how to play them on my own.

Jimi Hendrix was probably the greatest signpost I'd ever seen because he brought Blues and psychedelia together – and all he needed to add would have been added by the future. He admired Bob Dylan and was taking that influence in the direction of lyrical development. I could already see his sense of poetry emerging – and … maybe—just maybe—some *odd boy* could provide him with lyrics, just as Bernie Taupin had done for Elton John.[11] If Bernie Taupin could come out of nowhere – then Frank Schubert could do the same. Why not? Living within the gestalt of Jimi Hendix' creative genius, I became gripped by the idea that you could simply *be psychedelic* by being alive and being creative. It was a language that was understood just as the language of surrealism had been understood. I saw no great difference between Salvador Dali and Jimi Hendrix as world-class surrealists.

> *I have this one little saying, when things get too heavy just call me helium, the lightest gas known to man.* Jimi Hendrix

Jimi Hendrix had been *the future* – but his last public performance was an informal jam at Ronnie Scott's Jazz Club with Eric Burdon and War. He died on the 18th of September 1970. I arrived at Art School wearing a black arm band for Jimi Hendrix.

---

11 Bernard John Taupin – English lyricist, poet, and singer, best known for his long-term collaboration with Elton John. He wrote lyrics for the majority of Elton John's songs. In 1967, Bernie Taupin answered an advertisement in the NEW MUSICAL EXPRESS seeking new lyricists and was thus introduced to Elton John.

No one but Pete Bridgewater knew that there were two other world-class guitar heroes woven into the fabric of the band: Steve Bruce and Ron Larkin. I'd stepped out of the world of secondary school, into what was to have been an exciting new world of Art – but I came feeling somewhat ambivalent. In one respect I felt like a beggar living on the scraps of the feast that could have been. In another, I felt as I imagined Neil Armstrong felt when he placed his first foot on the Moon.

Bob Dylan said: *"People today are still living off the table scraps of the sixties. They are still being passed around – the music and the ideas."*

My story? That could be said to have been made of those scraps … but, it didn't taste that way to me. It still tasted like a tsog'khorlo[12]— a Vajrayana banquet—fresh and delicious.My table wasn't the famous Table Mountain, so the view would not seem so extraordinary. For me however – the view was immense and rich. I hoped, that my *table* would provide a Vajrayana Buddhist vision of some kind – at some point. I hoped it would be a Vajrayana vision that would open up vistas of *endless possible tables beyond mine* – laden with Art that would feed the world for centuries.

My view? Well … it's the view from the crossroads: the bardo. That's where it's always been. Whenever I arrived at *the next bardo* however, there was nothing there. Papa Legba didn't show when I was 12 – sitting naked, alone, and chilled with my appalling plastic guitar. Nothing of any lasting form had shown at any bardo since then: the bardo of the end of every romance; the bardo of the Dales' front room; the bardo of Ron's death; and, the bardo of Steve's death. These bardos always opened up some aspect of Vajrayana – and … the next direction that Vajrayana would take me.

As I surveyed the view from the crossroads of mid-September 1970, it occurred to me that I was probably lucky to have missed Legba when I was 12. What would've happened to a 12 year old boy confronted with the apparition of an African god – or his incarnation from Mississippi?

---

12 Tsog'khorlo (*tshogs 'khor lo / ganachakra*). A Vajrayana practice which employs the symbolism of a feast in terms of its profferment to a vast array of participants.

It would have made marvellous footage in a movie – but life never looks like that kind of movie. Then, the idea struck me … that maybe *Legba at the crossroads* was nothing more than a bardo – and the act of making a dramatic life-changing decision such as *'Others can play it safe – but I'm going for broke.'* Maybe it was the preparedness to *play the game to the end* – to throw everything I had onto that one last card?

Gambling brings to a mind a joke I was told about a fellow playing cards in some juke joint on the Thames Delta.[13] The game—the name of which I forget—is the one where you see how close you can get to 21 with the sum total of your cards. Getting 21 means you wipe the floor with the other players – unless one of them has a .45 Derringer boot-gun. Be that as it may, our gambling man's considering that, maybe … he ought to quit at a safe 14. He's had a bad run of luck – and if he pulled anything over a 7 he'd be out of the game—*and*—cleaned out of money. Just as he's weighing the dilemma, a diminutive demon appears on his shoulder with a quirky grimace and beady eyes. The demon whispers conspiratorially in a peculiar rasping voice *"Take another card!"* The fellow's wary about the suggestion … but hey, little demons don't suddenly appear on your shoulder every day bearing 'inside information' – so … he takes another card. Ace of Spades! He's delighted—he's up to 15— but the little demon immediately croaks *"Take another card!"* The fellow feels as if his luck may have changed … and … as the demon's so insistent, he takes another card, the 2 of Diamonds! Thrilled! He's now at 17 – but the little demon immediately cackles *"Go on! Take another card!"* The fellow's adamant he'll go no further – but the little demon commences to jabber *"Take another card! Go on! Go on! Take another card! Take another card! Go on! Take another card!"* With extreme reluctance—and almost crippling anxiety—he asks for another card, the 4 of Clubs! He has 21! He clears the other players out! He can't believe his good fortune!

---

13 The Thames Delta—and also the Wandle Delta—are names humorously given to the areas in which Blues thrived in Britain during the 1960s and early 1970s

Before raking in—*all*—the money on the table, he turns to thank the little demon – but is met with an unexpected response. The demon—looking inordinately surprised—squeaks *"You—lucky—lucky—bastard!"*

Maybe that's how it goes with Legba at the crossroads – or with some demon in a card game. Maybe the deal is just the deal you make when you won't back down. I knew that deal. I'd made it often enough. I'd made it often enough to know it wasn't a deal. It was just a decision. Some decisions had few consequences. Some were pivotal in precipitating volatile changes.

I'd had bad times. I'd had losses. I'd had tragedies too – but I'd also had more good times than the most demanding experiential glutton could wish. Life was good—as far as I could see—and, I'd lived more of it than anyone else I knew. The view at the bardo therefore, still seemed glorious to me: in every direction—in spite of everything—and, *because* of everything.

16

Lama Chime: the doors of perception

1970 – 1971

'And along with indifference to space, there was an even more complete indifference to time. "I could, of course, have looked at my watch but my watch I knew was in another universe. My actual experience had been, was still, of an indefinite duration. Or alternatively, of a perpetual present made up of one continually changing apocalypse."'
Aldous Huxley, The Doors of Perception / Heaven and Hell

Farnham Art School. Suddenly I was there. It was *close* to what I imagined – whilst, at the same time, being almost entirely other.

One day, I hope, I will be able to arrive somewhere—anywhere—with no preconceptions or expectations at all. Why do people go out and buy colour picture books of Ulaanbaatar[1] before going to Mongolia? Might they think they'd gone to Clacton-on-Sea if Ulaanbaatar didn't match the picture books?[2]

I was the kind of obstreperous young lunatic who would have such questions.

Courses are structured—true—but an Art School is made of people, rather than seminars and buildings. The Foundation Course at Hatch Mill was, therefore, something I was going to discover incrementally though the dramatis personæ. It would unfold as the other Art students made themselves apparent as characters in the living play.

---

1   Ulaanbaatar (Formerly Ulan Bator) means 'Red Hero'. It is the capital of Mongolia and lies in the North of central Mongolia at an altitude of about 4,350 feet in a valley on the Tuul River.

2   This was a note in an old Art School pocket notebook I used to carry to jot down ideas.

Hatch Mill—the Foundation Year Annexe building—was idyllic. An old mill house, redolent of down-at-heel splendour, sat on the Southern bank of the River Wey. It was an Art School as Art Schools *ought* to be – and still *should* be. And there I was, with some thirty confederates: all come from somewhere or other – but all alive to the fact that we were artists. Most of us had been oddities in our previous educational establishments – but now we were somehow conventional in our unconventionality.

I was happy to be in such a marvellous place – with so many fascinating people and possibilities. I could describe the course in detail – but that is not my purpose beyond the odd reference.[3] One of the first things that struck me was that I was not unusual in being a Buddhist. I didn't announce the fact – but it came out in everyday conversation, quite naturally.

Everyone was interested in anything concerning reality and the exploration of reality – and so although no one claimed to be definitively Buddhist, everyone had complete sympathy with the notion. Buddhist ideas were part of the lingua franca of the time and place – and it was taken for granted that one respected such ideas. Hatch Mill was an environment where 'interest in Buddhism' was taken for granted *"Me too, I've always been some kind of Buddhist"* but I wondered how serious some people were when they made that kind of statement. Still, at least I knew I could have conversations about reality and the nature of perception. It was woven into the structure of the act of painting. There was always a question hanging there – about *what was real*. What was the colour in front of your eyes? Was it the same for everyone? Was it a fixed experience? What was going on when the life model's skin looked almost green – as if flesh-pink and viridian were sparkling with each other?

It was not entirely unlike watching a play – apart from my being one of the actors; albeit an actor who only had the most rudimentary grasp of his lines. It was, at first, not easy to tell what or who was real or unreal. I knew that I wasn't acting a part – but some people seemed somehow larger than life. Where did they find their clothes?

---

3   See *'an odd boy'* Volume III by Doc Togden – ARO BOOKS WORLDWIDE.

There was a fellow who dressed like Gandalf and another dressed in buckskin leggings with a suede shirt and doublet. Several women were witch-inspired -and one seemed to have studied Cruella de Vil in close detail.[4]

Some students made me feel almost conservative in my dress. That was all to the good. I was glad of it. This was a brave new world – and I hoped I was going to be one of the heroes in the adventure. Pete Bridgewater was there, from Virginia Waters School. So was Rosemary Ryder – but they were not quite who they had been mere months earlier. They'd both shifted somehow – and I wondered if this was how they'd always been. They both seemed older and wiser than when I'd last seen them in July – as if years had passed.

People were reading every kind of book about every kind of philosophy and religion—the list was endless—and I wanted to read *everything* that *everyone* was reading.[5] Nessun Dorma!

People would quote out of the blue *"Y'know … 'Conscious faith is freedom. Emotional faith is slavery. Mechanical faith is foolishness.' … Gurdjieff said that."*

Then someone else would say *"You have to be comfortable to be on your own. 'If you are lonely when you're alone, you are in bad company.' … Jean-Paul Sartre wrote that."*

It was as if everyone had the wisdom of the world on tap and could let you in on the secret of it all at any moment.

---

4   Cruella de Vil is a character created by Dodie Smith as the main antagonist of her 1956 novel *The Hundred and One Dalmatians* and in Walt Disney Pictures' animated film adaptation *101 Dalmatians* (1961).

5   Plato; Socrates, Kierkegaard, Gaston Bachelard, Suzanne Bachelard, Simone de Beauvoir, Jean-Michel Berthelot, Maurice Blanchot, Francis Bacon, George Edward Moore, Martin Heidegger, Albrecht Wellmer, and Karl Popper. During tea breaks people's noses would be buried in: *La Nausée*, Jean-Paul Sartre; *The Metamorphosis*, Franz Kafka: *The Outsider*, Albert Camus; *Waiting for Godot*, Samuel Beckett; *One Flew Over the Cuckoo's Nest*, Ken Kesey; *Slaughterhouse-Five*, Kurt Vonnegut; *Notes from Underground*, Fyodor Dostoyevsky; *The Catcher in the Rye*, JD Salinger; *On the Road*, Jack Kerouac; *Rosencrantz and Guildenstern Are Dead*, Tom Stoppard; *Logic and Knowledge*, Bertrand Russell; *In Watermelon Sugar*, Richard Brautigan; *The Dice Man*, Luke Rhinehart; *The Electric Kool-Aid Acid Test*, Tom Wolfe; *Philosophical Investigations*, Ludwig Wittgenstein.

I wished I could quote Buddhism as well as they could quote almost anyone. Sometimes someone would just start reading something out loud – and everyone would stop reading and listen. *"So ... this is cool – this is what Aldous Huxley says: 'The mind is its own place, and the places inhabited by the insane and the exceptionally gifted are so different from the places where ordinary men and women live, that there is little or no common ground of memory to serve as a basis for understanding or fellow feeling. Words are uttered, but fail to enlighten. The things and events to which the symbols refer belong to mutually exclusive realms of experience.' That's from his book The Doors of Perception."*

Then there'd be some conversation before everyone went back to reading – and then the lunch break would come to an end and everyone would go back to their painting or sculpture or whatever it was. I wished that state education had been like this – but there was no room for regret of that kind. *This* was *what was happening* – and I could say *whatever I wanted* about *anything*.

The idea of rebirth was an accepted norm. Not everybody wanted to meditate – but everyone accepted that it was an entirely valid engagement with life. And *sure – I was going to India*. Who wouldn't want to go to India? And in fact, everyone was going at some point or other. It was the-done-thing. It was finishing school. You go to Art School – and, when it's over, you complete your education by heading East. It made sense. In terms of Art School, going to the East was entirely conventional behaviour.

It was an intriguing experience to feel part of a coherent culture. I might be a weirdo to society at large – but here I was, if anything, one of the less bizarre characters. I had no desire to be *more-bizarre-than-thou* – as it enabled me to be the *Blues Buddhist* I'd been for so long. There was no contradiction. There was nothing to prove.

Occasionally I went up to London to the Buddhist Society. Lama Chime Rinpoche gave talks there from time to time. It was marvellous to meet a Tibetan Lama at long last – and to be able to ask the questions after his talks. Lama Chime Rinpoche was extremely helpful with questions concerning silent sitting meditation – and he clarified many points for me. He mentioned David Bowie.

He told me *"David Bowie came to the Buddhist Society. That is how we met. I said 'Come in young man and sit down. So why have you come to see me?' David Bowie told me 'I want to be a monk.' So I asked 'But what is your talent?' He told me 'Music'. So, I said "Then you should not be a monk! You should be a musician!' And that's what he did. It was much better for him."*

David Bowie—who was 19 at that time—developed his interest in Buddhism from reading Heinrich Harrer's book *Seven Years in Tibet* which described Heinrich Harrer's encounter with the Dalai Lama. David Bowie had been inspired by Tibet and wrote the song *Silly Boy Blue* which made references to Tibet.

I asked Chime Rinpoche whether I could have a private interview and he was happy to oblige me. Once we had settled down in the small shrine room at the Buddhist Society, I asked him if he would give me the same advice as he'd given David Bowie and he replied *"Are you also talent with music like David Bowie?"*

I smiled *"No, not like David Bowie – and not Rock Music. I played Blues and I was mainly a singer."*

Chime Rinpoche asked for an explanation of Blues. I gave it. He asked whether it was as famous as the music David Bowie played. I replied, regretfully, that Blues had been famous in the late 1960s – but that now, it was waning. Chime Rinpoche shook his head *"No, I don't think so—not for you—but not monk. Monk is not good for you."* He said that he couldn't see so clearly where I should go – but *"... better you have khandro. Yes—not celibate—you must have khandro. This is better for you."* Chime Rinpoche thought I should go out to India and Nepal and then see what happened. I told him that this is what I had planned to do after the Foundation Year was over.

I asked whether I could take notes and he told me that was fine with him – then he asked *"What is it that you see when you look at the world?"*

"A mass of colours and shapes; sounds and textures; fragrances and tastes; and ... then I make sense of that according to what I know ... from what I have learned or absorbed through living."

"Yah, good" he replied. *"You sense – you see the relative. Phenomena, all the time, are changing. But how do you perceive phenomena as a whole?"*

251

That threw me a little because I was not quite clear where these questions were tending. *"Well—I'm sorry if this sounds stupid—but I see them as a whole simply by not seeing any artificial dividing lines between them."*

"Yah! Not stupid! The whole is only seen in the absolute. For example, if you are watching a river – how do you know it is a river? There is no continuity in the particles of water; from moment to moment the water changes and you do not see the same river twice. It only becomes a river through the absolute nature of flowing water – because there, the particles are undivided. Unless there is the absolute you can't see connection between particular phenomena. Is this clear to you?"

I said that it was. He waited 'til I'd finished writing.

"So ... we must never confuse relative with absolute. Mostly we see only the relative, and see it as being completely real. We become engrossed in particular things we are doing*; we* once did*, or we* will do *in the future. These particulars become so very real to us that we see nothing else. If some of these things seem to go wrong, we become agitated or sorrowful. This is like being tricked by an imitation snake. If you go into a room where there's a toy snake and you think it's real, you may be frightened – but as soon as you see it's not a real snake it ceases to be frightening. So ... what do you say to this?"*

"That it's the same with everything in the relative conditioned sphere of perception. If we see people as hostile then we relate to them as if they were hostile – or whatever our perception happened to be."

"Yes. So, by seeing that 'individual disconnected phenomena' are not 'the whole of reality' – we become free from attaching to them – as if they were true reality. Now, how do you come to see the absolute truth?"

"By silent sitting?"

"Yes, but what is your 'perception of the world' in that silent sitting?"

"Well ... I would not conceptualise about what I saw or what was happening in the sense fields."

"Yah—good—you can't see reality as a collection of objects. You can't find reality in one particular place. You can't find reality by making patches of relative truth next to each other until all vision is covered with patches. You can't find reality like that. The absolute is always free of conceptual patches.

"It's only because of the absolute that the relative exists – but you can't see the absolute as you would see a relative part of the absolute. It's like the eyes. They see – but they cannot see themselves. A knife cuts – but it can't cut itself. So, to see absolute reality – you must not cling to relative perception."

I suddenly had a question because there seemed to be something dualistic about the way in which the world was being relegated *"Would it be necessary to destroy the relative in order to see the absolute?"*

"No" he laughed. *"They're not in conflict. The relative comes from the absolute. The relative arises naturally and spontaneously. It's only our dualistic way of seeing that causes attachment. Where there is no attachment to relative phenomena—and, where we don't see relative as absolute—there is no division between relative and absolute. The absolute is like the moon – and the relative truth is like a reflection of the moon in the surface if a lake. In dualistic vision we think the reflection is the real moon – but we do not have to destroy the reflection to see the real moon. So—in your meditation—you have to be on the knife edge between affirming and denying the relative world. You can't make this happen though. You can only prepare – because it's beyond contriving."*

At this point, I asked Chime Rinpoche whether he would be my teacher – but he answered *"To be spontaneous with an open mind is good – but this, for you, is too soon, too early, too quick. You should go to the Himalayas first – to India and Nepal. You meet different Lamas and hear teachings. If you don't find a Lama, come back to me and I will be your teacher – but not before you have met other teachers. You must be sure you make the right choice."*

He then suggested that we sit in silence for a while. After maybe five minutes he continued *"In your life … you must remember that for the absolute, you have wisdom, and for the relative, you have compassion. Shakyamuni did not need to teach so that people would become wise – he taught to provide a method people could use to come to his understanding. So even though you may understand absolute truth, you need not be opposed to the outer relative religion – but find the best method that suits your personality."*

At this the interview was concluded and I walked off in the direction of Victoria Coach Station to catch my return to Farnham.

I saw Chime Rinpoche once more after that – and told him that I had a dilemma. I told him that at times I felt like a hypocrite as a Buddhist – because I had too much desire. I wanted too many things and had some sense that even though I occasionally disapproved of myself for wanting things – I knew that I might never change. I felt that there was something in my personality that simply did not want to be desireless. Was there a practice that would quell my desire?

Chime Rinpoche smiled. *"Look at me!"* he laughed. *"I have been meditating since I was a child – but I still desire things! I still desire good food to eat and clean clothes to wear. I desire a warm house and to be with good friends and family. The only difference between us, is maybe that when I don't get these things it doesn't matter very much. So—in this way—maybe at first it begins to matter less. Maybe you already notice this."*

"Somewhat, Rinpoche … I mean … I have been very sad about the deaths of my friends – but otherwise I don't get—that—upset when things don't go the way I want them to go."

"Sadness for death of friends—brother or sister, or parents—this is natural. This is not 'too much attachment'. But if never too upset when things are not what you desire – then, already, you have begun. Now all you need is to continue." Pause. *"There is much—much—misunderstanding about meditation. People are thinking 'many rules'. Many rules about just being still, sitting quietly with attention. Yet when mind is still, awareness allows inner treasures to come. In stillness-mind there is no aggression. It is relaxed, joyous, compassionate, and playful. These qualities exist already in everyone. Silent sitting simply allows them to manifest. You don't have to force yourself to be without desire. That is not the way. You will not be a monk – so there is no problem. Simply be as you are. Practise as you have already practised – then: no problem. Then when Art School is finished for this year: go to the Himalayas and see what you are finding. Then … maybe we will meet again – if it is necessary."*

The next day I'd be back at Hatch Mill. I was happy to be at Hatch Mill – even though I was eager to get to the Himalayas. Lama Chime Rinpoche—although he did not say a great deal—made the whole idea come alive.

A *real live Tibetan* had suggested I should go to the Himalayas. Meeting a Tibetan—let alone a Tibetan incarnate Lama—in England at that time, was like meeting King Solomon, Cleopatra, Leif Erikson, Boadicea, Barbara Strozzi[6] or Leonardo Da Vinci … The die was cast: I'd set out the following September.

In the meanwhile, there was Hatch Mill. Being in this new environment—where Art was the raison d'etre—threw me out of my habitual frames of reference. I expected to be haunted by Lindie —by Ron and Steve—but instead, I found myself carried by a wave of creative verve: blown by the winds of wonder. It's not that I had no thoughts of loss. They were there – but they were there in an environment that demanded so much in terms of time and energetic absorption that 'loss' was not what it once had been.

Virginia Water School seemed remote. I noticed the sense of the *Summer-just-gone* as belonging to a past decade. At first this notion made me a little uneasy. Was there something wrong with me? Surely, I should not be able to let go of past sorrows *so* very quickly? Of course, it was not long before I realised that the past *was* still with me. I could still shed a tear – but I could also let it wash through me. It was my choice whether I decided to indulge my sense of loss. My memories of Ron and Steve would always be cause for appreciation – but the rest of my life would have its own character and dynamics. I also realised that my life had changed quite radically from the ethos of being an *elderly school boy* to being a *young adult Art student*. I'd felt like an adult from the age of 14 – but the sense had been constrained by the secondary school environment. Now I was in a place where students and lecturers addressed each other by their first names. There were many mild shocks of that nature. They seemed desirably natural – but strikingly different from life up until that point. And Lindie?

---

6   Babara Strozzi (1619–1677) was the adopted daughter of poet and librettist Giulio Strozzi. He encouraged her musical talent and created an academy in which her performances could be displayed publicly. He thus exhibited her considerable vocal talents to a wider audience. Singing was not her only talent. She was also compositionally gifted, and her father arranged for her to study with composer Francesco Cavalli. She led a quiet, slightly unusual life, supporting herself through investments and her compositions.

Where was she in all this? Well … she'd have to live with the choice she felt forced to make. I wished her well with her life and hoped she'd find *in someone else* whatever she found most valuable about me. Did I miss her? Yes. I wished it had worked out otherwise – but I also knew that brooding about it was futile. Only idiots mourned too long about what could not be altered. I'd recovered from the loss of Alice, Mr Love, and Anelie – and I'd recover from the loss of Lindie.

The year passed with a rapidity that was almost alarming. I worked hard. I played hard in terms of the social whirl of Art School – tied up as it was with staying late in the evenings, working on projects and talking with the others. I soon found myself in a relationship with a Scots lady called Hell—Helen McGillvray—and that had various ramifications: both concupiscent and convoluted. It began delightfully – but became increasingly arduous in the second term. I might say *'Hell hath no fury like Helen McGillvray when Fine Art is not the be-all and end-all of everything'*.[7] It wasn't *fury* however, merely obdurate insistence on purism. Hell was a Fine Art purist. I was a Buddhist Bluesman – and decidedly multi-disciplinary in terms of the Arts.

I was not—in the end—*Hell's angel*. I had been, when she first made her move on me – but I gradually become an encumbrance. She began it – and, by the following early September, she ended it. I was somewhat sad about the end of the relationship – but it was an extremely short-lived sadness. By the end of our relationship – the fact that she wasn't Lindie, was glaringly obvious. She wasn't Buddhist and she only had a passing interest in Blues. She had no interest in Classical or Baroque music either. She had no interest even in exploring the notion of Buddhism.

I never blamed her for her lack of interest in Buddhism – but she certainly took against me for not being as devoted to Fine Art painting as she was.

---

7   See *'an odd boy'* Volume III by Doc Togden – ARO BOOKS WORLDWIDE. *'Hell hath no fury like a woman scorned'* is a revamped version of a line from *'The Mourning Bride'* a play by William Congreve – the original of which is *'Heaven has no rage like love to hatred turned, Nor Hell a fury, like a woman scorned.'*

Lama Chime: the doors of perception

By the end I realised that Lindie was—*very*—far from forgotten. I missed her as much as I ever had. So much for nonattachment …

So many events took place on the Foundation Year from 1970 to 1971. So many conversations. Even though I knew it was an illusion —to whatever extent—I enjoyed the texture of the illusion with rampant voracity. Being an Art student had the same quality as being on stage with the Savage Cabbage Blues Band – but here that quality of stage-performance was everyday life. Everyone was some sort of star performer – but there was no sense of competition. You could only outshine others by working harder and longer and by never being complacent about the quality of the work produced. No one was interested in outshining anyone. The idea was deemed crass. Only *philistines* and *cretins* competed. Now I was no longer absorbed with the WB Yates, James Joyce, Aldous Huxley, Virginia Woolf, Shakespeare, and Chaucer of English studies at school – I had more time to explore Buddhist books. Strangely enough there were some authors I'd not discovered: Anagarika Govinda,[8] Alexandra David-Néel,[9] and John Blofeld.

8   Lama Anagarika Govinda (1898–1985) was a painter, poet, and founder of the Arya Maitreya Mandala. In 1947 he married Li Gotami (1906–1988). She had been his student, in painting, at Shantinekan University. They became members of the Drukpa Kagyüd lineage and lived in a house rented from the writer Walter Evans-Wentz at Kasar Devi, near Almora in northern India. They went to Tibet in the late 1940s and produced a large number of drawings, paintings, and photographs. These travels are described in Anagarika Govinda's *Way of the White Clouds*. I corresponded with her in 1982 concerning her photographs of Ajo Répa Rinpoche and she was kind enough to send me copies of photographs of him.

9   Alexandra David-Néel (1868–1969) was a Belgian-French explorer, most known for her 1924 visit to Lhasa, Tibet. She wrote over 30 books about Eastern religion, philosophy, and her travels. In 1890 and 1891, she travelled throughout India. In 1911 she returned to India to study Buddhism. She went to Sikkim, where she met prince Tulku Namgyal. She met the 13th Dalai Lama in 1912, and had the opportunity to ask questions. From 1914–1916 she lived in a cave in Sikkim, learning together with the Sikkimese monk A'phur Yönten (Lama Yongden). She adopted him and he became a lifelong travelling companion. In 1937 they travelled to Tibet through Russia. They returned to France in 1946. A'phur Yönten died at age 56 in 1955. She continued to write at Digne-les-Bains, until her death at the age of nearly 101. The books I read: *My Journey to Lhasa*, 1929; *With Mystics and Magicians in Tibet*, 1930; *Initiations and Initiates in Tibet*, 1931; *The Superhuman Life of Gesar of Ling*, 1933; *In the Land of the Gentleman Brigands*, 1935; *Buddhism: Its Doctrines and Its Methods*, 1940; *The Secret Oral Teachings in Tibetan Buddhist Sects*, 1951.

These books were all far more readable than the books with which I'd struggled in previous years even though I only saw Anagarika Govinda as reliable in terms of authenticity. I found Anagarika Govinda's books [10] extremely helpful and felt inspired to follow his example. I read and re-read *Way of the White Clouds*. Alexandra David-Néel was too obsessed by the macabre and her books— although interesting and highly readable—were suspect, even to me. John Blofeld's books [11] were muddled and shallow, after Anagarika Govinda. They were light on technical information after Evens-Wentz.

From these books and other sources, I came to discover a wealth of literature on Tibet and realised that I had a great repository at my disposal. I therefore started ordering books from the library – being as I could not run to buying every book that took my interest. I decided to be canny in terms of what I decided to purchase. I'd read library copies first in order to establish whether owning a copy was essential. [12]

The books of Sir Charles Bell [13] were interesting and added to my knowledge of Tibetan culture – and, all told, I had a dozen books to absorb my attention when I was not engaged in my Art School work or playing Blues at the William Cobbet pub.

---

10 *Way of the White Clouds*, 1966; *The Psychological Attitude of Early Buddhist Philosophy*, 1937; *Psycho-Cosmic Symbolism of the Buddhist Stupa*, 1936; and, *Foundations of Tibetan Mysticism*, 1957.

11 John Blofeld (1913–1987) was a British writer on Asian religion who wrote: *The Tantric Mysticism of Tibet: A Practical Guide to the Theory, Purpose, and Techniques of Tantric Meditation*, 1970.

12 Over the course of time, every book proved essential. Many of them have now become the basis of the reference library at *Drala Jong* – the Aro gTér Nyingma Vajrayana Retreat Centre in Carmarthenshire: *Drala Jong*, Pant-y-Porthman, Banc-y-Ffordd, Llandysul, Sir Gærfyrddin, Wales, SA44 4RY, Britain.

13 Sir Charles Alfred Bell (1870–1945) was a British-Indian Tibetologist educated at Winchester College who became British-India's ambassador to Tibet. In 1908 he joined the Indian Civil Service and was appointed Political Officer in Sikkim. In 1910 he met the 13th Dalai Lama and came to know him quite well. He later wrote his biography *Portrait of the Dalai Lama*, 1946. He also wrote: *Tibet, Past and Present*, 1924; *The People of Tibet*, 1928; and, *The Religion of Tibet*, 1931.

With all this—and Helen McGillvray—there was no time to dwell on the past; even though it percolated through from time to time when I was riding my motorcycle to and from Hatch Mill.

I was soon looking back at Art School from Sir Lindsay Parkinson's Scaffolding Yard in Aldershot where I was living the life of a recluse. I simply worked all the hours available—and read books in my spare time—waiting for the end of the Monsoon when I could take the money I'd saved and head out to India. It was whilst I was working at Sir Lindsay Parkinson's Scaffolding Yard that I ploughed my way through *Theory and Practice of the Mandala*—and other works —by Giuseppe Tucci.[14]

I had nothing to do when I was awake and not working or sleeping other than meditate and study – so that became my life for a while. Through the books of Gisseppe Tucci, I discovered Fosco Maraini[15] whose book *Secret Tibet* was a fascinating insight – full of marvellous photographs. Books just kept coming to light from references in the books I'd initially found. Each led to the next. Not all of them were that marvellous – but I felt that every trail was worth following. Other books I found were Heinrich Harrer's [16] *Seven Years in Tibet* and AH Savage Landor's [17] obscure tome *In The Forbidden Land*. So many books—so little time—I had a whole list going after a while.

14 Giuseppe Tucci (1894–1984) an Italian scholar of oriental cultures, specialising in Tibetan Buddhism, was one of the founders of the field of Buddhist Studies. He was fluent in Tibetan, Sanskrit, Bengali, Pali, Prakrit, and Chinese. He taught at the University of Rome La Sapienza until his death. He wrote: *The Theory and Practice of the Mandala*, 1961; *To Lhasa and Beyond*, 1956; *Tibetan Folksongs from the District of Gyantse*, 1966; *Tibetan Painted Scrolls*, 3 volumes, 1949; and, *Secrets of Tibet. Being the Chronicle of the Tucci Scientific Expedition to Western Tibet*, 1935.

15 Fosco Maraini (1912–2004) Italian photographer, anthropologist, ethnologist, mountaineer, and writer known for his accounts of travels with Tibetologist Giuseppe Tucci during two expeditions to Tibet in 1937 and 1948.

16 *Heinrich Harrer* (1912–2006) Austrian mountaineer, geographer, and author best known for his books *Seven Years in Tibet*, 1952; and *Tibet is My Country* – autobiography of the Dalai Lama's older brother, Thubten Jigme Norbu, 1961.

17 *Arnold Henry Savage Landor: In the Forbidden Land: an Account of a Journey into Tibet*, 1898.

I knew that much of the list would have to wait to some future point, as time was running out.[18] Most of these books were out-of-print and could only be ordered through libraries – but I had been told that there were Antiquarian Book-Finding Services of which I could avail myself should I ever have funds to cover the growing number of books I wished to have as a reference library. I made many notes – but the more notes I wrote the more questions I had.

I made a trip to Edinburgh before I left Britain. That's where Helen McGillvray had gone. She had a place in Fine Art at the Art School there. I hadn't been entirely aware that our relationship was over when I set out – but it was explained within ten minutes of my arrival. She'd gotten painfully thin from the slightly rounded lady I'd first met. She had taken to smoking Gauloises[19] – a sure cure for any romance. Smoking was anathema to me—as she well understood—and so keeping my distance was evidently implied. In terms of her emaciation, I suspected she'd taken to *something* that dampened her appetite. Other than contracted pupils, however, I had no evidence. I thought I was sad at first – but my sadness was illusory. We both knew we were unsuited. We both knew that we weren't even friends. We had almost nothing in common, other than we'd once attended the Foundation Year at Farnham Art School. I took it more-or-less in my stride. I left early in the morning before Hell had awoken. There's no need to say 'goodbye' when it's goodbye forever.

---

18 *An Account of Tibet, The Travels of Ippolito Desideri,* 1931; *Journey of William of Rubruck to The Eastern Parts of the World,* by William Woodville Rockhill, 1900; *Account of an Embassy to the Court of the Teshoo Lama in Tibet,* by Samuel Turner, 1800; *Narrative of a Journey to Lhasa,* 1885; *Narrative of a Journey Round Lake Yamdo, Lhokha, Yarlung, and Sakya,* 1887; *Three Years in Tibet,* by Ekai Kawaguchi, 1909; *Tibet: A Chronicle of Exploration,* John MacGregor, 1970; *Pioneering in Tibet,* by Annie Taylor, 1898 and *My Diary in Tibet and Travel and Adventure in Tibet,* 1902; *An Adventurer in Tibet,* by Sven Hedin, 1904; and *Narratives of the Mission of George Bogle to Tibet,* and *Journey of Thomas Manning to Lhasa,* 1876.

19 Gauloises—launched in 1910—were short, wide, unfiltered cigarettes containing dark tobaccos from Syria and Turkey famous for their strength.

17

perchance to dream

late september 1971

I passed through Carlisle on the way back to Farnham. I'd met a young lady on the road. She—like me—had been hitching. The hour had been getting late and she'd offered me a place to lay my head. Her name was Emily. There was no romantic inclination in either of us – and we were so unalike that conversation was not easy. Whilst staying with Emily in Carlisle overnight however, I was persuaded to extend my sojourn. Emily told me about a venue where I could play a set. I stayed and played and met her two friends Rose and Valerie who'd come up from Exeter Art School to spend a short weekend with her.

They were all Fine Art students and had attended the same Foundation course. Emily's friends were strikingly different. I got on with them so well that they persuaded me to make a detour through Exeter on my way home. That was quite some detour – but, as I'd planned to spend the best part of a week in Edinburgh, I was not exactly in any tearing hurry. Fine. I'd travel back to Exeter with them. The set I played went well. Rose and Valerie were evidently Blues enthusiasts and so they wanted me to play a set on the Exeter Art School Folk and Blues night. Certainly, if I could borrow a guitar – and, if I could borrow some tools to make a nut-raiser. The laughed about what they imagined a 'nut-razor' to be – and asked me *"D'you plan to play sans-culottes, then?"*[1]

To which I replied *"You hum it and I'll play it."*

---

1 Sans-culottes, in contemporary slang usage, means 'naked'. Originally the sans-culottes (*literally 'without knee-breeches'*) were the common people in late 18th century France who were partisans of the French Revolution. The name refers to the fact culottes were the fashionable silk knee-breeches of the nobility and the working class 'sans-culottes' wore pantaloons (*trousers*).

They howled with laughter at that. Then I explained that *nut-raiser* was not a *nut-razor* – and that it would be necessary to make one in order to play lap slide.

'It was fine on Emily's nylon strung guitar. Spanish guitars have a high action – so all I needed to do was sling an ultralight steel set on it for the night. If I borrow a steel-strung however – I'd need to make a device to raise the nut: hence nut-raiser.'

'… but … wouldn't that be difficult?' Valerie asked.

'No … If I could borrow the right tools. It wouldn't need to look pretty – and I'm sure I could get away with something fairly simple.'

And so it was settled: I was due to be back on stage again – just when I thought those days were over. We bade goodbye to Emily and took off for South Devon: *to fresh woods, and pastures new.*[2] On the steps of Exeter Art School, I sat down and … smiled.[3]

I smiled, as soon as Rose and Valerie appeared. I'd been sitting—meditating—as was my custom whilst waiting anywhere. No one ever seemed to notice anything unusual in that. I never made it obvious by placing my hands in the meditation mudra.[4] Some people adopted mudras to let other people know that they were 'doing something special'. I found that decidedly creepy. Perfect in the appropriate setting – but pretentious when sitting on a park bench.

---

2 From *Lycidas* written by John Milton in 1637. A monody in which he bemoans a friend, drowned during his passage from Chester on the Irish Sea.

3 This is a reference to *By Grand Central Station I Sat Down and Wept* – a prose-poetry novel by Elizabeth Smart (1913 –1986) published in 1945. The title of the book is an allusion to Psalm 137: *'By the waters of Babylon we lay down and wept …'*

4 Mudra (*chag-gya / phyag rGya*) means gesture. Samten chag-gya (*bSam gTan phyag rGya / dhyana dudra*) the gesture of meditation. The hands are placed on the lap, left hand on right with fingers fully stretched (*four fingers resting on each other and thumbs facing upwards towards one another diagonally*). Palms facing upwards – hands and fingers make a triangle symbolic of the Three Jewels. This mudra is used in representations of Shakyamuni Buddha and 'ö-Pag-mèd (*'od dPag med / Amitabha*).

"You weren't contemplating your navel,[5] *were you Vic?"* Rose smiled as she loomed, seemingly out of nowhere.

"Someone's maybe – but not mine" I replied – which made both Rose and Valerie burst out laughing. They pulled up their T-shirts and said *"You can contemplate ours if you like."*

"A pleasure and a privilege …" I replied *"… but my contemplation can be somewhat lengthy – so maybe we'd better get some lunch."* It was indeed lunch time. They'd come to join me—enjoying the cool October sunshine—and we were shooting the breeze about anything and everything. They were a conversational whirlwind.

"It's strange …" I began *"… being on the outside."*

"We often sit out here at lunchtime" Rose grinned.

That made me laugh. Rose and Valerie looked at me with slight confusion. *"That's not quite what I meant – I meant outside vis-à-vis my not being an Art student at the moment. It hadn't really hit me 'til now."* Pause. *"I don't mean 'strange' as in 'unpleasant' … just … strange."*

"Glad it's that kind of strange …" Valerie chuckled *"… when you sounded like you were laughing for no reason at all we wondered if you'd been at the dope."*

"No … but funny you should think that – because people do sometimes think I'm stoned, when I'm just enjoying colours and sounds."

"So how far out d'you get when you do get stoned?" Valerie enquired, laughing in delight at what seemed to her a far-out statement.

"I don't get stoned – in fact I've never touched the stuff or anything else for that matter. I like a nice glass of red wine when I can afford it – but, I've never experimented with drugs."

"Never!?" the two ladies yelped in tandem. *"That's gotta be the weirdest thing for an Art student to say"* Rose continued.

"Well certainly – but then … I'm a—weird—Art student."

---

5   Omphaloskepsis. *'Gazing at your navel'* is mildly derogatory English idiom for taking inordinate time in introverted reflection.

"You were never curious …" Rose asked with some incredulity. *"I mean … everybody seems to try it, at least."*

"Yes … well … I was curious back in 1966 *when the Beatles 'Revolver' album came out – but … not curious enough. For me … the curiosity was all based on the backwards guitar of* I'm Only Sleeping *and* Tomorrow Never Knows. *Once I listened to that enough times I discovered that those kinds of sounds were … here there and everywhere, as it were. You see … I'm naturally psychedelic. I see sounds and hear colours without having to rearrange my brain chemistry – and … from what I've seen of people on dope and acid … I wouldn't want to be there. They just get silly and laugh at nothing – as I did, when I laughed in response to your saying that you enjoyed being outside."*

"Right … well that's novel" Valerie mused. *"Don't get us wrong, we've both smoked a little—to see what it was like—but neither of us have any interest in it. As you said, it makes people stupid. It makes them slow. What we notice about the dope-heads in Fine Art is that they don't really do a lot of work."*

"Right" Rose cut in. *"We're here to work – I mean we've only got three years – and if we can't get on a Master's degree somewhere – the fun's over."*

*"That's—*exactly*—how I see it"* I agreed with a vehemence that even caused me slight surprise *"Carpe diem. No choice about it. Carpe diem. If you're not passionate you're dead. Carpe diem. You have to live it. If you can't live it—if you can't suck it down like oxygen—you end up as factory fodder, or growing mould in your eyebrows in some office somewhere."*

Rose and Valerie were in tears of laughter at the end of my tirade. *"Are you sure you're not on something?"* Rose cackled.

That made me cackle *"I'm on everything! I'm mainlining life! I'm shooting up Blues, inhaling Art, and snorting Vajrayana!"* Pause – and in a more sedate tone *"… but … as I said before it's not that I was—*never*—curious. You'd have to be dead not to be curious."* Pause. *"It's … a promise I made to myself when my father backed down on throwing me out of the house unless I cut my hair."*

Then, of course, I had to tell them the whole story about how my father thought guitars and long hair led to heroin and a life of crime and homosexuality and perversions he couldn't even bring himself to mention.

"That's … quite a story – not the whole thing with your father – but making a promise like that to yourself that you'd never break" commented Valerie. *"It's really … like something out of Robert Louis Stevenson or something – the honour thing, I mean – not that there's anything wrong with that … I mean … Ah … I'm sorry how that came out … I didn't mean it to sound like that, or whatever."*

Valerie was obviously embarrassed and so I did my best to put her at ease *"No need to be sorry … I am vaguely old fashioned in some ways … and strangely enough … it's not the first time that someone's mentioned me being a little like something out of Robert Louis Stevenson."*

"But what about Vajrayana Buddhism?" asked Rose *"I didn't take you for a religious type?"*

"Nor did I" I smiled. *"I'm probably not the—*typical—*religious type; just as I'm not a typical Art student or typical hippie."*

"Good for you!" laughed Valerie. *"Who'd want to be typical – but if you're not typical, as a Buddhist … well, what does that mean to you?"*

"Well, to me … it means that I'm not some-sort-of-convert. I don't want to convert anyone. It means … I'm not particularly pious, devout, spiritual, holy, mystical, unworldly, or otherworldly. I've met 'spiritual types' –and, what I notice mainly, is that they tend to find me … too 'un-spiritual'. I like to laugh." I burst into song: *"I like to laugh, and when the sun is out – I've got something I can laugh about. I feel good, in a special way. In Exeter and it's a sunny day. Good day, sunshine; good day, sunshine; good day, sunshine; good day, sunshine; good day, sunshine; good day, sunshine … or, something like that."*[6]

That made Rose and Valerie almost cry laughing until Rose finally said *"Alright—we believe you, we believe you—you're not spiritual – and thank the Fancy Christmas Duck for that!"*[7]

---

6   Partial parody of *Good Day Sunshine* by the Beatles from the *Revolver* album (1966) – written mainly by Paul McCartney and credited to Lennon–McCartney.

7   *Thank the Fancy Christmas Duck for that!'* was a personal linguistic coinage of either Rose or Valerie as a euphemistic version of *'Thank the Fuck for that!'*

I was glad that Rose and Valerie asked me no more, because they obviously had no interest in Vajrayana – or any other religion for that matter. I never liked answering questions about Vajrayana unless people were genuinely interested. Throwaway information in casual conversation just never suited me where Vajrayana was concerned.

After some moments of silence—Art students were usually good at social silence—Valerie asked *"Last night … I got the faint impression that you weren't that keen on John Mayall and Alexis Korner … and I was wondering …"*

"Right … well … yes – it could only have been a faint impression because I don't like to be down on musicians other people enjoy – and … it's not even that I have anything to say against them. It's just that … well, they don't really represent Blues as I know it can be. I suppose I'm something of a purist … I prefer Muddy Waters – y'know the main man – the lineage holder of Robert Johnson's legacy – through Son House."

"Yes …" Valerie replied *"… but I thought you were grieving the death of the British Blues Boom?"*

"I am …" Pause. *"… but … apart from a few tracks on a few albums … the British Blues Boom was more-or-less the British Rock & Roll Boom. There was a lot of Blues played early on in clubs and pubs – but when it came to albums … Blues was just a little scarce. Don't get me wrong – I admire John Mayall and Alexis Korner and I like a fair selection of their material – but they played Blues too fast … and … when you increase the tempo of Blues beyond a certain point – you've more-or-less got Rock & Roll …"* Pause. *"… and … it's not even that I don't like Rock & Roll. It's just not Blues – and, Blues is my passion."*

"But!" Rose cut in with a gleam in her eye *"You told us that Savage Cabbage used to play the odd Beatles' number and psychedelic numbers like Itchycoo Park!"*

"Quite right. So did Cream. *I never said that Blues was the—only—music I liked or wanted to play. Savage Cabbage was fundamentally—and almost completely—a Blues band. When we played Blues—and that was* 90 percent *of the time—it was always slow.*

"We played the long Cream-style improvisations with each number—and they admittedly owed much to Jazz and JS Bach—but we never played Rock & Roll. We played Blues – with a few Acid Rock numbers for variety. A fair few of the Black American Blues people played the odd out-of-genre number – you wouldn't be a real musician if you were never tempted to use other material from time to time."

Rose and Valerie sat silent for a moment – obviously thinking about what I'd said – and finally Valerie responded *"Alright … yeah … I can see that in terms of Rock&Roll … I s'pose that's why Cyril Davies[8] broke away from Alexis Korner's band …"* Pause. *"I can see what you mean now – and … really … it's the authentic Chicago Blues we'd rather hear – I just never thought of there being such a big difference."*

"Well … maybe there isn't. Maybe it's just me" I volunteered.

"No, I think Vic's right …" said Rose *"… there really is quite a difference when you really look at it. I mean if you listen to Muddy Waters and most of the people from the British Blues Boom back to back … I suppose you'd have to come to that conclusion."* Pause. *"I suppose it must be a little more obvious to you because you've played in a band and you'll have given the thing a lot of thought."*

"There were some fantastic moments in it all though … Led Zeppelin were a brilliant Blues band in the beginning – very much like Cream in some ways – then … they moved into Progressive Rock—which I like—but I'd rather they'd stayed with Blues. Edgar Broughton too – they were once the Edgar Broughton Blues Band. Of course … when Cream split up Jack Bruce moved back into Jazz. I loved his 'Songs For A Tailor' album – because I love his bass playing and Pete Brown's lyrics – but I was sad not to hear him sing Blues as he sang it with Cream. Ginger Baker always was a Jazz musician, even in Cream – so he moved out into Jazz-Rock fusion. Eric Clapton seems to have given up Blues altogether. Maybe he'll come back to it again one day. I hope so." Pause. *"The Stones started out as a Blues band too."* Pause. *"The adjectival thing, that irks me … is … why did they—have—to move on? What was—wrong—with Blues? Muddy Waters never 'moved on'. Howling Wolf never 'moved on'. Buddy Guy never 'moved on' – where's the loyalty-to-genre gone?"*

8   Cyril Davies (1932–1964), one of the first British Blues harp players. He also played banjo and 12-string guitar.

"Well Vic" said Valerie as if she was making the most obvious statement in the world to a simpleton *"The people who stayed in genre – they're all Black Americans aren't they … It's their music – so it's their tradition to keep up."*

"Yes … now—I know this is going to sound ridiculous—but … I thought— we—were all Black too … In some way I thought we'd all escaped from being English or something. It's utterly crazy—and I've never put it into words before —but there was this sense of having crossed the Rubicon. Jimi Hendrix and Buddy Guy grew long hair – so it was happening the other way round too. There was this sense that we were all in it together. I suppose … you must think I'm utterly—utterly—naïve."

"Maybe …" Valerie grinned *"… but, as* you *said 'if you're not passionate you're dead' and maybe you need to be a little naïve to be that passionate."*

"I think …" added Rose *"… that we'd both rather be naïve too – if that's what it takes to be passionate."*

"So …" I sighed *"… where has all the flour gone? Gone to make bread I suppose …"*

"Oh! Very droll – but very true" laughed Rose.

*"What happened to the—*conviction*—that created the British Blues Boom?"*

"As you said: commercialism happened – there was more bread in Progressive Rock" Rose snorted.

"Yeah …" I sighed *"Commercialism happened alright …"*

"Commercialism happened and Jimi Hendrix died" added Valerie. *"That's what happened."*

Lunch break over, I was glad to discover that I could be wangled into the sculpture department to make my nut-raiser. A 12-string guitar had been borrowed from a very willing young lady—also a Blues enthusiast—who Rose and Valerie had convinced that I was *somebody vaguely famous*. I was not entirely pleased by that. I knew they meant well – and so I said nothing to dismantle their promotional work.

I'd found a piece of hard old mahogany in a skip—from an old section of bannister—and in two hours I made a rather nice nut-raiser. It was far nicer than I'd imagined possible – so I was mightily pleased with my work. I had the length of chromium towel rail that I'd made into a slide for my gig in Carlisle – and so I was ready to roll in as the Hoochie Coochie Man.

The gig went well. I enjoyed myself immensely – even though I felt as if I was in a play, where I was acting the part of *one aspect of who I was*. After the gig we returned to Rose and Valerie's flat. We spent the evening together talking and playing Blues albums. Rose and Valerie then surprised me—at the end of the evening—by springing spontaneous torridity upon me. They'd vanished for a few minutes and returned sans-culottes. I then surprised myself by being unable to object to what they had in mind.

Eventually Rose and Valerie went to sleep on either side of me. I lay awake wondering how it had all happened. Well, I knew how it had happened. They'd simply disrobed and made their intentions unavoidable. I should have realised that there was something in the air. Rose and Valerie had made a few sexually tinged rejoinders. I'd taken it as free-spirited badinage. After all it *had* to be possible for men and women to engage in banter without it having to betoken *more than jocularity*. In any case I was an extremely poor womaniser. I found the process of deliberate seduction entirely distasteful. If I liked a lady I'd simply engage in conversation – and, if she liked me, the conversation would become invigorating. There'd be more conversation and eventually the situation would become obvious. Romance simply happened of itself – by being natural. Maybe I was just naïve. Maybe? No, there was no 'maybe' about it: I *was* naïve.

What follows verges on chaos – random, even as stream-of-consciousness prose. It is a depiction of one night in terms of sleeping, dreaming, and intermittently waking.

Headings are supplied to indicate approximate mind-states: *déjà vu*, *jamais vu, presque vu, quotidian nocturnal reality*, and, *quotidian diurnal reality*.[9]

Déjà vu: As I lay there, I became aware of Rose and Valerie asleep on either side of me. How could I be experiencing déjà vu? Why was there the sense of the situation being customary – as if this was *just how I lived* on a day-to-day, or night-to-night, basis? I fell asleep.

Jamais vu: I woke up. The room wasn't entirely dark – and, in any case, my eyes had grown accustomed to the dark. I'd always had good night-vision. The situation was reasonably clear to me at first – but suddenly I was aware that I was not in a room. I was not in the bedroom where my amorous liaison with Rose and Valerie had so recently occurred.

I looked around. I seemed to be seeing what looked like the sides of a tent. The impression didn't dissipate. I scanned my surroundings. For reasons entirely unknown, I was not disconcerted by what was obviously hallucinatory. I was awake and so it must have been some-sort-of hallucination. It didn't seem unnatural that I should be in a tent – but I felt no sense of that *in itself* being unnatural. That sense would have been more typical of the dream state – but I was definitely awake. The strange turn of events with Rose and Valerie – was not in my mind. There was nothing at all in my mind but the sense of having suddenly woken from sleep. I went back to sleep.

I don't know how long I'd been asleep – but I woke rather suddenly; again. I became aware that I was looking up at the night sky.

---

9   Déjà vu (French – *already seen*) is the strong sensation that an event currently experienced has been experienced in the past. Déjà vu is apparently caused by a brief glimpse of an object or situation, before the brain has completed constructing a conscious perception, resulting in an anomalous familiarity. Science rejects déjà vu as precognition or prophecy – but it cannot rule it out. Approximately two-thirds of the population have déjà vu experiences, but frequent or prolonged—and associated with hallucinations—may indicate neurological or psychiatric illness. Jamais vu (French – *not seen*) is the opposite of déjà vu. It is the feeling of not knowing how one came to be in a previously unknown place. Presque vu (French – *almost seen*) is a failure to remember something, but feeling as though it is imminent. In other words it is 'on the tip of the tongue'.

This again seemed customary because I seemed to remember that I often slept outside at night – but who was the 'I' in question? I did not form the question in words – It was more a vague sense of being experientially distant from the 'I' who was in Exeter en route to the Himalayas via Farnham in Surrey. One was always en route to somewhere – but in each place that 'one' was always a result of the surroundings and the circumstances.

Presque vu. I thought that if I simply lay still for long enough: the words, ideas, or information would simply come back to me – from wherever they were before they slipped my mind. I had no sense, in that moment that I'd never slept outside at night.

There was something in my consciousness that seemed at odds with another sense of memory – as if the memories of more than one person were attempting to cohabit in the same consciousness. I was having memories that were not my own – but which one was I? Or were there more than two streams of memory? Was it a ménage à trois of memories? Was I somehow telepathically sharing memories with Rose and Valerie? Was that possible? Could people have *adjacent dreams*? I fell asleep.

I woke up, needing a drink. The room was again the room in Exeter in which I'd gone to sleep. Rose and Valerie sound asleep. Just gone 1.00 am on the luminous dial of Rose's alarm clock. For some moments I wondered if my experiences of *waking* and *sleeping* had both been dreams. That was possible. Maybe I was just over-tired from travelling. Too many late nights. Two Blues performances and other exhilarating diversions. Dwelling on these imponderables I fell asleep.

Déjà vu: I woke after twenty minutes – but I was in some environment that was nothing like the room in which I had fallen asleep. It was the tent again. Again? Yes … I had been there before – and it seemed as if it had not been a dream. Was this another dream? No … the bed covering seemed thick and heavy. These were not the bedcovers under which I'd gone to sleep. The air felt colder than it should have been. Weird.

I turned onto my left side and went back to sleep – being too tired to investigate the anomalies of the situation yet again. There was no sense in thinking about it – it was all too bizarre. Thinking did not help with anything that was happening. I was tempted to get up and move to another room where I could turn on the light and puzzle the matter in what might be more like a 'real life environment'. A mere velleity. I fell asleep.

Presque vu: I woke up again. Just gone 2.30 a.m. I went back to sleep. Then I seemed to know that I was asleep. A lucid dream. My body was lying down but I seemed to be able to see straight ahead as if I was sitting up. I sensed the wind. There was some rocky outcrop vaguely illuminated by a gibbous Moon. There was something strange happening that I needed to comprehend. It seemed that I was on the verge of knowing who I was – and where I was. I was on the verge of knowing – because it was obvious; I was on the verge of knowing because nothing was obvious. I remained in that state of presque vu where obvious and non-obvious seems to have the same taste.

I woke up. The room was a tent again – but made of tiger hides. I fell asleep.

I woke up – and this time I forced myself to sit up in bed. I was actually awake—as far as I could ascertain—and sitting in a normal room rather than a tent. I wondered whether Rose and Valerie had spiked my drink with LSD. Entirely unlikely – but it felt as if I was going through the paranoia that had been described to me on various occasions. However, it wasn't paranoia that I was experiencing – merely a mild bafflement that occasionally teetered on the brink of amusement.

Waking and sleeping kept alternating – but I was never quite certain which was which. If I'd not found the condition restful, I would have been concerned that such a night would have left me exhausted the next morning. On that thought I fell asleep.

Having fallen asleep however I entered a lucid dream again.

I dreamed that I'd been asleep: dreaming about a room in Exeter that kept turning into a tent and that I had woken up *(in the lucid dream)*. Then I was back in the strange situation in which I had found myself before falling asleep, but there was a night sky above me.

It felt as if I was in some sort of hall of mirrors in which *dream* and *reality* kept mirroring each other – except that *the reality was like a lucid dream* and *the lucid dream* alternated with *dreams* in which the configuration of the Exeter bedroom was what I thought to be reality.

Quotidian nocturnal reality: Suddenly, absolutely sure I was awake, I looked around the room and identified objects. There were my Levi 501 Serge de Nîmes trousers beneath my Levi shirt neatly draped over a chair. My boots stood beneath the chair. Everything accorded to quotidian reality.

Jamais vu: I looked alternately at Rose and Valerie – but they were not Rose and Valerie. They both had dark hair—almost black—that was clear, in the full moonlight. I couldn't see their faces because they both had their backs to me – but I knew they were not the two young English ladies with whom I had retired for the night. I decided it was best to go to sleep. Waking them to ask who they were did not seem to be a good idea – but why was I not curious? I did not ask myself that at the time. That only became a question the next morning when I remembered. I didn't ask them who they were because I knew who they were – but on waking I no longer knew.

After seeing the two dark-haired ladies I'd fallen immediately into a dream about sky – a vast sky that kept expanding and getting brighter until it turned into the surface of a lake. Then I lost the lucidity.

I woke up sometime later. It was still dark. I opened my eyes to investigate the situation and Valerie's blond hair was clearly visible. Which of the previous episodes had been a dream? Had I actually been awake when I saw those two dark-haired ladies – or had it been a lucid dream?

273

I could not tell what was *waking experience* and what had been *lucid dreams* – but there had also been dreams which were not lucid … and I tried to recall what they were, and what had occurred in them. Someone had been speaking. It was one of the dark-haired ladies – but I could not recall what she had said. It was a question. I had answered – or someone had answered. Daylight had been streaming into the tent in which I had been sleeping. Maybe the dream had been ignited by the crescent Moon having traversed the sky.

At one point in the night the Moon had started shining into the bedroom. However … when I'd woken up sensing I was in a tent … it had been dark with no trace of the Moon. Then it occurred to me that I'd seen the Moon in different phases on the same night – so if I checked on the Moon phase the next day, perhaps I could tally it with what happened. The aspects of the night's visions which equated with *the actual Moon phase in common-or-garden quotidian Exeter* would have been what I saw when I was awake – and all the other visions would have been dreams. On that dizzying height of futile conjecture I fell asleep.

I awoke quite early from a dream that had been vivid – but not a lucid dream.

There was no story line to the final dream of the night – I'd simply been sitting in an alpine meadow watching two young girls riding extremely large dogs. They cantered the dogs around the various tents which sat regally-placed below a range of mountains. There were sounds I recalled from the dream—some kind of music—but the nature of the music was no longer clear when I awoke. All I remembered was that the sounds were enjoyable – although 'enjoyable' is rather an approximate word.

The dream had set itself in Tibet. I was used to that. It had happened many times before: when I was very young – and then later, in my teenage years, consequent to beginning to meditate. The White Lady had enabled me to *walk into Tibet from my bedroom* as a child – and from time to time—over the years—the same thing had happened. I could never tell when it would happen.

274

After each time it happened, I tried to look for signs of what it was that triggered those dreams, or daydreams, or daydreams in the night – or whatever they were. I could find no answer to that question.

Quotidian diurnal reality: I finally arose feeling rested and surprisingly perky. I fixed breakfast for Rose and Valerie. Eggs Florentine with toast. Rose and Valerie greeted me – but both launched into telling me that I'd been talking in my sleep.

"What was I saying?" I laughed.

"No idea" They replied. *"You weren't speaking English."*

"Maybe it was German."

"No … it didn't sound German – it sounded more as if you were ordering something at a Chinese restaurant."

"Maybe I was hungry" I dissimulated, laughing. I was not too keen on talking about the previous night's dreams. *"I certainly am pretty hungry now – which is why I've fixed us all a feast-of-a-breakfast."*

"Well I can't say you didn't work hard for it last night" Rose cackled.

"So what were you dreaming about?" Valerie laughed. *"People always dream when they talk in their sleep."*

I told them about the dream over breakfast but I placed the scene in Switzerland to avoid the complications that could arise when anything verged on the spiritual – and I knew that Rose and Valerie weren't wildly keen on anything spiritual. I'd picked that up from the way they made fun of Emily.

"Were they wearing lederhosen?" Rose laughed *"Y'know like Heidi or whatever?"*

"No …" I pondered *"… now that you mention it … they weren't wearing anything."*

"Well that doesn't surprise me!" laughed Valerie – who—noticing the question on my face—continued *"Dreams usually connect with what's happening in your life – so two naked girls kinda-makes-sense."*

275

"Yes … 'We are such stuff as dreams are made on; and our little life is rounded with a sleep' " [10] I replied in order to steer the subject away from my dreams.

"Shakespeare?" Rose enquired.

"Yes … Shakespeare … There's a Shakespeare quote for almost everything – and if you add Blues to the assortment there's almost nothing for which you can't find a suitable reference."

"Do you look for meanings in dreams?" asked Valerie.

"No … That's more in your friend Emily's line." Pause. *"Light, seeking light, doth light of light beguile; So ere you find where light in darkness lies, Your light grows dark by losing of your eyes."*

"Yet more Shakespeare!" laughed Rose. *"Where's this from?"*

"Speech by Berowne from 'Love's Labours Lost' – the whole thing runs like this – if I can remember it properly:

> *Why, all delights are vain – but that most vain / Which, with pain purchased, doth inherit pain – As, painfully to pore upon a book / To seek the light of truth, while truth the while / Doth falsely blind the eyesight of his look. / Light, seeking light, doth light of light beguile; / So ere you find where light in darkness lies, / Your light grows dark by losing of your eyes.'* [11]

I've always liked those lines."

"Yeah – but 'All delights are vain' eh …" laughed Valerie *"… that's a … sombre perspective. It's not yours I hope."*

"By no means." I smiled somewhat wanly. *"I was just thinking of the one line 'So ere you find where light in darkness lies, Your light grows dark by losing of your eyes.' That 'light in darkness' sounded like the dream-world – and it occurred to me that trying to find meaning in dreams was like losing your eyes. There is no sense in trying to analyse dreams."*

"So you don't go along with Jung and all that psychoanalytical stuff?"

---

10 William Shakespeare, The Tempest, Act IV, Scene i.

11 William Shakespeare, Love's Labour's Lost, Act I, Scene i.

"Not really—no—because all you analyse when you analyse a dream is the waking mind that remembers the dream. You can only attempt to analyse a dream when you are dreaming."

"But ..." opined Valerie *"... that would mean you'd have to be conscious that you were dreaming – when you were dreaming. Is that possible?"*

"Yes ..."

"Can you—do—*that, I mean: have you ever done that?"* asked Rose.

"Yes ..." I replied, realising that I'd said more than I wanted to say *"... not often – but I have had experiences of being conscious in dreams."*

"I think you're more like Emily than you let on, Vic."

"Yes ... in some ways, perhaps – but I tend to think of myself as a realist – even though '... there are more things in heaven and earth, Horatio, than are dreamt of ...'[12] *et cetera ..."*

"Hamlet!" chirped Rose – delighted that she'd pinned the reference.

"... 'Oh day and night – and it was wondrous strange!' ..."[13] Valerie misquoted and laughed.

"... 'And therefore as a stranger give it welcome.' ..."[14] I concluded with a wistful yet serviceable grin.

What was it about the creature I seemed to be? The esoteric Emily found me too pragmatic – too unspiritual. The pragmatic Rose and Valerie had me pegged as a closet woo-woo.[15] Still, I'd thrown them off the trail with Shakespeare – and so we talked until it was time to hit the road and see what lifts might come my way. I'd decided— early in the morning—I'd better leave for Farnham.

I'd have been open to a relationship with either lady – but a scene with both was not exactly part of my vision of what I did with my life.

12 William Shakespeare, Hamlet, Act I, Scene v.

13 Ibid

14 Ibid

15 Woo-woo (slang) A person readily accepting spiritual, supernatural, or occult phenomena.

The fact that I was unable to refuse a situation that wasn't *something I would have considered;* somehow disturbed me. I thought I had some idea of who I was – even though there was no *solid, permanent, separate, continuous, or defined 'I'* in the Buddhist sense.

I pondered. So … there really was no 'I' – and 'I' could be a surprise to *the 'I' of any moment in time.*

It wasn't that my torrid night with Rose and Valerie was something I failed to enjoy; or something that I came to regret. It was not so simple. I wouldn't go that way again – but the chances were that a situation like that would never come into being again. I started pondering the nature of karma and what my karmic patterning was.[16] Rose and Valerie were the secondary causes which had facilitated behaviour of which I would have otherwise disapproved. For whatever reason, I have always been entirely monogamous – and have never thought, as some fellows did, that a harem would be ideal. I just wanted a ladyfriend who would be my friend in all senses – and we'd have a life together as friends. The word friend had always been important to me – and I valued my friends. That was *what I was* – but obviously *what I was,* was capable of mutating according to the secondary causes the world presented. I'd have to be on my guard in that respect. Secondary causes were a minefield.

Mr Love—back when I was eight years old—had been the cause of my love of Blues. Had Mr Love been a secondary cause? Had I been primed to love Blues? Had I had a previous re-birth in the Mississippi Delta? A romantic thought no doubt – and I had no time for such fanciful speculations. There were too many lunatics who imagined they were the rebirth of someone or other and I had no interest in swelling their ranks. It was curious however, that Blues had grabbed me the way it did at the age of eight.

---

16 Karma means action. It refers to the principle of causality where perception and intention influence future perception and intention. Karma is psychological habit. Karmic seeds create further habits (*vasana*), and habits create perception. Karma seeds self-perception, and perception influences how one experiences life events. Both habits and self-perception affect the course of one's life. Breaking negative habit is not easy; it requires conscious effort for release from the cycle of dualism.

The Vikings had also grabbed me – but that interest had faded into insignificance by the time I left Junior School. It was maybe only the things that grabbed a person life-long that meant anything. Would Blues always be the big deal it was? And what about Vajrayana? The two religions—as I sometimes thought of them—seemed hard-wired in me, so there seemed little chance of either vanishing.

Rose and Valerie were a little disappointed that I had to head back to Farnham – and, to tell the truth, so was I. The thought of further nights with the two lovely ladies was not relinquished without regret – but it felt entirely unwise to remain. That was *not* really 'me' – but it wasn't *entirely* alien either. How could that be?

I knew that both polygyny and polyandry [17] had existed in Tibet because I'd read about those modes of marriage in *Mipam* – a Tibetan novel by Lama Yongden, the adopted son of Alexandra David-Neel.[18] Funnily enough, Rose and Valerie styled themselves as sisters – but they were entirely humorous about it. Rose was on the short side with dark curly hair and Valerie was tall with straight blond hair. They couldn't have been more different in appearance – Rose could have been French and Valerie Scandinavian. Part of their sister-act was to wear identical clothes as often as they could – but whatever their concept may have been, I did not see myself as a polygynist, whatever the Tibetan system might be in rural areas.

17 Polyandry is a form of polygamy in which a woman has multiple husbands. In Tibet those husbands were brothers (*fraternal polyandry*). One brother—usually the eldest—was nominally regarded as the father of the children, his brothers being designated as uncles. This system was a mode of marriage designed to keep farming land from being divided. The same was true in terms of one man marrying a group of sisters (*sororal polygyny*).

18 Yongden is a vague phonetic for Yönten (*yon tan / guna*) meaning attribute, quality, excellence, taste, effect). *Mipam* (*mi 'pham*) is a novel ostensibly by Lama Yongden which seeks to portray Tibetan life. It has however, obvious slants that could only have come from the pen of Alexandra David-Neel: a pretentious astrologer to whom Mipam is apprenticed, greedy monks, self-righteous missionaries, an arrogant prince, a powerful Bhutanese sorcerer, and an entirely skewed presentation of Bön. *Mipam* was published in 1938. In an introduction (*purportedly written by Lama Yongden*) Alexandra David-Neel writes: '*I hesitated, in my heart, as to what form my notes should take, when one evening, while camping with my mother by adoption, the explorer Alexandra David-Neel, amid the vast solitudes of Northern Tibet, I happened to speak once more of the distress I had experienced on seeing the people and things of my native land so travestied. She urged me, then and there, to attempt a faithful description of the people and their ways, in the form of a novel … never was a writer's vocation more unforeseen than in my own case.*'

Neither did I intend to drift through life becoming whatever the world made of me through fluke circumstances. Shakespeare flitted through my conceptual infrastructure:

> Romeo: *I dreamt a dream tonight.*
> Mercutio: *And so did I.*
> Romeo: *Well, what was yours?*
> Mercutio: *That dreamers often lie.*
> Romeo: *In bed asleep, while they do dream things true.*
> Mercutio: *Oh, then I see Queen Mab hath been with you.*
> William Shakespeare, *Romeo and Juliet,* Act I, Scene iv

Yes … *Queen Mab had been with me* – and she'd been a *White Incandescent Space of Meaning* since I was an infant. Be that as it may— and whether Rose and Valerie were Queen Mab's færies or not—I wanted to be at the driving wheel, as much as that was possible. So, I made my way homeward with the help of my thumb and a cardboard sign that read: 'Reading / Farnham'.

I got lucky. I didn't get to Reading but I got as far as Newbury. Then I picked up a lorry that was bound for Aldershot – and the driver was kind enough to change his customary route in order to pass the bottom of Woodsfield Lane. I had *all* the luck. Now, if I'd been an eternalist,[19] I would have read this as a sign that I'd made the right decision vis-à-vis not staying longer with Rose and Valerie in Exeter. As I wasn't—I didn't—but I did check the phase of the Moon as it was on the *night of visions* in Exeter.

> *'I have had a most rare vision. I had a dream, past the wit of man to say what dream it was… The eye of man hath not heard, the ear of man hath not seen, man's hand is not able to taste, his tongue to conceive, nor his heart to report, what my dream was.'*
> William Shakespeare, Bottom, *A Midsummer Night's Dream,* Act IV, Scene i

What I discovered made no sense at all.

---

19 Eternalism is one of the 'Four Denials' in Buddhism: Monism, Dualism, Nihilism, and Eternalism. Eternalism includes the misconception that everything has meaning and that nothing happens by accident.

'Why, thou hast put him in such a dream – that when the image of it leaves him, he must run mad.'
William Shakespeare, Sir Toby Belch, *Twelfth Night*, Act II, Scene v

The phase of the Moon when I saw the two dark-haired ladies was the actual phase of the Moon on the night. It had been a full Moon. The crescent Moon and gibbous Moon I saw were not the reality of that night – and yet I'd thought the two dark-haired ladies had been a dream I remembered on waking. It was what I thought I'd seen when I was awake that had been a dream.

'I have heard my daughter say, she hath often dreamed of unhappiness and waked herself with laughing.'
William Shakespeare, Leontes, *Much Ado About Nothing*, Act II, Scene i

I looked around me at the familiar world of my parental home and laughed. It looked entirely as I might have expected it to appear.

18

into India

Rose and Valerie—*whatever the phase of Moon had been in Exeter*—were eclipsed by the glaring Sun of India. I'd send a card—naturally—but our continued close association was not prudent; given my fundamentally monogamous determination. What however, had happened to *monogamy* on the night in question? I was a hypocrite – or at least that night had made me a hypocrite.

There were two options in terms of abjuring hypocrisy. I either had to accept that I was not entirely monogamous – or, I had to know that such a night could never recur. I had decided immediately after the event that such a thing would never recur. Of that I was certain – but some years would have to pass before I could feel that I was capable of governing myself under all circumstances. Would the notion of 'youthful folly' lend leniency to self-judgement? Possibly. The ménage à trois hadn't been *my* idea. I'd simply acquiesced to it. Having acquiesced, however, I'd not been noticeably reserved. Acquiescence was not a valid justification. On the other hand, it had been too late to show reserve. It would have been gauche in the extreme to have had a panic attack and fled the bedchamber. Life was for learning – or so I'd heard.

What *did* I learn? I had no idea. Maybe I learned nothing. Most people don't 'live and learn'. There is nothing automatic about learning as part of living. Learning is possible, certainly – but one has to gain an understanding sufficiently cogent as to preclude further folly. I was still quite capable of further folly – visions and meditation notwithstanding.

Be that as it may – whatever I failed to learn, I had experienced a welter of dreams that challenged my sense or reality. More than dreams, there had been lucid dreams, and quasi-visionary experiences – and they remained far more vivid than the riotous romp and circumstance of nocturnal concupiscence.

I felt that the tent that I had seen, had been real. The two dark-haired young ladies in the tent were in some way connected with me. I remembered *knowing* that they were sisters. That might have been an impression in hindsight – based on Rose and Valerie acting the part of being sisters.

No. That was not how it was.

I really *knew* that they were sisters – but I had no idea how I could possibly know such a thing to be a fact. I knew the difference between factual knowledge and intuition – and was careful not to confuse the two. I therefore knew *the sisters* existed somewhere—or that they *had* existed somewhere—and that I was somehow related to them.

I decided after a great deal of self-critical evaluation that, although I should *not* have gone along with Rose and Valerie's picaresque proposal – It had served as the basis of unearthing a plethora of dreams and visionary experience.

Would those dreams have occurred in any case? They could have been ripe to occur. And what of the visions – or the 'hallucinations' as a psychiatrist might diagnose them? I struggled with the idea of 'visions' and 'hallucinations' and came to the conclusion that if they had been hallucinations, I would not be able to function as a relatively normal person. Psychiatric cases were probably not adequate building-site workers or reliable vocalists in Blues Bands. I may have been weird in many ways—in terms of conventional society—but I was more functional than many hippies I'd met. I decided in the end that these were questions for a Lama. They were not dilemmas I could unravel on my own.

Whatever the case was, I would avoid complying with the creation of secondary causes that conflicted with my fundamental ethics. The whole question of primary and secondary causes is a serious matter. I'd read about primary and secondary causes – but was shocked by the fact that I'd been ambushed by a primary cause of which I seemed to have no foreknowledge.

Everyone—apart from realised beings—is *programmed with primary causes* – and they inhabit a *minefield of secondary causes*. Some primary causes can be relatively harmless – but others can be lethal. What if somewhere—in my perceptual biochemical karmic makeup—there was a primary cause for murder? That was unlikely as I'd only acted violently once by punching Adrian Parrot on the nose at the age of nine. I had been sorry that I had felt there was no choice but to resort to physical violence. I had only done so to defend myself – and was sorry afterwards. So, I was probably safe there. When it came to accidental amorous assignations however – what was the primary cause there? What habit from what past life had caused me to act against my current convictions? Having thought about it for a while, it struck me as amusing. I was agonising about the possibility of being concupiscently waylaid by another two young ladies. That was extremely unlikely. Such an event wouldn't recur unless I sought it out—and even then, it was improbable—because although I wasn't ugly, I knew I wasn't any more than averagely desirable.

After my return from Exeter, temporal reality had telescoped. I'd spent the Summer working on a building site as a hoddie[1] and—one morning, after two-and-a-half-months hodding bricks—I had more than money enough for the long journey. Months had become weeks. Weeks became days – and I was on a train to London, headed for Heathrow Airport, to board an æroplane.

Suddenly—almost unexpectedly—I was in India. India was both *what I expected* – and something else entirely. India was the consequence of a long series of choices – but now the situation was choiceless. I'd heard about 'culture shock', naturally – but had no idea whether I was experiencing it. I was saddened by the poverty and disease – but delighted by the everyday-gentility of ordinary people. I met dishonesty and outstanding genuineness – avarice and unprecedented generosity. India teemed with unexpected prodigies: some diminutive, some immense.

---

1 A brick hod is a three-sided box with a long handle for carrying bricks on building sites. It is carried over the shoulder. Twelve bricks can be carried if a hoddie has the strength and sufficient stamina. Hoddies are part of a bricklaying team – with two bricklayers for each hoddie.

It seemed hard to imagine how a country functioned with the degree of chaos that characterised most aspects of life. This, I realised, was the main cause of culture shock: *the chaos* – and that *chaos* was *emptiness. Emptiness* is 'The Great Lesson that India Teaches'. Anyone willing to embrace uncertainty, insecurity, improbability, ambiguity, equivocality, dubiety, diffidence, and implausibility – can allow India to change their life-perspective. It didn't take long to come to this understanding. All I had to do was to observe people living their everyday lives, without the degree of certainty that I took as normal. I could see that it was entirely possible to entertain ever decreasing levels of security. The customary need for security was conditioned by society. It wasn't hard-wired – therefore one could acclimatise to insecurity just as one acclimated to heat. Improbability edged its way to becoming *a cause of delight* – rather than *a cause of anxiety*. Anxiety could dwindle— if one allowed it—into disquiet; uneasiness; vague apprehension; and—finally—into a relaxed inquisitiveness. That process could take months – but I managed to leave culture shock behind after a day or two by employing the good old-fashioned 'pull yourself together and stop being a wimp' method.

I booked my ticket at Old Delhi Railway Station and—having six hours to occupy—I went to visit the Red Fort.[2] The Red Fort was the residence of the emperors of the Mughal dynasty for 200 years, until 1857. It houses a number of highly interesting museums and an arcade with three extensive Tibetan antique shops. I entered each of them and boggled. Here were things I'd seen in museums in Britain – and in old photographs of Tibet.

---

2   The Red Fort was built in 1639 by the 5th Mughal Emperor Shah Jahan as the palace of his fortified capital Shahjahanabad. It is named for its massive walls of red sandstone and is adjacent to the older Salimgarh Fort, built by Islam Shah Suri in 1546. The palace was planned according to Mughal architecture; displaying a Timurid and Persian synthesis. The fort was plundered during Nadir Shah's invasion of the Mughal Empire in 1747. Most of the marble structures were destroyed by the British following the Sepoy Mutiny of 1857. The defensive walls remained and the fortress was used as a garrison – and the site where the British tried the last Mughal Emperor before exiling him to Rangoon in 1858.

I had limited finances and duly had items put aside for my return to Britain – leaving myself lighter of hard earned resources. Money was to be sent out to me in the form of British postal orders from the sale of my musical equipment: a MARSHALL bass amplifier, PA system, and sundry instruments. I would survive – but I wished I had more resources for the wonderful Vajrayana appurtenances I had seen. Some things, after which I had lusted, were non-essential – and so I told myself that 'avaricious obsession' was not a healthy state of mind for a Buddhist. I decided that I was extremely lucky to have found what I found – and was soon most content with what I had acquired for future practice.

The overnight train from Old Delhi Station took me to Pathankot. I'd been advised that 2nd Class Air Conditioned 2-tier was superior to 1st Class. The Air Conditioning was simply a fan – but it worked well enough.

Hot and humid. I'd expected that – but not the oppressive omnivorous omnipresent intensity it could reach. It cooled however, as the ramshackle bus to Upper Dharamsala ascended higher into the ameliorative coniferous-green of the Himalayan foothills. I'd not expected the brown sky of the plains – and to my relief the sky gradually became an understandable blue. Mote by mote, the dust of the lower altitudes disappeared – as the foothills of Himachal Pradesh drew closer.

On reaching Upper Dharamsala I took another bus of further decrepitude a thousand feet higher, to McLeod Ganj. That was my destination. I'd escaped the heat and dust. I was relieved to alight from the bus, in the mist—or cloud—whichever it was. To my great joy, I was met by Yeshi Khadro, the wife of Amji Pema Dorje.[3]

3   Yeshi Khadro was how she spelled her name. It would usually be written Yeshé Khandro (*ye shes mKha' 'gro*). Amji Pema Dorje (1950–2015) was born in in Lhodrag, Central Tibet. He fled to India with his parents when he was nine years old. He completed his medical studies in 1974 under Amji Barshi Phüntsog at the Men-tsé Khang, the Tibetan Astro-Medical Institute. He was selected to complete his internship under Amji Yeshé Dhonden and held many prestigious appointments. After completing his internship, he directed various branch clinics of the Men-tsé Khang in Bodha, Nepal,: New Delhi, McLeod Ganj, Itanagar, Calcutta, and Siliguri, West Bengal. He and Yeshi Khadro had two daughters, and a son.

I had corresponded with her as a pen-friend[4] – and she took me to Amala Norga's house where I was to reside; for an extremely low rent that included breakfast. Amala Norga was Yeshi Khadro's aunt and she was also the chang lady – one of the Tibetan barley-beer brewers of the village. She proved to be an entirely dear late-middle-aged lady with a wonderful laugh and a lovely voice. She sang mantra most of the time: Om Mani Pemé Hung – the awareness-spell of Chenrézigs.[5]

After a few days—acclimatising to life in McLeod Ganj—I started taking classes with Geshé Ngawang Dargye at Gangchen Kyishong.[6] I realised from the first class that my insatiable Tibetological reading was largely irrelevant. The books I'd researched and studied had built a picture in my mind which was quite dissimilar from what I found. My previous study proved to be little help. One afternoon walking back to McLeod Ganj, I chuckled. I'd arrived with some sense of being knowledgeable – but realised I was an ignoramus. Not that the books I'd read were not factual – but the ethos I felt them to have purveyed, had little to do with where I was in any practical sense. I wasn't disappointed – far from it. I was merely slightly discombobulated. I was ready to learn, however – and set to with zeal, to gain a whole new outlook.

---

4   *The Tibetan Friendship Group* in Bromley, Kent, organized Tibetan pen-friends. It was established by Ani Tsultrim and Ani Wangchuk—two Kagyüd nuns of Cockney extract—a mother and daughter who had been ordained as nuns by the 16th Gyalwa Karmapa.

5   sPyan ras gZigs (*Avalokiteshvara or Padmapani*) is a changchub sempa bodhisattva who embodies compassion. He is portrayed in different cultures as either male or female. In Chinese Buddhism, Avalokiteśvara has evolved into the female figure Guanyin, also known in Japan as Kanzeon or Kanno.

6   Geshé Ngawang Dhargyey (1921–1995) was born in Tré-hor, Kham, Eastern Tibet and studied at the Dhargye Gompa. When he was 18, he transferred to Séra Gompa in Lhasa. He fled Tibet in 1959 – and, in 1971, was appointed head teacher at the Library of Tibetan Works and Archives, Gangchen Kyishong. He remained in post until 1985. Gangchen Kyishong (*gangs can sKyid gShongs / Snow Mountain Happy Valley*)—the National Tibetan Library, Museum, and Archive—is a centre for education – and is associated with many scholars and Tibetologists. Educational programmes in language, philosophy, and culture occur there on a regular basis. The library is officially recognised by Himachal Pradesh University as a Centre for Tibetan Studies.

I would say I wasn't disappointed – but that's not entirely true. I'd expected a situation similar to the one I'd known at Art School. I'd expected a sense of camaraderie with fellow students. I thought I'd find them to be brothers and sisters in arms – but no. They were curiously aloof and somewhat unapproachable and I wondered how much ganja they'd ingested to be so emotionally attenuated.

They had a way of conversing – and I found myself on the outside of it. Unlike Art School, I was often found to have ideas and attitudes that were not acceptable – and subject to lethargic languorous ridicule. It felt a little like speaking with Lindie Dale's parents – where I was working class and they were middle-upper-middle class. The *Dharmites*—as I came to call them—were elitists of another sort completely. With the Dales it was not my ignorance of culture – but my long hair and love of Blues. That I also loved JS Bach cut no ice with them. With the Dharmites, my long hair was at first entirely acceptable. The fact that I loved Blues, Bach, and Shakespeare however, was regarded with suspicion. They seemed to hold the opinion that nothing of Western culture had any worth. That I was knowledgeable in terms of Tibetan culture and history cut no ice either – because *all that,* was merely academic.

The knowledge I lacked was *inside information* concerning Lamas. Where was the Dalai Lama travelling next? Had I taken certain empowerments or not? The other Dharmite characteristic was—to my mind—the infantile pretensions to 'egolessness'. They were all 'sick of samsara' – whereas, I had to admit, I was merely suspicious of it. I found life to be fun in general – the deaths of my closest friends notwithstanding. My commitment to Vajrayana was valid from my own point of view – but not from theirs. I was always willing to question myself – and even willing to look at myself as they looked at me. However, the conclusions I drew were, in the end, my own. I was no great practitioner – but neither was I the dilettante of their narrow imaginings.

For some reason most Western people called the village of McLeod Ganj, 'Dharamasala'. The town of Dharamsala however, lies some miles below the smaller town of Upper Dharamasala.

Upper Dharamasala, in turn, lies some miles below McLeod Ganj. McLeod Ganj—to my relief—is a thousand feet higher than Dharamasala – and therefore cooler. I could not discover why Western Buddhists misname McLeod Ganj – but suspect they don't relish the British Raj associations. McLeod Ganj—and the nearby Forsyth Bazaar—were British Raj Hill-stations.

Whilst not being a supporter of British imperialism, I *am* interested in history – and that interest put me in the way of a heart-warming conversation with an Indian Army major on the train to Pathankot from Delhi. He shared his goat curry with me – and a fine meal it was. I told him of my father having been in India in 1927 in the Khyber. He told me, proudly but with genuine delight, that the Indian Army maintained traditions that were forgotten in the British Army. I thoroughly enjoyed conversing with the major – but the reference to it was met with derision when recounted to Western Buddhists. Armies and soldiers were bad per se—as was the British Raj—and no interest was found in the delightful human connection that had been made possible by both. There was obviously something wrong with me … Was I too simplistic? Was I ethically vague? I shall not dwell on this aspect of my stay in the Himalayas – because there are other matters of far greater import to relate.

After the morning Buddhist classes at Gangchen Kyishong, I'd have lunch and then explore the area around McLeod Ganj. I had not taken into account that I would find myself in a mainly Gélug area, in terms of Vajrayana. That was no problem in itself—as I have never been sectarian—but what I was hoping to find were Nyingma ngakpas. Yeshi Khadro told me that there were two in the area – but could not be precise about where they were. I had a photograph in the back of my mind—Ajo Répa Rinpoche from Anagarika Govinda's book *Way of The White Clouds*—and I wanted to meet someone like him. I pronounced his name wrong at first – because the book had spelled the name awkwardly as Ajorepa Rinpoche – so that it read, to me, as 'Ajore-pa'.

I later discovered that Ajo Rinpoche was a *répa*—a master of gTummo—hence his name was Ajo Répa.[7] These names became easier once I started learning Tibetan from Sônam Wangdü, an older student at the Tibetan School of Medicine and Astrology. The Tibetan alphabet was a delight. I enjoyed learning to make the shapes – even though the spellings were baffling at first. That *sPrul sKu* was pronounced *trülku* seemed capricious, until I realised it was no worse than *psalm, pneumatic, mnemonic, diarrhoea, xenophobia, phlegm, pulchritude, callipygous, or bathykolpian.* At least Tibetan spelling was consistent. In English **ough** can make a variety of sounds: **cough, rough, though, through, thought,** or **bough** – and there is no way —if one is not British—to understand how these words are pronounced without remembering the individual pronunciation of each variant. I then learned how to pronounce *sNgags pa* – and went off in search of one of the two who lived in the area.

It didn't take long. I'd been watching a dance performance by the children at the Tibetan school in Forsyth Bazaar and on my way back to McLeod Ganj I saw a figure advancing from the distance on the narrow track. As we approached each other he began to look increasingly like Ajo Répa Rinpoche – but with none of the severity of the face in the photograph. As we came close enough for words to be plainly heard – he looked at me with a merry expression—and a certain mischievousness—and exclaimed *"Yes!"* That was his only word of English. The ngakpa in question was Ngakpa Yeshé Dorje[8] – and this meeting marked the beginning of my training as a member of the gö kar chang lo'i dé – *the class of those with white skirts and uncut hair.*[9]

---

7 Répa (*ras pa*) or réma (*ras ma*) are the male and female practitioners of gTummo (*gTum mo / chandali*) the spatial heat yoga.

8 sNgags pa yes shes rDor rJe. The first and subsequent meetings are recounted in *Wisdom Eccentrics,* Ngakpa Chögyam, Aro Books Inc., New York.

9 Gö kar chang lo'i dé (*gos dKar lCang lo'i sDe*). Gö means skirt; kar means white; chang lo pertains to willow branches that hang down – representing long hair.

I went to his home-cum-temple and met his sangyum—spiritual wife—Khandro Ten'dzin Drölkar,[10] who was as astonishing as he was. She was younger by some 20 years and utterly radiant. She was a disciple of a Lama called Kyabjé Künzang Dorje Rinpoche – and sometimes she would travel somewhere to see him for short periods of time.

There were several meetings at the home of Ngakpa Yeshé Dorje and Khandro Ten'dzin Drölkar before it became obvious that I had entered into a period of formal training. It unfolded quite naturally without arrangement or discussion. It was taken for granted that I would wish to practise Tröma Nakmo – the Black Wrathful Mother.[11] I should really have practised tantric ngöndro first – but Ngakpa Yeshé Dorje—through Sônam Wangdü my translator—told me that I could practise ngöndro in parallel with Tröma Nakmo.[12] Then, suddenly, from having all the time in the world – my day was entirely taken up. I had to give up the classes at Gangchen Kyishong and spend my morning performing prostrations in the Tsug-la Khang.[13] Sônam Wangdü helped me with transcribing the text into English and phonetic Tibetan. It was not a lengthy text so it did not take long. It was the shorter ngöndro from the Düd'jom gTérsar – a treasure or practice discovered by Kyabjé Düd'jom Rinpoche.

---

10 Khandro Ten'dzin Drölkar (*mKha' 'gro bsTan 'dzin sGrol dKar*) was also a disciple of Kyabjé Düd'jom Rinpoche and his son Dung-sé Thrin-lé Norbu Rinpoche. She is a Dzogchen yogini who had spent many years in retreat – but that was information that was only discovered much later. She rarely spoke in a didactic manner.

11 Tröma Nakmo (*khros ma nag mo*), the Black Wrathful Mother – the black Dorje Phagmo (*rDo rJe phag mo / Vajra Varahi*).

12 Tantric ngöndro (*sNgon 'gro*) consists of the preliminary practices for engagement with the inner tantras. These general outer preliminaries are: reflections on precious human rebirth, impermanence and death, karmic perception and response, and the self-defeating cycle of samsara. The tantric preliminaries are the fourfold hundred-thousand practices of: prostration accompanied by recitation of the refuge and Bodhicitta verses, kyil'khor (mandala) profferment, 100-syllable Dorje Sempa (*rDo rJe sems dPa' / Vajrasattva*) recitation, and Lama'i Naljor (*bLa ma'i rNal 'byor / guru yoga*) unification with the mind of the Lama. See *Torch of Certainty* by Jamgön Khongtrül Lodrö Thayé, Shambhala.

13 gTshug lag khang

Kyabjé Düd'jom Rinpoche was the incarnation of Düd'jom Lingpa,[14] and a great Nyingma Lama and gTértön whose visionary revelations amount to twenty huge volumes. He was the incarnation of Khyéchung Lotsa, one of the 25 disciples of Padmasambhava.

As soon as I heard the name *Kyabjé Düd'jom Rinpoche*, an uncanny exhilaration swept over me. Maybe it is because I write poetry, that word sounds can be unusually powerful in my ears. On analysis however, the sounds—in themselves—were not what I would usually consider evocative, resonant, resounding, or poignant. Something else carried the sense of awe – but I could not identify it. Maybe was the reverence in Ngakpa Yeshé Dorje's voice. Maybe there were other reasons connected with the time and place that I heard the name. I could not cognise any relevant signifier. However the deduction was delved—and from whatever direction—I deduced that *Kyabjé Düd'jom Rinpoche – Jig'drèl Yeshé Dorje* was the *Emperor of Vajrayana*. It was there in my mind when I segued into sleep. It arose when I awoke in the morning. It was a blazing beacon that drew me into an unknown future – a space in which anything could happen.

That the prostrations involved with the Düd'jom gTérsar Ngöndro were painful at first, is a meaningless statement – even from a person who is not violently keen on exercise. Suffice it to say that the pain subsided fairly quickly – and the number of prostrations I could perform increased. The fact that it was the Düd'jom gTérsar Ngöndro somehow made it worthwhile whatever pain was involved. Ngakpa Yeshé Dorje suggested that I perform all four aspects of the ngöndro each day, in order that I wouldn't become too exhausted by the prostrations. The advice worked out well. By the time I returned to Britain I had completed the Shorter Düd'jom gTér Ngöndro and the prostrations of the Longer Düd'jom gTér Ngöndro.

---

14 *bDud 'joms gLing pa* was also known as Chakong gTertön (*lCags sKong gTer sTon*) 1835–1904). Düd'jom Lingpa had five incarnations: Sonam Détsen (1910-1958); *body incarnation*; Dzong-gTér Künzang Nyima (1904-1958) *speech incarnation*; Dud'jom Rinpoche – Jig'drèl Yeshé Dorje (1904-1987) *mind incarnation*; Tulku Pednam, *qualities incarnation*; Tulku Natsok Rangdröl (1904-1958) *activity incarnation*.

I would practise in Farnham and complete the longer ngöndro before I went to whatever Art School accepted me for a degree course. Then, during my time at whichever Art School I attended I would complete the Tröma Ngöndro – as, thanks to Sônam Wangdü, I had the text translated and converted into phonetic in order that I could chant it.

The afternoons were mainly spent with Ngakpa Yeshé Dorje – either with Sônam Wangdü to translate; on my own just observing him making gTormas;[15] or, engaging in ritual preparations. I was shown how to make many things on this extended tantric crafts course. These skills have been valuable over the years in terms of being able to show my own students how to make practically anything they need: drum and bell cases; chö'phens; robes; and the entire assemblage of what members of the gö kar chang lo'i dé might require. Much of this craft-learning was conducted without Sonam Wangdü – because all that was required was that I observe Ngakpa Yeshé Dorje and copy whatever he did. When I made mistakes, he put me right because he observed me in the way I worked to emulate his skills.

This education differed entirely from my expectations – but I was delighted by it. I dove in at the deep-end – and found myself swimming in a situation, in which everything felt natural. This was nothing like anything I'd found in the books I'd read. It was nothing like my previous practice of silent sitting. When I asked about silent sitting, Ngakpa Yeshé Dorje said that I would need to receive teachings of that nature from Düd'jom Rinpoche – and that, in fact, I should go to see him in any case; as I would need to receive the empowerment of Tröma Nakmo. It was also put to me that Düd'jom Rinpoche would be my Tsawa'i Lama – as he was the Tsawa'i Lama of all Nyingmas.

That statement came as a jolt—a glorious shock—but a shock nonetheless. I was suddenly a member of the Nyingma Tradition. It was what I had wanted for years.

---

15 gTor ma (*balingta / votive sculptural symbol*) sculptures either edible or made of metal or wood. The Vajrayana embodiments of visualised awareness beings.

I had wondered whether it would ever be possible – but had classified that *wondering* as mere wishful thinking. It had been a fantasy: such things could not happen. Now, not only was it possible – but it had already happened, without being able to identify when it had happened. It had been taken for granted – as had everything else. Naturally I would wish to practise Tröma Nakmo. Naturally I would want to complete tantric ngöndro. Naturally I would wish to enter a three-month solitary retreat. Naturally? Well yes ... Ideally I would. Ideally, I wanted to be the person for whom that would be natural. It had been *who I thought I could be* – but ... *was* I that person? Was I that person, now that the opportunity was there for the asking? I found the idea of three months in isolation daunting – but, I was sure I'd take it on, as soon as I could manage it.

And so it was, that I was to set out for Nepal to meet Kyabjé Düd'jom Rinpoche, Jig'drèl Yeshé Dorje – the Supreme Head of the Nyingma Tradition. In Ngakpa Yeshé Dorje's view, he was none other than Padmasambhava – a Lama of such preëminent status that everyone looked to him as the source of inspiration. This was so fabulously exciting that I couldn't really conceive what was happening to my life. I'd taken a trajectory when I was eight years old and I'd followed it at a modest pace 'til now – even with all my reading. Now the circumstantial vector was escalating: intensifying at a rate that was hard to comprehend, emotionally.

I'd lost control of my life – but, I was happy to have lost control of it. It was like the moment of taking a plunge from a high diving board or the edge of a cliff. There's the moment in the air before you crash into the water. It was my choice to dive – so the outcome was obvious. It's just that I thought it would have taken a lot longer. Maybe it *had* taken a long time. From eight years old to 19 years old is 11 years. Is that a long time? The adolescent years are long in terms of experience – far longer than the years of one's 20s or 30s. Looking back, those 11 years seemed like decades – and now the world was accelerating. In the first month of being in India, the speed of the trajectory became exponential – and suddenly I arrived in Nepal.

It seemed sudden when I got there – but it took nine days by bus and train. It was far from pleasant. When I finally got to Bodhanath in Nepal however, I knew *that* was exactly where I needed to be. My first sight of the Great Chörten left an impression on me that has never dwindled.[16] I have seen far more ostensibly imposing architectural Buddhist features – but none have had the impact of the Great Chörten of Bodha.

16 The mChod rTen chen po (*Great Chörten* / *chörten*) the Jarung Khashor (*bya rung kha shor*) of Bodhanath enshrines remains of Kassapa Buddha. It is about seven miles from the centre of Kathmandu. It is one of the largest chörtens in Nepal, situated on the ancient trade route from Tibet. Tibetan merchants have rested and practised there for a millennium. Many refugees from Tibet in the 1950s settled in Bodhanath.

19

demon destroyer

october 1971 to november 1972

Bodhanath was quiet. More dulcet—by evident decibels—than
McLeod Ganj. It was conspicuously ancient – removed from the
conventional 20th Century flow of time. A bus arrived and departed
each day: morning and evening. Other than the two buses, there was
no traffic: no sound other than birdsong and a few dogs.

The Great Chörten of Bodhanath was surrounded by fields. The
road outside the Chörten precincts was a dirt track with three small
shops – hardly more than stalls. One sold eggs, butter, ghee, and
bread. One sold vegetables. The other sold simple kitchen hardware,
paper, pencils, and cheap Indian ballpoint pens that leaked. Opening
hours were limited to a few hours in the morning. They were not
open every day. Opening hours—and days—seemed sporadic; as
would befit an easy-going lifestyle, not primarily concerned with
profit and loss. Out amongst the fields were a few gompas – but the
Düd'jom Gompa was across the road from the main entrance to the
Chörten precinct.

Having arrived I found a place to stay quite easily and settled in. The
next morning, I set out to find where Kyabjé Düd'jom Rinpoche
might be living. First, I went to the Düd'jom Gompa. I felt that I
should sit there for a respectable period of time – before asking
whether it was possible to have an audience with Düd'jom
Rinpoche. I sat for two hours. I had been noticed as I sat – but in a
cheerful way. They could see that I was engaged in meditation so the
monks simply smiled in passing. Then I asked about Düd'jom
Rinpoche—when I'd concluded my meditation session—and
discovered that he didn't live at the gompa, or in any place attached
to the gompa. He lived in one of the houses that surrounded the
Great Chörten.

I'd meditated in the Düd'jom Gompa because I'd wanted to absorb as much as possible in terms of a sense of the *Demon Destroyer* I hoped to meet. I'd learned that Düd'jom meant 'demon destroyer'. Jig'drèl Yeshé Dorje – his personal name meant Fearless Thunderbolt of Primordial Wisdom. It was a powerful name – but Ngakpa Yeshé Dorje had told me that Düd'jom Rinpoche was the living evidence of the name.

I walked around the Great Chörten three times before I enquired after Düd'jom Rinpoche – and, somehow surprisingly, I was directed to his house. It was easy to find.[1]

'I have come from McLeod Ganj …I've been studying with Ngakpa Yeshé Dorje. I have been practising Düd'jom gTérsar Ngöndro with him and also Tröma Nakmo – and he's advised me to come to Nepal to see Kyabjé Düd'jom Rinpoche. Is it possible for me to meet Düd'jom Rinpoche?"

"Yes—welcome—you are coming inside."

And there was Kyabjé Düd'jom Rinpoche – smiling as he always smiled thereafter. It is not really possible to explain how I witnessed the presence of Düd'jom Rinpoche – how he appeared to a young Englishman. I'd been pre-empted. I was going to meet Padmasambhava. With that introduction, I could have been disappointed – but I was not. I was staggered. On first meeting, Düd'jom Rinpoche didn't seem supernatural – but he was *super-real*. He was the most *utterly* real human being I'd ever met. That however, was only my first impression – which was quickly shattered.

Düd'jom Rinpoche seemed to know who I was – and, to have expected me.

It was like waking up from a dream in which I'd imagined myself to have been a young English Bluesman and Art student – but on waking, I was someone I didn't know. My previous life suddenly melted.

1   Düd'jom Rinpoche's house was at 9 o'clock around the Chörten in the site now occupied by the Padma Hotel. As of 2011 almost all the original houses around the Chörten had been demolished to make way for hotels.

I was simply *extant* in the presence of Düd'jom Rinpoche – *being what I really was* in a waking life that was foreign to me. It was as if I'd dreamed my entire life history up 'til that point.

Suddenly Tara—the White Lady of my childhood dreams and visions—flashed on the surface of my mind. Her image lasted only a moment – but it had a strange effect on me. Once the visual aspect of her was gone, it was as if everything in my visual field had become imbued with her. She became everything I saw. That is not to say that anything looked any different from what it was – but that everything I saw seemed to be emanated from her. Whenever I had seen her in the past, I knew that she had always been there. She had been there even when I'd not been aware of her. She had been there even when I'd apparently forgotten her.

This sense of Tara did not distract me from Düd'jom Rinpoche because they were the same experience. As soon as I felt her presence however, Düd'jom Rinpoche looked at me intently and then smiled. *'Oh Yah!*[2] *Khandro Karmo in mind arriving!*[3] *She with you always staying. This is good. But first you study with me. You will come every day—when I am free—and we shall speak of her. We shall many things speaking. Today I say only Khandro Karmo is your mind knowing. She is your mind knowing – and I am your mind knowing. In this we are undivided. This is why you here coming and finding."* The translator unpacked the words *Khandro Karmo*. Khandro was *dakini* – which meant *enlightened lady* or *nondual lady*. Kar meant *white* – and *mo* was a female suffix. An unexpected Tibetan lesson and an explosion of information. Düd'jom Rinpoche had explained the major questions of my life in a few minutes.

I was shocked. It was one of many shocks. These instances of Düd'jom Rinpoche's unimpeded clairvoyance were glorious – yet disorientating.

---

2   Oh Yah (*'ong yag*) is a Tibetan expression which can mean various things according to tone: happiness, surprise, appreciation, suspicion, weariness, et cetera. It can only be understood in context.

3   mKha' 'gro dKar mo

He told me that there was no time on this particular occasion to talk with me about *Khandro Karmo* – but that he had wanted to establish the fact that this was something I needed to explore, and to discuss with him. *"There is something you must developing. She is very early for you. Many years passing since visions first appearing."* He looked a little grave at that point. *"There obstacles coming – but always obstacles arising possible. For Dzogchen practice, obstacles not negative. Obstacles, aspects of the path becoming. Much for you learning necessary. Much practising – then revelations fulfilled coming. Then one day you will your own sangha Khandro Karmo's teaching giving."*

I did not quite understand what Düd'jom Rinpoche meant or intended by what he had said – and this day was evidently not the time to ask further questions. He indicated that our first audience was concluded and I took my respectful departure.

So – I really *was* to study with Düd'jom Rinpoche. Obviously, I *wanted* to study with him – but I was astonished that it was taken for granted. I was accepted without even having to ask. Fortunately, the monk—whose name was Tséring Dorje—spoke English and even though his syntax was Tibetan – his English pronunciation was better than average. I had *all* the luck.

In the first full meeting after my first brief introductory audience, Düd'jom Rinpoche told me that I'd had many dreams—especially when I was young—of Khandro Karmo. He said these were important dreams – but that no one had been able to help me understand these dreams or develop them. *"Maybe for Roman Catholic parents, 'Virgin Mary' thinking – but mother: only dreams thinking. Father …"* he laughed *"myonpa thinking."*[4]

This was profoundly shocking. There was no way that Düd'jom Rinpoche could have known that my father questioned my sanity by any other means than a metaphysical microscope combined with a time-telescope.

---

4 Myonpa (*sMyon pa*) madman.

"Yah … this happens many times before in Tibet. Often with daughters – parents are not always happy when visions arising – but in West countries … often people not knowing visions meaning. Anyway, now in Bodha arriving – many visions coming. Then time coming – and you everything Khandro Karmo discovery telling. Then advice giving. Before then ngöndros practising."

Düd'jom Rinpoche was silent for a while then—gazing at me intently—said *"We must together meditation sitting. Maybe possible every day. Some days not possible – but not two days passing without together sitting."* Düd'jom Rinpoche told me that he would know more once we had spent more time together, but that I should take careful note of all my dreams and visions from that point on – and, tell him of anything that related to Khandro Karmo.

Düd'jom Rinpoche assured me that there had been no risk of my becoming a myonpa because of my dreams and visions of Khandro Karmo – but that because these phenomena were not understood, development had not been possible. I had suffered confusion and pain because obstructions had been caused. Düd'jom Rinpoche said that he was glad that there had been good friends with good parents in my life – because this had given me confidence. He said that my mother was good religious woman. My father had limited religious understanding – but was not fundamentally a bad man, even though he was ignorant of anything beyond the domain of material understanding.

He told me that he would help me with the development I needed – but that it would require some years before fruition would occur. First it was necessary that I practise more specifically to establish the ground from which my childhood visions could be of value. He told me that he had dwelt upon the nature of Khandro Karmo and that she also had the name *Garuda who Tastes the Primordial A*.[5] She was a gTértön. She had taken Ja'lü[6] earlier in the century. I had been her son in my previous life. My name had been Aro Yeshé.

---

5   gTértön Khyungchen Aro Lingma (*gTér sTon khyung chen a ro gLing ma*) 1886–1923.

6   Ja'lü (*'ja' lus*) rainbow body. The great accomplishment that comes at death as the realisation of the practice of Dzogchen togal (*Thod rGal*) – where the physical body dissolves into the essence of the elements as a display of light.

That was what he knew at the present time – but when he knew more, he would tell me. He said that gTértön Aro Lingma was known to him—and had been known by Düd'jom Lingpa—but no Lama to whom he had spoken had heard of her apart from Kyabjé Dilgo Khyentsé Rinpoche, who had said that he had heard the name many years before as a yogini who had realised Ja'lü in Southern Tibet. Dilgo Khyentsé Rinpoche had known no other details.

Düd'jom Rinpoche told me that I should go out around the chörten and make a few circumambulations. Whilst doing so I should acquire a damaru and a dorje and drilbu and bring them back to him. I found a small wooden damaru and a nine-prong dorje and drilbu set. I don't know what attracted me to the nine-prong set – but Düd'jom Rinpoche was delighted by the choice and explained that this variety was good for a ngakpa to use. He said that the damaru was nothing special – but that it was sturdy and well made. He advised me to make my own chö'phen—as decent chö'phens were hard to find—but before that I could get one made by one of the Tibetan tailors who made the brocade thangka frames. He then showed me how to use the dorje, drilbu, and damaru in the practice of Dorje Tsigdun – the Seven Line Song of Padmasambhava.

It was not coincidental, that—thus equipped—I began to have dreams again. Dreams I remembered from my childhood reappeared as if they had remained somewhere unchanged whilst I was otherwise occupied.

One day Düd'jom Rinpoche asked me to recount what I remembered of my childhood dreams and visions. I told him about the return of a childhood dream. It was the dream of the White Lady. Rinpoche asked me whether I had told anyone about the dream and I told him that beyond my parents, I had never told anyone apart from Steve Bruce – but he had died. He told me it was good that no one living knew about it – and that I should never discuss my dreams with anyone but himself and Dilgo Khyentsé Rinpoche. He told me that I would have further dreams—and that I should keep a careful record of all their details—but that in the meantime I should complete the ngöndros.

The completion of the ngöndros would establish the basis for what the dreams would reveal in the future. This was mysterious and I wanted to ask what it portended – but Rinpoche told me that it was better not to discuss anything in detail until later. It would create obstacles, he told me, if too much was said of my dreams. Düd'jom Rinpoche seemed to know exactly what would unfold – but he would only provide a synopsis on this occasion. What he felt useful to tell me was that I was to inherit Aro Lingma's gTérma—her cycle of teachings—and that these would manifest at a future time when I had created the auspicious circumstances for their revelation. I was content to leave my many subsequent questions unasked.

My second task was to have robes made. I was to find a tailor and the tailor would tell me how much fabric to buy. I would have to go to Thamel to buy the fabric as there was nowhere in Bodha at that time where fabric could be purchased. I was to have a white robe-skirt and a red waistcoat.

Robes … A month before I had been looking for a ngakpa whom I would recognise by his gö kar chang lo robes – and now I was shopping for fabric from which my own robes could be made. This was entirely unexpected. This was a possibility that I had not imagined. I was already long-haired – but now I was never again to cut my hair. I bought the fabric—the robes were made—and I was soon to be wearing them consequent to receiving empowerment from Düd'jom Rinpoche that would authenticate my appearance as a member of the gö kar chang lo'i dé. Düd'jom Rinpoche was to give me the 14 Root vows and all the ancillary vows – as well as the full empowerment of Tröma Nakmo.

The Fourteen Root Vows of Vajrayana are:

1. *Never denigrating the Lama.*

2. *Never denigrating the Lama's teaching.*

3. *Never harbouring animosity toward tantrikas.*

4. *Never deviating from acting for the benefit of all beings.*

5. *Never distorting the spatial essences through sexual aberrance.*

6. *Never denigrating the teachings and paths of other spiritual systems.*

7. *Never revealing tantric teachings to those who are not ready to receive them.*

8. *Never viewing the five elements of the psycho-physical body as 'impure' or 'defiled'.*

9. *Never developing doubt about the inner tantras in oneself or others.*

10. *Never failing to act in potentially disastrous situations.*

11. *Never holding the four philosophical extremes: monism; dualism; nihilism; and eternalism.*

12. *Never refusing to teach those who seek instruction.*

13. *Never refusing to partake of the symbolic meat and alcohol offerings.*

14. *Never mentally or verbally denigrating the other gender.*

The first three vows were accompanied by the wearing of the white shamthab, the gö kar chang lo shawl, and yogic waistcoat. The fourth vow required bell and vajra rings. Then there were other requirements such as saving combed-out hair as symbols of dPa'wos for women and khandros for men.[7]

The next time I saw Düd'jom Rinpoche he told me that I would need to study Vajrayana – but that there were too few books in English and sometimes they contained errors. There seemed to be many books on Sutra – but little on Tantra and nothing on Dzogchen. Someone had quoted from these books on Tantra – and he'd had to tell them they were in error.

Düd'jom Rinpoche knew that my time in the East was limited and that my time in Nepal was shorter still. He had contemplated my situation and he saw that much of my learning would need to come from my own visionary experience. He told me that, with practice, I would come to know what I needed to know over a period of time – and that, when my practice and knowledge had ripened, visions would arise that were 'complete in themselves'. Before then however, I would gain memories of previous incarnations.

7   dPa'wo *(dPa' bo / daka)*. Khandro *(mKha' 'gro / dakini)*

I would need to return to Nepal to see him as soon as my Art degree course was completed. He would then give me more detailed instructions – as I would be able to stay for a longer period.

I asked whether I should simply abandon my Art education – but he shook his head. He said that this was good because it showed my seriousness – but that qualifications were needed in the West if one were to earn a living. One could be an itinerant yogi in the East – but not in the West. I explained that I was used to manual labour – but at this he laughed, explaining that this was fine for a young man – but that I too would grow older *"Then many bricks carrying every day not possible."* Düd'jom Rinpoche had asked me about the labouring work in which I'd engaged to take me out to the Himalayas and had seemed unusually interested in what I told him about hodding. He had made a joke about my being like Milarépa – but concluded that it would not be necessary for me to work as hard as that. He considered that the experience of hodding would prove highly beneficial in terms of performing the hundred thousand prostrations and that I would develop even more strength than I already had. It seemed delightfully whimsical that Düd'jom Rinpoche should have such a marked appreciation of physical strength – and more so when he asked Tséring Dorje to investigate the biceps in my right arm. Tséring Dorje seemed impressed and Düd'jom Rinpoche told me that it was good that I was strong – because I would need to be strong in body, speech, and mind. *"When obstacles arising: much strength needing – much, much strength needing. Düd'jom Lingpa—many, many obstacles—overcoming necessary. Great strength is needed when mikha dominating."*[8] Silence for a moment, then he continued *"Yah … mikha will be dominating. Much mikha. For almost two cycles of years mikha will make obstacles – but, then"* he beamed *"mikha finished. Then all joys coming."*

Twenty-four years of slander, disparagement, vilification, and calumny? Or maybe just malicious gossip? I thought of asking why – but felt somehow that this was not a question I could ask.

---

8   mi kha *(literally 'bad mouth')*: slander, defamation of character, contrived calumny, fabricated scandal, malicious gossip, criticism from the ignorant.

If Düd'jom Rinpoche thought I should know – he would tell me. He knew everything there was to know – and so asking would seem discourteous. It would also make me seem nervous – self-protective. It felt stronger simply to accept that I'd be bad-mouthed for a while. What did it matter what the subject matter might be? To ask could only come from some notion that it was possible to avoid mikha – so I simply assumed that it could not be avoided.

The next time I saw Kyabjé Düd'jom Rinpoche I asked him about Düd'jom Lingpa. Kyabjé Düd'jom Rinpoche Jig'drèl Yeshé Dorje's incarnation line is a wonder and inspiration to all who receive teachings from him. He told me about his life – with additional material supplied by the translator.[9]

I had plunged into another world – yet felt at home there. I felt natural in Bodhanath – but did not understand why. It was almost dreamlike. Such events occur in dreams. One could find oneself in places one had never visited – and act as if one lived there. One could be conversing with esquimaux husky-sled riders in an Arctic blizzard. One could find oneself in movies or scenes in novels without questioning the situation. In dreams everything was accepted as it was – unless they were lucid dreams. Bodhanath felt somewhat like a lucid dream. There was no resistance. Visions were spoken of as events that were real. Düd'jom Rinpoche was familiar with the nature of 'hallucination' and assured me that my visions had not been hallucinations. He told me that some of my dreams were good but not entirely reliable. Other dreams had been dreams of clarity – and he clarified the difference according to his own insight.

I went to bed entirely delighted at the end of each day in which I had spent time with Düd'jom Rinpoche.

9   See Appendix I.

20

the beginning of mind

Nondual emptiness is undivided from nondual form. Therefore, everyone and everything everywhere has the intrinsic nature of nondual awareness – the spontaneously arisen universe of pure qualities.
Kyabjé Düd'jom Rinpoche Jig'drèl Yeshé Dorje

A week passed in which I received teachings – but mainly I sat with Kyabjé Düd'jom Rinpoche whilst he gave audiences and conferred with various Lamas. I asked if I was superfluous to requirement but Düd'jom Rinpoche said that he had decided that he wanted me to be there every day. That was perfect for me – and if he'd told me that was how I was going to spend the rest of my life, I would have been entirely content.

At the end of the week my ngakpa robes were ready to collect. There were no gö kar chang lo shawls available so I was advised to have a white section sewn into a standard monastic maroon shawl.

When I'd collected my robes from the Tibetan tailor, Düd'jom Rinpoche performed the empowerment. Tséring had shown me how to wear the shamthab – the white skirt of the gö kar chang lo'i dé. It's basically a large tube-like garment—sewn in six sections— with a double band about a hand's breadth at the top and bottom.[1] The skirt is pleated front and back – and I was advised to use a wall to hold the back pleats in place whilst I was folding the front pleats.[2] Once the pleats were set in place, the assemblage was bound together at the waist by a sash.

---

1   Shamthab (*sham thabs*). The shamtab worn by the gö kar chang lo'i dé is exactly the same as the monastic shamtab apart from being white rather than the monastic maroon. The six panels of the shamthab represent the six classes of Vajrayana. The doubled band at the bottom represents the indivisibility of emptiness and form and the doubled upper band is the indivisibility of samsara and nirvana.

2   The front pleats of the shamthab are the union of wisdom and method. The rear pleats of the shamthab are the union of relative and absolute.

I took the gö kar chang lo vows with Düd'jom Rinpoche and began wearing the robes. It was at that point that I started to feel like *Chöying Gyamtso*. That was the name the Ngakpa Yeshé Dorje had given me. Düd'jom Rinpoche then gave me the empowerment of Tröma Nakmo—and gave me the name Ögyen Togden—and I was instructed to obtain a gCod damaru and kangling.[3] Chöying Gyamtso Ögyen Togden seemed quite a long name – and I tentatively enquired of Düd'jom Rinpoche whether I could contract Chöying Gyamtso to Chögyam. He replied *"Like Trungpa Rinpoche coming?"* and then chuckled *"Oh-yah then two Chögyams—Kagyüd Chögyam and Nyingma Chögyam—I think good. Yes. Chögyam – this name is like you."*[4]

The next day Düd'jom Rinpoche was joined by another Lama, whose name was Lama Künzang Wangdü – also known as Nyinkula Lama[5] He was a ngakpa who wore a red shawl with a white stripe down the middle.

---

3   A *gCod* (pronounced 'chöd') damaru (*gCod rNga*) is a double-sided drum of around 12 inches in diameter with two strikers on thick threads. The drum is played by turning it in the hand. A kangling (*rKang gLing*) is a thigh bone trumpet made from a human femur.

4   I did not realise till years later that in the case of Chögyam Trungpa Rinpoche his name was not a contractions of Chöying Gyamtso – but Chökyi Gyamtso. I also did not realise that it is an unusual contraction as Gyamtso is spelled rGya mTsho and the 'm' at the end of Chögyam should not really be there. It should be Chögya, as the 'm' belongs to the syllable mTsho

5   Kyabjé Nyingkhula Rinpoche (Lama Künzang Wangdü, 1942–2018) was born in Pangthang village in Bartsham, Tashigang. Nyingkhula (*sNying khu la* – heart essence) was his parent's endearment name for him – but he retained it throughout his life. His grandfather, Nyöndo la, taught him when he was a child and he grew up in the old Chador Lhakhang in Bartsham – becoming one of the most learned and meditatively profound Lamas of his time. He was ordained into the gos dKar lCang lo'i sDe tradition and received teachings from Kyabjé Düd'jom Rinpoche Jig'drèl Yeshé Dorje, Dung-sé Thrin-lé Norbu Rinpoche, Dilgo Khyentsé Rinpoche, Lama Sonam Zangpo Rinpoche, Lama Pema Wangchen, and Lama Norbu Wangchuk. He received many unique gTérma legacies from Düd'jom Rinpoche, through working closely with him for more than a decade: 1971 to 1986 in Bodhanath Nepal. As the chief scribe and editor during that period he received many empowerments, transmissions and instructions. He worked on various projects of writing, editing, and anthologies under the tutelage and guidance of Kyabjé Düd'jom Rinpoche. These monumental writing projects included collected works of Düd'jom Lingpa in 27 volumes, and the collected works or Kabum of Kyabjé Düd'jom Rinpoche in 25 volumes.

It was similar to mine – and he indicated, with a broad smile, that it was good that we wore the same shawl. He took great pleasure in this simple fact – which made me feel more at ease than I would otherwise have been.

Düd'jom Rinpoche was unexpectedly interested in my early life and in my early interest in Buddhism. He was curious concerning my autodidactic exploration of Buddhism – and found explanations of my silent sitting experience worthy of probing. I explained how I'd begun meditation with the help of the book by Rear Admiral EH Shattock. Then I'd been lucky enough to obtain Shunryu Suzuki's *Zen Mind Beginners Mind* which had provided a far more expanded view of the practice of silent sitting.[6] I'd written down a list of quotations from Shunryu Suzuki – and so I was able to read them out to Düd'jom Rinpoche. He found them interesting and gave commentary on them which constituted the commencement of my education. I soon learnt to rephrase the quotations in order that the translator would find them intelligible.[7]

> Shunryu Suzuki: *Treat every moment as your last. The moment is not preparation for something else.*

Düd'jom Rinpoche, nodding momentarily, smiled *"I think you already have knowledge of silent sitting – and this is why you are liking and notes writing. When you were very young you were already meditation I think?"*

"I did do something like meditation when I was young Rinpoche – but I cannot say it actually was meditation. I would just sit quietly and stare into what was in front of me. I used to do that in the woods behind my home."

Düd'jom Rinpoche confided *"Yah – this meditation."*

---

6 *Zen Mind, Beginner's Mind* by Shunryu Suzuki (*published in* 1970) became a spiritual classic, which serves to steer meditators away from the trap of intellectualism. This book was strongly advocated by Chögyam Trungpa Rinpoche.

7 The following discussion with Kyabjé Düd'jom Rinpoche was committed to a notebook at the time – and Düd'jom Rinpoche's responses are word-for-word what was translated by Gélong Tséring (*dge slong tshe ring*). A Gélong is a monk who has taken full ordination.

Then, with a slow downward chopping movement of his left hand *"Shi-nè: basis approaching to Dzogchen sem-dé. What describing in shi-nè—in young experience—has value for your life. Read more from Japanese Lama."*

Shunryu Suzuki: *If your mind is empty, it is always ready for anything, it is open to everything. In the beginner's mind there are many possibilities, but in the expert's mind there are few.*

Düd'jom Rinpoche nodded. *"Emptiness-mind is where beginning. This beginner's mind is like 'beginning mind' – from beginning always pure. This is maybe meaning. Expert with pride can tied down becoming – too much information-knowledge having. Dzogchen not academic. Meditation not academic. Academic knowledge value having – but value is limited. When directly from experience speaking – then everyone understanding. When from academic knowledge speaking – then only academics understanding."*

Ngak'chang Künzang Wangdü laughed heartily at this point – in fact he laughed so loudly and lengthily that Düd'jom Rinpoche also began to laugh and I was unable to prevent myself laughing. Somehow this seemed the funniest thing I had ever heard – but what was funny was that it was glaringly obviously true. After the laughter had calmed – Düd'jom Rinpoche indicated that I should read another quotation.

Shunryu Suzuki: *Wherever you are, you are one with the clouds and one with the sun and the stars you see. You are one with everything. That is truer than I can say, and truer than you can hear.*

Düd'jom Rinpoche nodded *"Maybe ..."* then furrowing his forehead *"... Japanese Lama meaning 'not separate' – then meaning is good coming. Otherwise this mu-teg tag ta-wa thinking."*[8]

I had to ask what this meant – as I was unfamiliar with this term, mu-teg tag ta-wa. *'I know that ta-wa means 'view' as in view, meditation, and action – but I don't know the meaning of mu-teg tag?'*

---

8   Mu-teg tag ta-wa (*mu sTegs rTag lTa ba*): Tirthika view which is predominantly monist/eternalist – comprising of the idea that we are 'all one' in that we are all aspects of God. From this view we cease to be individual when we are 'God-realised'. This can sometimes be seen in the way certain spiritual teachers say 'I am God' – meaning that they are *indistinguishable from God* or *part of God.*

Tséring the translator suggested *'Tirthika'* but I did not understand that either – so he said *"Something like Hindu – but maybe more 'non-Buddhist' because many ideas and many different religions of India. Same as 'heretic' translating – but mainly eternalism and monism believing. This is where 'all is one' – 'we all part of God' saying. This mu-teg tag ta-wa."*

I nodded in token of understanding.

Düd'jom Rinpoche continued to comment on the quote. *"These eyes that see – not separate from what is seen. No separation between seer and seen – yet multiplicity remaining. Buddhist nonduality – not monist. Everything empty – yet multiplicity manifesting. My emptiness; Künzang Wangdü's emptiness; Tséring's emptiness; Chögyam's emptiness – no difference. Same emptiness – but different forms showing. Emptiness is emptiness. If more than one emptiness; this not emptiness. Form arising from emptiness and every form different coming. Emptiness and form not divided – but this not 'everything same' making."* Pause. *"Now more reading."*

> Shunryu Suzuki: *Nothing we see or hear is perfect – but right there, in the imperfection, is perfect reality.*

Künzang Wangdü laughed.

Düd'jom Rinpoche grinned broadly *"Oh yah! Samsara and nirvana – not separate. This is Dzogchen."*

> Shunryu Suzuki: *I discovered that it is necessary, absolutely necessary, to believe in nothing. That is, we have to believe in something which has no form and no colour: something which exists before all forms and colours appear.*

Düd'jom Rinpoche simply nodded. *"Yah – this you are knowing."* He had no other comment to make – but motioned to me to read another quotation.

> Shunryu Suzuki: *Even though you try to put people under control, it is impossible. You cannot do it. The best way to control people is to encourage them to be mischievous. Then they will be in control in a wider sense. To give your sheep or cow a large spacious meadow is the way to control him. So it is with people: first let them do what they want, and watch them. This is the best policy. To ignore them is not good. That is the worst policy.*

The second worst is trying to control them. The best one is to watch them, just to watch them, without trying to control them.

"*Oh yah!*" Düd'jom Rinpoche laughed "*With people—I do not know—sometimes controlling necessary – when bad people harm causing; but with arising thoughts – this is perfect teaching.*"

Shunryu Suzuki: *What we call 'I' is just a swinging door which moves when we inhale and when we exhale.*"

"*Oh yah … this shi-nè*" Düd'jom Rinpoche announced with glee. "*And like this—I see—you practising when very young – when trees climbing and sitting.*"

"*Yes, Rinpoche. Something like that – but I don't think it was shi-nè when I sat in the woods at the age of five.*"

Düd'jom Rinpoche looked quizzically amused and asked "*Why this saying?*"

"*Well Rinpoche … I had no idea what I was doing. It wasn't any kind of discipline – I think I just liked looking at … the colour of nature.*"

Düd'jom Rinpoche laughed and exclaimed "*Yet this Japanese Lama same saying!*" He slapped both thighs with the palms of his hands "*Beginning mind – many possibilities! But expert's mind possibilities more difficult!*" Pause. "*Anyway, how long formal shi-nè practising?*"

"*Since I was 14 years old, Rinpoche.*"

Then Rinpoche looked at me intently for maybe a minute – but it seemed a long time. He nodded with what seemed akin to expressionlessness – and finally smiled "*But very long every day practising.*"

"*At first only half an hour – but later for an hour. Then I started practising more than once a day – and finally over the last few years I have tried to practise whenever there was time: on buses and when I had to wait somewhere.*"

"*And then?*" Rinpoche grinned "*Thoughts always coming – or emptiness coming?*"

"*Always thoughts at first, Rinpoche – but then slowly after some time the thoughts died down and sometimes, they ceased completely.*"

"But not sleeping?" Rinpoche laughed – but shaking his head seemingly to negate the possibility.

"No, Rinpoche – not sleeping. Sometimes sleepy – but when I get sleepy, I do something else. I don't like to sit when I'm drowsy. I like to be alert and awake."

"Then now shi-nè sitting" Düd'jom Rinpoche concluded and we all sat in silence. I do not know how long we sat – but it did not seem longer than ten minutes. At the end of that period of time Düd'jom Rinpoche chanted a short passage of Tibetan in which he was joined by Ngak'chang Künzang Wangdü and Tséring. I had not known the chant and so I sat in silence.

"Shi-nè and lhatong later teaching." Düd'jom Rinpoche smiled, then pointed to my notebook again, indicating that I should read another passage.

> Shunryu Suzuki: *Life is like stepping onto a boat which is about to sail out to sea and sink.*

"Oh yah!" Düd'jom Rinpoche laughed again *"… but to India flying!"*

Somehow this seemed extremely funny and I laughed. Ngak'chang Künzang Wangdü and the translator laughed as well. Then Düd'jom Rinpoche continued *"Anyway – birth happens then death follows. This always knowing. We must all be knowing. It is good that you write this – are you often reading?"*

"Yes, Rinpoche – I wrote these quotations down so that I could remind myself of what I should be doing. There are no Vajrayana teachers in Britain – and so I have had to do whatever I could to gain experience."

Düd'jom Rinpoche looked sad for a moment and commented to the effect that I had not met with friends. I didn't understand at first – but then it became clear that he was referring to the Western Buddhists in McLeod Ganj and Bodha.

313

To clarify that I was understanding correctly, I gave some short account of my communication difficulties with Western Buddhists in the East – to which he nodded and said *"These not needing. These always coming and going – first serious then forgetting. Like this not needing."* Pause. *"But also friends losing – and music playing, this also losing."*

I replied that I had indeed lost my two best friends who were excellent musicians – and he asked *"So now, no music playing possible?"*

"Not much, Rinpoche. I do play alone—but it is not the same—and anyway I'm not that good a musician."

"Yah …" Rinpoche sighed *"Always you must music playing. You must know … 'good' and 'not good' – only subjectivity. There is no meaning to these ideas for a yogi. You simple keeping. Chögyam doing what Chögyam doing. Other people—'this and that' saying—only nonsense coming. Too many people ideas having and judgements making. You judgements not needing from others. You only—my—judgement listening. Then no problems coming."* Pause. *"Now more reading possible?"*

"Yes, Rinpoche."

Shunryu Suzuki: *When something dies is the greatest teaching.*

I also added *'when someone dies'* as that was a statement, personal to me.

"Yah … then we know reality." Düd'jom Rinpoche sighed – but evidently not for himself. *"You have death knowing since young. This has great meaning – very great meaning. This not merely intellectual understanding. It is important. Death very sad. Death also very normal. Everyone born must be also be dying. Everyone dying must be rebirth taking. We all dying. We all rebirth taking, countless times. What is important is awareness keeping. Awareness keeping through bardos. Awareness into next life taking."*

I had indeed known death from an early age. I never attended a wedding as a child – but I had attended a series of funerals. My father was 50 years old when I was born and was the youngest of his family. I saw my grandparents die when I was quite young. They were followed by uncles and aunts.

I felt somehow comforted by the fact that Düd'jom Rinpoche seemed to know my entire life simply by looking at me. I wondered how much detail he knew – but felt it would be impolite to ask. Did he know about Alice, Anelie, and Lindie? Did he know about my naked journey to the crossroads to meet Papa Legba? I construed that he probably did – and wondered what on earth he'd make of all that. Then I caught Rinpoche's nod – motioning me to read another quotation.

Shunryu Suzuki: *In the meditation posture, mind and body have great power to accept things as they are, whether agreeable or disagreeable.*

Düd'jom Rinpoche nodded and his expression expressed that this was self-evident.

Shunryu Suzuki: *If you understand real practice, all other activities are meditation. If you don't understand how to practice in the real sense, then even though you practice very hard, what you acquire is just technique.*

"Yah" Düd'jom Rinpoche stated most deliberately tapping the table with his forefinger three times. *"This important. Especially in Dzogchen important. You must be every day coming—when I have time—and you must tell about practice so that I will know how continuing and what method using."*

Shunryu Suzuki: *While you are continuing this practice, week after week, year after year, your experience will become deeper and deeper, and your experience will cover everything you do in your everyday life. The most important thing is to forget all gaining ideas, all dualistic ideas. In other words, just practice. Do not think about anything. Just remain on your cushion without expecting anything. Then eventually you will resume your own nature. That is to say, your own nature resumes itself.*

Düd'jom Rinpoche glanced out of the window for a few moments and commented *"Deeper, wider... Yah ... these words have no great meaning. Meditation everyday life becoming. That is Dzogchen. Then nature is there of-itself. This is rangdröl: self-liberation. Tomorrow returning. Then Dzogchen speaking. gCèrdröl, shardröl, and rangdröl speaking."*[9]

9   gCèrdröl, shardröl, and rangdröl (*gCer grol, shar grol, and rang grol*) gCèrdröl: liberated as soon as it appears; shardröl: liberated as it arises; and Rangdröl spontaneously self-liberated, of itself.

After a pause Düd'jom Rinpoche asked *"More coming?"*

I replied that there was a little more and Rinpoche enquired as to how much. I said that there were only four more excerpts – and he asked me to read them and commented on each one in order that I could make annotations from him that would serve me in developing the view.

> Shunryu Suzuki: *When you accept everything, everything is beyond dimensions. The earth is not great nor a grain of sand small. Picking up a grain of sand is the same as taking up the whole universe. To save one sentient being is to save all sentient beings.*

"View, meditation, and action …" Rinpoche began *"… central to Dzogchen. When nondual awareness – each action complete and perfect coming. Everything accepted because everything perfect in its own arising."*

> Shunryu Suzuki: *Meditation is not some fancy, special art of living. The teaching is just to live, always in reality, in its exact sense. To make effort, moment after moment, is the way.*

"Making effort …" Rinpoche mused momentarily *"… this is important at the beginning – but when meditation integrated with life, then effort not necessary. Without reference points – no dissatisfaction coming. Free from referentiality – anxiety is unnecessary, and relaxing possible. Appearances infinitely pure—so discrimination unnecessary—serenity having. When self-existent wisdom is total, effort unnecessary – and cheerfully resting."*

> Shunryu Suzuki: *Even though you read much Dharma, you must read each sentence with a fresh mind. You should not say 'I know what Dharma is' … this is also the real secret of the Arts: always be a beginner.*

"Yah …" Rinpoche smiled *"… you must Vajrayana like artist studying – because you are an artist. Always senses and sense-fields remembering. This is where awareness finding. There—resting—nowhere further going necessary. Nothing seeking necessary."*

> Shunryu Suzuki: *When you are sitting in the middle of your own problem – which is more real to you: your problem or you yourself? Awareness here, right now, is the ultimate fact.*

Rinpoche laughed *"Maybe mosquito net buying."*

Somehow that was one of the funniest things anyone had ever said to me – and also entirely practical. I had been suffering from the mosquitoes in Bodha – but had no idea that mosquito nets were available there. The statement was also directly related to the quote from Shunryu Suzuki – but in a way that was both entirely down-to-earth and indescribably mysterious. It probably reflects a great deal about my state of mind when I was with Düd'jom Rinpoche – because, at face value, there is nothing remarkable about what he said. It was just the way he tied in a piece of pertinent practical advice with the quote from Shunryu Suzuki and concluded our discussion on a hilarious note at the same time.

After a few days had passed, Düd'jom Rinpoche spoke of rigpa and asked me to transcribe everything in my own words in order that it could be translated back to him – in order to check my understandings.

This is my teaching to you on Dzogchen and the nature of vision.

The vision of Dzogchen sees reality as it actually is. Reality inseparable from the nature of Mind: the natural state, where there are no distinctions, demarcations, or discriminations. This awareness is rigpa: naked presence of awareness in each point-instant.

We cannot express this awareness in words – and there is nothing with which to compare it, in terms of description. It is not the mundane condition of emotional turmoil and conflicted thoughts – but neither is it the emptiness that is the cessation known as nirvana.

Rigpa cannot be assembled, constructed, or developed. It cannot be interrupted, discontinued, or extinguished. One is never separate from rigpa – nor does dualistic derangement disturb the nondual state.

In terms of rigpa, it is impossible to say that we are existent in the moment – but neither can we say that we are non-existent.

Rigpa is neither infinite nor temporary. It cannot be established though specifics such as experiences or activities. It is the original face of nonduality which is beginninglessly pure, all-pervasive, and all-pervaded.

The unobstructed luminosity of nonduality – and the entire spectrum of experience—whether deranged or liberated—is as the sun and its rays.

Nondual emptiness is undivided from nondual form. Therefore, everyone and everything everywhere has the intrinsic nature of nondual awareness – the spontaneously arisen universe of pure qualities.

Recognition of the presence of rigpa, as the primordial natural ground of being, gives innate cognisance of the three spheres of being as the intrinsic awareness of the union of luminosity and emptiness. This is the vision of Dzogchen.

I always found Düd'jom Rinpoche to be poetic – a work of art in himself. There was grace in every movement and gesture – a sonorous lilt to his voice. He had light-heartedness in which great seriousness resided – a solemnity that oscillated with mirth. His surroundings were always simple, yet perfect – and he was obviously, always, the master of circumstances. I went to see him almost every day – and he explained many aspects of the Nyingma Tradition. I had no idea how unusual this was at the time – but I did know I was extremely fortunate. He possessed a sense of utter conviction as to where I needed to go – and he was never wrong.

21

born in a dragon year

november 1971

When I next met Kyabjé Düd'jom Rinpoche, I asked him if he would be so kind as to tell me something about his life. I expected a relatively brief picture – but he was most generous with his time and attention to detail. *"O yah … in future times …"* he commenced *"… there are many things you must know."*

Tséring gave the introduction telling me that in the remote past, in a previous world-age – Kyabjé Düd'jom Rinpoche had been the Awareness Holder Nuden Dorje; and in the future, it was predicted that he would take incarnation as the Buddha Möpa Tha-yé. In the present he manifested as the representative of Padmasambhava.[1]

His previous incarnation, Dud'jom Lingpa, told disciples as he approached death *"Whoever relies on me, go to Pemakö – but before you youngsters arrive, I will already be there."* This occurred exactly as predicted. Düd'jom Rinpoche was already three years old when he was discovered as a direct emanation of Düd'jom Lingpa – and could thus remember his previous lives clearly.

"This" Tséring added *"is why Düd'jom Rinpoche, all Chögyam's life and lives knowing."* I had no doubt of it. I had no reason for my lack of doubt. It was like accepting that the M4 led to London. It was there on the sign and all you had to do was keep driving—or hitching—and arriving in London would be no monumental surprise.

"At age five, gTér discovering." Düd'jom Rinpoche laughed *"At age five you treasure khandro discovering."* Then he asked *"You one girlfriend then finding?"*

"Yes Rinpoche, her name was Alice."

---

1   For the details of Kyabjé Düd'jom Rinpoche's life and incarnation line given in this conversation, see Appendix II.

"Yah, good – but now, no girlfriend?"

"No, Rinpoche."

"But many girlfriends before having?"

I answered in the affirmative – knowing that there was no need of an answer, as Kyabjé Düd'jom Rinpoche already had my entire biography in his intuitional library.

"You must one sangyum finding – or gTérma not finding and teaching not possible." Düd'jom Rinpoche told me that I had seen my sangyum in a dream before leaving England – and that I would recognise her when she appeared in my life. He told me that this was his prediction and that all I had to do was practice and be observant. There would be obstacles to our being together – but these would be overcome.

"Past incarnation name: Aro Yeshé. Not Aro Yeshé Jung-né – but similar, like him, Dzogchen sem dé much teaching."

The name Aro Yeshé didn't immediately have a great effect on me. It was more that it didn't sound unusual. I could say that it simply sounded like my name – but that is not quite right either. It was actually some minutes after Düd'jom Rinpoche mentioned the name that I started to take it in. Düd'jom Rinpoche had put a name to my previous life. The impact of that wasn't as startling as it should have been – it was more a pervasive wave of something that I couldn't define. It was like someone describing the house on Frognal Crescent, Aldershot, in which I had lived as a baby before my family moved to Woodsfield Lane. The staircase would be described, the hall, the first-floor landing, the front door, the drawing room … As each aspect would be described I'd hear it – and it would not sound *unfamiliar*. This would not mean that I'd remembered it – but there'd be a sense in which the information was registering, albeit in an amorphous manner. Then at a later point there'd be a tiny flash of recognition – some small detail would become real. Aro Yeshé. It was not I name I would forget. I wrote it out in Tibetan U-chen script.

I'd begun to learn the alphabet in McLeod Ganj and so I wrote the name and showed it to Düd'jom Rinpoche. Wonder of wonders … I'd spelled the name correctly. Or maybe it wasn't that surprising – because I already knew the Yeshé was spelled *ye shes* – and my guess at Aro as *a ro* was straightforward as it has no silent letters.

Düd'jom Rinpoche smiled at my writing—made no comment—and continued with the account of his life.

"At your age: Padmasambhava meeting, and gTérmas writing." Düd'jom Rinpoche smiled *"Now you are here and meeting. This is good because later you also gTérma writing – maybe when you my age now becoming. Maybe not so long. Maybe earlier. Yes – maybe earlier. First students must be coming—then sangyum finding—then gTérma teaching."*

Clearly no reply was required. I did have questions – but Düd'jom Rinpoche continued to relate aspects of his life.

His experience of Dorje Tröllö practice inspired him to visit Paro Taktsang in Bhutan where there were many auspicious signs – and he discovered the Phurba Pu-dri Rekpung, the Tso-kyé Thug-thig and the Khandro Thug-thig. *"Paro Taktsang is Tiger Nest meaning. This is where Guru Rinpoche as Dorje Tröllö manifesting. Last incarnation you also to Taktsang pilgrimage making – with sangyums travelling."*

"With sangyums?" I asked *"Did I mishear, or did Düd'jom Rinpoche say sangyums – that is to say, more than one?"*

Düd'jom Rinpoche laughed on hearing my question *"No need two sangyums now having – this not necessary for you. This not good in your country. There only one wife having possible."*

I told him I was happy to hear that as I had no wish to be a bigamist or have some sort of open relationship. That would not suit me.

"This is good – but one time for you—in Tibet—this situation coming." He laughed *"Now two khandros not necessary. Chögyam not desiring. This is better. This for you is perfect."*

Then he laughed again – and went on to explain that having two sangyums was not completely unusual in Tibet.

Aro Yeshé's sangyums had been sisters – but he knew no more about them at that time apart from the fact that I had seen them once in a dream. Maybe he would know more in the future when I returned to see him again at the end of my Art School course.

Was Düd'jom Rinpoche seeing my dreams in Exeter? That felt extremely strange. It suddenly flooded back: waking in a tent; two dark haired young ladies lying, one on each side of me; my talking in my sleep in some foreign language; and, my sense of having someone else's memories in my mind.

"And now here in Bodha staying ..." he laughed *"... and young ngakpa long list giving."* Pause. *"Yah – so ... this now is enough."* He smiled *"Then when Chögyam old becoming – long list also giving."*

Düd'jom Rinpoche then asked me whether I remembered the subject on which he said he would elucidate.

"Yes, Rinpoche" I replied. *"gCèrdröl, shardröl, and rangdröl."*

"Good. These are methods within the drol-lug-zhi: the four modes of liberation."

Then Düd'jom Rinpoche elaborated *"First mode gCèrdröl. This liberation through naked awareness meaning. Second is shardröl. This meaning liberation on arising. Third is rangdröl. This meaning of-itself liberated. These three are ways to bring yédröl in dimension of practice. Yédröl meaning primordial liberation. gCèrdröl, is liberation through recognising namtogs."* Pause. *"You know 'namthog' meaning?"*

"Yes, Rinpoche. It means 'that which arises in mind' – and that can either be thought or image or whatever moves in mind."

"Yah—good—then next we look at function."

"gCèrdröl like meeting person whom you have met before. You know person and so no question having. You not 'Who are you?' asking."

Düd'jom Rinpoche went on to explain that shardröl is where thoughts liberate themselves after they arise. There was a way of explaining this through the coiling and uncoiling of a snake. Shardröl is where a snake uncoils itself from its coils.

"Snake is knot appearance having – but then … knot gone. Knot is made from snake – but knot not part of snake. Where knot gone? Knot never existing. Now meditation."

We sat for a few minutes and then Kyabjé Düd'jom Rinpoche recommenced.

"Next, rangdröl. This self-liberation meaning. Namtogs arising and with arising: immediate spontaneous liberation. Nothing happening needing. No detriment and no advantage in arising and namtogs self-liberating. These first three modes of liberation are practice of namtogs liberating. But then yédröl— primordial liberation—this is unborn nature of rigpa. This never different coming – from beginninglessness liberated."

Düd'jom Rinpoche paused whilst I caught up with my notes.

"Now further looking. gCèrdröl is insignificant perceptual activity. Attention turning to whatever namtogs arising – and immediately: recognition of namtog. This is like seeing a stranger in the bazar – suddenly you recognise stranger as old friend."

"Maybe for you …" Rinpoche laughed *"… old girlfriend!"*

With this mention of girlfriends, I was presented with another occasion where Düd'jom Rinpoche knew far more about me than he could have known by any normal means.

"So …" Rinpoche continued *"… although this inevitable in your practice becoming – there is a small gap."* Here Rinpoche showed how his thumb and index finger could be so close that they appeared to be touching *"… between namtog arising and becoming aware of presence of namtog."* Pause. *"Finally recognition of the namtog. Then the namtog dissolving. At this time—and maybe, for some months or maybe years—this your practice defining. But after this, practice obstacle becoming if not shardröl practising.*

"Then there is shardröl. With shardröl, namtog liberates – soon as arising. Like drawing pictures on lake surface. Drawing dissolves into clarity surface of lake – as soon as drawing making. Drawing and dissolution simultaneous. So arising, this is called shar-wa.[2] *Then liberating, this dröl-wa.*[3]

2   Shar-wa (*shar b*a).

3   Dröl-wa (*grol ba*).

"Shar-wa and dröl-wa simultaneous. No gap. No discontinuity between self-arising and self-liberation of namtogs. So, manner is different from gCèrdröl: liberation through naked awareness – and shardröl: liberation immediately on arising. In gCèrdröl there is minute appearance of disunion between the arising and liberation – but with shardröl, is no sense of namtogs suppressing. Effort not invested in anything. Liberation is spontaneous effortless reflex. This tsol'mèd."[4]

Kyabjé Düd'jom Rinpoche explained that, with the practice of gCèrdröl, there is the minute effort in terms of maintaining naked awareness – but with Shardröl, no effort exists. Whatever namtogs arise, they immediately move—according to their own energy—into the natural state. This occurs because this is the nature of namtogs.

He elucidated that arising namtogs are pure in themselves. He said that this was due to their own potentiality which is none other than the energy of Chö-ku.[5] Namtogs come into being effortlessly and liberation occurs effortlessly through the natural momentum of their arising. So this is the snake unknotting. When a namtog—or strongly charged thought arises, such as obsession or anger—then the awareness which manifests in the moment of liberation will be extremely strong and clear. In this way obsession becomes a friend of rigpa, instead of an adversary or obstacle. In this way, conceptualisation becomes a manifestation of the inherent energy of rigpa.[6] So, in this way, you continue in the state without accepting or rejecting.[7]

At this point Kyabjé Düd'jom Rinpoche looked at me intently – and asked *"You are everything clearly understanding?"*

"I understand as you speak Rinpoche – and I hope that what I understand will not slip away."

---

4   Tsol-mèd *(rTsol med).*

5   Chö-ku *(chos sKu / Dharmakaya)* the sphere of unconditioned potentiality.

6   Rigpa zangthal gyi-ngang lé-rang rTsaldu 'charwa *(rig pa zang thal gyi ngang las rang rTsal du 'char ba).*

7   Lang dor-mèd par kyangpa *(bLang dor med par bsKyangs pa).*

Rinpoche nodded and continued *"Anyway – I see that all is in Mind staying. So ... then ... although holding recognition of Chö-ku—so Chö-ku continuing—it is still as if duality and nonduality separate remaining. This Drölcha'i Chö-ku ngö-zung[8] – this meaning still exists subtle duality remaining. This because practice and everyday life not yet seamless. Then third stage. This is rangdröl. Distinction between arising and liberating is gone. This is journey in which destination same as point of departure. You bus boarding that takes immediately to where you are. So, when namtogs arising: instantaneously self-liberating. Not state of nonduality leaving. Their arising is their liberation. Division no longer existing. Liberation is instantaneous spontaneous effortlessness. This is rangdröl. Namtogs liberate as arising. Their very arising is nature of liberation."* Düd'jom Rinpoche paused for a moment gazing into space. Then he said *"Now we sit."*

After some time had elapsed Düd'jom Rinpoche said *"Face of nondual awareness recognising ... Although experiencing, description not possible. Like a mute, dreams describing."*

Rinpoche told me that I should write these words down in my note book and read them back to him. He asked me to write them in the English that I would use and that Tséring would then translate it back into Tibetan for him. This is what I wrote.

It is impossible to distinguish between oneself resting in nondual awareness and the nondual awareness one is experiencing. When one rests naturally—nakedly —in the boundless state of nondual awareness, the urgency of injudicious hyperactive conceptuality, memories, and troublesome plans – evaporates and disappears in the spacious sky of awareness. Referentiality collapses and vanishes into nondual awareness.

At the end – Düd'jom Rinpoche seemed pleased *"Always these words of Düd'jom close in heart keeping – then never dispirited becoming."*

Then we sat in silence again. I do not know how long we sat – but our meetings were often concluded in this way. After a month— which was the extent of my Nepalese visa—I had to return to McLeod Ganj. The conclusion of my sojourn in Bodha with Kyabjé Düd'jom Rinpoche was drawing closer.

8   Drölcha'i Chö-ku ngö-zung *(grol cha'i chos sKu ngos bZung)*.

One thing only troubled me during this time. I had begun to have serious doubts about Art School. I found that I'd lost enthusiasm for the idea of an Art degree – especially as it would take three years. It seemed that what I really should do was simply work every Summer and return to Nepal for the rest of the year in order to continue my studies and retreat commitments.

I put this problem to Düd'jom Rinpoche and he replied *"You must Art School. Nepal coming, good – but first examinations and qualifications obtaining. Otherwise poor old man becoming. This result must not be coming in the West. For Tibetans—no problem—but for Western peoples, unwise. You must good circumstances making."* He had explained this before – but this time he gave greater emphasis to my not giving up Art School. He said that I would have a longer time of living in the West ahead of me – and that living in the East was not easy for Western people. It was by no means certain that British citizens would always be allowed to come to India without visas – or stay as long as they wished. It would not always be so cheap to live in India and Nepal – and I had my old age to consider. Life was not easy in the West if one did not have qualifications – and one day I would be too old for hard manual labour.

I was not expecting this advice and was somewhat taken aback by it – however Düd'jom Rinpoche's advice made complete sense. He appreciated my fervour in wishing to abandon all my previous life-plans and dedicate myself to Vajrayana – but my work in the future would be to transmit Vajrayana to the West. I would therefore have to know the West well – and to make a life in the West. There were those who found ways of living in the East for decades – but this, he explained, was not for me. My job was to understand what was needed in the West and to be able to speak to Western people.

It seemed to be taken for granted—as far as Düd'jom Rinpoche was concerned—that I would eventually teach my own students. I found that idea as remote as realisation or discovering I could fly – but Düd'jom Rinpoche was in earnest about my future. What was more – I was to establish the gö kar chang lo'i dé in the West. That would be my life's work.

I had come to the East to find the gö kar chang lo'i dé – and I was to return in order to establish it in the West. Staying in the East therefore, was not an option.

I imagine that many people would not find it easy to have their lives laid out for them. I am actually a person who, in all other circumstances, would never comply or bow to authority. I certainly didn't comply with my father's efforts to steer me in my life – but when it came to Düd'jom Rinpoche, I simply accepted his direction without the slightest demur. If he had suggested studying for the Mathematic 'O' level—that I was deemed too arithmetically retarded to take at 16—I would have taken it on with pleasure. There was nothing I would not have taken on at Düd'jom Rinpoche's suggestion.

Düd'jom Rinpoche listed nine indications in respect of my life that confirmed his view that I could undertake something for him:

Firstly: *I was, like him, born in a Dragon Year – and I'd had authentic visions as a young child.*

Secondly: *I'd had dreams of clarity in which I'd seen vignettes of my past life.*

Thirdly: *I'd seen the photograph books of Tibet and later a photograph of Ajo Répa Rinpoche. These had made a significant impression on me.*

Fourthly: *The cumulative connections with the Nyingma Tradition had brought me to India in search of ngakpas.*

Fifthly: *I'd studied with the first ngakpa I met and taken all the advice that I had received.*

Sixthly: *I'd come to Nepal to meet him immediately, as I had been advised.*

Seventhly: *Having arrived in Nepal, I'd meditated in his gompa, circumambulated the Great Chörten – and then come directly to see him.*

Eighthly: *I'd taken all his instructions to heart.*

Ninthly: *I'd taken gö kar chang lo ordination – and he saw that I would keep these vows for the rest of my life.*

In addition to these indications he had personal recognition of my past lives. He foresaw that I was a person who could make the gö kar chang lo'i dé known in the West. This was important to him as the gö kar chang lo'i dé had become weakened after the exodus from Tibet. Even in Tibet it was not what it once was during the Early Spread of Vajrayana in Tibet. It had been famous and highly influential during the Early Spread – but since the second spread it had been repressed and neglected. Düd'jom Rinpoche wanted that to change – and saw me as a person he could trust to effect that change. If the gö kar chang lo'i dé could be seen and understood in the West, then it would be preserved in the East – and this is why I had to make my life in the West rather than jeopardising my future by devoting too much time to being in the East.

This then, was to be my life. Not only was there to be a training—and a life of study and practice—but there was Düd'jom Rinpoche's mission for me to preserve the gö kar chang lo'i dé by establishing it in the West. I promised Düd'jom Rinpoche that I would do everything in my power to fulfil his wishes – and he was pleased at my acceptance of his prediction.

It was a prediction – but the Tibetan idea of a prediction is that when one's Lama gives one a prediction, one does everything one can to make sure the prediction is fulfilled. Obviously, the Lama who makes the prediction has to have foresight and a profound understanding of the individual who receives the prediction – but there was no doubt in my mind that this was the most enormous honour as well as the most enormous responsibility.

Düd'jom Rinpoche did not accept my promise immediately however. He explained that it was a difficult task. Many people would stand against me in trying to make the gö kar chang lo'i dé known. It would not be an easy life if I chose to do as he had asked – but he would always think of me and always keep me in his heart. I should never feel separate from him.

"What could happen?" I asked rhetorically. *"They can't kill me – so I will survive. I've found that I am quite good at surviving – in fact surviving is what I seem to do best."*

Düd'jom Rinpoche looked quite serious when I said that – and told me that they could not kill me in the West, but that was not so certain in the East. Lamas had been assassinated in Tibet – and it was not impossible in India or Nepal. Evading the consequences of the law was far easier in India and Nepal than it was in Western countries.

Kyabjé Düd'jom Rinpoche then told me that it might be useful for me to know something of his life history. *"After Tibet leaving, then Kalimpong living. Then many teachings and empowerments in Kalimpong and Darjeeling giving."* These teachings and empowerments had been much appreciated by the Tibetan community. Availability on the part of a great Lama, such as Düd'jom Rinpoche, was much needed and cherished as a support for Tibetans in exile. It made them feel that their culture could survive. Sadly, it seems that Düd'jom Rinpoche's accessibility was interpreted as a political threat. It did occur to me to ask *who* saw it as a threat and *why*. I decided however – that, had Düd'jom Rinpoche wanted to be specific, he would have made it clear.

Having been raised by a Victorian father, I knew that there were certain questions it was impolite to ask – if one were addressing one's elders and betters. Those elders around me when I was a child were not necessarily my betters – but Düd'jom Rinpoche was in a category far beyond 'betters'. I simply trusted that he would tell me what I needed to know. If he did not tell me, there was no need to ask. I therefore only asked questions when there were points of Vajrayana that I did not understand.

Düd'jom Rinpoche told me that he had been subject to hostility 10 years previously. It had occurred on a train journey. He'd been in McLeod Ganj discussing the Tibetan refugee situation in relation to the exiled Nyingma peoples.[9]

9   Düd'jom Rinpoche did not mention with whom he discussed these matters. The author did not enquire because it did not seem necessary to know more than Düd'jom Rinpoche explained.

The situation had caused him concern – vis-à-vis the wish, in certain quarters, to make all traditions subject to centralised authority. This proposed policy—he felt—was not in keeping with Tibetan culture prior to the exodus. He was concerned about the future of what had always been independent lineages. With respect to this concern, he had asked Kathog Ontrül Rinpoche to perform a mélong divination [10] whilst on the train – and Ontrül Rinpoche, scrying the mélong, saw a statue of Padmasambhava bound in barbed wire. This did not bode well.

The train had to stop for a while at Siliguri. In the interim, whilst the train was stationary, Düd'jom Rinpoche was apprehended and subsequently incarcerated by the Indian Police. This had occurred because the Indian Intelligence Service had been informed—by certain Tibetan sources—that Düd'jom Rinpoche was a salaried Chinese collaborator.

I naturally wondered who the source could have been. One would have to be in some position of authority to make contact with the Indian Intelligence Service. I could have asked for more details – but again, I did not know how to frame such a question. To what end would I need such information?

Düd'jom Rinpoche gazed peacefully around the room *"Yah ... news very fast spreading – and disciples too shocked and sad. They hear from Siliguri to Panchimari prison sending. Then many disciples from Darjeeling, Kalimpong, Sikkim, and Bhutan, say: must be preventing necessary."* Their preventative measure was to be extraordinary – and in the style of Mahatma Gandhi. At any sign of Kyabjé Düd'jom Rinpoche being transported to the Panchimari prison, hundreds of people would lie on the railway lines. The number prepared to do this escalated by the hour – and the Indian authorities were aware that a crisis was mounting.

---

10 Mirror of clairvoyance (*me long rGyang gSal*). A circular mirror used for many purposes – one being mirror scrying. The mélong is an important Dzogchen device which symbolizes the reflective quality of internally manifested energy.

The Chögyal of Sikkim, the Royal Family of Bhutan, prominent Nepalese and Indian dignitaries, and thousands of students, wrote letters to Nehru – and within days Düd'jom Rinpoche was released and returned to his home in Kalimpong.

"This everyone in Nepal, Sikkim, and Bhutan knowing – but no one speaking. No one publicly saying. This is for you—not in this time for others hearing—only when you, my age becoming. Then this can be spoken. This you must decide. This is now, only for you hearing – so nature of politics you very well understanding. Dangerous people Chögyam harming." Düd'jom Rinpoche sighed *"So care must be taking. Always great care taking."*

And so … this was why I could not venture East for lengthy periods. I could only ever make short visits – and it could never be known in advance by anyone when I was coming—where I was going—or for how long.

I asked Düd'jom Rinpoche if there were any words of support he could offer me – that I could remember when things seemed difficult. He paused for a moment – then gave me an extremely broad smile *"Just think of me."* Then after a moment of silence that seemed to seethe like the sea, he said *"This is my Heart advice. This is self-sufficient."*

As before with such special teachings, Kyabjé Düd'jom Rinpoche wanted me to write it down and then hear my translation translated back into Tibetan.

Fervently invite the presence of Padmasambhava. Then settle in the space of Padmasambhava in which your mind and my mind are inseparable.

The relaxed openness of Padmasambhava is uncontrived naturalness – and does not curtail, reject, cultivate, or ignore.

Relax without grasping at the state of Padmasambhava – and whatever arises will self-liberate.

This is the nature of Padmasambhava. It abides in the natural state. It's not a new attainment because it has never been separate from you.

Although not separate, you have not recognised it 'til now. It is this non-recognition that is the only delusion. There is endless delusion and non-delusion — so whatever arises in Mind, look directly at its essence.

When examining it cannot be seen — so throw away the external examiner. The space where the examiner is abandoned is chö-ku: the essential nature; all-pervasive unconditioned potentiality. In this space of chö-ku, where can one go or stay? Understand this. Realise its meaning. Sustain it effortlessly in practice. The result is to be without hope or fear.

Düd'jom Rinpoche remained silent for a minute and continued

"Having attained this confidence ..." he laughed *"... has made this old man satisfied."*

Then he concluded *"I believe this young ngakpa also satisfied becoming."*

22

parting words

december 1971 to january 1972

The day arrived. I was to bid farewell to Kyabjé Düd'jom Rinpoche. It was sad to contemplate his absence in my life – but I knew that I would see him again in three years. In those three years I would have completed the ngöndros and various other practices on which he had given me instruction.

Before I left his presence however, Düd'jom Rinpoche said *"Before England going – we Arts speaking."* He said this as he knew I was going back to study at Art School. He wanted to say a few words about Art – and about *the Arts* in general. He knew I was interested in music and poetry as well as painting – and asked *"What music playing and singing?"*

"It's called Blues, Rinpoche. It comes from America – but before that, it came from West Africa."

He then asked me if I would sing him something so that he could hear what it sounded like, so—feeling slightly uneasy—I launched into 'Hoochie Coochie Man'. It didn't take more than the first line to feel entirely natural because Düd'jom Rinpoche gave me a broad grin.

> *Gypsy woman told my mother before I was born*
> *Y'got a boy childs coming, gonna be a son-of-a-gun*
> *Gonna make pretty women's jump and shout*
> *Then the world wanna know – what's it all about?*
> *'cause I'm here – ever'body knows I'm here*
> *I'm the hoochie coochie man – ever'body knows I am.*

Then he asked me what the words meant.

"That is something of a problem, Rinpoche – because ... parts of it are untranslatable."

Düd'jom Rinpoche smiled when my answer was translated for him *"Yah ... but many words in Tibetan you must be English translating. Then much more difficulty. You poetry writing – so for you it is not too difficult. So now you poetry-system using – and meaning telling."*

I asked if I might think about it for a while because I'd have to work out a form of English that would translate into Tibetan whilst retaining a meaning that was representative of the original. After a minute of scribbling I worked out something in English that could be translated into Tibetan.

> *A nomad khandro told my mother, before I was born*
> *You will have a boy child and he will be strong and charismatic*
> *He's going to cause beautiful women joyful fascination*
> *And everybody is going to be extremely curious about him*
> *Because I'm here – everybody knows I'm here*
> *I'm the man with siddhis – everybody knows I am.*

Once this had been translated Düd'jom Rinpoche laughed appreciatively *"Good song! This song very much liking! Very strong! Very powerful! Always you must be singing like this in your country!"*

I explained that I'd had to change the words—and they were sometimes a long way from the original—but that the original Black American language would have made no sense in Tibetan.

Düd'jom Rinpoche chuckled about that *"You poetry writing since child. So natural coming, you good translation making!"* He said he felt confident that I had translated the meaning. He said that this was an important part of the work that lay ahead of me as I would have to translate the meaning of the most profound Vajrayana teachings I received. *"No purpose word-for-word translation giving. This Sarma style. You must Nyingma style teaching."*

Düd'jom Rinpoche explained that the Arts were crucial to Vajrayana – and not simply the *Vajrayana Arts* in terms of thangkas, statues, gTormas, vajra dance, and so forth. The secular Arts—both Tibetan and Western—were also important. It was through the secular Western Arts that I could reach out to people.

"Secular Arts by ngakpa practising, not secular coming. Secular Arts by ngakpa practising, Vajrayana coming! Ngakpa everything into dimension of Vajrayana transforming! People not 'Vajrayana only for monks and recluses' thinking. This is wrong thinking. You must strongly 'this wrong' always saying."

He told me that in Tibet and Bhutan the ordinary people lived their lives very much within the dimension of Vajrayana and some ordinary people with ordinary working lives had achieved ja'lü.[1] Then he asked me whether I could earn a good living through the Arts and I replied that with painting it was more difficult unless one took the route I planned to take, in terms of becoming an Art School lecturer. He then asked about poetry and I replied that this was the most difficult course to take. Then he said *"Yah – but music everyone is liking."* And he asked me what the future was there. I replied that some people could become extremely wealthy through music – but that I had lost my chance in that direction. Düd'jom Rinpoche looked quizzical for an instant and asked me to explain how that came to be – so I provided a potted history of Savage Cabbage. He nodded—gave me a penetrating look—and said *"You must—always—music playing. This I see. This important – very important. Always painting. Always poetry writing. Always Arts in every part of life. In this way, changchub sem always manifesting.[2] This prediction I am making. Always Arts making. Never difference in Vajrayana and Art coming! Always together manifesting. In this way peoples are nature of Vajrayana understanding."*

This came as something of a surprise to me. I thought I was giving up my life as a Blues performer – but Düd'jom Rinpoche thought this definitely was not a good idea.

---

1   'ja' lus – rainbow body. At the time of death, the Dzogchen practice of Togal (*thod rGal – direct crossing / passing over the summit*), allows the five elements which form the physical body, to dissolve into their essence as light of the five colours – leaving only hair, nails, and nasal septum.

2   Changchub sem (*byang chub sems / bodhicitta*) mind of pure and total presence. In relative terms this relates to active compassion / empathetic appreciative awareness and engagement.

He said that it was 'most necessary' in terms of realising my potential for the benefit of others. He said that every human being has potential and that potential must be realised for the benefit of the world. If I gave up playing Blues, how could those who loved Blues come to know about Vajrayana? If I gave up writing poetry what connection would there be for those who loved poetry? The same was true for all the Arts with which I engaged.

This then, would be how I would teach in the West. What a staggering idea. This would be my métier and forté – because if Vajrayana was to be established in the West it would have to engage with Western culture. This was not to say that Vajrayana would change to suit the West – but that Vajrayana would be discovered as naturally inherent within the Arts. This would be seen because I was an Artist. This was the bridge I was to build.

This was—really—not what I was expecting to hear. I had somehow taken on a renunciate view without realising that Vajrayana concerned *transformation* rather than *renunciation*. This advice from Düd'jom Rinpoche changed my life—right there—in that moment.

On the afternoon I left Bodha, Düd'jom Rinpoche gave me a final teaching. Again, he asked me to write it down in my own English so that it could be translated back to him.

What is considered to be Mind, is not what it is imagined to be. This is because people try to understand Mind with thought. It is better simply to allow Mind to see itself – and for there to be no difference between Mind and seeing.

Past mind no longer exists. Future mind is not yet present. Whatever arises in the moment is indecipherable because it cannot be translated by thought without turning it into thought.

Let thoughts of past, present, and future settle in the present moment – and, in that moment, simply experience what is naturally there. Visual projections appear in meditation if one distracts oneself with here and there or then and when. If it is considered that Mind is nothing, it will become 'the prison of numb emptiness' – and the richness of the nature of Mind cannot self-emerge.

Mind can be investigated with the intellect for the duration of one's life – but one would be no closer to realisation. The real meaning of Dzogchen is natural immediacy in which the presence of awareness is without limit. Whatever is perceived is radiantly clear like the changeless blue of the sky. Whatever arises in Mind is inseparable from primordial radiant clarity-awareness. It is unborn and unceasing in splendour –and joyously manifests in every aspect of phenomenal reality.

When namtogs arise, stare directly into their arising. When namtogs dissolve stare directly into their dissolution. It is the same, in life. With each life-circumstance: whatever is enacted, stare directly into the enactment – with all the senses. Considering this will make you happy.
Be of great good cheer. É: Ma: Ho:

This teaching has remained with me and supported me through everything that has occurred – good, bad, and indifferent. I read it every day on my travels and at home – and each time I read it Düd'jom Rinpoche seemed close at hand. Even today when I read it Düd'jom Rinpoche seems close at hand.

The journey back across the industrial belt of Northern India was arduous. What did I expect? Whenever I resented the arduous nature of the journey, I'd read Düd'jom Rinpoche's text and laugh at myself. I'd have liked to have remained longer in Nepal – but I'd have had to have gone to Delhi to acquire another Nepalese visa. My money would not have stretched to that journey *and* to the train and bus ride back to Nepal. The finances required would not have been great – but my reserves were severely limited.

It would be three years before I could see Düd'jom Rinpoche again. That fact was not a happy one, even though I knew he would always be with me. He had said he would always be with me – and I knew that his statement *should* carry all the sense of closeness I required; as a ngakpa. I should therefore not indulge in infantile notions of feeling 'separated'. After all, I was supposed to be some sort of *ancient time traveller* who'd migrated through various bodies.

I had no doubt of Düd'jom Rinpoche's word on the matter – but I did not feel like a tulku.[3] I could not see my past lives—apart from strange dreams and fragmented images—and I did not feel as if I had any special qualities aside from insane enthusiasm.

I'd put this point to Düd'jom Rinpoche, and he told me that there were many tulkus who had no memory of their previous incarnations – so I had no need to be concerned. He said that I had already had more memories than some tulkus – and that I'd therefore have more memories in the future. He said that these memories were not so important in themselves. What was important was understanding Vajrayana and experience of practice. It was this that was valuable to others rather than stories of a generation that was gone. Tibetans were always excited to hear these stories and to hear of wonders. The *real wonder* however, was the nondual state – and the ability to give transmission of that state.

Then—unusually—he looked rather sad. He explained that memories of previous incarnations could always be called lies – but that changchub sem could never be disparaged. It could not be denied. *"No one saying 'Chögyam kindness* not *having!'"* he pronounced quite forcefully. *"No one saying 'Chögyam generosity* not *having, gentle* not *doing, friendly* not *doing, laughing* not *doing'. This—I believe—people are* never *saying."* Then he laughed *"Same, like 'Chögyam* not *powerful singing' saying!"* Then Düd'jom Rinpoche laughed rather loudly *"This* no one *can be saying – because nomad khandro, mother telling! Chögyam, man with siddhis becoming and everybody knowing – also khandros much liking!"*

This was deeply moving but also amusing. Düd'jom Rinpoche was quoting Muddy Waters back to me from my singing of Hoochie Coochie Man. Two apparently separate worlds had become undivided. Düd'jom Rinpoche and Muddy Waters were far from irreconcilable.

At that moment however—hearing those words—I felt both the burden of a huge responsibility – and a strange confident lightness.

---

3   Tulku (*sPrul sKu* / *nirmanakaya*) a recognised incarnation who has maintained an awareness of the realised state – however tenuous.

It was as though Düd'jom Rinpoche was empowering me not only to be a decent human being – but a creative human being. It's not that I doubted my capacity to be decent – but I did not know I was capable of guaranteeing that under all circumstances. I did not know that it was possible for me to be a Buddhist Bluesman with adequate integrity.

With Düd'jom Rinpoche's words however, I felt that it had become a viable challenge. I *could* be a decent honourable artist. I *would* be a decent honourable artist. I'd try my level best to carry through with the promises I'd made – and attempt to accomplish the practices. I absolutely had to become what Düd'jom Rinpoche believed I could become. I would do whatever it took not to disappoint him.

Of course … the passion of youth is given to such staunchly devout declarations – but then 'life happens'. What would happen then? That was a serious question – but it was not in my mind at that point. Sitting with Kyabjé Düd'jom Rinpoche – everything was possible.

23

there and back again

december 1971 to january 1972

Looking back, I recognised I'd been more than merely fortunate. I'd spent an inordinate period of time with Kyabjé Düd'jom Rinpoche. I'd also spent time with Dilgo Khyentsé Rinpoche.[1] I'd gone to see him at the advice of Kyabjé Düd'jom Rinpoche – who felt it would be good if I made this connection. This was on the basis that Dilgo Khyentsé Rinpoche had also heard of Khyungchen Aro Lingma.

I had audiences with Dilgo Khyentsé Rinpoche several times. He was wonderfully kind and generous – and meetings with him were always encouraging, and inspiring.

On our third meeting, he presented me an ivory damaru, teng'ar, and phurba. He told me that I should keep these items reserved for the future when I gave empowerments to my own students. This was something of a shock – even though Kyabjé Düd'jom Rinpoche had told me I would teach. But how could I possibly— ever—give empowerments? It was like hearing him tell me that I'd rival Leonardo Da Vinci in painting, Shakespeare in poetry, and Bach in music. I checked that I had not misheard or misunderstood – but no. I was assured that as I had given empowerments as Aro Yeshé in my previous life – that I would eventually give them again. It was not something I needed to think about at the moment – or for some years to come. It would all take care of itself – all I needed to do was practise.

Düd'jom Rinpoche would indicate when I should begin to use these ivory implements – but that in the meantime I should acquire a bodhi seed teng'ar, and an iron phurba. I had already acquired a bell and vajra.

---

1   *dil mGo mKhyen brTse*

I'd visited the local traders and found a bell and damaru I could afford: it was unusual – and I wondered whether it was suitable. Both Düd'jom Rinpoche and Dilgo Khyentsé Rinpoche told me that it was more than suitable. It was perfect and was not of recent make. The bell and vajra were nine-pronged and these were ideal for a Nyingma.

I asked Dilgo Khyentsé Rinpoche whether he would be so kind as to tell me about his life in order that I could read it for inspiration as I travelled back to Britain. He was happy to oblige and gave me a far longer account than I imagined. I was delighted. I took copious notes and the translator, Ngawang,[2] was kind enough to see me later to give me all the Tibetan spellings for the names I had mutilated with my primitive phonetics. This process took over three hours – but I learned a great deal from the experience.

"Oh yah …" Dilgo Khyentsé Rinpoche said *"… Sangyum you must be having. Kyabjé Düd'jom Rinpoche is Chögyam sangyum speaking?"*

"Yes Rinpoche."

"Then good – but great care taking. Sangyum must be auspicious – serious practitioner, or many problems coming." He smiled at this point and continued *"But now, very young – so no difficulty. Maybe some girlfriends having, then seeing if suitable becoming."*

After the long and detailed discourse on his life, Dilgo Khyentsé Rinpoche laughed *"So … no more telling. Then Ngakpa Chögyam in Bodha arriving. Kyabjé Düd'jom Rinpoche recognising – and all things teaching."*

Dilgo Khyentsé Rinpoche asked me whether I recited the Seven Line Song of Padmasambhava.[3] I replied that I did – and he asked me to chant it for him.

---

2   *ngag dBang.*

3   The Tsig-dun sol'dep (*tshig bDun gSol 'debs*) or the Dorje Jö-dun (*rDo rJe brJod bDun*) the Seven Vajra Verses.

"Hung: Ögyen yul gyi nub chang tsam: / Pema ké-sar dong-po la: / Ya tsan chö-gi ngö-drüp nyé: / Pema Jung-né Shé-su drag: / Khordu khandro mang-pö khor:/ Khyé kyi jé-su dag drüb kyi: / Chin gyi lob chir shèg su sol: / Guru Pema Siddhi Hung:"

"Yah ..." he grinned at me *"... so maybe you should know the path of the hidden meaning – the path of liberation."* Then he began to expound the root meaning. *"The first word is the syllable* Hung. *This awakens the nature of self-arisen wisdom. Then the first line:* Ögyen yul-gyi nub chang tsam. *Sem-nyid is the* nature of Mind – *but when sem, conceptual mind, is misunderstood as being divided from it; this is dualism. Sem-nyid is identical with Ögyen yul. This is the freedom:* tsam; *from the extremes of samsara:* nub; *and nirvana:* chang. *Samsara is cyclic experience and nirvana is the release form cyclic experience into emptiness. These are known as extremes because although nirvana is the release from samsara – it abandons form. The nature of Mind is not disturbed by the forms that arise because it is the nature of space to give rise to form.*

"So, then – the next line coming?" at which Dilgo Khyentsé Rinpoche motioned me to recite.

"Pema ké-sar dongpo la."

"This meaning: realisation of union: dongpo; *of primordial sphere:* pema; *and intrinsic awareness:* ké-sar.*"*

Dilgo Khyentsé Rinpoche motioned me again.

"Ya-tsan chö-gi ngö-drüp nyé."

"Dzogchen is Great Completeness. This is marvellous: ya-tsen; *attainment:* nyé; *of supreme accomplishment:* chö-gi ngödrup.*"*

"Pema Jung-né shé-su drag."

"This is wisdom of primordial nature, renowned as: zhesu trag; *the ultimate ground:* jung-né; *of Buddhahood:* pema. *This is nondual ground of Being."*

"Khordu khandro mang-pö 'khor."

"This wisdom: 'khor; *is multiple power of manifestation:* mangpo; *emanating:* dro; *in primordial sky:* kha; *as attributes of nondual realisation:* 'khordu. *This is primordial purity of phenomenal world."*

"Khyé kyi jé-su dag drüb kyi."

"I develop firm confidence: dag drub kyi; *in nature of nondual primordial wisdom:* khye kyi je su.*"*

"Chin gyi lob chir shèg su sol."

"In order to purify: chir; *all attachments to appearances as primordial wisdom:* chin gyi lob; *may I realise the ultimate nature:* shèg-su sol.*"*

"Guru Pema Siddhi Hung."

"Essence of primordial wisdom is emptiness of chö-ku: Guru; *Nature of primordial wisdom is clarity of long-ku:* Pema; *Energy of primordial wisdom is all-pervasive compassionate power of trülku:* Siddhi; *manifested by the fivefold wisdom of the elements:* Hung.

"Yah … and so … the verse begins with the seed syllable of the nature of Mind—Hung—which awakens self-arisen primordial wisdom – which is the actual nature of samsara and nirvana.

"The country of Ögyen[4] *is a unique source of Vajrayana. In relation to the path, your Mind—the nature of Mind—is the unique source of Vajrayana. This is the meaning of Ögyen. The nature of Mind is free from descending samsara and ascending nirvana. This descending and ascending are meaningless because the* nature of Mind *is not partial to the extremes. It has no addiction to either form or emptiness.*

"Pema is the lotus—and signifies chö-ying—the sphere of the creative space of phenomena. This is the nature that must be realised. It doesn't dwell anywhere. It's beginninglessly pure – just as the lotus flower is unstained by the impurity of the mire in which it grows.

---

4 O rGyan *(o rGyan / Uddhiyana / Oddiyana)* is an area associated with early medieval India that is of great importance in the development and dissemination of Vajrayana. It is commonly thought to be the Swat District of Pakistan, but it was a much larger area that spread into Afghanistan. There is still a central province of Afghanistan that is called Oruzgan. The area that can be considered as Ögyen is mainly defined by the Silk Road and the confluence of trade routes through a large area of wilderness.

"Ké-sar *is the pistil, and signifies the vajra: the luminosity of intrinsic awareness*[5] – *the method of realising the nature of Mind. This is spontaneously-accomplished and realised as self-radiant intrinsic-awareness, primordial wisdom. It blossoms with clarity – and for that reason it resembles the pistil of a lotus.*

"Dongpo *is the stem which supports the pistil and the lotus petals. This is the self-arisen primordial wisdom of unconstrained ebullience that resides as the union of the sphere of phenomenal reality*[6] *and sphere of primordial wisdom,*[7] *and it is the ultimate nature of mind or the innate luminosity of mind. Mind is the luminous spontaneously-born Great Completion,*[8] *the primordial wisdom of the absolute nature. This is the meaning of the fourth empowerment of inner tantra – and it is this which is marvellous. The nature of Mind is the ground of all Buddhas of the three times, who have blossomed like lotus flowers – so the nature of Mind is renowned as the basis of Pema: the Buddhas. This recognition is known as Pema Jung-né—Padmasambhava—the absolute Buddha. In terms of this state or realisation, there are five spectral rays of primordial wisdom* [10] *which naturally manifest. To realise the nature of nondual primordial wisdom and to integrate it into everyday life with unchanging confidence, we say 'I shall follow your practice.'*

"Guru: *If you become experienced and discover the ultimate nature*[11] *you will realise the view*[12] *and complete this realisation through meditation.*

5   Rigpa'i dorje (*rig pa'i rDo rJe*).

6   Chö-ying (*chos dByings / dharmadhatu*).

7   Yeshé (*ye shes / jnana*).

8   Dzogchen (*rDzogs chen / rDzogs pa Chenpo / mahasandhi*).

9   The fourth empowerment is the ngowo-ku (*ngo bo nyid kyi sku / Svabhavikakaya*) empowerment.

10 The yeshé-nga (*ye shes lNga*) are: the primordial wisdom of evenness – of equanimity and equality; the primordial wisdom of mirror-like discriminative awareness; the primordial wisdom of pure empathetic appreciation; the primordial wisdom of self-accomplishing activity; and the primordial wisdom of ubiquitous intelligence in all-encompassing space.

11 Né-lug (gNas lugs).

12 Tawa (*lTa ba*).

"Then you will transform all attachments into the pure appearances that radiate from the essential sphere.[13] *Primordial wisdom is the emptiness essence of Being.*[14]

"Pema: The nature of primordial wisdom is luminosity.[15] *It is spontaneously accomplished as the sphere of realised appearances,*[16] *which are a ceaseless display of power in being inseparable from the sphere of unconditioned potentiality.*[17] *So Pema is the lotus which is unstained by dualism. The inseparability of the essence and nature*[18] *is the empathetic appreciative activity display,*[19] *which arises independent of samsara and nirvana. Through this the needs of endless beings are fulfilled. This is known as the attainment of siddhi.*

"Hung—the final Hung—is the self-arisen primordial wisdom – and the seed syllable of Mind which possesses the five primordial wisdoms."

Dilgo Khyentsé Rinpoche gave a series of teachings pertaining to the Seven Line Song of Padmasambhava and it took me years to unpack what he taught. I took copious notes and studied them each day. Düd'jom Rinpoche answered a great many questions that arose from the teachings I'd received from Dilgo Khyentsé Rinpoche – and by the time I left Nepal I felt as if I'd undergone a doctoral degree course in Vajrayana. My head often swam with the density of the teachings and I realised that I had to move beyond the intellect if I was ever to understand what I had been taught. To Düd'jom Rinpoche and Dilgo Khyentsé Rinpoche these teachings were self-explanatory because they were speaking from the point of view of realisation.

13 Ngowo tongpa (*ngo bo sTong pa*).

14 Chö-ku (*chos sKu / Dharmakaya*) the sphere of unconditioned potentiality.

15 Rang-zhin sèl-wa (*rang bZhin gSal ba*).

16 Long-ku (*longs sKu / Sambhogakaya*).

17 Chö-ku (*chos sKu / Dharamakaya*).

18 The inseparability of ngowo and rangzhin (*ngo bo* and *rang bZhin*) essence and nature; tongpa and sèl-wa (*sTong pa* and *gSal ba*) emptiness and clarity; chö-ku and long-ku (*chos sKu* and *longs sKu*); and, guru and pema (*bLa ma* and *pa dMa*), the Lama and the lotus – Padmasambhava.

19 Rolpa (*rol pa*) the play of realisation.

What they related to me was only difficult because I was having to grapple with *intellect* – where *intellect* was out of its depth. I realised that much of what I was being taught had to be seen as transmission. It occurred to me that this was material that would serve me later when I had the meditative experience to authentically comprehend what I had been taught.

Nine days of travel back to McLeod Ganj with my notes, allowed me to ferment in a vast carboy of Vajrayana terminology. I understood the words – but the meaning was sometimes hidden within them. Both Düd'jom Rinpoche and Dilgo Khyentsé Rinpoche had advised me to make the Seven Line Song one of my major practices—and so, I chanted it whenever I wasn't studying it —and, eventually, I staggered out of the bus in McLeod Ganj; weary – but whelmed with wonderment.

I spent another month with Ngakpa Yeshé Dorje and Khandro Ten'dzin Drölkar. They were delighted to see me in gö kar chang lo robes. They were delighted that Düd'jom Rinpoche had accepted me as a disciple – and that he had given me so many teachings. Ngakpa Yeshé Dorje told me that he could not help me with the Dzogchen teaching because—as he put it—only Kyabjé Düd'jom Rinpoche could teach on such a subject. He also told me that what I had studied of the Seven Line Song with Dilgo Khyentsé Rinpoche was also beyond his scope. Ngakpa Yeshé Dorje was a master of Mahayoga ritual and symbolic activity so I settled, gratefully, to learn whatever I could of the practices of Tröma Nakmo.

I read the notes I had taken in Nepal every day – and every day I sat. At Düd'jom Rinpoche's advice I continued with my practice of the shorter Düd'jom gTérsar Ngöndro and then the longer Düd'jom gTér Ngöndro – and by the time I left India I had completed 200,000 prostrations.

I was painfully thin—yet muscular—when I arrived home. My mother took a moment to recognise the figure standing—slightly baffled—at the front door. I hadn't taken a front-door key with me –so I'd rung the bell and stood there feeling almost as if I were a ghost come to haunt my previous home.

I had no idea what I was going say when the door opened. Ridiculous. Of course, I knew what to say. Of course, I knew how to be. It was all second nature. The door opened and I was simply who I was, with the mother I knew so well.

My father looked from his desk and smiled his usual slight smile. *"Home is the sailor, home from sea, And the hunter home from the hill."* [20]

I almost replied *"There and back again – a Hobbit's holiday ..."* but my father would not have understood the reference.[21]

A bizarre notion entered my mind.

As I took in the scene before me – I simultaneously recollected my time in the Himalayas.

The first notion that formed itself was of two movies running concurrently. I could be in either, alternately.

The second aspect was more intricate. The only real scenes of the movie were the ones I was inhabiting in the moment. The movie I was not inhabiting merely ran on—just as scripted—including some vaporous version of me who acted according to the vague logic demanded by the story. This was not to demean the other characters in the movies – it was more a notion that undermined the concept of my own reality as a uniform continuum. The other characters were real – but I was a superimposition.

The third aspect was that there was a state in which the movies came to an end. There was also a state before the movies had been made. This gave rise to the question: who I was when there was no movie and no script. That question was surprisingly easy to answer. Of course! There was no movie playing in the presence of Kyabjé Düd'jom Rinpoche – not at any time. Those were times when I'd stepped sideways – out of the movie.

---

20 From *Requiem* by Robert Louis Stevenson (1850–1894).

21 *The Hobbit* or *There and Back Again* is a novel by JRR Tolkien published in 1937. It is set within a fictional universe and follows the journey of Bilbo Baggins, to win a share of the treasure guarded by Smaug the dragon. Bilbo's journey takes him from bucolic Hobbiton to lands of sinister danger. Bilbo names his account of the journey as *There and Back Again – a Hobbit's Holiday*.

The memory of those times could, of course, easily become fictionalised by distance and converted into movies – but there'd always remain a sense of potency; of fundamental reality.

Then the notion vanished and I had no notion of what had occurred in my mind.[22] It did return later and was present from time to time – but at the moment there was the voice of my father.

"Home is the sailor, home from sea, And the hunter home from the hill."

My father looked pleased to see me. The past vanished. I realised that I had no functional memory of an 'overbearing father'. There I was – and there was the first sign of the world of literature I'd left behind. My father didn't quote a great deal – but I always enjoyed it when he did. I think he enjoyed it when I could not place the quote. He had to remind me *"Robert Louis Stevenson."*

"Ah yes, of course" I replied. *"It's been a long time since I've been called upon to quote English literature – but I shall enjoy familiarising myself."*

I heard the distant sound of Jimi Hendrix emanating from the bedroom. My brother Græham was busy with an essay. The track was *Voodoo Chile (slight return)*. The title made me smile: *slight return*; I was *slight*; I had *returned*. I'd once imagined I might be a Hoodoo child, back in the 1960s. At the age of 12, I'd sat at the crossroads in Runfold at midnight. I was waiting for Papa Legpa – but that old African Djinn never appeared.

I'd arrived home just before dinner. My father had cooked his own remarkable version of Welsh Rarebit – which, apart from cheese, had little connection with Welsh Rarebit. I was famished – and ate more than I'd eaten in a long time. My father seemed to gain unusual pleasure from seeing me tucking in with such gusto – and said *"You don't miss the curries, then?"*

"No indeed not, Dad" I replied. I'd actually only eaten half a dozen curries in the entire extent of my stay in India – and one had been with the Indian Major on the train ride north to Pathankot. I'd tell my father about that meeting over the next few days.

22 The notion would have vanished had I not written it down and unearthed it half a century later. It is included here as an example of my thinking at that time.

Whilst in India I'd always been with Tibetans—and had therefore eaten Tibetan food—but there was no need to upstage my father with such a statement.

It occurred to me that I'd taken the first step into the life of dual-identity. I was a little surprised that it was so easy to be *who I had been before I left for India* – and yet … *being the same* was *different*. It was as if I had grown older – whilst having time-travelled to my childhood, in respect of the presence of the White Lady. I now had a name for her: Khyungchen Aro Lingma. She had been my mother in my past life as Aro Yeshé. Kyabjé Düd'jom Rinpoche Jig'drèl Yeshé Dorje had made sense of those strange childhood dreams – and now all that was left was for me to … fill in the pieces? No, there was no way of doing that. I couldn't simply will myself to remember. Maybe I'd have further dreams? Or maybe I'd have to wait until I saw Düd'jom Rinpoche again. He told me that I would probably have further dreams and remember more as time went on.

The fact that I'd taken gö kar chang lo vows was always with me. It affected everything I did or said. I had become careful: far more careful than I had ever been before – but also curiously carefree. The vicissitudes of life were vaguely like a pantomime: they were scenarios with which I had to engage with whatever earnestness seemed suitable to the occasion. It was possible to be earnestly light-hearted in the face of whatever came along.

Something or someone had died and been reborn – but that seemed to be happening all the time. The vocalist of the Savage Cabbage Blues Band seemed remote. He was there if I cast my mind back – but he was as real as my dreams of Tibet. I felt like a space that was inhabited by different *persona dramatis*. I wondered whether I could actually stand on a stage again and be the Bluesman I was. I had been able to sing *Hoochie Coochie Man* for Düd'jom Rinpoche – so anything was possible.

Apart from the sense of bemusement, there was an inherent obligation to be kindly rather than indulgent – whenever the choice lay before me. People *were* as they *were* – and mostly could not help themselves.

I had come to understand that I *could*—and therefore *should*—step outside the framework in which I had to take offence at anything. There was so much that I could not say or explain to *anyone* – unless I went to see Lama Chime Rinpoche at Kham House. I had once asked Lama Chime Rinpoche to be my teacher – but he told me *"… this, for you, is too soon, too early, too quick. You should go to the Himalayas first … You meet different Lamas and hear teaching. If you don't find a Lama, come back to me and I will be your teacher – but not before you have met other teachers. You must be sure you make the right choice."*

He had given the perfect advice and I'd made the right choice. It was probably stupid on my part – but it seemed as if it would be churlish to visit Lama Chime Rinpoche and say *'I've found my Tsa-wa'i Lama. Kyabjé Düd'jom Rinpoche has accepted me as a student – but can I call round and bend your ear from time to time?'* Of course, Lama Chime Rinpoche would have been happy to talk with a student of Düd'jom Rinpoche – but, I still had foolish ideas that prevented me from asking for support, where support would have been cheerfully forthcoming.

I *had* been able to talk to Steve about my visions – and he'd neither treated me as if I had a mental condition or as if I was a poseur. Now, however, I was on my own. There was great joy and colossal loneliness.

I wordlessly contemplated the loneliness for an indeterminate period of time – after which I laughed almost imperceptibly. I felt unaccountably unassailable. I laughed briefly without irony – but with a naturally assured sense of merriment. The mirth had welled up out of a *space that I seemed to know* – and to have known for a thousand years.

Appendix I
Düd'jom Lingpa
1835–1904

The details of Düd'jom Lingpa's life were told to me by Kyabjé Düd'jom Rinpoche – with additional material supplied by the translator. Kyabjé Düd'jom Rinpoche was clearly not interested in glorifying his incarnation line – so it was left to the translator to add whatever he felt it was necessary for me to know. This information is available elsewhere – but I provide it here because of the manner in which I received it.

Kyabjé Düd'jom Rinpoche Jig'drèl Yeshé Dorje's incarnation line is a wonder and inspiration to all who receive teachings from him: Nuden Dorje Chang *(who vowed to appear as Buddha Möpa 'ö Thayé— Adhimukta—the* 1,000[th] *and last Buddha of this Aeon)*; Shariputra; Saraha; Krishnadhara *(chief minister of Indrabhuti of Ögyen)*; Hungkara; Khyé'u-chung Lotsa; Smritijnana; Rongzom Pandita Chökyi Zangpo; Dampa Desheg; Palden Ling-jé Répa *(one of the founders of the Drukpa Kagyüd)*; Sakya Tri'dzin Chögyal Phakpa; Drum-khar Nagpopa *(a Khampa Naljorpa who meditated in dark retreat for 18 years)*; Héwa Chöjung *(Khampa magician and subjugator of demons)*; Traktung Düd'dül Dorje; Kathog Gyalsé Sônam Détsen *(head of Kathog)*; Düd'dül Rolpa-tsal *(teacher of Jig'mèd Lingpa)*; Düd'jom Lingpa; and Kyabjé Düd'jom Rinpoche Jig'drèl Yeshé Dorje.

Düd'jom Lingpa was also known as Chakong gTertön. Düd'jom Lingpa had five incarnations: Sonam Détsen – *body incarnation*; Dzong-gTér Künzang Nyima – *speech incarnation*; Dud'jom Rinpoche Jig'drèl Yeshé Dorje – *mind incarnation*; Tulku Pednam – *qualities incarnation*; and Tulku Natsok Rangdröl – *activity incarnation*.

Düd'jom Lingpa was a great Nyingma Lama and gTértön whose visionary revelations amount to twenty huge volumes. His immediate incarnation—born even before his physical life ended—was Dud'jom Rinpoche Jig'drèl Yeshé Dorje.

Khenpo Jig'mèd Phüntsog's family is also related to Düd'jom Lingpa since Khenpo Jig'mèd Phüntsog's great-great-grandfather was Cha-khung Chö-gyé – the younger brother of Düd'jom Lingpa.

Düd'jom Lingpa was born in 1835 in the Sérta Valley of Golok.

He belonged to the A-chak Dru lineage of the Nub clan of the Chakong people and was an incarnation of Nuden Dorje, and the Imperial era figure, Khye'u-chung Lotsa, who was one of the 25 disciples of Padmasambhava.

Throughout his life Düd'jom Lingpa had direct visionary experiences of Padmasambhava, Yeshé Tsogyel, Dorje Phagmo, Chenrézigs, Chana Dorje, Jampalyang, Saraha, and Longchenpa Drimèd 'ö-Zér from whom he received transmissions. Also in visionary experience Düd'jom Lingpa journeyed to the visionary dimension of the Copper-Coloured Mountain where he received transmissions directly from Padmasambhava.

Düd'jom Lingpa lived mainly amongst the ordinary people and behaved in an ordinary manner – but he was never perceived as ordinary by anyone. He received only a few teachings and transmissions from human teachers – but received most of his knowledge directly from the nature of reality.

At the age of 23, Düd'jom Lingpa left his native home and settled in the Mar Valley. He stayed there for a lengthy period with the support of the Gili family, and so became known as Gili gTértön.

At age 25 Düd'jom Lingpa retrieved a revelatory or prophetic guide—kha-jang—from the rock escarpment of Ba-tér in the Mar Valley which contained instructions on how he should discover and reveal his gTérmas. In that same year, he began to discover and reveal his own major Earth gTérmas from Ngala Tak-tsé in the Sérta Valley.

He revealed twenty volumes of earth and mind gTérmas, hidden in the ninth century by Padmasambhava. fourteen of these came to be known as the Düd'jom gTérsar, the New Treasures of Düd'jom. Amongst the most famous texts of his revelations are the Tröma Nakmo Cycle and the Nè-lug Rangjung, a Dzogchen cycle of teaching and transmission. He established Dar-tsang Kèlsang Gompa in Sérta, which became a seat for several of his sons.

Düd'jom Lingpa had a strong body, with a reddish-brown complexion, a fierce face, and large powerful eyes. He dressed in gö kar chang lo robes with all appropriate ornaments and conch earrings. Half his uncut hair was coiled into a topknot, while his remaining hair hung loosely down his back.

During his life, Düd'jom Lingpa faced many obstacles from various vituperate bigoted hierophants but was able to transform all circumstances into supports for Vajrayana. He did not always have good health in the later years of his life – but he was able to heal many people through his single gestures.

While he was looking straight ahead, even the closest disciples of Dud'jom Lingpa did not dare to look at him – because of the power of his staring eyes. People in Golok recited the words *"Hung! Physical Presence of Düd'jom!"* instead of reciting the usual liturgy which included mind and speech as well as body. This testifies to his vast charismatic presence as having been utterly extraordinary.

Dud'jom Lingpa was invited by Jamyang Khyentsé Wangpo and Jamgön Kongtrül the Great to include his gTérmas into their collection of the Rinchen gTérdzöd – but he declined their request, telling them that wherever the Rinchen gTérdzöd would be spread, the Düd'jom gTér would also spread.

In his last years of life—apart from two brief journeys to Dza-chukha—Düd'jom Lingpa spent his time only in three main places in Eastern Tibet: the Sérta Valley, the mDo Valley, and the Mar Valley.

Düd'jom Lingpa wished to reveal the Hidden Land of Pemakö in Kongpo. This is one of the four major Hidden Lands authenticated by Padmasambhava as vividly potentiated domains for Vajrayana practitioners when general circumstances would become less conducive. Being unable to go there himself, Düd'jom Lingpa predicted that his incarnation would be born there and reveal it. Düd'jom Lingpa passed away in 1904, and took rebirth In Pemakö as Kyabjé Düd'jom Jig'drèl Yeshé Dorje – the Second Düd'jom Lingpa.

Notes:

The transliteration and details of people and places are given here, in order of appearance.

Düd'jom Lingpa *(bDud 'joms gLing pa,*1835–1904) was also know as Chakong gTertön *(lCags sKong gTer sTon).*

Sonam Détsen *(bSod nams lde btsan,* 1910–1958); the *body incarnation* of Düd'jom Lingpa.

Dzong-gTér Künzang Nyima *(rDzong gTer kun bZang nyi ma,* 1904–1958); the *speech incarnation;* of Düd'jom Lingpa.

Dud'jom Rinpoche Jig'drèl Yeshé Dorje *(bDud 'joms Rin po che 'jigs bral ye shes rDo rJe,* 1904–1987); the *mind incarnation* of Düd'jom Lingpa.

Tulku Pednam *(sPrul sKu pad nam,* the *qualities incarnation* of Düd'jom Lingpa.

Tulku Natsok Rangdröl *(sPrul sKu sna tshogs rang grol,* 1904-1958); the *activity incarnation* of Düd'jom Lingpa.

Khenpo Jig'mèd Phüntsog *(mKhen po 'jigs med phun tshog,* 1933–2004).

Cha-khung Chö-gyé *(lCag khung chos brGyad).*

Nuden Dorje Chang *(nus lDan rDo rJe 'chang,* 1655–1708), a famed Nyingma master from Kham, East Tibet.

Shariputra (568–484 BCE) – a disciple of Gautama Buddha.

Saraha – an 8ᵗʰ century Mahasiddha.

Khye'u-chung Lotsa *(khye'u chung lo tsa ba)*– one of the 25 disciples of Padmasambhava.

Smritijnana (Tib. Drenpa Yeshé Drakpa – *dran pa ye shes grags pa*).

Rongzom Pandita Chökyi Zangpo *(rong zom chos kyi bZang po, 1012–1088).*

Dampa Desheg *(dam pa bDe gshegs, 1122–1192).*

Drukpa Kagyü *('brug pa bKa' brGyud)* – a branch of the Kagyu School founded in Tibet in the 12ᵗʰ Century.

Palden Ling-jé Répa *(dPal lDan gLing rJe ras pa),* one of the founders of the Drukpa Kagyü school.

Sakya Tri'dzin Chögyal Phakpa *(sa sKya khri 'dzin chos rGyal 'phags pa, 1235–1280).*

Nagpopa *(nag po pa).*

Héwa Chöjung *(he ba chos 'byung).*

Traktung Düd'dül Dorje *(khrag 'thung dud 'dul rDo rJe, 1615–1672).*

Kathog Gyalsé Sônam Détsen *(ka thog rGyal rSas bSod nams lde btsan).*

Düd'dül Rolpa-tsal *(dud 'dul rol pa rTsal).*

Jig-mèd Lingpa *('jigs med gLing pa).*

Khyé'u chung Lotsa *(khye'u chung lo tsA).*

Sérta *(gSer thal)* Valley, Golok *(mGo log).*

A-chak Dru *(A lCags 'gru).*

Nub *(gNubs)* clan of the Chakong *(lCags sKong)* people.

Padmasambhava (Guru Rinpoche).

Yeshé Tsogyel *(ye shes mTsho rGyal).*

Dorje Phagmo *(rDo rJe phag mo; Skt. Vajravarahi).*

Chenrézigs *(sPyan ras gZigs, Skt Avalokiteshvara).*

Chana Dorje *(phyag na rDo rJe, Skt. Vajrapani).*

Jampalyang *('jam dPal dByangs, Skt. Manjushri).*

Longchenpa Dri-mèd 'ö-Zér *(kLong chen pa dri med 'od zer,* 1308–1363).

Kha-jang *(kha byang)* – revelatory or prophetic guide.

Earth gTerma *(sa gTér)* and **Mind gTerma** *(dGongs gTer).*

Ngala Tak-tsé *(sNags la sTag rTse).*

Düd'jom gTérsar *(bDud 'joms gTer gSar).*

Tröma Nakmo *(khros ma nag mo).*

Nè-lug Rangjung *(gNas lugs rang byung).*

Dzogchen *(rDzogs chen)* – the three series of Dzogchen are **sem-dé** *(sems sDe* – the series of Mind); **long-dé** *(kLong sDe* – the series of space; and **men-ngak-dé** *(man ngag sDe* – the series of Secret Instruction.

Dar-tsang Kèlsang Gompa *(brDa tshang bsKal bZang dGon pa).*

Gompa *(dGon pa)* – monastery.

The sons of Dud'jom Lingpa:

> **DoDrüpchen Jig'mèd Tenpé Nyima** *(rdo grub chen 'jigs med bstan pa'i nyi ma,* 1865–1926); **Tulku Pema Dorje** *(sPrul sKu pad med rDo rJe,* 1867–1934) – an incarnation of Dra'gyür Marpa Lotsawa *(sGra bsGyur mar pa lo tsA ba).* **Khyentsé Tulku Dzamling Wang-gyal** *(mKhyen brTse sPrul sKu dzam gLing dBang rGyal,* 1868–1907) – an incarnation of DoKhyentsé Yeshé Dorje *(mDo mKhyen brTse ye shes rDo rJe),* and father of Dzong-tér Künzang Nyima *(rDzong gTer kun bZang nyi ma);* **Namtrül Mi'pham Dorje** *(rNams sPrul mi 'pham rDo rJe)* – tulku of **Ché-yö Rig'dzin Chenmo** *(che yol rig 'dzin chen mo,* b. 1879); **Tulku Dri-mèd 'ö-Zér** *(sPrul sKu dri med 'od zer,* 1881–1924); **Tulku Lhatop** *(sPrul sKu lha 'thob,* 1884–1942) – an incarnation of Shéchen A'phang Tulku *(zhe chen A 'phang sPrul sKu);*

Tulku Namkha Jig'mèd *(sPrul sKu nam kha'i 'jigs med,* 1888–1960) of Dzachukha *(rDza chu kha)* – an incarnation of Dza Paltrül Rinpoche *(Dza dPal sPrul rin po che)*; **Tulku Dorje Dra'dül** *(sPrul sKu rDo rJe dGra 'dul,* 1891–1959); **A'phang Tertön** *(A 'phang gTer sTon,* 1895–1945) – miraculously conceived through Düd'jom Lingpa's nondual intent *(dGongs pa)*.

Jamyang Khyentsé Wangpo *(jam dByangs mKhyen brTse dBang po,* 1820–892).

Jamgön Kongtrül *('jam mGon kong sprul,* 1813–1899).

Rinchen gTérdzöd *(rin chen gTer mDzod)* – the collection of gTérmas compiled by Jamgön Kongtrül.

Pemakö *(pad ma bKod)* in Kongpo, Southeast Tibet.

Appendix II

Kyabjé Düd'jom Rinpoche

1904–1987

Tséring gave the introduction telling me that in the remote past, in a previous world-age – Kyabjé Düd'jom Rinpoche had been the Awareness Holder Nuden Dorje; and in the future, it was predicted that he would take incarnation as the Buddha Möpa Tha-yé. In the present he manifested as the representative of Padmasambhava. His previous incarnations included Shariputra, Saraha, and Khyé'u Chung Lotsa. Tséring said that in the texts of prediction of Ögyen Déchen Lingpa it was revealed that Kyabjé Düd'jom Rinpoche would appear in order to reveal gTérma.

Düd'jom Rinpoche was of royal lineage, descended from Nyatri Tsènpo, the first king of Tibet, and from Powo Kanam Dépa, the Gyalpo of Powo. His father, Kathog Tulku Norbu Ten'dzin, was a famous Lama of the Pemakö region. His mother Namgyal Drölma was descended from Ratna Lingpa. Düd'jom Rinpoche was born in the Wood Dragon Year (1904) early in the morning of the tenth day of the sixth month, with many amazing signs. His previous incarnation, Dud'jom Lingpa, told disciples as he approached death *"Whoever relies on me, go to Pemakö – but before you youngsters arrive, I will already be there."* This occurred exactly as predicted. Düd'jom Rinpoche was already three years old when he was discovered as a direct emanation of Düd'jom Lingpa – and could thus remember his previous lives clearly.

Düd'jom Rinpoche had studied for sixteen years with Tulku Gyür-mèd. He'd studied the Dzogchen men-ngag-dé of the Sangwa Nyingthig from Khyentsé Rinpoche. He also received the gTérmas of Düd'jom Lingpa and other Dzogchen teachings from Jé-drung Thrin-lé Jampa Jung-né and Gyür-mèd Wangpo.

Gyür-mèd Wangpo told him that the Rinchen gTér-dzöd represented the activity of Khyentsé and Kongtrül.

At age 18 he met Padmasambhava and was writing gTérmas. In his twenties he received the Dzogchen Nyingthig Yabshi—the lineage of Nyoshül Lungtok Tènpa'i Nyima—the Ka'gyür lung, Dam-ngag Dzöd, Sangchen Ngépa'i Nyingthig Yabshi, from Togden Tènpa. From Tulku Künzang Thegchog Tenpa'i Gyaltsen and Ngagtsün Géndün Gyatso he received the teachings of gTértön Pema Lingpa. After taking transmission from many other Lamas, he went to Phüntsog Ga'tsal and accomplished Dorje Phurba. At Sang-gyé Tsé Phuk, he practised Tsé-drüp and his Tsé-chang boiled when he practised the gong gTér of Düd'dül Tröllö.

This experience of Dorje Tröllö inspired him to visit Paro Taktsang in Bhutan where there were many auspicious signs – and he discovered the Phurba Pu-dri Rekpung, the Tso-kyé Thug-thig and the Khandro Thug-thig.

His teachers prophesised that he would give transmission of Rinchen gTér-dzöd ten times – and Pema Lingpa's gTérmas, as well as Nyingma Gyüd Bum and many other teachings.

Düd'jom Rinpoche wrote twenty-five volumes of gong gTér—all of which have been printed—and established many new retreat places in Pemakö.

After leaving Tibet, he lived in Kalimpong, and gave many teachings and empowerments in Kalimpong and Darjeeling. These teachings and empowerments had been much appreciated by the Tibetan community. Availability on the part of a great Lama, such as Düd'jom Rinpoche, was much needed and cherished as a support for Tibetans in exile. It made them feel that their culture could survive. Sadly, it seems that Düd'jom Rinpoche's accessibility was interpreted as a political threat.

Düd'jom Rinpoche had been subject to hostility in 1961. It had occurred on a train journey. He'd been in McLeod Ganj discussing the Tibetan refugee situation in relation to the exiled Nyingma peoples.

(Düd'jom Rinpoche did not mention with whom he discussed these matters. The author did not enquire because it did not seem necessary to know more than Düd'jom Rinpoche explained.) The situation had caused him concern – vis-à-vis the wish, in certain quarters, to make all traditions subject to centralised authority. This proposed policy—he felt—was not in keeping with Tibetan culture prior to the exodus. He was concerned about the future of what had always been independent lineages. With respect to this concern, he had asked Kathog Ontrül Rinpoche to perform a mélong divination whilst on the train – and Ontrül Rinpoche, scrying the mélong, saw a statue of Padmasambhava bound in barbed wire. This did not bode well.

The train had to stop for a while at Siliguri. In the interim, whilst the train was stationary, Düd'jom Rinpoche was apprehended and subsequently incarcerated by the Indian Police. This had occurred because the Indian Intelligence Service had been informed—by certain Tibetan sources—that Düd'jom Rinpoche was a salaried Chinese collaborator.

This news spread very fast, and Düd'jom Rinpoche's disciples were shocked and sad. They heard of his imprisonment from Siliguri to Panchimari, and many disciples from Darjeeling, Kalimpong, Sikkim, and Bhutan, took extraordinary preventative measures – in the style of Mahatma Gandhi. At any sign of Kyabjé Düd'jom Rinpoche being transported to the Panchimari prison, hundreds of people would lie on the railway lines.

The number prepared to do this escalated by the hour – and the Indian authorities were aware that a crisis was mounting. The Chögyal of Sikkim, the Royal Family of Bhutan, prominent Nepalese and Indian dignitaries, and thousands of students, wrote letters to Nehru – and within days Düd'jom Rinpoche was released and returned to his home in Kalimpong.

Notes:

The transliteration and details of people and places are given here, in order of appearance.

Tséring – the translator monk Gélong Tséring (*dGe sLong tshe ring*).

Ögyen Déchen Lingpa (*O rGyan bDe chen gLing pa*).

Nyatri Tsènpo (*gNya' khri bTsan-po*) – the first king of Tibet, in the 2nd century BC.

Powo Kanam Dépa (*sPo bo kaH gNam sDe pa*) – the Gyalpo (*rGyal po* – king) of Powo.

Kathog Tulku Norbu Ten'dzin (*ka thog sPrul sKu nor bu bsTan 'dzin*).

Namgyal Drölma (*rNam rGyal sGrol ma*).

Ratna Lingpa (*rat na gLing pa*, 1403–1471).

Tulku Gyür-mèd (*sPrul sKu 'gyür med*).

Sangwa Nyingthig (*gSang ba sNying thig*).

Khyentsé Rinpoche (*mKhyen brTse rin po che*).

Jé-drung Thrin-lé Jampa Jung-né (*rJe drung 'phrin las byams pa 'byung gNas*).

Gyür-mèd Wangpo (*'gyur med dBang po*).

Kongtrül (*kong sprul*).

Dzogchen Nyingthig Yabshi (*rDzogs chen sNying thig ya bZhi*).

Nyoshül Lungtok Tènpa'i Nyima (*smyo shul lung rTogs bsTan pa'i nyi ma*, 1829–1901).

Ka'gyür lung (*bKa' 'gyu rLung*).

Dam-ngag Dzöd (*gDams ngag mDzod*).

Sangchen Ngépa'i Nyingthig Yabshi (*gSang chen nges pa'i sNying thig ya bZhi*).

Togden Tènpa (*rTogs lDan brTan pa*).

Tulku Künzang Thegchog Tenpa'i Gyaltsen (*sPrul sKu kun bZang theg mChog brTan pa'i rGyal mTshan*).

Ngagtsün Géndün Gyatso (*ngag tsun dGe 'dun rGya mTsho*).

Phüntsog Ga'tsal (*phun tshog dGa' rTsal*).

Dorje Phurba *(rDo rJe phur ba)*.

Sang-gyé Tsé Phuk *(sangs rGyas tshe phug)*.

Tsé-drüp *(tshe sGrub)* – long life practice.

Tsé-chang *(tshe chang)* – amrita, long life wine.

Düd'dül Tröllö *(dud 'dul gro lod)* – the Dud'jom Dorje Tröllö gong gTér.

Paro Taktsang *(sPa ro sTag tshang)* – Tiger's Nest.

Phurba Pu-dri Rekpung *(phur ba sPu gri reg phung)*.

Tso-kyé Thug-thig *(mTsho sKye thugs thig)*.

Khandro Thug-thig *(mKha' gro thugs thig)*.

Pema Lingpa *(pad ma gLing pa)*.

Nyingma Gyüd Bum *(rNying ma rGyud 'bum)*.

Kathog Ontrül Rinpoche *(ka thog 'ong khrul rin po che)*.

mélong *(me long)* – mirror. A mirror of clairvoyance *(me long rGyang gSal)* is a circular mirror used for many purposes, one being mirror-scrying.

Chögyal *(chos rGyal)* – Dharma king.

Appendix III
Dilgo Khyentsé Rinpoche
1910–1991

I asked Dilgo Khyentsé Rinpoche whether he would be so kind as to tell me about his life in order that I could read it for inspiration as I travelled back to Britain. He was happy to oblige and gave me a far longer account than I imagined. I was delighted. I took copious notes and the translator, Ngawang, was kind enough to see me later to give me all the Tibetan spellings for the names I had mutilated with my primitive phonetics. This process took over three hours – but I learned a great deal from the experience. The many notes that follow were culled from this session with Ngawang.

Dilgo Khyentsé Rinpoche was born in 1910 in Denhok Valley, Der-gé, in Kham. He was born into a family descended from Chögyal Trisong Détsen. His father, Tashi Tséring was the son of a Der-gé minister, Tashi Tsépel, and both were disciples of Khyentsé Wangpo. His mother, the daughter of a Der-gé minister, was named Lhaga. He was born on the third day of the third month of the Iron Dog Year, while Ju Mi'pham Gyamtso was teaching the Dü-kyi 'Khorlo to the family. When he was one month old, Ju Mi'pham named him Tashi Pal'jor. Ju Mi'pham frequently gave Jampalyang empowerments to Dilgo Khyentsé Rinpoche and his family, until his death. Dilgo Khyentsé Rinpoche's elder brother was the 9th Benchen Sang-gyé Nyènpa, Karma Shédrüp Tenpa'i Nyima. He was a major incarnation of the Karma Kagyüd Gompa, Ga Benchen in Yu-shu. Dilgo Khyentsé Rinpoche loved and respected this brother – and composed his biography. The eldest son of the family, also named Shédrüp, was a life companion.

Circumstances before his birth led several Lamas (including Dzogchen Khenpo Zhenga Zhenpen Chokyi Nangwa and Adzom Drukpa Pawo Dorje) to believe that Dilgo Khyentsé was the incarnation of his father's Tsawa'i Lama, Önpo Ten'ga. An older brother had previously been identified as the tulku. He however, had died – and the 14th Karmapa, Tekchok Dorje, declared the incarnation would be a son of Tashi Tséring. Prior to Dilgo Khyentsé's birth, his mother miscarried, unknown to the Lamas looking for the rebirth of Önpo Ten'ga, which was why Tashi Pal'jor was not recognised.

Tashi Paljor's father did not wish his son to be recognised as a Lama, despite repeated indications that he was a tulku. When Dilgo Khyentsé Rinpoche was just one-year old, Jamyang Lo-gTér Wangpo declared him to be an incarnation of Khyentsé Wangpo and asked that he be taken into training. Ju Mi'pham advised Tashi Tséring to refrain from accepting the identification and keep Dilgo Khyentsé Rinpoche at home. Along with Lo-gTér Wangpo, the 5th Dzogchen Tulku,Thubten Chökyi Dorje, and Khangsar Khenpo, also requested the boy for their monasteries.

In addition, the 3rd Kathog Situ, Chökyi Gyatso, declared that he was the incarnation of the 3rd Karma Kuchen, Ögyen Do-ngak Chyi Nyima.

In 1912, the 4th Shéchen Gyaltsab, Pema Namgyal, visited the Dilgo family during the funeral services for Ju Mi'pham, and asked Tashi Tséring to give Tashi Pal'jor to Shéchen Gompa. He accepted this request, although Tashi Pal'jor remained for several more years with his family.

In 1916, while the Dilgo family was on pilgrimage in Tibet, the 5th Taklung Matrul, Ngawang Ten-pa'i Nyima, told Tashi Pal'jor that his son was an incarnation, and asked whether he would make him a monk or a ngakpa. Tashi Pal'jor declared that his son should not be a monk, stressing that the family line needed to continue.

In 1919, Tashi Tséring brought his family to Shéchen to meet with A'dzom Drukpa – who dispelled obstacles for the family.

A'dzom Drukpa gave Dilgo Khyentsé transmission for the Longchen Nyingthig preliminary practices.

In 1924, Dilgo Khyentsé and his elder brother travelled to Shéchen to meet the 4th Shéchen Gyaltsab, Padma Namgyal, who was in retreat in the hills above Shéchen. He gave the Mindröl Ling Dorje Sempa of gTér-dag Lingpa Gyür-mèd Dorje and Guru Chöwang's Phurba Yang-sang Pu-tri. They also received empowerments from Shéchen Kongtrül Pema Dri-mèd, and Tashi Pal'jor memorised the root text of the Sangwa Nyingpo Gyüd. Shéchen Gyaltsap also taught Ju Mi'pham's collected works.

Following his Lama's death, Dilgo Khyentsé went into retreat. He resided in a cave in Denhok with his brother Shédrüp. They were occasionally importuned by bears – but the cave was only accessible by ladder, so they were mostly left in peace.

In 1934, Dilgo Khyentsé developed a fever which almost caused his death. It was decided at this point by Jamyang Khyentsé Chökyi Lodrö and Karma Chökyi Nyingche, that taking a consort would both improve his health and enable him to discover gTérma. Shortly thereafter, he married Khandro Lhamo with whom he had two daughters: Sémo 'Chi-mèd Wangmo and Sémo Déchen Wangmo.

The following year he revealed the first section of one of his most widely practised gTérmas – the *Lotus Heart Life Essence*. The revelation was completed the following year at Pema Shelpuk, a gTérma site near Dzongsar Gompa opened by Khyentsé Wangpo and Chog'gyür Lingpa.

In 1944, Dilgo Khyentsé spent an extended period of time at Dzongsar with Jamyang Khyentsé Chökyi Lodrö, who gave him transmission of the Nyingma Kama and Jamgön Kongtrül's *Treasury of Knowledge*. They visited the pilgrimage places in Meshö Jong where—in the 19th century—Jamyang Khyentsé Wangpo, Jamgön Kongtrül, and Chog'gyür Lingpa revealed gTérmas. Dilgo Khyentsé performed tsog'khorlos and transcribed gTérmas that three earlier Lamas had only partially revealed.

In 1945, he received the transmission and empowerments for the Rinchen gTérdzöd from Jamyang Khyentsé Chökyi Lodrö.

In 1946, Dilgo Khyentsé traveled through Kham, visiting sites of Chog'gyür Lingpa's gTérmas. In Nangchen he met the holders of Chog'gyür Lingpa's lineage, including gTér-sé Tulku Gyür'mèd Tsé-wang Ten'phel, the incarnation of Chog'gyür Lingpa's son Wangchuk Dorje. He also met the two incarnations of Chog'gyür Lingpa, Tsi-ké Chogling and Pema Gyür-mèd, whom he had befriended during the Rinchen gTérdzöd transmission at Dzongsar. Examining the gTérma objects of Chog'gyür Lingpa, Dilgo Khyentsé found a text sheet of khandro cypher which he transcribed as the Ka'gyèd gTérma cycle.

During the initial years of Chinese military rule in Kham, Dilgo Khyentsé travelled to Nangchen and received teachings at Zurmang Düd-tsi Thil and Trangu Gompa *(khra 'gu dGon)*. In Dér-gé he performed rites for the well-being of the population. He stayed in Repkong for a year, where he gave the Rinchen gTérdzöd transmissions and opened a pilgrimage site at A-myé Ma-chen. On returning to Dzongsar, he received teachings from the 41st Sakya Tri'dzin, Ngawang Kunga Tekchen Pelbar. Dilgo Khyentsé gave him a long-life empowerment from one of his gTérmas. Dilgo Khyentsé Rinpoche resided at Dzongsar for a year with his sangyum and daughters, giving teachings to all who came to see him.

In 1956, Dilgo Khyentsé left Kham for Lhasa. While staying at Khampa Gar however, Chinese soldiers had come to Sa-kar looking for him. His sangyum, Khandro Lhamo, delayed them for several weeks, telling them Dilgo Khyentsé was travelling and that she would send messengers to tell him about their request to see him. After several such delaying tactics Khandro Lhamo decided it was not safe for her to remain and set out herself to find Dilgo Khyentsé – taking only a small bag of food for the journey in order not to arouse Chinese suspicions.

When she found Dilgo Khyentsé they made immediate plans to travel to Lhasa, interrupting teachings he was giving with the 8th Khamtrül Tulku, Don-gyüd Nyima.

Jamyang Khyentsé Chökyi Lodrö had already left for Sikkim and Dilgo Khyentsé and his sangyum Khandro Lhamo used their pilgrimage as a means of escape from Tibet. They remained in Lhasa for several years, until the situation became critical. In Lhasa, in 1956 he gave Sangwa Nyingpo teachings for four months. At Tsur-phu Gompa he gave the transmission for the gTérmas of Chog'gyür Lingpa. He visited Mindröl Ling for a month, where he met Kyabjé Düd'jom Rinpoche for the first time. Not long after that, Dilgo Khyentsé, Khandro Lhamo, and their family left Tibet. They fled to Bhutan with other families and Kham guerrillas – but stayed only a few weeks before continuing to Kalimpong, India, where they stayed with Kyabjé Düd'jom Rinpoche.

Dilgo Khyentsé remained in Kalimpong for several years, shifting occasionally to Bhutan and Sikkim to visit the remains of Jamyang Khyentsé Chökyi Lodrö, who died there in 1959 – and to give the transmission and empowerments for the Rinchen gTérdzöd to his incarnation. In 1961 he was invited to Bhutan to serve as the Lama in Thimphu – and remained until 1962, when he received the news that his brother Sang-gyé Nyènpa had died in Sikkim. There, he learned that his youngest daughter Sémo Déchen Wangmo was ill. She died in Lucknow in 1963.

In 1965 Pema Dorje of Nyima-lung Gompa in Bumthang invited Dilgo Khyentsé to Bhutan. There had been serious unrest before he arrived – and so he began his visit with rites of pacification. With the success of his rites he was immediately given a Bhutanese passport – and Bhutan became his main residence.

Then later, Dilgo Khyentsé Rinpoche had dreams of clarity of Shéchen Rabjam, Shéchen Kongtrül, and Shéchen Gyaltsap appearing all together. (They had all died in Chinese prisons.) They told him that all three together would appear as one Lama. And so Shéchen Rabjam Jig-mèd Chökyi Seng-gé was born to his daughter 'Chi-mèd Wangmo. He became the 7th Shéchen Rabjam.

For the next 30 years Dilgo Khyentsé Rinpoche was dedicated to preserving the Nyingma Tradition in Bhutan, India, and Nepal – giving teachings, transmissions, and empowerments.

He first visited the West in 1975. He made three journeys to America and numerous visits to Europe. In France he established a three-year retreat centre in the Dordogne. He was one of the main teachers of Chögyam Trungpa, whom he regarded extremely highly. He died in Bhutan in 1991.

His lineage holder is his grandson Shéchen Rabjam. Dilgo Khyentsé Rinpoche's incarnation, Dilgo Yangsi, was born in 1993 and enthroned at Shéchen in 1997. He is the son of the 4th Tsi-ké, Chogling Min'gyür Dé-wa'i Dorje, and the grandson of Tulku Ögyen Tsé-wang Chog-drüp Pal'bar.

Notes:

The transliteration and details of people and places are given here, in order of appearance.

Dilgo Khyentsé Rinpoche *(dil mGo mKhyen brTse rin po che,* 1910–1991) .

Ngawang *(ngag dBang).*

Denkok Valley, Der-gé *(sDe dGe),* in Kham.

Chögyal Trisong Détsen *(chos rGyal khri srong lDe bTsan).*

Tashi Tséring *(bKra shis tshe ring,* d. 1932).

Tashi Tsépel *(bKra shis tshe 'phel).*

Lhaga *(lha dGa').*

Ju Mi'pham Gyamtso *('ju mi 'pham rGya mTsho,* 1846–1912).

Dü-kyi 'Khorlo *(dus kyi 'khor lo rGyud; Kalachakra Tantra – Wheel of Time).*

Tashi Pal'jor *(bKra shis dPal 'byor).*

Benchen Sang-gyé Nyènpa *(ban chen sangs rGyas mNyan pa).*

Karma Shédrüp Tenpa'i Nyima *(karma bShad sGrub bsTan pa'i nyi ma,* 1897–1962).

Karma Kagyüd *(karma bka' brGyud).*

Ga Benchen Gompa *(sGa ban chen)* Yu-shu *(yul shul).*

Dzogchen Khenpo Zhenga Zhenpen Chokyi Nangwa *(rDzogs chen mKhan po gZhan dGa' gZhan phan chos kyi sNang ba, 1871–1927)*.

Adzom Drukpa Pawo Dorje *(A 'dzom 'brug pa dPa' bo rDo rje, 1842–1924)*.

Önpo Ten'ga *(dBon po bsTan dGa' o rGyan bsTan 'dzin nor bu)* of Gemang Monastery *(dGe mang dGon pa)* in Dza-chuka, Kham.

Tekchok Dorje *(theg mChog rDo rje, 1798–1869)*.

Jamyang Lo-gTér Wangpo *(jam dByangs bLo gTer dBang po)* – a disciple of Khyentsé Wangpo.

Khangsar Khenpo *(khang gSar mKhen po)* – of Ngor É-wam Chö-dé *(ngor e wam chos sDe)*.

Dzogchen Tulku *(rDzogs chen sPrul sKu)*.

Thubten Chökyi Dorje *(thub bsTan chos kyi rDo rje, 1872–1935)*.

Kathog Situ *(ka thog si tu)*.

Chökyi Gyatso *(chos kyi rGya mTsho, 1880–1925)*.

Karma Kuchen *(kar ma sKu chen)*.

Ögyen Do-ngak Chyi Nyima *(o rGyan mDo sNgags chos kyi nyi ma, 1854–1906)* of Palyul Gompa *(dPa' yul dGon)*.

Shéchen Gyaltsab *(zhe chen rGyal tshab)*.

Pema Namgyal *(pad ma rNam rGyal, 1871–1926)*.

Taklung Matrul *(sTag lung ma sPrul)*.

Ngawang Ten-pa'i Nyima *(ngag dBang bsTan pa'i nyi ma)*.

A'dzom Drukpa *(A 'dzom brug pa)*.

Longchen Nyingthig *(kLong chen sNying thig)*.

Padma Namgyal *(zhe chen rGyal tshab pad ma rNam rGyal)*.

Mindröl Ling *(sMin grol gLing)*.

Dorje Sempa *(rDo rJe sems dPa')*.

gTér-dag Lingpa Gyür-mèd Dorje *(gTer bDag gLing pa 'gyur med rDo rje,* 1646–1714).

Guru Chöwang *(gu ru chos dBang).*

Phurba Yang-sang Pu-tri *(phur ba yang gSang sPu gri).*

Pema Drimèd *(pad ma dri med,* 1901–1960).

Sangwa Nyingpo Gyüd *(gSang ba sNying po rGyud).*

Jamyang Khyentsé Chökyi Lodrö *(Jam dByangs mKhyen brTse chos kyi bLo gros).*

Karma Chökyi Nyingche *(kar ma chos kyi nying byed,* 1879–1939) – the 10th Zurmang Trungpa *(zur mang drung pa).*

Khandro Lhamo *(mKha' gro lha mo,* 1913–2003) – a highly accomplished yogini, skilled doctor, and a witty raconteur, with a trove of fascinating stories about her life with Dilgo Khyentsé Rinpoche.

Sémo 'Chi-mèd Wangmo *(sras mo 'chi med dBang mo).*

Sémo Déchen Wangmo *(sras mo bDe chen dBang mo).*

Lotus Heart Life Essence (Pema tsé-yi Nying-thig – *pad ma tshe yi sNying thig)* – discovered at Do-ti Gangkar *(rDo ti gangs dKar),* near La-dro Samdrüp Lhaden Cho-khör Ling *(gLa gro bSam 'grub lha lDan chos 'khor gLing)* in Nangchen *(nang chen).*

Pema Shelpuk *(pad ma shel phug).*

Dzongsar Gom *(rDzong gSar dGon).*

Chog'gyür Lingpa *(mChog 'gyur gLing pa,* 1829–1870).

Nyingma Kama *(rNying ma bKa' ma).*

gTér-sé Tulku Gyür'mèd Tsé-wang Ten'phel *(gTer sras sPrul sKu gyur med tshe dBang bsTan 'phel).*

Wangchuk Dorje *(dBang phyug rDo rJe).*

Tsi-ké Chogling *(rTsi ke mChog gLing,* 1940–1952) – the young 3rd Tsi-ké *(rTsi ke).*

Pema Gyür-mèd *(pad ma 'gyur med,* 1928–1974) – the 3ʳᵈ Né-tèn Chogling *(gNas brTan mChog gLing).*

Ka'gyèd *(bKa' brGyad).*

Zurmang Düd-tsi Thil *(zur mang bDud rTsi mThil).*

Trangu Gompa *(khra 'gu dGon).*

A-myé Ma-chen *(a mYes rMa chen).*

Sakya Tri'dzin *(sa sKya khri 'dzin).*

Ngawang Kunga Tekchen Pelbar *(ngag dBang kun dGa' theg chen dPal 'bar).*

Khampa Gar *(khams pa sGar)* in Nangchen.

Khamtrül Tulku *(khams sprul sPrul sKu).*

Don-gyüd Nyima *(don brGyud nyi ma,* 1930–1979).

Tsur-phu Gompa *(mTshur phu dGon).*

Lucknow *(Lakhnau)* – the capital city of Uttar Pradesh, India.

Shéchen Rabjam *(zhe chen rab 'byams).*

Shéchen Kongtrül *(zhe chen kong sprul).*

Shéchen Rabjam Jig-mèd Chökyi Seng-gé *(zhe chen rab 'byams 'jigs med chos kyi seng ge,* born 1966).

Dilgo Yangsi *(dil mGo yang srid).*

Chogling Min'gyür Dé-wa'i Dorje *(mChog gLing min 'gyur bDe ba'i rDo rJe,* born 1953).

Tulku Ögyen Tsé-wang Chog-drüp Pal'bar *(sPrul sKu o rGyan tshe dBang mChog grub dPal 'bar,* 1910–1996).